Deep Learning in Action: Image and Video Processing for Practical Use

Deep Learning in Action: Image and Video Processing for Practical Use

Abdussalam Elhanashi
Department of Information Engineering, University of Pisa, Pisa, Italy
Sergio Saponara
Department of Information Engineering, University of Pisa, Pisa, Italy

ELSEVIER

Elsevier
Radarweg 29, PO Box 211, 1000 AE Amsterdam, Netherlands
125 London Wall, London EC2Y 5AS, United Kingdom
50 Hampshire Street, 5th Floor, Cambridge, MA 02139, United States

ISBN: 978-0-443-30078-3

For Information on all Elsevier publications
visit our website at https://www.elsevier.com/books-and-journals

Publisher: Mara E. Conner
Acquisitions Editor: Neil Craig Smith
Editorial Project Manager: Debarati Roy
Production Project Manager: Anitha Sivaraj
Cover Designer: Greg Harris

Typeset by MPS Limited, Chennai, India

Dedication

This book is dedicated to the unwavering support and love of my parents, whose guidance and encouragement have been the foundation of my journey. To my mother and father, your belief in me has been a constant source of strength and motivation. Your sacrifices and unwavering faith have propelled me forward, and for that, I am eternally grateful.

To my friends, thank you for your endless encouragement and for being my pillars of support throughout this endeavor. Your confidence in my abilities, your patience, and your constant cheering have been invaluable. You have shared in my triumphs and offered solace in moments of doubt, and this achievement is as much yours as it is mine.

I also extend my deepest gratitude to the academic experts who reviewed this book. Your insightful feedback, constructive criticism, and thoughtful guidance have been instrumental in shaping the final manuscript. Your dedication to excellence and your willingness to share your knowledge have elevated the quality of this work immeasurably.

Abdussalam Elhanashi & Sergio Saponara

Contents

Foreword

The realm of artificial intelligence (AI) has witnessed unparalleled advancements, fundamentally altering the landscape of technology and its applications. At the forefront of this revolution is deep learning—a transformative branch of AI characterized by its ability to process and analyze vast datasets, uncover intricate patterns, and deliver solutions with extraordinary precision. *Deep Learning in Action: Image and Video Processing for Practical Use* by Abdussalam Elhanashi and Sergio Saponara masterfully bridges foundational theory with hands-on practice, offering a unique road map for those aspiring to harness deep learning in real-world scenarios.

This book is more than an academic text; it is a comprehensive guide that delves into lightweight, resource-efficient AI methodologies tailored for image and video processing. It explores a spectrum of applications ranging from surveillance systems to healthcare diagnostics, emphasizing approaches suitable for resource-constrained environments like Internet of Things (IoT) and embedded systems. Through in-depth case studies, such as COVID-19 safety measures and real-time stroke detection, readers are introduced to state-of-the-art algorithms, practical deployment strategies, and the ethical implications of AI.

Elhanashi and Saponara succeed in demystifying complex AI concepts, making them accessible to intermediate and advanced audiences alike. Whether you are a researcher aiming to push the boundaries of computer vision or an engineer striving to develop efficient deep learning solutions, this book equips you with the tools to translate theoretical knowledge into impactful innovations.

In a rapidly evolving field, this text invites readers not only to understand the power of deep learning but also to contribute meaningfully to its future development.

Prof. Maria Sabrina Greco

Preface

In *Deep Learning in Action: Image and Video Processing for Practical Use*, the journey begins with a comprehensive exploration of artificial intelligence and its evolution, laying the groundwork with fundamental concepts in deep learning. The power of deep learning unfolds through an in-depth examination of neural networks, particularly convolutional neural networks (CNNs), pivotal for tasks like object detection and classification. Autoencoders and their role in computer vision applications, alongside the integration of deep learning into embedded systems, underscore the transformative potential in real-world scenarios. Understanding the nuances of image and video data, from formats to processing methods, sets the stage for practical applications across diverse industries, bridging theoretical concepts with pragmatic solutions. Each chapter unfolds with a strategic focus: from enhancing safety measures through AI-powered video analysis in scenarios like fire detection and social distancing enforcement to leveraging deep learning for tasks as nuanced as fingerprint image restoration and medical image analysis. Real-time stroke detection emerges as a critical application area, demonstrating the synergy of deep learning and federated learning in healthcare settings. This book concludes by addressing industry-specific challenges, such as efficient bag breakup detection in continuous airflow via video analysis, highlighting robust methodologies and experimental results. Throughout, the integration of NVIDIA platforms underscores the computational backbone crucial for real-time inference and system implementation. This book serves as a comprehensive guide, equipping readers with both theoretical insights and practical strategies to harness the transformative power of deep learning in image and video processing applications.

Acknowledgments

We gratefully acknowledge the University of Pisa for its unwavering support and commitment to advancing research and education in the field of artificial intelligence and deep learning. The collaborative efforts and resources provided by the University have significantly enriched the content and depth of this book, *Deep Learning in Action: Image and Video Processing for Practical Use*.

We extend our sincere appreciation to the Society for Imaging Informatics in Medicine (SIIM) for its invaluable contributions to medical imaging research and its continuous efforts to promote innovation in healthcare technology. The insights and datasets shared by SIIM have greatly enhanced the chapters dedicated to medical image analysis and diagnostic applications.

Their support has been instrumental in shaping this comprehensive guide, which aims to bridge academic knowledge with real-world applications, benefiting researchers, practitioners, and enthusiasts alike.

Nomenclature

- **Clustering: -** An unsupervised learning task where the algorithm groups a set of objects in such a way that objects in the same group (cluster) are more similar to each other than to those in other groups.
- **Edge Computing: -** A distributed computing paradigm that brings computation and data storage closer to the location where it is needed to improve response times and save bandwidth.
- **Gabor Filter:-** A linear filter used for texture analysis, which is particularly useful for detecting edges and textures in images.
- **Graph-based Methods: -**Techniques in machine learning that utilize graph structures to represent data and discover patterns, particularly useful in semisupervised learning.
- **Histogram of Orientation Gradients (HOG): -**A feature descriptor used in computer vision and image processing for the purpose of object detection. It counts occurrences of gradient orientation in localized portions of an image.
- **Local Binary Pattern (LBP):-**A visual descriptor used for texture classification in computer vision. It labels the pixels of an image by thresholding the neighborhood of each pixel and considers the result as a binary number.
- **Local Ternary Pattern (LTP):-**An extension of local binary pattern (LBP) that considers three possible values (positive, negative, and zero), making it more robust to noise.
- **Principal Component Analysis (PCA): -** A statistical technique used for simplifying data by reducing its dimensions while retaining most of the variation in the dataset.
- **Transfer Function:-** A function used in neural networks to determine the output of a neuron given a set of inputs, typically involving an activation function such as sigmoid, tanh, or ReLU.
- **IoT-based Framework**: An Internet of Things framework enabling remote visual feedback and real-time alerts, integrated with cloud computing via iCloud for fire and smoke detection in smart cities.
- **Region of Interest (ROI)**: Extracts suggestions for object bounding boxes from input images.
- **ReLU Layers**: Introduce nonlinearity by converting negative image values to zero.
- **Pooling Layers**: Downsample images using max-pooling and average-pooling.
- **Dropout Layer**: Prevents overfitting.
- **Fully Connected Layer**: Final classification decision layer.
- **SoftMax Layer**: Computes the probability of the predicted class.
- **Batch Normalization**: Normalizes values across layers to enhance model regularization.
- **Top-Down View Transformation**: Converting camera perspectives into a uniform overhead view to eliminate distortions in distance measurement.
- **Perspective Correction**: Adjusting visual representations to ensure objects are shown in true proportions and positions.
- **Visual Data Reliability**: Improving the accuracy and usability of visual information for better decision-making in fields like cartography, architecture, and surveying.
- **COVID-19 Mitigation**: The primary goal of the research is to reduce the spread of COVID-19 and its impact on public health and the economy.

- **Ground Truth Labeler**: A MATLAB application used to annotate individuals in thermal images for accurate model training.
- **Fingerprint Recognition: -**A biometric process that involves identifying and verifying individuals based on the unique patterns of their fingerprints.
- **Kullback-Leibler Divergence: -** A measure used in machine learning to quantify the difference between two probability distributions. In sparse autoencoders, it is used to enforce sparsity by penalizing deviations from a desired activation distribution.
- **Efficient Net**: A scalable and efficient convolutional neural network architecture.
- **Backpropagation: -** A training algorithm for neural networks that involves a forward pass to compute the prediction and a backward pass to compute the error gradient, which is then used to update the model weights.
- **Faster R-CNN**: Faster Region-based Convolutional Neural Network
- **YOLO**: You Only Look Once
- **Cropping**: Removing the outer parts of an image to focus on a specific area.
- **Localization**: The process of identifying the location of objects in an image.
- **Pulmonary Abnormalities**: Irregularities or deviations from normal lung anatomy or function.
- **Acute Stroke:** A condition characterized by the sudden onset of neurological deficit due to a disturbance in the blood supply to the brain.
- **CBS:** A combination of Convolution, Batch Normalization, and SiLU (Sigmoid Linear Unit) operation used in neural networks.
- **CSPDarknet53:** A core framework used in YOLOv8 architecture, derived from Darknet-53, that incorporates cross-stage partial connections to improve learning efficiency.
- **Gradients:** Derivatives of the loss function with respect to the model parameters, used to update the parameters during training.
- **Residual Connections:** Links in a neural network that bypass one or more layers, helping to mitigate the vanishing gradient problem and improve training of deep networks.
- **Synthetic Data:** Artificially generated data that mimics real-world phenomena, used to augment training datasets when limited real-world data is available.

CHAPTER

Introduction

1

1.1 Overview

Many image classification techniques in computer vision rely on the detection and extraction of the local features in the images; as a result, most of the computer vision literature is devoted to this topic, dwelling extensively on discovering, understanding, describing, and enhancing features that can be extracted from the images. A vast number of features reported in the literature were manually developed, or "handcrafted," to address specific challenges such as variations and occlusions in the scale illuminations (Kumar & Bhatia, 2014). The handcrafted design usually implies the right trade-off between computational cost and performance. Several steps are involved in computing handcrafted features (Nanni et al., 2017). Hand-craft feature extractors are used in image recognition. The selection is based on their outlined performance in various applications for object recognition (Emeršič et al., 2017, 2020; Hassaballah et al., 2019; Pflug et al., 2014). These extractors encode the replicated patterns and classify the image characteristics, such as shape, color, and orientations, in the given images. There are different types of manual feature extraction that have focused on the use of handcrafted image features designed by experts, such as the Gabor filter (Kashyap & Mishra, 2017), local binary pattern LBP (Khaleefah et al., 2020), local ternary pattern LTP (Ren et al., 2013), and histogram of orientation slopes HOG. For the handcrafted design, effective feature extraction is a lengthy process. The handcrafted features were investigated in previous relevant studies that lacked the ability to extract the targeted and effective features throughout automatic learning (Hsu & Zhuang, 2020). This meticulously written book delves into the heart of modern deep learning (DL), taking readers on a journey from fundamental concepts to real-world applications. Beginning with a solid foundation in DL fundamentals, including neural networks, convolutional neural networks (CNNs), and autoencoders, the book guides readers through progressively complex topics, ensuring a firm grasp of the underlying principles. The authors offer in-depth insights into the latest advancements in computer vision, from image classification and object detection to segmentation, with practical hands-on examples and code samples in popular frameworks such as MATLAB and Python. Moving beyond static images, the book extends its reach into the dynamic realm of video processing, covering topics such as action recognition, video captioning, and video generation, making it a valuable resource for both beginners and experienced practitioners. Moreover, the book explores the integration of DL techniques with emerging technologies such as edge computing and IoT, showcasing their applicability in real-world scenarios such as autonomous vehicles, surveillance systems, and medical imaging. The authors also emphasize the ethical considerations and potential biases associated with DL in image and video processing, providing readers with a holistic understanding of the field. "Deep learning in action: image and video processing for practical use" is a comprehensive and detailed guide essential for anyone interested in DL applications in image and video processing. It is ideal for students, researchers, and

Deep Learning in Action: Image and Video Processing for Practical Use. DOI: https://doi.org/10.1016/B978-0-443-30078-3.00001-9

professionals who aim to fully utilize DL in these constantly changing fields. The book is valuable for both beginners starting their DL journey and experts aiming to remain updated in this fast-paced area. It provides the necessary insights and resources to significantly contribute to the field of image and video processing.

1.1.1 Definition and evolution of artificial intelligence

Artificial intelligence (AI) is a field of computer science that aims to establish intelligent systems capable of simulating human cognitive functions such as learning, solving problems, perception, and understanding the language. Artificial Intelligence endeavors to endow machines with the ability to process the data, make decisions, and adapt to changing circumstances similar to the human brain. While AI involves a wide range of techniques and approaches, one of its most prominent and practical branches is DL, which encompasses the use of artificial neural networks to recognize and analyze complex patterns and relationships within vast datasets, particularly in the domain of image and video processing. AI systems can be categorized into three main types: narrow or weak AI, which is designed for specific tasks and lacks general intelligence; artificial general intelligence (AGI), which aims to create machines with human-like reasoning abilities across a wide range of tasks; and artificial superintelligence, a hypothetical level of AI surpassing human intelligence. AI's practical applications are vast and rapidly expanding, with image and video processing being crucial domains where DL techniques have achieved remarkable success. These applications include image recognition, object detection, facial recognition, natural language processing, autonomous vehicles, medical image analysis, and more. Deep learning, characterized by its deep neural networks with multiple layers, has significantly advanced the state-of-the-art in image and video processing, enabling tasks such as image classification, image generation, and video analysis with unprecedented accuracy and efficiency. As AI continues to evolve, its integration into everyday life becomes increasingly apparent, from virtual personal assistants such as Siri and Alexa to autonomous drones, healthcare diagnostics, recommendation systems, and even self-driving cars. However, the field also faces ethical and societal challenges, such as bias in AI algorithms, data privacy concerns, and the potential for job displacement due to automation. Despite these challenges, AI holds immense promise for improving our lives, transforming industries, and unlocking new possibilities in the domain of image and video processing, making it an essential field for both researchers and practitioners alike.

The evolution of AI is an interesting journey, which illustrates the intersection of human ingenuity, technological advancement, and the quest to replicate human intelligence in machines. This narrative begins in the 19th century and extends into the present day, chronicling key milestones and breakthroughs that have shaped the field. In 1837, the seeds of AI were put in the ground with Charles Babbage's design of the first programmable machine. Babbage was regarded as the "father of the computer," who collaborated with Ada Lovelace and was recognized as one of the first computer programmers. Lovelace's contributions are significant, as she realized that the machine had applications beyond pure calculation, planting the earliest ideas of algorithmic processing in computing. Fig. 1.1 illustrates the evolution of AI: this figure illustrates the journey of AI, tracing its historical milestones and transformative developments from its conceptual origins to the technologies of today.

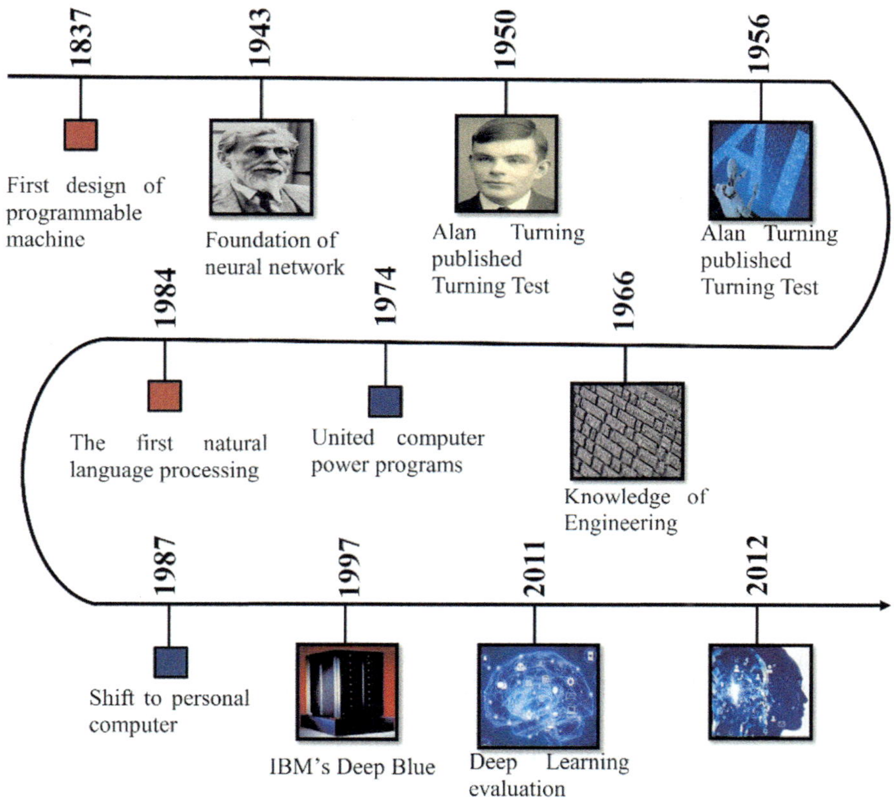

FIGURE 1.1

Evolution of artificial intelligence. This figure illustrates the journey of AI, demonstrating its historical milestones and transformative developments from its conceptual origins to the technologies of today. Each node represents a significant breakthrough, highlighting the continuous growth, challenges, and paradigm shifts that have shaped the landscape of AI over the decades. *AI*, Artificial intelligence.

In 1943 (ENIAC, 2023), the concept of neural networks entered the scene. Warren McCulloch and Walter Pitts made groundbreaking strides by drawing parallels between the brain and computers. Their work laid the foundational principles of how networks of artificial neurons could simulate human thought processes, leading to the development of modern neural networks. In 1950 (History of Artificial Intelligence, 2023), the field took a philosophical turn with Alan Turing's landmark paper proposing a test to see if humans could not distinguish AI from a human in conversation. This "turing test" became a seminal concept in AI, setting a benchmark for machine intelligence and stimulating further exploration into human-like AI. The Dartmouth Conference of 1956 is widely recognized as the seminal event that marked the birth of AI as a field of research (Dartmouth Workshop, 2023). Organized by John McCarthy, Marvin Minsky, Nathaniel Rochester, and Claude Shannon, the conference was held at Dartmouth College in Hanover, New Hampshire.

The main objective of this event was to explore how machines could be made to simulate aspects of brain intelligence. John McCarthy, who is credited with coining the term "artificial intelligence," proposed the conference in a grant proposal to the Rockefeller Foundation, emphasizing the concept that "every aspect of learning or any other feature of intelligence can in principle be so precisely described that a machine can be made to simulate it." This ambitious statement set the tone for the conference and for the field of AI research for decades to come. By 1966, AI had expanded into the realm of natural language processing. This development meant that computers could begin to understand and reciprocate human language, a significant step toward machines that could interact with humans in a more natural and intuitive way. However, the journey wasn't always upward. Between 1974–80, the first "AI winter" occurred, characterized by a lack of funding and interest in AI research. This period underscored the challenges of limited computer power and the need for more foundational knowledge in programming and computing. The 1980s experienced a resurgence in AI interest, particularly in the area of expert systems. These systems utilized expert-derived knowledge to answer questions and solve problems within specific domains. This era, known as "knowledge engineering," showcased the practical applications of AI in various industries, from medicine to finance. Yet another AI winter loomed during 1987–93, brought on by financial constraints and a shift toward more personal computing. This period was a time of reflection and recalibration in the AI community, as researchers and developers sought to overcome the limitations of previous approaches. A significant milestone was achieved in 1997 when IBM's Deep Blue defeated Chess World Champion Garry Kasparov. This event was more than just a victory in a game; it symbolized AI's capability to process large amounts of information and make strategic decisions—a feat previously thought to be exclusive to human intelligence. In the 21st century, AI made considerable strides toward the concept of general intelligence. This paradigm envisioned an AI system capable of solving any problem, not just those it was specifically programmed for. The development toward this goal was symbolized by technologies that resembled intricate networks or brain-like structures, indicating the increasing complexity and adaptability of AI systems. Fig. 1.1 illustrates the Journey of AI, tracing its historical milestones and transformative developments from its conceptual origins to the technologies of today.

Throughout these years, AI has transformed from a theoretical concept to a practical tool that spreads through many aspects of modern life. It has evolved from simple programmable machines to complex systems capable of learning and outperforming humans in specific tasks. This journey reflects the technological advancement and changing understanding of what it means to think, learn, and be intelligent. As AI continues to advance, it promises to redefine the boundaries of what is possible, blurring the lines between human and machine intelligence.

1.1.2 Machine learning fundamental

Machine learning (ML) is a subset of AI. It is an approach to data analysis that automates analytical model building. It's based on the techniques that can learn from the data. It identifies the patterns and performs decisions with minimal human intervention. Machine learning involves feeding data into algorithms to design models that can predict or classify outcomes. These algorithms, varying from simple linear regression to complex models, are the engines of ML. The process begins with data collection and preparation, a crucial step as the data quality influences the accuracy of the model. Input variables are selected based on their relevance to the prediction task. The next step is choosing the right model, which depends on the type of problem (classification, regression, clustering, etc.), the size and type of data, and the desired outcome. Supervised learning is used to train the model on labeled data. It is the most common approach. It involves providing the algorithm with input-output pairs, enabling it to learn the relationship between them. Unsupervised learning, on the other hand, deals with unlabeled data, discovering hidden patterns or intrinsic structures. A newer approach, reinforcement learning, involves training models to make a sequence of decisions by rewarding or penalizing them for the actions they take in an interactive environment. Once an algorithm is selected, the model is trained by feeding it the training dataset. This phase is where the model learns from the data, adjusting its weights and biases to minimize errors. The performance of the model is then assessed using a different dataset, the test set, which was not seen by the model during training. This evaluation helps in understanding the model's accuracy and generalizability to new data. Overfitting, where a model performs well on the training data but poorly on new data, and underfitting, where a model is too simple to capture the underlying trend, are common challenges in this phase. Techniques such as cross-validation and regularization and choosing the right complexity for the model help in mitigating these issues. Once a model is trained and evaluated, it can be deployed in real-world applications, from recommending products to users based on their browsing history to detecting fraudulent transactions in banking.

Machine learning is evolving rapidly, with new models and techniques being developed to tackle increasingly complex problems. Deep learning, a subset of ML, has gained prominence for its ability to handle large volumes of unstructured data such as images and text. It uses neural networks with many layers (hence 'deep') to learn features and tasks directly from data, eliminating the need for manual feature extraction. The success of DL in areas such as image and speech recognition has led to its widespread adoption in various fields. However, ML is not without its challenges. Issues such as bias in data, interpretability of models, and the need for large amounts of data for training are ongoing challenges. Ethical considerations, particularly in the use of ML for decision-making in sensitive areas such as healthcare and criminal justice, are increasingly coming to the forefront. Researchers and practitioners are working on these challenges, striving to make ML more transparent, ethical, and efficient. The future direction of ML is promising, with advancements to drive significant changes in various industries and modern life. As the field continues to grow, the importance of understanding its fundamental concepts and methodologies cannot be overstated, making it an essential area of study and research in the realm of AI.

1.1.3 Machine learning types

Machine learning can be categorized into four types based on the nature of the learning systems and data availability, which are as follows:

- **Supervised learning** is a type of ML that enables computers to learn from and make decisions based on labeled data. It works under the paradigm where models learn from labeled training data. This setup imitates a student-teacher relationship, where the model, such as a student, learns from given examples. The primary aim of supervised learning is to create an algorithm that can make accurate decisions when fed new data. This is achieved through a process known as training, where the model iteratively tunes its parameters to minimize the difference between its predictions and the actual outputs in the training data.

The performance of a supervised learning model is measured using metrics such as accuracy, precision, recall, or mean squared error, depending on the nature of the task. There are two main types of tasks in supervised learning: classification and regression. Classification involves categorizing data into predefined classes. For instance, a classification model might be trained to recognize whether an email is spam or not. On the other hand, regression deals with predicting continuous values, such as forecasting the price of a house based on various features such as size, location, and age. The process of training a supervised learning model includes several steps. First, the data is preprocessed, which involves cleaning, normalizing, and features. The next step is to split the dataset into training and testing sets. The algorithm learns from the training set, while the testing set is used to evaluate its generalization performance. Common algorithms used in supervised learning include linear regression for regression tasks, logistic regression, support vector machines, decision trees, and neural networks for classification tasks. Each algorithm has its strengths and weaknesses and is chosen based on the specific requirements of the task at hand. One of the critical aspects of supervised learning is overfitting, where a model becomes too tailored to the training data and performs poorly on new data. To combat this, techniques such as cross-validation (where the training set is split into smaller sets to validate the model multiple times), regularization (which adds a penalty to the model complexity), and pruning (for decision trees, to remove unnecessary branches) are used.

- **Unsupervised learning** focuses on identifying patterns in data without the guidance of labeled outcomes or predictions. Unlike supervised learning, where models are trained on data with labeled outputs, unsupervised learning operates with data that has no labels, leaving the algorithm to discover the inherent structure within the data itself. The primary aim of unsupervised learning is to explore the underlying patterns, such as groupings or associations, in a dataset. This exploration can reveal hidden features that might not be immediately apparent, leading to valuable insights, especially in complex datasets. Two main types of tasks in unsupervised learning are clustering and dimensionality reduction. Clustering involves grouping data points so that those within each group (or cluster) are more similar to each other than to those in other clusters. Common clustering algorithms include K-means, hierarchical clustering, and DBSCAN. These methods are widely used in market segmentation, social network analysis, and as a preprocessing step in complex data analysis pipelines. Dimensionality reduction, on the other hand, is about reducing the number of variables under consideration. It's a crucial step in data preprocessing, especially when dealing with high-dimensional data. Techniques such as principal component analysis (PCA) and t-distributed stochastic neighbor embedding (t-SNE) are commonly used to simplify data, enhance visualization, and improve the efficiency of subsequent analysis or supervised learning tasks. Another significant aspect of unsupervised learning is association rule learning, which is about discovering interesting relations between variables in large databases. This technique is particularly useful in market basket analysis, where retailers can uncover associations between products purchased together by customers. A unique challenge in unsupervised learning is the lack of clear performance measures. Since there are no correct answers or labels to compare against, it can be difficult to objectively evaluate the quality of an unsupervised model. Measures such as the silhouette coefficient for clustering or explained variance for dimensionality reduction are used, but these metrics often rely on subjective interpretation.

- **Semisupervised learning** is an approach in ML that sits between supervised and unsupervised learning. It includes training algorithms using a limited dataset of labeled data supplemented by a substantial volume of unlabeled data. This method is particularly useful when acquiring labeled data is expensive or time-consuming, but there's an abundance of unlabeled data available. The fundamental principle behind semisupervised learning is that even though the unlabeled data doesn't have explicit outputs, it still carries valuable information about the structure of the data space. Through the integration of labeled and unlabeled data, semisupervised learning models can attain superior accuracy and generalization performance compared to exclusively supervised or unsupervised models within specific contexts. There are various techniques used in semisupervised learning, with some of the most common being self-training, cotraining, and graph-based methods. In self-training, a supervised model is initially trained with the small, labeled dataset and then used to label the unlabeled data. The most confidently predicted labels are then added to the training set, and the process repeats. Cotraining, on the other hand, uses two different views of the data to mutually enhance learning. Graph-based techniques leverage the connections among data points to disseminate labels across the entire dataset. Semisupervised learning is particularly beneficial in domains where labeling data requires expert knowledge or extensive effort, such as in medical imaging and speech recognition. For example, in medical imaging, labeled data might be limited due to the need for expert radiologists to annotate images, but there may be a vast amount of unlabeled medical images available. One of the critical challenges in semisupervised learning is ensuring that the model doesn't reinforce its own erroneous predictions. This is known as confirmation bias and can occur during self-training if the model starts to confidently predict incorrect labels, subsequently training itself on these inaccuracies.
- **Reinforcement learning (RL)** is a type of ML where the central concept revolves around agents learning to make decisions by interacting with their environment; the essence of RL lies in the idea of learning from the consequences of actions rather than from being told explicitly what to do; it sets itself apart significantly from other learning approaches, such as supervised or unsupervised learning. In reinforcement learning, an agent—which can be anything from a robot, a software program, or a more complex system—learns to achieve a goal in an uncertain, potentially complex environment; it operates through a process of trial and error, wherein the agent takes actions and, in return, receives rewards or penalties (reinforcements) based on the outcomes of these actions, the rewards and penalties serving as signals that guide the learning process. The aim of the agent is to learn a strategy for taking actions based on its current state that maximizes the cumulative reward it receives over time, which involves exploring the environment to discover which actions yield the most reward and exploiting this knowledge to make better decisions in the future; this exploration versus exploitation dilemma is a key challenge in reinforcement learning, requiring a balance between trying new actions to improve future rewards and using known actions that already yield high rewards. The learning process in RL is often modeled as a Markov Decision Process (MDP), a mathematical framework that provides a formalization of decision-making situations where outcomes are partly random and partly under the control of a decision maker; an MDP is defined by its states, actions, transition probabilities (the probability of moving from one state to another given an action), and rewards, and solving an MDP typically involves finding a policy that maximizes some aspect of long-term reward. A widely used approach in RL is Q-learning, a model-free algorithm that learns

the value of an action in a particular state without requiring a model of the environment; it works by estimating the values of the action-state pairs, denoted as Q-values, and updating them using a form of temporal difference learning, which adjusts the Q-values based on the difference between the expected reward and the actual reward received.

1.2 The power of deep learning

Deep learning is a technology that has made significant advancements in recent years, impacting various fields and industries. Deep learning is a subset of AI that automates discovering the intricate patterns in large datasets. One of DL's most remarkable accomplishments is in the field of computer vision. Deep Learning algorithms have enabled computers to interpret images and videos with extraordinary precision. This breakthrough has transformed industries like healthcare, where DL-based medical imaging systems can detect diseases such as cancer and diabetic retinopathy earlier and more accurately than human experts. In the automotive sector, self-driving cars rely heavily on DL to understand their surroundings, making them safer and more efficient. In the realm of natural language processing (NLP), an area where DL excels, computers possess the capability to comprehend and produce text that closely resembles human language. This has led to the development of conversational AI systems and chatbots, revolutionizing customer service, language translation, and content creation. This innovation has transformed the field of surveillance systems, where DL-powered technologies can automatically detect and track objects, individuals, or suspicious activities in real time, enhancing security measures and reducing human intervention. Deep learning's prowess also extends in the area of medical imaging. Deep learning algorithms are capable of interpreting complex X-ray images with a level of accuracy that rivals or even surpasses human radiologists. This advancement has a profound impact on healthcare, as DL assists in diagnosing various medical conditions, such as fractures, tumors, and infections, leading to faster and more precise patient care.

1.2.1 Deep learning fundamental

Deep learning involves the use of artificial neural networks to model and process complex data structures. These artificial neural networks draw inspiration from the structure and operations of the human brain, particularly in how neurons signal to each other. Deep learning networks are characterized by their depth, that is, the number of layers through which data is transformed. The most basic unit of a DL model is the neuron, or node, which imitates the function of biological neurons. Each neuron receives input, processes it, and passes on its output. In artificial neural networks, these neurons are organized into layers. There are three types of layers: input, hidden, and output. The input layer receives the initial data, the hidden layers process the data through various transformations, and the output layer produces the final result. One of the main features of DL is its ability to learn the tasks directly from the data, be it images, text, or sound. This is in contrast to traditional ML, which relies on manual feature extraction. Deep learning automates this process, making it more efficient and often more accurate. Training a DL model involves adjusting the weights of the connections between neurons. This is typically done using a method known as backpropagation, which involves a forward pass through the network to generate a prediction and a backward pass where the error between the prediction and the actual value is used to adjust the weights. This process is repeated over many iterations with the aim of minimizing the error. One common type of DL model is the CNN, widely used in image recognition and processing. CNNs are particularly adept at identifying patterns in images, such as edges and textures, and can handle varying sizes of input images. The recurrent neural network (RNN) stands out as another widely embraced model, particularly well-suited for handling sequential data like time series or natural language. RNNs possess a distinctive capability—the ability to retain internal memory, enabling them to grasp contextual information within the data. Deep learning requires a large amount of data to perform well. This is because the models need to learn from as many examples as possible to make accurate predictions. Furthermore, DL models are computationally intensive, requiring powerful graphics processing units (GPUs) to train and deploy the models effectively.

1.2.2 Deep neural network

Deep neural network (DNN) is a complex computational model inspired by the human brain's neural structure. The role of artificial neurons is akin to that of a miniature processing unit receiving and processing signals to make decisions. While biological neurons in the brain can fatigue and be influenced by various biological factors, artificial neurons excel in their ability to operate for extended periods without fatigue and handle digital data with precision. Fig. 1.2 illustrates the structure of biological neurons. An artificial neuron receives input signals from multiple sources, assigning a specific weight to each signal during the learning process. The neuron aggregates these signals with their designated weights. Subsequently, the resulting value is passed through a transfer function, which transforms the signal into a new signal or value representing a specific decision. The transfer function is a crucial component in artificial neurons, determining the output based on input values. Transfer functions act as the pulsating heart of neural networks, specifying when and how neurons should be activated, thereby determining the final output of the entire network. A neural cell (neuron) operates through several essential parts that work harmoniously to achieve desired outcomes, as shown in figure. These parts include:

1. Dendrites: These branches play a crucial role in receiving inputs that arrive in the form of charges.
2. Cell body (Soma): This part manages the processing of values and charges received from dendrites, deciding whether they should pass through the neural axon or not.
3. Axon: The function of this part is to transmit neural signals across the neural cell.
4. Synapses: Responsible for releasing outputs from the cell, synapses determine the effectiveness and impact of these signals on the receiving cell.

On the other hand, as depicted in the illustration of the artificial neuron, it is structured by receiving multiple inputs (symbolized by X in the figure). These inputs are processed using weights (symbolized by W in the figure), which will be discussed later. Subsequently, the values undergo processing through a mathematical function known as the sigmoid function (symbolized by σ in the figure) to generate a value ranging between one and zero. This value constitutes the outputs of the neuron (symbolized by Y in the figure). When numerous artificial neurons are aggregated, whether in tens, hundreds, or even thousands, they form what is known as artificial neural networks

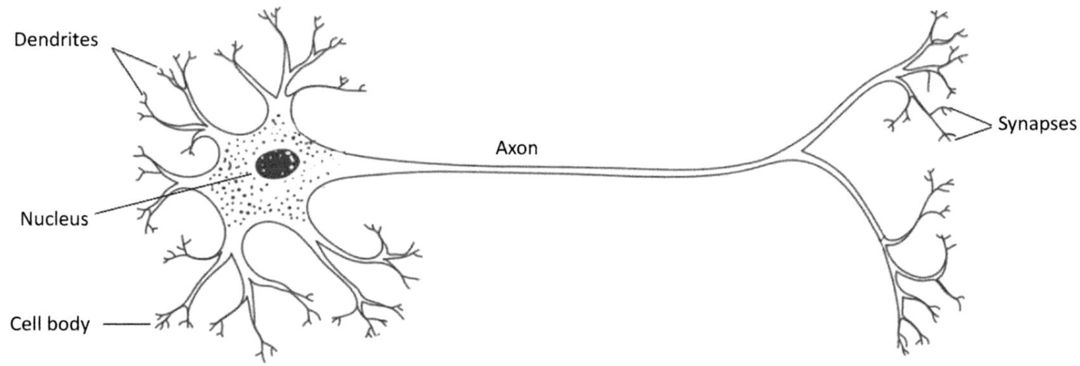

FIGURE 1.2

The structure of human neurons. This figure illustrates the neuron, which is composed of dendrites, which receive signals; a cell body, containing the nucleus; and an axon, transmitting signals to other neurons. Synaptic terminals enable communication between neurons, forming the basis of neural networks critical for information processing in the brain.

(ANNs). In the realm of artificial neural networks, the interplay of inputs, weights, and the activation function (such as the sigmoid function) is foundational. This intricate interconnection allows neural networks to learn and adapt, making them integral to various applications, including ML and pattern recognition.

Understanding the architecture of artificial neurons and their arrangement into neural networks is crucial for delving into the broader field of AI. Fig. 1.3 illustrates the artificial neuron. These networks exhibit remarkable capabilities in processing complex information, recognizing patterns, and making predictions. The significance of artificial neural networks extends across diverse domains, from image to natural language processing. The weights assigned to inputs play a pivotal role in shaping the network's ability to discern patterns and make accurate predictions. Moreover, the sigmoid activation function, by confining outputs within the range of zero to one, facilitates the network's decision-making process. As we explore the intricate dynamics of these artificial neurons and their collective formations, it becomes evident that the essence of AI lies in the sophisticated interplay of mathematical functions, weights, and inputs within neural networks. This holistic understanding is fundamental for researchers and practitioners seeking to harness the full potential of artificial neural networks in advancing AI applications.

Thus, the interaction between multiple neural cells is capable of creating a biological neural network, performing a specific function with high density and accuracy. This is achieved by receiving and processing multiple inputs, followed by the issuance of outputs for a response. At its core, a DNN consists of multiple layers of interconnected nodes, or neurons, organized into an input layer, hidden layers, and an output layer. Each connection between neurons is associated with a weight, representing the strength of the connection. During training, the DNN learns to adjust these weights based on input data to make accurate predictions or classifications. The depth of the network, achieved through numerous hidden layers, enables it to capture intricate patterns and representations in the data. This depth is crucial for handling high-dimensional and nonlinear relationships, making deep neural networks effective in many tasks such as object detection and speech recognition. The learning process involves forward and backward passes, where data is fed through the network and errors are backpropagated to update weights. The success of DNNs can be attributed to

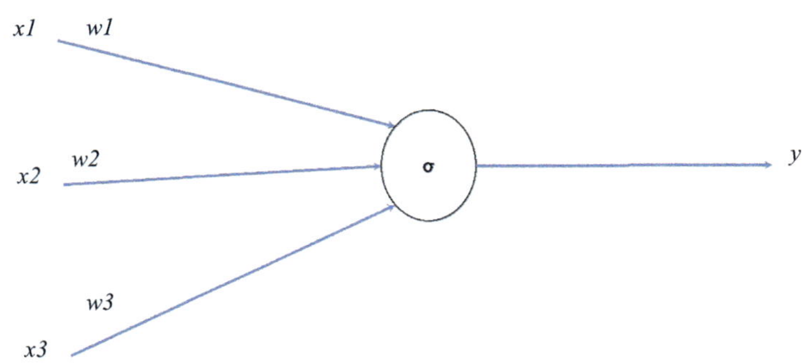

FIGURE 1.3

The structure of an artificial neuron. This figure illustrates the artificial neuron, represented by the reception of inputs (*X*) and their processing through weights (*W*), resulting in an output (*Y*) by utilizing the sigmoid function. This fundamental element is integral to the structure of artificial neural networks.

their ability to automatically extract hierarchical features from raw data, learning complex representations that would be challenging to engineer manually. Despite their power, DNNs pose challenges, including the need for substantial amounts of labeled data and computational resources for training. Ongoing research focuses on addressing these challenges, exploring new architectures, and optimizing techniques to enhance the efficiency and generalization capabilities of deep neural networks, making them invaluable tools in modern AI applications.

1.2.3 Convolutional neural network

A CNN is a type of DL model designed for image processing and recognition tasks. At its core, a CNN employs convolutional layers to learn spatial hierarchies of features automatically and adaptively from input images (Yamashita et al., 2018). This hierarchical learning is crucial for capturing complex patterns and representations present in visual data. Unlike traditional neural networks, CNNs use convolutional filters to scan input images, allowing them to identify local patterns such as edges, textures, colors, and shapes. These filters are applied across the entire image, enabling the network to recognize these patterns irrespective of their location. Additionally, CNNs often include pooling layers to reduce spatial dimensions and computational complexity. The combination of convolutional and pooling layers makes CNNs robust to variations in scale, orientation, and position of the input features. The learned features are flattened and passed through fully connected layers to make predictions. CNNs have demonstrated remarkable success in various computer vision tasks, including image classification, object detection, and facial recognition. Their ability to automatically learn hierarchical representations makes them highly effective in extracting meaningful features from visual data, contributing to their widespread use in diverse applications across industries such as healthcare, autonomous vehicles, and security systems. As a powerful tool in the realm of DL, CNNs continue to drive advancements in image understanding and recognition.

CNNs represent a groundbreaking advancement in the field of DL, particularly tailored for tasks involving image analysis. The architecture of CNNs draws inspiration from the human visual system, implementing a sophisticated hierarchy of layers to automatically learn and discern intricate patterns within images. The core components of a CNN include convolutional layers, pooling layers, and fully connected layers. Convolutional layers employ filters that traverse input images, enabling the network to capture spatial hierarchies of features such as edges, textures, and complex patterns. This ability to extract meaningful features from raw pixel data distinguishes CNNs from traditional neural networks, making them exceptionally proficient in image-related tasks.

Pooling layers are used to downsampling the spatial dimensions of the data, effectively reducing computational complexity and enhancing the network's resistance to variations in input. By aggregating information from neighboring pixels, pooling layers contribute to the creation of more abstract representations, further aiding the network's capacity to recognize patterns at different scales. Fully connected layers, often located at the end of the network, establish connections between every neuron in one layer to every neuron in the next. This facilitates high-level feature learning and classification, allowing CNN to make decisions based on a combination of learned features. One of the remarkable strengths of CNNs lies in their proficiency in tasks such as image classification, object detection, and facial recognition. The hierarchical feature learning process, combined with the ability to automatically extract relevant patterns, empowers CNNs to excel in scenarios where traditional computer vision approaches may fall short. The training process involves forward and backward passes, during which the network adjusts its internal weights using optimization algorithms such as gradient descent. This iterative optimization refines the network's ability to accurately classify and interpret images. Several notable CNN architectures have played pivotal roles in shaping the landscape of DL. LeNet-5 (Lecun et al., 1998), introduced by Yann LeCun and his colleagues, was among the pioneering CNNs designed for handwritten digit recognition. Subsequent architectures such as VGG (Sapijaszko & Mikhael, 2018), AlexNet (Alom et al., 2018), GoogLeNet (Szegedy et al., 2015), and ResNet50 (He et al., 2016) have pushed the boundaries of image processing capabilities, demonstrating the adaptability and scalability of CNNs. Transfer learning, a practice where pretrained CNN models are fine-tuned for specific tasks, has become a standard approach. This approach exploits the knowledge that has been obtained from training on large datasets, allowing the model to generalize better to new tasks while mitigating the need for extensive computational resources.

Despite their remarkable successes, CNNs have challenges that researchers are actively addressing. Adversarial attacks, where small, imperceptible modifications to input data lead to misclassifications, pose a significant concern. Researchers are exploring techniques to enhance the robustness of CNNs against such attacks. Additionally, the dependence on large, labeled datasets for training can be a limitation, particularly in domains where acquiring annotated data is challenging. Ongoing research is focused on addressing these issues and further refining CNN architectures to extend their applicability to a broader range of tasks.

1.2.4 Overview of object detection, classification, and segmentation

In the initial stages of development, DL structures were conceived primarily to maximize task accuracy, with less emphasis on considering implementation complexity (Sze et al., 2017). Contemporary research underscores the importance of designing DL models to optimize accuracy and minimize power requirements and computational complexity. This shift in focus aims to enhance the practical applicability of DL approaches (Chen et al., 2020). Object detection has emerged as a crucial research area, benefiting from the availability of powerful learning tools that facilitate the recognition and prediction of deeper features (Zou et al., 2023). Notably, recent advancements have seen a significant integration of object detectors in extracting high-level features from images, surpassing the performance of traditional algorithms. The evolution of these features has transitioned from global representations to local representations designed to be invariant to changes in translation, scale, rotation, illumination, viewpoint, and occlusion (Murase & Nayar, 1995). The popularity of handcrafted local invariant features began with the introduction of the scale-invariant feature transform (SIFT) (Lowe, 2004). Subsequently, progress in various visual recognition tasks heavily relied on the utilization of local descriptors, such as Haar-such features (Viola & Jones, 2001), SIFT, histogram of orientation (HOG) (Dalal & Triggs, 2005), local binary patterns (LBP) (Ojala et al., 2002), and region covariance (Tuzel et al., 2006). These local features are typically aggregated through methods such as simple concatenation or feature pooling encoders, such as the bag of visual words approach (Sivic & Zisserman, 2003) and spatial pyramid matching (SPM) of bag of visual words models (Lazebnik et al., 2006). To illustrate the developmental trajectory of DL and traditional algorithms for object detection over time, refer to Fig. 1.4. The road map of advancements in DL detection and the traditional algorithms of object detection models over a period of time.

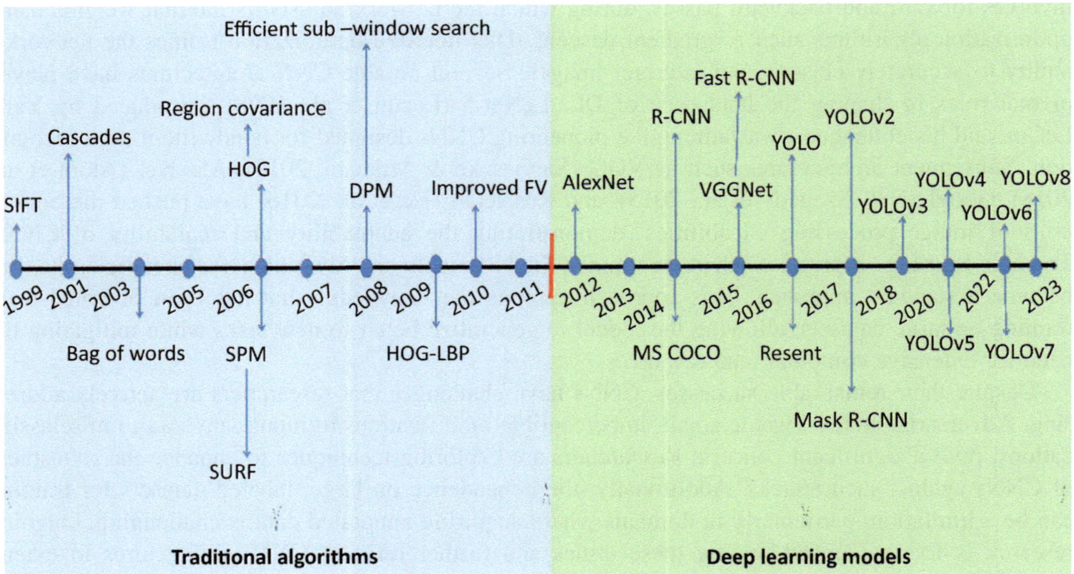

FIGURE 1.4

Road map development for object detection and feature extraction techniques. This figure illustrates the development of traditional versus deep learning models for object detection and feature extractions from the images.

The DL methodology represents an object detection approach designed to address challenges associated with computational complexity. This approach emulates the task of predicting objects within images. Specifically, CNN stands out as a neural network type adept at efficiently detecting patterns in multidimensional spaces. In the realm of DL architectures for object detection, CNNs are commonly employed. This algorithm operates by taking an input image and assigning biases and learnable weights for distinct classes in the images. This enables the differentiation of objects from one class to another. Various CNN models find application in different object detection scenarios. Notably, Ross Kirchick introduced a regional CNN detector, denoted as R-CNN, which comprises four distinct stages. The first stage involves inserting images into the input layer to detect regions of varying sizes and aspect ratios. Subsequently, multiple bounding boxes are drawn on the input image, and region proposals are extracted. Each proposed region undergoes training by a CNN network, and the last layer's output serves as features. The feature extractor's final output corresponds to the number of proposed regions. To compute features for a region proposal, the image data in that region is converted into a format compatible with CNN layers. The CNN's architecture mandates inputs with a fixed size of 227×227 pixels. The feature vector generated by the CNN is then utilized by the binary support vector machine (SVM), trained independently for each class. This SVM model, which takes a feature vector generated in a preceding CNN architecture, returns a confidence value indicating the presence of an object in the corresponding region. R-CNN incorporates selective search algorithms to generate region suggestions, a process that is time-consuming due to the classification of regions per image (Girshick et al., 2014). Unfortunately, R-CNN is not suitable for real-time object detection and must be trained independently for each part. In contrast, Fast R-CNN represents an alternative version of the algorithm, aiming to address these limitations. The regional suggestion algorithm, authored by the same individual responsible for the R-CNN model (Girshick, 2015), was followed by the development of the Fast R-CNN, which aimed to address the limitations of the R-CNN and enhance the efficiency of object detection. This algorithm bears similarity to the regional convolutional neural network with the variation of feeding the input image directly into a convolutional neural network to generate a convolutional feature map, as opposed to providing region suggestions to the CNN. The suggested region undergoes distortion into squares within this model. Region of interest pooling layers are then employed to transform these areas into a fixed size that can be input into a fully connected layer. The softmax layer is utilized in this architecture to predict region class and bounding box offset values. Fig. 1.5 illustrates the schematic diagram for the Fast R-CNN detector.

Both the R-CNN and Fast R-CNN algorithms utilize selective search to identify region suggestions. However, this method is effected by its slowness and time, which adversely impacts the performance of the neural network algorithm. Recent advancements in DL for object recognition introduce alternative algorithms, such as You Only Look Once (YOLO) detectors, which represent a state-of-the-art approach in DL object detection. Developed by Joseph Redmon et al. in 2016

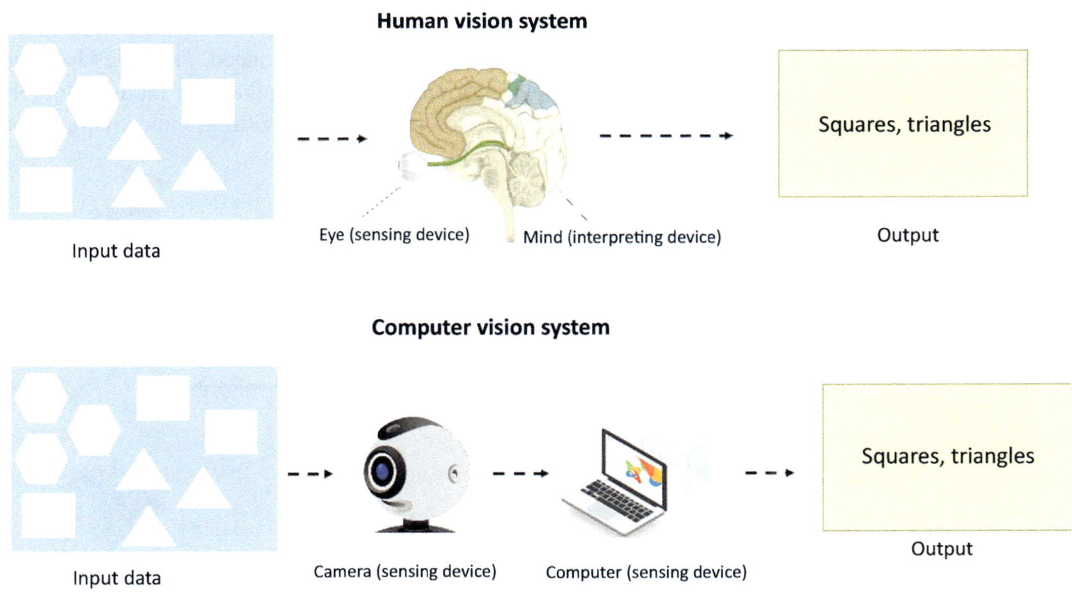

FIGURE 1.5

Human vision verses computer vision systems. This figure illustrates the distinction between the human vision system, employing eyes for sensing and the mind for interpretation, and the computer vision system, utilizing a video camera for sensing and a computer for data interpretation.

(Redmon et al., 2016), YOLO employs a single neural network for the entire image, dividing it into regions and predicting bounding boxes and probabilities for each region. These bounding boxes are weighted by predicted probabilities. Unlike other object detectors such as R-CNN, YOLO examines the entire image at once, allowing its predictions to be informed by the context in the image. Notably, YOLO makes predictions with a single network evaluation, in contrast to other detectors that necessitate thousands for a single image. YOLO algorithms take the input image and partition it into S × S grids, extracting features from each raster. Predictions for bounding boxes with confidence values for the predicted classes within the bounding boxes are made, as illustrated in Fig. 1.6. Each grid cell recognizes bounding boxes and confidence values, with the bounding box comprising five predictions represented by x, y, w, and h and the confidence value. The x and y coordinates denote the center of the bounding box of the grid cell, while w and h represent the width and height of the entire image. The confidence values reflect the certainty of the detector regarding whether the box contains the object to be predicted. The YOLO algorithm employs a grid-based approach for object detection, predicting multiple bounding boxes within each grid cell. During the training phase, a single bounding box predictor is assigned responsibility for each class, and this predictor is tasked with predicting an object based on the highest intersection over union (IoU) value with the ground truth. This specialization within bounding box prediction is achieved through the use of a cumulative squared error, encompassing classification, localization, and confidence losses.

To optimize YOLO's performance during training, a specific loss function is employed, as denoted by Eq. (1.1). YOLOv2, the second iteration of YOLO, is designed for real-time processing and addresses several shortcomings of its predecessor, as detailed in the YOLO9000 paper (Redmon & Farhadi, 2017). YOLOv2 enhances processing accuracy and speed, amplifies localization errors for predicted classes, and integrates batch normalization to regulate the model. Notably, YOLOv2 eliminates the need for dropout layers to mitigate overfitting, improving input

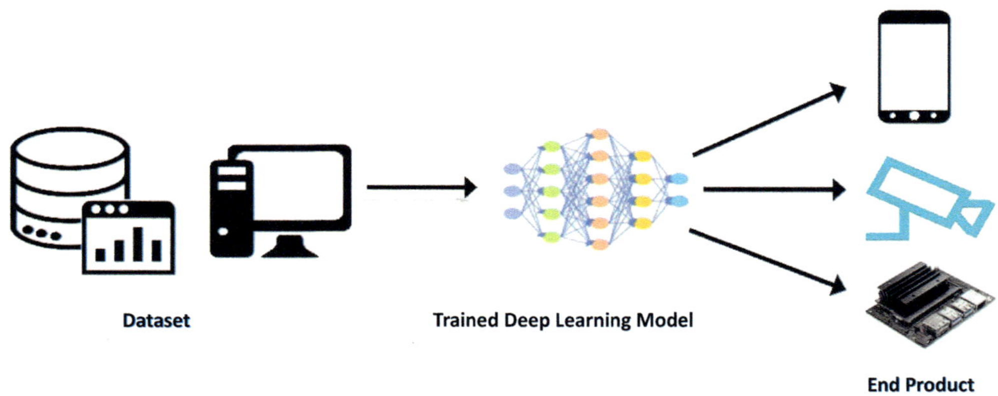

FIGURE 1.6

Typical development flow of a deep learning network. This figure illustrates a model of a neural network that has been created to solve a classification problem and is fed huge amounts of labeled data, from which it learns how to classify objects by end devices.

normalization by defining variance values and means over mini-batches. In 2020 (Bochkovskiy et al., 2020), YOLOv4 was introduced as an optimal speed and accuracy object detector, featuring significant improvements over previous versions.

$$
\begin{aligned}
&\lambda_{\text{coord}}\sum_{i=0}^{s^2}\sum_{j=0}^{B}\mathbb{1}_{i,j}^{\text{obj}}\left[(x_i-\hat{x}_i)^2+(y_i-\hat{y}_i)^2\right] \\
&+\lambda_{\text{coord}}\sum_{i=0}^{s^2}\sum_{j=0}^{B}1_{i,j}^{\text{obj}}\left[\left(\sqrt{w_i}-\sqrt{\hat{w}_i}\right)^2+\left(\sqrt{h_i}-\sqrt{\hat{h}_i}\right)^2\right] \\
&+\sum_{i=0}^{s^2}\sum_{j=0}^{B}\mathbb{1}_{i,j}^{obj}\left(C_i-\hat{C}_i\right)^2 \\
&+\lambda_{\text{noobj}}\sum_{i=0}^{s^2}\sum_{j=0}^{B}\mathbb{1}_{i,j}^{\text{noobj}}\left(C_i-\hat{C}_i\right)^2 \\
&+\sum_{i=0}^{s^2}\mathbb{1}_{i}^{\text{obj}}\Sigma_{c\in\text{class}}\left(p_i(c)-\hat{p}_i(c)\right)^2
\end{aligned}
\tag{1.1}
$$

where λ_{coord} is a constant used to increase the weight for the first two terms of the loss function. B is the number of prediction boxes for each cell. jth is a predictor of this cell and is the highest among the predictors of each cell. x_i and y_i represent the location of the centroid of the anchor box. w_i is the width of the anchor box. h_i is the height of the anchor box. λ_{noobj} weights down the loss when detecting background. C_i is the confidence score where there is an object or no.

YOLOv4 incorporates a state-of-the-art bag of freebies (BoF) and bag of specials (BoS) to enhance detector accuracy without increasing influence time and training cost. Despite a marginal increase in influence cost, BoS substantially improves object detection accuracy. YOLOv4, based on Darknet, achieved an AP of 43.5% on the COCO dataset with a real-time speed of 65 fps on Tesla 100, establishing itself as the most accurate model at the time. The subsequent release, YOLOv5, introduces a novel DL network structure comprising a backbone, neck, and head. It is a lightweight architecture, with a disk size of only 27 MB, distinguishing it from previous YOLO detectors. The CSP (cross-stage partial networks) modules, employed as a backbone in YOLOv5, facilitate the extraction of essential properties from input images. The Neck model, following the FPN (feature pyramid network) architecture, creates feature pyramids to generalize effectively across different object sizes and scales. Finally, the head model, responsible for the final detection step, utilizes anchor boxes to construct output vectors containing class probabilities, objectness scores, and bounding boxes. These models, such as FPN, BiFPN, and PANet, leverage diverse feature pyramid approaches to enhance the model's effectiveness with previously imperceptible data. Overall, these architectures enable convolutional neural networks to handle high-dimensional data and form the basis for robust object classification. YOLOv6 is a top-notch object detection system known for balancing speed and accuracy, making it a popular choice for real-time applications. It has improved architecture and training methods, including the use of a bi-directional concatenation (BiC) module, anchor-aided training (AAT) strategy, and better backbone and neck design, resulting in high accuracy on datasets like COCO. Moving forward, YOLOv7 sets a new standard in real-time object detection, outperforming previous detectors across a wide speed range (5–160 FPS) and achieving the highest accuracy (56.8% AP) among real-time detectors at 30 FPS or higher on GPU V100. It excels against competitors such as YOLOR, YOLOX, Scaled-YOLOv4, and YOLOv5 in both speed and accuracy. Recently, YOLOv8 takes the lead as the latest version, utilizing advanced DL and computer vision techniques for unmatched speed and accuracy in real-time object detection and image segmentation. Its user-friendly design allows easy adaptation across different applications and hardware platforms, from edge devices to cloud APIs.

Classification is the concept in the field of AI, serving as a cornerstone for organizing, categorizing, and making sense of vast datasets. At its core, classification involves the task of assigning predefined labels or categories to input data based on its inherent characteristics. This process is akin to teaching a computer to recognize patterns and relationships within the data, allowing it to make informed decisions about new, unseen instances. The beauty of classification lies in its versatility, with applications spanning a myriad of domains, from image to spam filtering and medical diagnosis. At the heart of the classification paradigm are algorithms that learn from historical data, iteratively refining their ability to differentiate between classes. Two main types of classification emerge: binary classification, where the data is divided into two distinct categories, and multiclass classification, where the task involves assigning data to multiple predefined classes. Popular algorithms, such as decision trees (de Ville, 2013), support vector machines (Suthaharan, 2016), and neural networks, play pivotal roles in training models to become adept at classification tasks. The success of classification hinges on features—the distinctive attributes of the data that inform the model's decision-making process. Feature selection and extraction are crucial steps in refining the input data to enhance the model's accuracy. Furthermore, evaluating classification models involves metrics such as accuracy, precision, recall, and F1 score, providing a comprehensive understanding of their performance. As the field of ML continues to evolve, advancements in classification techniques, including ensemble methods and DL architectures, are pushing the boundaries of what is achievable. The significance of classification transcends its technical intricacies, as its real-world applications are transforming industries, offering solutions to complex problems, and contributing to the evolution of AI. Classification is a foundational concept in the fields of data science and ML, serving as a fundamental building block for organizing and making sense of large datasets. At its core, classification involves the task of assigning predefined labels or categories to input data based on its inherent characteristics. The versatility of classification is evident in its applications across various areas, from recognizing images and speech to filtering out spam emails and assisting in medical diagnoses.

In the heart of the classification process are special algorithms that learn from past data, continuously refining their ability to tell the difference between different classes. There are two main types of classification: binary, where data is split into two distinct categories, and multiclass, where data is assigned to multiple predefined classes. Algorithms such as support vector machines, decision trees, and neural networks are effective to be trained and become good at classification tasks. The success of classification depends on features—the unique characteristics of the data that guide the model's decision-making. Selecting the right features and transforming raw data are vital steps to improve the accuracy of the model.

When evaluating classification algorithms, we use metrics such as recall, precision, F1 score, and accuracy to get a full picture of how well they perform. Accuracy looks at overall correctness, precision checks how well the model avoids false positives, recall measures its ability to catch true positives, and the F1 score gives a balance between precision and recall. These metrics help us understand the strengths and weaknesses of a classification model, guiding us in making it better over time. As ML keeps advancing, new techniques such as ensemble methods (combining strengths of multiple algorithms) and DL architectures (inspired by the complexity of neural networks) are pushing the limits of what we can achieve. The continuous exploration of these advanced techniques promises better accuracy, scalability, and adaptability, positioning classification as a dynamic and ever-evolving field within the broader scope of AI. In simpler terms, classification is more than just a complex technical concept. Its real-world applications are transformative, driving progress in various industries, solving complex problems, and playing a big role in how AI is evolving. Classification shows us the power of using data to make smart decisions, providing a way for us to understand and navigate the complexities of a world increasingly shaped by data.

In the field of ML, segmentation involves the division of a dataset or input into distinct and meaningful segments or groups based on specific criteria. The primary objective is to partition the data in a manner that facilitates easier analysis, understanding, and extraction of valuable insights. This technique finds widespread application in various fields, such as image processing, natural language processing, and marketing. Depending on the nature of the data and the problem at hand, there are different types of segmentation. For instance, in computer vision, image segmentation divides an image into meaningful regions for tasks such as object recognition. In natural language processing, text segmentation breaks down textual content into smaller segments, aiding tasks such as summarization and sentiment analysis. Marketing utilizes customer segmentation to group customers based on characteristics, facilitating tailored strategies. Time series segmentation, crucial for time series analysis, involves dividing temporal data into intervals for trend detection. Clustering, a form of segmentation, groups similar data points using unsupervised learning, with K-means clustering being a common example. The significance of segmentation in ML lies in its ability to simplify complex datasets, allowing for more focused analysis or modeling of each segment, with methods chosen based on data characteristics and analysis goals.

1.2.5 Autoencoders

The autoencoder is a type of neural network that operates without the need for data labeling, making it an unsupervised learning algorithm. Its primary objective is to acquire an input function capable of reconstructing input data into an output of reduced dimensions. Essentially, it aims to approximate the identity function, mimicking the input through the output. In mathematical terms, denoting the input as x (referred to as the encoder), the network is represented by x as well (referred to as the decoder). The autoencoder achieves dimensionality reduction through nonlinear optimization, as illustrated in Eqs. (1.2) and (1.3), where h denotes the hidden layer. The hidden layer is computed by multiplying weights and the vector x, then adding the bias to the activation function:

$$h = \sigma(W \times x + b) \tag{1.2}$$

$$x' = (W \times h + b) \tag{1.3}$$

Various autoencoder types exist, such as sparse autoencoders, denoising autoencoders, complete autoencoders, and convolutional neural autoencoders. A study, detailed by Sewani and Kashef (2020), demonstrated that the reconstruction of input data is more straightforward when a relationship or basic structure is present. Autoencoders find applications in diverse fields, including the analysis of brain disorders in clinical neuroimaging studies. Autoencoders are often employed as a preprocessing step before feeding data into another classification model, particularly due to the high dimensionality of genetic and neuroimaging data. Wang et al. (2016) evaluated autoencoder performance by comparing it with other models for reduction tasks, including principal component analysis, linear discriminant analysis (linear models), locally linear embedding, and isomap (nonlinear models). The impact of the number of hidden layer nodes on autoencoder performance was explored. Optimal performance was observed when the hidden nodes were set around the inherent dimensionality of the datasets, as demonstrated with the Modified National Institute of Standards and Technology (MNIST) dataset. Additional investigations involved the Olivetti dataset and a synthetic dataset.

Experimental analysis of the synthetic dataset revealed stable performance by PCA, linear discriminant analysis (LDA), and Isomap, while the autoencoder and locally linear embedding exhibited instability. Despite this, the unstable models retained the geometric properties of the original data, yielding acceptable results. Experiments with the MNIST dataset indicated that the autoencoder outperformed PCA. The autoencoder tended to project dots representing the digit 1, projecting images of the same class onto edges and corners. These results highlighted that the autoencoder aids in dimension reduction. It contributes to recognizing recurring structures. The low-dimensional data generated during the encoding process, containing valuable patterns from the original input, can be utilized in a convolutional neural network or another ML algorithm.

1.2.6 Computer vision applications

Computer vision is a subfield of AI that employs advanced techniques in DL to imbue computers with the capacity to perceive, recognize, and scrutinize visual content, mirroring the cognitive processes of human vision. This burgeoning discipline finds increasing prominence in various domains, including automated AI vision inspection, remote monitoring, and automation. Traditionally, computer vision relied on established techniques such as feature descriptors for tasks such as object detection. Before the advent of DL, a crucial step called feature extraction was integral to tasks such as image classification. Features, denoting small, distinctive, descriptive, or informative patches in images, were extracted through diverse algorithms, encompassing edge detection, corner detection, and threshold segmentation. The culmination of these features defined each object class. During deployment, these feature-defined object classes were compared with features in other images. The classification of an image hinges on the presence of a significant number of features corresponding to a specific object class. However, the conventional approach faced challenges, particularly in the manual selection of pertinent features for each image. As the number of classes increased, the feature extraction process became increasingly cumbersome, necessitating manual intervention and an extensive trial-and-error process to identify optimal characteristics for different object classes. Moreover, each feature definition entailed meticulous adjustment of a multitude of parameters. In this book, we harnessed the power of DL across diverse computer vision applications, spanning surveillance, fire and smoke detection, social distancing for COVID-19, fingerprint analysis, and medical imaging. Deep learning, characterized by its ability to enhance accuracy and robustness across various applications, also demonstrates proficiency in addressing image-based challenges that elude traditional methodologies. Notably, it excels in the classification of intricate patterns in surface recognition, marking a departure from the limitations of conventional approaches. Fig. 1.5 shows the difference between the human vision system, employing eyes for sensing and the mind for interpretation, and the computer vision system, utilizing a camera for sensing and a computer for data interpretation.

1.2.7 Deep learning for embedded systems

Recently, the integration of DL into embedded systems has emerged as a transformative force, revolutionizing how intelligence is processed and applied at the edge of various devices. Embedded systems, ranging from smart cameras and IoT devices to automotive components, are equipped with the power to make complex decisions, thanks to the advent of DL algorithms tailored for resource-constrained environments. Embedded systems are dedicated computing devices that are designed to perform specific tasks, often with constraints such as power consumption, memory usage, size, and real-time processing. They are omnipresent in our daily lives, found in smartphones, smart home devices, medical instruments, and even within the intricate systems of modern automobiles. The traditional approach to embedding intelligence in these systems involved rule-based methods or simpler machine-learning algorithms. However, the rise of DL has ushered in a new era of capability, allowing these devices to handle more sophisticated tasks. Embedded systems typically operate in resource-constrained environments, where limitations in terms of processing power, memory, and energy consumption are inherent. Deep learning, with its appetite for computational resources, initially seemed incompatible with such systems. However, the field has witnessed a paradigm shift with the development of lightweight models and optimized algorithms tailored for embedded environments. To make DL feasible for embedded systems, researchers and engineers focus on creating models with reduced complexity and computational demands. Techniques such as model quantization, pruning, and knowledge distillation are employed to shrink the size of neural networks without compromising their performance significantly. Moreover, specialized hardware accelerators, such as GPUs and TPUs, are integrated into embedded devices to execute DL computations. The concept of edge computing involves processing data closer to the source of generation rather than relying on a centralized cloud infrastructure. Deep learning in embedded systems plays a crucial role in enabling edge intelligence, allowing devices to make rapid decisions locally without the need for constant communication with the cloud servers. This reduces the latency and addresses the privacy concerns by keeping sensitive data on the device. Embedded DL is revolutionizing the field of computer vision in smart cameras. These cameras can interpret video feeds, detect objects, recognize faces, and even predict potential security threats in real time. Internet of Things (IoT) devices benefit from embedded DL for tasks such as voice recognition, natural language processing, and personalized user experiences. This local processing enhances the efficiency and responsiveness of these devices. Deep learning algorithms embedded in the processing units of autonomous vehicles enable real-time analysis of the surrounding environment. This includes object detection, path planning, and decision-making, contributing to safer and more efficient self-driving capabilities. In healthcare, embedded DL facilitates the analysis of medical images, monitoring vital signs, and predicting potential health issues. Portable medical devices with embedded intelligence provide timely insights for both patients and healthcare professionals. While significant progress has been made, challenges persist in the integration of DL into embedded systems. Power efficiency remains a concern, as energy consumption must be minimized for prolonged device operation. Additionally, the ongoing exploration of novel architectures and algorithms aims to balance between model performance and complexity. The future of DL in embedded systems holds promise for advancements in natural language processing, reinforcement learning, and the seamless integration of AI into diverse applications. As research continues, we can expect even more sophisticated and efficient models tailored to the unique constraints of embedded environments.

Deep learning for embedded systems marks a transformative leap in the capabilities of everyday devices. The synergy between powerful neural networks and resource-constrained embedded systems has opened doors to a new era of intelligent and responsive technologies. From enhancing the vision of smart cameras to enabling autonomous decision-making in vehicles, embedded DL is shaping the landscape of AI at the edge. As technology continues to evolve, we can anticipate a future where embedded systems seamlessly integrate sophisticated deep-learning capabilities, bringing intelligence closer to the point of action and enriching our daily lives in ways previously unimaginable. Fig. 1.6 shows a typical workflow of a DL framework deployment system.

1.3 Understanding image and video data

Images are composed of pixels, the smallest units of a digital image. Each pixel represents a tiny element and is characterized by its color and intensity. In digital images, colors are represented using the RGB (red, green, blue) color model, where each pixel's color is a combination of these three primary colors (Bovik, 2010). The resolution of an image is determined by the number of pixels it contains, with higher resolutions providing greater detail. Grayscale images, on the other hand, use a single channel to represent intensity, with pixel values ranging from black to white. Image data is often stored in formats such as JPEG, PNG, or TIFF, each with its own compression and quality characteristics. Understanding image data involves extracting features that capture important information about the content. Feature extraction can involve identifying edges, textures, shapes, or more complex patterns. Techniques such as CNNs have proven highly effective in automatically learning and extracting meaningful features from images, enabling tasks such as image classification, object detection, and segmentation.

Video data extends the principles of image data to a sequence of frames. A video is essentially a series of images displayed in rapid succession, creating the illusion of motion. Each frame is a complete static image, and the combination of frames over time produces the dynamic visual experience we associate with videos. Video data introduces the dimension of time, making it more complex than still images. Temporal information becomes critical in understanding motion, tracking objects across frames, and recognizing patterns over time. Video data is represented using codecs such as H.264 or H.265, which compress the data to reduce file size while maintaining visual quality. Similar to image data, the analysis of video data often involves feature extraction. However, it added emphasis on temporal features. Tracking algorithms, optical flow techniques, and RNNs are commonly employed to model temporal dependencies in video sequences. These methods enable applications such as action recognition, video summarization, and activity detection.

Despite the progress made in image and video analysis, several challenges persist. One major challenge is the variability in visual data. Images and videos can exhibit diverse lighting conditions, viewpoints, occlusions, and background clutter, making it difficult for algorithms to generalize effectively. Robustness to these variations is crucial for the success of computer vision applications in real-world scenarios. Another challenge is the need for large, labeled datasets for training ML models. Creating comprehensive and diverse datasets is a time-consuming, labeled resource-intensive process. Insufficient datasets can lead the models to be biased and fail to generalize to unseen data. Interpreting the semantics of visual content, understanding the context, and reasoning about the relationships between objects in an image or video pose additional challenges. While strides have been made with advanced deep-learning architectures, achieving a human-level understanding of visual scenes remains an open research problem.

1.3.1 Overview of the importance of image and video data in various real-world applications

Image and video data play a pivotal role in real-world applications, permeating diverse fields and impacting how we interact with technology significantly. In the field of healthcare, medical imaging leverages the power of visual data to diagnose and treat ailments, with technologies such as MRI and CT scans providing intricate insights into the human body. Surveillance applications, powered by video data, enhance security measures in public spaces, airports, and critical infrastructure, aiding in threat detection and prevention. Moreover, image and video data serve as the lifeblood for training ML and DL models, allowing computers to recognize patterns, objects, and even emotions. E-commerce platforms exploit visual data for image recognition, facilitating efficient product searches and enhancing the user experience. Social media platforms thrive on visual content, with images and videos driving engagement and communication. Augmented reality (AR) and virtual reality (VR) applications rely heavily on visual data to create immersive and interactive experiences, transforming the way we perceive and interact with the digital world. Environmental monitoring utilizes satellite imagery and video feeds to track changes in landscapes, study climate patterns, and manage natural resources. The entertainment industry, from filmmaking to gaming, is fueled by the creative deployment of image and video data to captivate audiences and tell compelling stories. As technology continues to evolve, the importance of image and video data in shaping our daily lives becomes increasingly evident, underscoring the need for robust systems to capture, process, and interpret visual information across a spectrum of applications. From revolutionizing healthcare diagnostics to enhancing the capabilities of self-driving cars, the impact of image and video data is both profound and multifaceted, reflecting a fundamental aspect of our interconnected digital age.

1.3.2 The evolution of visual processing

The development of visual processing has undergone a significant transformation, reflecting the sophisticated abilities of the human visual system. From basic image recognition systems in early computers to advanced AI neural networks today, progress has been marked by improvements in computational power, algorithmic advancements, and a deeper understanding of how visual information is processed. Initially, efforts to enable machines to understand visual data faced challenges, as early attempts struggled to make sense of pixelated input. However, as technology advanced, the methods used in visual processing also improved. The introduction of feature-based recognition allowed systems to identify specific patterns and shapes in images. A major shift in visual processing occurred with the incorporation of neural networks inspired by the human brain. CNNs emerged as a groundbreaking approach, mimicking the hierarchical processing observed in the human visual cortex. These neural networks demonstrated an unprecedented ability to recognize detailed features, identify objects, and even generate realistic images. As computational resources increased, so did the depth and complexity of these networks, resulting in architectures such as ResNet and Inception capable of handling complex visual tasks with high accuracy. The evolution continued with the rise of generative adversarial networks (GANs), unlocking the potential for AI systems to recognize and create visually compelling content. The impact of these advancements in visual processing on AI has been transformative across various fields. In healthcare, AI-powered image analysis has revolutionized medical diagnostics, allowing for the detection of anomalies in medical images with remarkable precision. The ability of AI models to analyze large datasets of medical images has significantly sped up the diagnosis process, providing invaluable support to healthcare professionals in critical decision-making. Similarly, in vehicles, the evolution of visual processing has played a crucial role. Advanced perception systems, equipped with sophisticated visual recognition algorithms, empower self-driving cars to navigate complex environments, identify pedestrians, and anticipate potential hazards. This improves the safety of vehicles. However, it contributes to the realization of a future where transportation is seamlessly integrated with AI technologies. The entertainment industry has also experienced a revolution fueled by the evolution of visual processing in AI. Deep learning models, capable of generating realistic images and videos, have opened up new possibilities in virtual reality and gaming. The synthesis of visual content that blurs the line between reality and simulation has enhanced the immersive experience for users, offering unprecedented levels of realism. Additionally, content creation has become more accessible and efficient, with AI algorithms assisting in tasks such as image editing, style transfer, and even the generation of entirely new visual content based on user preferences. Beyond these specific applications, the impact of visual processing on AI extends to the core of human-computer interaction. NLP systems, combined with advanced visual understanding, enable AI models to comprehend and respond to text, images, and videos. This multimodal capability enriches how humans interact with machines, creating a more intuitive and inclusive user experience. Virtual assistants and smart devices, equipped with enhanced visual processing, can interpret gestures, recognize objects, and respond to visual cues, creating a seamless and integrated interaction between humans and AI. However, as AI continues to advance in visual processing, ethical considerations come to the forefront. Issues such as bias in training data, privacy concerns related to image recognition, and the potential misuse of AI-generated visual content raise important questions about the responsible development and deployment of these technologies. Balancing innovation with ethical considerations is crucial to ensuring that the benefits of visual processing in AI are realized without compromising fundamental principles of fairness, accountability, and transparency.

1.3.3 The differentiating between image and video data

Understanding the fundamental disparities between image and video data is vital in various fields, particularly in the realm of computer vision and multimedia analysis. The image represents a static, two-dimensional depiction of visual information, encapsulating a single moment in time.

In contrast, video data encompasses a dynamic sequence of frames constituting a temporal dimension that unfolds over time. The discrete nature of images allows for focused analysis of individual frames, each serving as an isolated entity for examination. In the context of video data, the interplay of consecutive frames introduces a dynamic aspect, wherein temporal relationships and motion patterns become critical considerations. While images primarily rely on spatial features for interpretation, videos necessitate the integration of both spatial and temporal cues. Additionally, the temporal dimension in videos introduces challenges related to compression, storage, and efficient retrieval, demanding specialized methodologies for optimal processing. Furthermore, the inherent complexity of video data extends beyond the summation of individual frames, as it involves the nuanced exploration of temporal coherence, motion trajectories, and the potential presence of dynamic events. Distinctive approaches are thus required in handling image and video data, emphasizing the necessity for tailored algorithms and techniques to extract meaningful insights from these diverse modalities. Comprehending the nuanced disparities between image and video data fosters a refined understanding of visual information. It facilitates the development of targeted methodologies for improved analysis and interpretation within academic and technological fields.

1.3.4 The common image formats and their properties

Common image formats play a vital role in digital communication and visual representation, serving as the cornerstone of diverse applications ranging from web design to medical imaging. Among the plethora of image formats, JPEG (Joint Photographic Experts Group) stands out as a widely adopted standard, renowned for its efficient compression algorithms that balance image quality and file size. JPEG's lossy compression makes it ideal for photographic images, where a slight loss in fidelity is acceptable. However, this format is not suitable for images requiring precise detail preservation, such as diagrams or text. On the contrary, PNG (Portable Network Graphics) employs lossless compression, ensuring impeccable image quality but often resulting in larger file sizes. This makes PNG preferable for graphics that demand transparency or intricate details, albeit at the expense of increased storage requirements. The GIF (Graphics Interchange Format) format, renowned for its support of animations and transparency, employs lossless compression but is limited in color depth compared to other formats. Emerging as a versatile option, the WebP format, developed by Google, combines both lossy and lossless compression, offering high-quality images with smaller file sizes. With a focus on the preservation of transparency and animation features, WebP is gaining traction as a modern alternative to traditional formats. In the realm of professional graphic design and print media, the TIFF (Tagged Image File Format) format reigns supreme. TIFF's lossless compression ensures that no image data is sacrificed, making it a preferred choice for tasks demanding the utmost image fidelity, such as printing and archival purposes. However, the resulting larger file sizes make TIFF less suitable for web applications, where swift loading times are paramount. As digital technology advances, the HEIF (High-Efficiency Image Format) emerges as a modern contender, offering superior compression efficiency without compromising image quality. Embraced by Apple's ecosystem, HEIF provides an excellent balance between reduced file sizes and exceptional visual fidelity. Nevertheless, widespread adoption across various platforms remains a work in progress.

In the context of scientific and medical imaging, the DICOM (Digital Imaging and Communications in Medicine) format takes precedence. Tailored to meet the specific requirements of the healthcare industry, DICOM ensures standardized storage and sharing of medical images, crucial for diagnostic and research purposes. Furthermore, the SVG (Scalable Vector Graphics) format revolutionizes the representation of graphics on the web by utilizing vector graphics, ensuring scalability without compromising image quality. SVG is particularly advantageous for logos, icons, and illustrations that demand adaptability across various screen sizes. Despite its merits, SVG is not the optimal choice for complex photographic images, where raster formats such as JPEG or PNG excel. As the digital landscape evolves, considerations for image formats extend beyond mere visual appeal. Accessibility and responsiveness in web design, efficient storage in medical databases, and fidelity in graphic design are all paramount factors influencing the choice of image format. The dynamic interplay between these formats continues to shape the visual language of the digital era, ensuring that each image finds its most suitable and effective representation, whether in the vast expanse of the internet, the intricacies of medical diagnostics, or the finesse of graphic design. Thus, understanding the nuances of common image formats and their properties becomes imperative for individuals navigating the multifaceted realm of visual communication in the 21st century (Ansari et al., 2019).

1.4 Importance of real-world applications

The significance of real-world applications in various domains cannot be overstated, as it serves as the litmus test for the practical utility of theoretical concepts. In the realm of technology and AI, the emergence and proliferation of DL have remarkably transformed the landscape of real-world problem-solving. Deep learning, a subset of ML, has demonstrated unparalleled capabilities in processing and interpreting complex data, enabling it to tackle intricate challenges across diverse sectors. One salient aspect of its importance lies in the field of healthcare, where the accurate diagnosis of diseases and the identification of potential treatment options demand a nuanced understanding of intricate patterns within medical data. Deep learning algorithms, equipped with the capacity to discern subtle correlations and anomalies, contribute significantly to enhancing diagnostic accuracy and treatment efficacy. Similarly, in the financial sector, the ability of DL architectures to analyze vast datasets in real time has proven instrumental in detecting fraudulent activities and optimizing investment strategies. The dynamic and evolving nature of financial markets necessitates sophisticated tools, and DL emerges as a beacon in navigating this complexity. Moreover, in the field of autonomous systems, the practical application of DL algorithms is indispensable. These approaches, trained on large datasets of real-world scenarios, empower vehicles to make informed decisions, ensuring safety and efficiency on the roads. The fusion of DL with real-world applications extends its influence to diverse fields such as natural language processing, image recognition, and speech synthesis, underpinning advancements in human-computer interaction and information retrieval systems. Real-world applications act as proving grounds, validating the robustness and adaptability of DL models in addressing multifaceted challenges. The translation of theoretical advancements into tangible solutions for real-world predicaments reinforces the credibility and practicality of DL methodologies. This bridge between theory and application is crucial for the maturation of the field, fostering a symbiotic relationship where real-world challenges inspire and refine theoretical frameworks, while theoretical insights, in turn, provide innovative solutions for practical problems. Moreover, the importance of real-world applications is underscored by the societal impact of technological advancements. The deployment of DL in areas such as climate modeling and prediction facilitates a proactive approach to environmental challenges, offering insights into the mitigation of natural disasters and the development of sustainable strategies. The seamless integration of DL into real-world scenarios also contributes to the democratization of technology, ensuring that its benefits are accessible across diverse demographics. As DL continues to permeate various facets of our daily lives, from virtual personal assistants to personalized recommendations on online platforms, the emphasis on real-world applications becomes paramount. The efficacy of DL algorithms in processing and understanding complex patterns positions them as indispensable tools in an era characterized by data deluge and technological complexity. In conclusion, the importance of real-world applications in validating and refining the capabilities of DL cannot be overstated. The symbiotic relationship between theoretical advancements and practical implementations propels the field forward, fostering innovation and addressing real-world challenges across diverse domains. As technology continues to evolve, the seamless integration of DL into various sectors that enhances efficiency and accuracy holds the promise of transformative societal impact, shaping a future where intelligent systems contribute meaningfully to our daily lives.

1.4.1 Bridging the gap between theory and practice

The connection between theoretical frameworks and practical applications in DL for image and video processing emerges as a vital pursuit in modern research, responding to the increasing demand for translating theoretical advancements into tangible real-world solutions. However, as the theoretical landscape of DL flourishes, translating these complex models and algorithms into tangible solutions remains a critical challenge. For instance, consider the theoretical underpinnings of CNNs designed for image classification. While the foundational principles of CNNs are well-established, the translation of such architectures into real-world applications demands a nuanced understanding of parameters, data preprocessing, and model fine-tuning. In image processing, one illustrative example of bridging this gap lies in medical diagnostics. Theoretical advancements in image segmentation algorithms, leveraging DL architectures, have significantly improved the accuracy of identifying and delineating anomalies in medical images such as MRIs. The theoretical foundation might revolve around semantic segmentation using U-Net architectures; however, the practical implementation involves domain-specific fine-tuning to adapt the model to the intricacies of medical imagery. This synergy between theory and practice enhances diagnostic precision and underscores the importance of tailoring DL models to the unique challenges posed by specific domains. Extending this paradigm to video processing, theoretical breakthroughs in action recognition using RNNs and long short-term memory (LSTM) networks have paved the way for practical applications in surveillance systems. The theoretical framework might emphasize the temporal dependencies captured by these networks; however, their deployment in real-world scenarios involves addressing challenges such as occlusions, variable lighting conditions, and diverse camera perspectives. By integrating theoretical insights with practical considerations, researchers can develop video processing solutions that are robust and reliable in dynamic, uncontrolled environments. Furthermore, the bridging of theory and practice is essential for addressing ethical considerations in DL applications. Theoretical models for facial recognition, for instance, encounter challenges in real-world deployment due to biases inherent in training data. Bridging this gap involves refining theoretical models and implementing strategies for ethical and unbiased data collection and preprocessing. In the realm of autonomous vehicles, the fusion of theoretical insights and practical implementation is exemplified by advancements in computer vision for object detection. Theoretical models based on region-based convolutional neural networks (R-CNNs) or one-stage detectors such as YOLO provide the conceptual foundation, but adapting these models to the real-world complexities of varied traffic scenarios demands continual refinement. Effective bridging of the gap ensures that autonomous vehicles can accurately detect and respond to diverse objects, weather conditions, and unexpected obstacles, thereby enhancing safety and reliability. Moreover, the synergy between theory and practice extends beyond the confines of specific applications to encompass model interpretability and explainability. Theoretical advancements in interpretable DL, such as attention mechanisms and saliency maps, are instrumental in elucidating the decision-making processes of complex models. However, translating these theoretical insights into practical tools for stakeholders, such as healthcare professionals relying on diagnostic models, requires a user-friendly interface and clear interpretability metrics. Bridging this gap ensures that end-users can trust, understand, and effectively utilize DL models in their respective domains. The imperative task of Bridging the Gap Between Theory and Practice in Deep Learning for Real-World Applications in Image and Video Processing necessitates a holistic approach that integrates theoretical advancements with practical considerations. Examples ranging from medical diagnostics to autonomous vehicles underscore the multifaceted nature of this endeavor. Researchers and practitioners alike must navigate the intricate interplay between theoretical models and real-world complexities to unlock the full potential of DL in addressing the challenges of contemporary applications. As the field continues to evolve, the seamless integration of theory and practice remains pivotal for the development of robust, ethical, and impactful solutions.

1.4.2 Solving real-world challenges

The application of DL in video and image processing has revolutionized various industries, offering innovative solutions to complex real-world challenges. As technology advances, the demand for efficient, accurate, and scalable methods to handle large volumes of visual data has become increasingly critical. One of the primary challenges in image and video processing is accurate object recognition and detection. Deep learning models, particularly CNNs, have demonstrated exceptional capabilities in this domain. These models can automatically learn hierarchical representations of features, enabling them to identify and localize objects within images and video frames with remarkable precision. This has significant implications for industries such as autonomous vehicles, surveillance, and healthcare, where the accurate detection of objects is crucial for decision-making processes. Traditional methods of image and video classification often rely on handcrafted features and rule-based algorithms, making them less adaptable to diverse datasets. Deep learning, on the other hand, excels at automatic feature learning, allowing models to discern intricate patterns and variations in visual data. This has led to advancements in content-based image and video classification, enhancing applications such as content recommendation, video indexing, and image retrieval. The ability of DL models to generalize well across different categories contributes to their versatility in solving real-world challenges. Semantic segmentation involves classifying each pixel in an image or video frame and assigning it a specific label to understand the context and relationships within the visual data. Deep learning techniques, especially semantic segmentation models such as U-Net and DeepLab, have substantially improved the accuracy and efficiency of segmentation tasks. This has implications in various fields, such as medical imaging for organ delineation, environmental monitoring for land cover classification, and augmented reality for precise object interactions. Video action recognition poses unique challenges due to the temporal dimension involved. Deep learning architectures, including RNNs and 3D CNNs, have been designed to capture temporal dependencies in video sequences. This enables accurate recognition of complex actions and activities, making it invaluable for applications such as video surveillance, brain-computer interaction, and sports analytics. Deep learning's ability to learn temporal patterns has significantly improved the robustness and reliability of video action recognition systems. Deep learning has alleviated the data scarcity issue in many real-world applications by leveraging transfer learning. Pretrained models on large datasets, such as ImageNet, can be fine-tuned for specific tasks with limited labeled data. This approach has proven effective in domains such as medical imaging, where obtaining annotated datasets is challenging. Transfer learning accelerates model development and enhances the performance of DL models on diverse and specialized tasks.

One of the challenges faced in deploying DL models, especially in applications involving low-cost embedded systems, is the computational intensity and memory requirements of traditional architectures. These constraints often hinder the feasibility of implementing sophisticated models in resource-limited environments. To address this, researchers have developed lightweight architectures tailored for efficiency and reduced computational complexity, making them well-suited for deployment in low-cost embedded systems. These lightweight models, such as MobileNet and EfficientNet, strike a balance between model performance and resource utilization, allowing them to operate seamlessly on devices with limited processing power and memory. The advent of lightweight architectures has had a profound impact on various applications, including those in video and image processing. In scenarios such as edge computing, IoT devices, and surveillance systems, where cost-effectiveness is paramount, deploying lightweight DL models has become a game changer. These architectures enable real-time processing and decision-making directly on the device, reducing the need for constant communication with centralized servers. This enhances the speed of inference and mitigates issues related to latency, bandwidth, and privacy concerns. Furthermore, the implementation of lightweight architectures has facilitated the integration of DL into a myriad of low-cost embedded systems. Applications ranging from smart cameras for home security to wearable devices for health monitoring can now leverage the power of DL without compromising on cost or energy efficiency. This democratization of DL capabilities has paved the way for innovative solutions in sectors where the affordability and accessibility of technology are crucial factors. The application of DL in video and image processing continues to reshape industries and provide innovative solutions to longstanding challenges. From improving object recognition and semantic segmentation to enhancing video action recognition, DL's versatility and adaptability make it a powerful tool in addressing real-world complexities. As technology evolves, the integration of DL methodologies is expected to push the boundaries of what is possible, opening new avenues for advancements in visual data analysis and interpretation. The ongoing research and development in this field promise a future where DL plays a central role in solving intricate problems across various domains.

1.4.3 Industry relevance and innovation

In recent years, the application of DL in the fields of video and image processing has undergone significant advancements, leading to groundbreaking innovations with far-reaching implications across various industries. This surge in innovation has been driven by the continuous evolution of DL models, increased computational power, and the availability of vast datasets. Let's explore some of the most recent industry relevance and innovation in applying DL to video and image processing. One of the noteworthy advancements is in the realm of computer vision, where DL models are being leveraged for object detection, recognition, and segmentation in images and videos. CNNs have emerged as powerful tools in this domain, enabling machines to learn hierarchical representations of visual data. Recent innovations in CNN architectures, such as the introduction of attention mechanisms and transformers, have significantly improved the accuracy and efficiency of object detection algorithms. In the healthcare industry, DL has made remarkable strides in medical image analysis. Radiology, pathology, and other diagnostic imaging fields have witnessed the development of sophisticated deep-learning models capable of detecting anomalies, identifying diseases, and providing more accurate diagnoses. These models enhance the speed and accuracy of medical imaging and contribute to early disease detection, ultimately improving patient outcomes. Another area experiencing rapid innovation is autonomous vehicles. Deep learning plays a pivotal role in enabling vehicles to perceive and understand their surroundings through image and video data. Advanced driver-assistance systems (ADAS) (Haas et al., 2019) rely on DL algorithms for lane detection, object recognition, and pedestrian tracking tasks. The continuous evolution of DL models ensures that autonomous vehicles become increasingly proficient at navigating complex and dynamic environments. In the entertainment and media industry, DL has transformed content creation and delivery. Generative models (Creswell et al., 2018) are being used to create realistic images and videos, revolutionizing the fields of computer graphics and special effects. These models can generate high-quality, synthetic content, reducing the need for extensive manual labor in creative processes. Security and surveillance have also benefited significantly from DL applications. Video analytics powered by DL algorithms enable more effective monitoring and threat detection in public spaces, airports, and critical infrastructure. Facial recognition technology, enhanced by DL models, has seen widespread adoption for identity verification and access control, raising concerns about privacy and ethical considerations. In e-commerce, the integration of DL in image recognition and recommendation systems has transformed the online shopping experience. Retailers utilize DL algorithms to analyze customer preferences, enabling personalized product recommendations and improving overall user satisfaction. This enhances the customer shopping experience and contributes to increased sales and customer loyalty. Moreover, the fusion of DL with natural language processing has given rise to innovative applications in multimedia understanding. This enables machines to comprehend and generate textual descriptions of visual content, making it easier to index and search vast collections of images and videos. While the recent innovations in applying DL to video and image processing offer immense potential, they also pose challenges related to ethical considerations, bias, and privacy. Striking a balance between technological advancements and responsible deployment is crucial to ensuring that these innovations benefit society without compromising fundamental values. OpenAI's groundbreaking multimodal language model, GPT-4, represents a significant leap in AI capabilities by seamlessly integrating both image and text inputs. This development opens up a myriad of possibilities across diverse fields such as entertainment, education, and healthcare. The expansive scope of GPT-4 applications allows users to harness its power through code, instructions, and images, enabling the creation of remarkable projects on the GPT-4 API.

Initially accessible to developers, the GPT-4 API has subsequently been extended to ChatGPT Plus subscribers, democratizing access to this innovative technology. A noteworthy development in the realm of AI-generated images is Microsoft's unveiling of Bing Image Creator, now available in select countries. The core functionality of GPT-4 lies in its ability to process both image and text inputs, facilitating responses to natural language, code, instructions, or artificial opinions. For the average user, this translates to the ability to submit an image along with instructions and receive a well-structured response. The versatility of GPT-4 extends from instructing the model to comprehend the context of an image to analyzing data represented in a graphical format. While GPT-4 doesn't inherently possess the visual processing capabilities of a dedicated computer vision model, it can be seamlessly integrated with such models. Through collaboration, GPT-4 can extract relevant information from images, enhancing its contextual understanding and subsequently influencing its responses. ChatGPT, although not inherently designed to process image inputs directly, exhibits the capability to generate textual descriptions of images. These textual descriptions become valuable input for image-generating tools such as DeepAI, DALL · E, and Midjourney (OpenAI, 2023).

The industry relevance and innovation in applying DL to video and image processing are reshaping various sectors, from healthcare and autonomous vehicles to entertainment and security. The continuous evolution of DL models, coupled with the availability of vast datasets, is driving transformative changes, paving the way for a future where machines can perceive, understand, and interact with visual information in ways previously thought impossible. As these technologies mature, it is essential to address ethical concerns and establish responsible guidelines to harness the full potential of DL in video and image applications.

1.5 Book outline

In **Chapter 1**, the book commences with an introduction, providing a foundational overview that sets the stage for the subsequent chapters. This initial section serves as a comprehensive introduction to the overarching themes and establishes the context for the exploration of innovative applications and advancements in AI, particularly within the realm of image analysis and DL.

Chapter 2, "Image analysis for surveillance," delves into an intelligent approach to fire and smoke detection. This chapter meticulously examines two different deep-learning object detectors, aiming for heightened accuracy and enhanced real-time detection capabilities. The intricate examination of these detectors sets the stage for robust advancements in surveillance technology.

Chapter 3 propounds innovative deep-learning techniques for setting up a surveillance system dedicated to people detection, social distancing classification, and body temperature measurement, aiming to mitigate the spread of COVID-19. By leveraging advanced AI algorithms, this chapter explores how real-time analysis of video data can enhance safety measures, providing a comprehensive solution for public health challenges.

Chapter 4 delves into "Deep learning approaches for fingerprint image restoration," delving into the intricate process of recreating fingerprint images using diverse autoencoder architectures, encompassing sparse and convolutional neural network models. The algorithms are subjected to rigorous testing across four datasets, systematically demonstrating their resilience and robust performance in reconstructing fingerprint images with precision and effectiveness.

In Chapter 5, the exploration of "Deep learning for classification and localization of multiple abnormalities on chest X-ray images" unfolds, delving into the realm of advanced medical image analysis. This chapter elucidates the intricacies of employing DL techniques for discerning and localizing diverse abnormalities on chest X-ray images and contributes valuable insights into the ever-evolving field of diagnostic imaging.

Chapter 6 delves into the integration of DL and federated learning techniques, offering a sophisticated real-time solution. It explores the synergies between these technologies, pushing the boundaries of stroke detection and significantly advancing timely intervention strategies in healthcare.

Chapter 7, titled "Efficient identification of bag breakup in continuous airflow via video," presents an in-depth exploration of video-based detection methods. This chapter scrutinizes strategies for accurately and efficiently identifying instances of bag breakup within a continuous airflow setting. Various technological approaches and their implications are meticulously analyzed, providing valuable insights for applications requiring precise object recognition in dynamic environments.

Chapter 8 concludes the book, summarizing key findings and providing recommendations for future research endeavors.

References

Alom, M. Z., Taha, T. M., Yakopcic, C., Westberg, S., Sidike, P., Nasrin, M. S., van Essen, B. C., Awwal, A. A. S., & Asari, V. K. (2018). The history began from AlexNet: A comprehensive survey on deep learning approaches. *arXiv*. Available from https://doi.org/10.48550/arxiv.1803.01164, https://arxiv.org.

Ansari, A. S., Mohammadi, M. S., & Parvez, M. T. (2019). A Comparative Study of Recent Steganography Techniques for Multiple Image Formats. *International Journal of Computer Network and Information Security*, *11*(1), 11–25. Available from https://doi.org/10.5815/ijcnis.2019.01.02.

Bochkovskiy, A., Wang, C.-Y., & Liao, H.-Y. M. (2020). YOLOv4: Optimal speed and accuracy of object detection. *arXiv*. Available from https://doi.org/10.48550/arXiv.2004.10934.

Bovik, A. C. (2010). *Handbook of image and video processing* (p. 974) Academic press.

Chen, C., Zhang, P., Zhang, H., Dai, J., Yi, Y., Zhang, H., & Zhang, Y. (2020). Deep learning on computational-resource-limited platforms: A survey. *Mobile Information Systems*, *2020*, 1–19. Available from https://doi.org/10.1155/2020/8454327.

Creswell, A., White, T., Dumoulin, V., Arulkumaran, K., Sengupta, B., & Bharath, A. A. (2018). Generative adversarial networks: An overview. *IEEE Signal Processing Magazine*, *35*(1), 53–65. Available from https://doi.org/10.1109/MSP.2017.2765202.

Dalal, N., & Triggs, B. (2005). Histograms of oriented gradients for human detection. *Proceedings – 2005 IEEE Computer Society Conference on Computer Vision and Pattern Recognition, CVPR, France*, 886–893. Available from https://doi.org/10.1109/CVPR.2005.177.

Dartmouth Workshop. (2023). Available from https://en.wikipedia.org/w/index.php?title = Dartmouth_workshop& oldid = 1168445773.

de Ville, B. (2013). Decision trees. *Wiley Interdisciplinary Reviews: Computational Statistics*, *5*(6), 448–455. Available from https://doi.org/10.1002/wics.1278.

Emeršič, Z., Meden, B., Peer, P., & Struc, V. (2017). Covariate analysis of descriptor-based ear recognition techniques. *International Work Conference on Bio-Inspired Intelligence: Intelligent Systems for Biodiversity Conservation, IWOBI 2017 – Proceedings*. Available from https://doi.org/10.1109/IWOBI.2017.7985520.

Emeršič, Ž., Meden, B., Peer, P., & Štruc, V. (2020). Evaluation and analysis of ear recognition models: Performance, complexity and resource requirements. *Neural Computing and Applications*, *32*(20), 15785–15800. Available from https://doi.org/10.1007/s00521-018-3530-1.

ENIAC. (2023). *Wikipedia, The Free Encyclopedia*. Available from https://en.wikipedia.org/w/index.php?title = ENIAC&oldid = 1183611103.

Girshick, R. (2015). Fast R-CNN. *Proceedings of the IEEE International Conference on Computer Vision, Institute of Electrical and Electronics Engineers Inc. United States*, 1440–1448. Available from https://doi.org/10.1109/ICCV.2015.169, http://ieeexplore.ieee.org/xpl/conhome.jsp?punumber = 1000149.

Girshick, R., Donahue, J., Darrell, T., & Malik, J. (2014). Rich feature hierarchies for accurate object detection and semantic segmentation. *Proceedings of the IEEE Computer Society Conference on Computer Vision and Pattern Recognition, IEEE Computer Society United States*, 580–587. Available from https://doi.org/10.1109/CVPR.2014.81.

Haas, R. E., Bhattacharjee, S., & Möller, D. P. F. (2019). *Advanced driver assistance systems smart technologies: Scope and applications* (pp. 345–371). Springer Singapore. Available from https://link.springer.com/book/10.1007/978-981-13-7139-4, https://doi.org/10.1007/978-981-13-7139-4_27.

Hassaballah, M., Alshazly, H. A., & Ali, A. A. (2019). Ear recognition using local binary patterns: A comparative experimental study. *Expert Systems with Applications*, *118*, 182–200. Available from https://doi.org/10.1016/j.eswa.2018.10.007.

He, K., Zhang, X., Ren, S., & Sun, J. (2016). Deep residual learning for image recognition. *Proceedings of the IEEE Computer Society Conference on Computer Vision and Pattern Recognition, IEEE Computer Society, United States*, 770–778. Available from https://doi.org/10.1109/CVPR.2016.90.

History of Artificial Intelligence. (2023). Available from https://en.wikipedia.org/w/index.php?title = History_of_artificial_intelligence&oldid = 1185714359.

Hsu, P.-H., & Zhuang, Z.-Y. (2020). Incorporating handcrafted features into deep learning for point cloud classification. *Remote Sensing*, *12*(22), 3713. Available from https://doi.org/10.3390/rs12223713.

Kashyap, S. K., & Mishra, J. K. (2017). A review paper on gabor filter algorithm for the application of texture segmentation. *IJARCCE*, *6*(4), 476–480. Available from https://doi.org/10.17148/IJARCCE.2017.6492.

Khaleefah, S. H., Mostafa, S. A., Mustapha, A., & Nasrudin, M. F. (2020). Review of local binary pattern operators in image feature extraction. *Journal of Electrical Engineering and Computer Science*, *19*(1), 23–31. Available from https://doi.org/10.11591/ijeecs.v19.i1.pp23-31, http://ijeecs.iaescore.com/index.php/IJEECS/article/view/21493/13861.

Kumar, G., & Bhatia, P. K. (2014). A detailed review of feature extraction in image processing systems. *International Conference on Advanced Computing and Communication Technologies, ACCT, Institute of Electrical and Electronics Engineers Inc. India*, 5–12. Available from https://doi.org/10.1109/ACCT.2014.74, http://ieeexplore.ieee.org.

Lazebnik, S., Schmid, C., & Ponce, J. (2006). Beyond bags of features: Spatial pyramid matching for recognizing natural scene categories. *Proceedings of the IEEE Computer Society Conference on Computer Vision and Pattern Recognition, United States*, 2, 2169–2178. Available from https://doi.org/10.1109/CVPR.2006.68.

Lecun, Y., Bottou, L., Bengio, Y., & Haffner, P. (1998). Gradient-based learning applied to document recognition. *Proceedings of the IEEE*, *86*(11), 2278–2324. Available from https://doi.org/10.1109/5.726791.

Lowe, D. G. (2004). Distinctive image features from scale-invariant keypoints. *International Journal of Computer Vision*, *60*(2), 91–110. Available from https://doi.org/10.1023/B:VISI.0000029664.99615.94.

Murase, H., & Nayar, S. K. (1995). Visual learning and recognition of 3-d objects from appearance. *International Journal of Computer Vision*, *14*(1), 5–24. Available from https://doi.org/10.1007/bf01421486.

Nanni, L., Ghidoni, S., & Brahnam, S. (2017). Handcrafted vs. non-handcrafted features for computer vision classification. *Pattern Recognition*, *71*, 158–172. Available from https://doi.org/10.1016/j.patcog.2017.05.025.

Ojala, T., Pietikainen, M., & Maenpaa, T. (2002). Multiresolution gray-scale and rotation invariant texture classification with local binary patterns. *IEEE Transactions on Pattern Analysis and Machine Intelligence*, *24*(7), 971–987. Available from https://doi.org/10.1109/TPAMI.2002.1017623.

OpenAI. (2023). *GPT-4*. Available from https://openai.com/gpt-4.

Pflug, A., Paul, P. N., & Busch, C. (2014). A comparative study on texture and surface descriptors for ear biometrics. *Proceedings – International Carnahan Conference on Security Technology, Institute of Electrical and Electronics Engineers Inc., Germany*. Available from https://doi.org/10.1109/CCST.2014.6986993.

Redmon, J., Divvala, S., Girshick, R., & Farhadi, A. (2016). You only look once: Unified, real-time object detection. *Proceedings of the IEEE Computer Society Conference on Computer Vision and Pattern Recognition, IEEE Computer Society, United States*, 779–788. Available from https://doi.org/10.1109/CVPR.2016.91.

Redmon, J., & Farhadi, A. (2017). YOLO9000: Better, faster, stronger. *Proceedings – 30th IEEE Conference on Computer Vision and Pattern Recognition, CVPR 2017, Institute of Electrical and Electronics Engineers Inc., United States*, 6517–6525. Available from https://doi.org/10.1109/CVPR.2017.690.

Ren, J., Jiang, X., & Yuan, J. (2013). Relaxed local ternary pattern for face recognition. *IEEE International Conference on Image Processing, ICIP 2013 – Proceedings, IEEE Computer Society, Singapore*, 3680–3684. Available from https://doi.org/10.1109/ICIP.2013.6738759.

Sapijaszko, G., & Mikhael, W. B. (2018). An overview of recent convolutional neural network algorithms for image recognition. *Midwest Symposium on Circuits and Systems, Institute of Electrical and Electronics Engineers Inc., United States*, 743–746. Available from https://doi.org/10.1109/MWSCAS.2018.8623911.

Sewani, H., & Kashef, R. (2020). An autoencoder-based deep learning classifier for efficient diagnosis of autism. *Children*, *7*(10), 182. Available from https://doi.org/10.3390/children7100182.

Sivic, J., & Zisserman, A. (2003). Video google: A text retrieval approach to object matching in videos. *Proceedings of the IEEE International Conference on Computer Vision, Institute of Electrical and Electronics Engineers Inc. United Kingdom*, 1470–1477. Available from https://doi.org/10.1109/iccv.2003.1238663, http://ieeexplore.ieee.org/xpl/conhome.jsp?punumber = 1000149.

Suthaharan, S. (2016). Machine learning models and algorithms for big data classification: Thinking with examples for effective learning. *Integrated Series in Information Systems*, *36*. Available from https://doi.org/10.1007/978-1-4899-7641-3.

Sze, V., Chen, Y.-H., Yang, T.-J., & Emer, J. S. (2017). Efficient processing of deep neural networks: A tutorial and survey. *Proceedings of the IEEE*, *105*(12), 2295–2329. Available from https://doi.org/10.1109/jproc.2017.2761740.

Szegedy, C., Liu, W., Jia, Y., Sermanet, P., Reed, S., Anguelov, D., Erhan, D., Vanhoucke, V., & Rabinovich, A. (2015). Going deeper with convolutions. *Proceedings of the IEEE Computer Society Conference on Computer Vision and Pattern Recognition, IEEE Computer Society United States*, 1–9. Available from https://doi.org/10.1109/CVPR.2015.7298594.

Tuzel, O., Porikli, F., & Meer, P. (2006). *Region Covariance: A Fast Descriptor for Detection and Classification* (3952, pp. 589–600). Springer Science and Business Media LLC. Available from http://doi.org/10.1007/11744047_45.

Viola, P., & Jones, M. (2001). Rapid object detection using a boosted cascade of simple features. *Proceedings of the IEEE Computer Society Conference on Computer Vision and Pattern Recognition, United States*, I511–I518.

Wang, Y., Yao, H., & Zhao, S. (2016). Auto-encoder based dimensionality reduction. *Neurocomputing*, *184*, 232–242. Available from https://doi.org/10.1016/j.neucom.2015.08.104.

Yamashita, R., Nishio, M., Do, R. K. G., & Togashi, K. (2018). Convolutional neural networks: An overview and application in radiology. *Insights into Imaging*, *9*(4), 611–629. Available from https://doi.org/10.1007/s13244-018-0639-9, http://www.springer.com/medicine/radiology/journal/13244.

Zou, Z., Chen, K., Shi, Z., Guo, Y., & Ye, J. (2023). Object detection in 20 years: A survey. *Proceedings of the IEEE*, *111*(3), 257–276. Available from https://doi.org/10.1109/JPROC.2023.3238524, http://ieeexplore.ieee.org/xpl/RecentIssue.jsp?punumber = 5.

CHAPTER 2

Image analysis for surveillance: detecting fire and smoke incidents

In recent years, the surge in smoke and fire incidents has emerged as one of the foremost disasters, giving rise to substantial social and economic consequences. The growing incidence of fire-related incidents has ignited a pressing need for a comprehensive reevaluation of safety measures in various settings, prompting a paradigm shift toward advanced fire and smoke prevention systems.

The conventional reliance on heat and smoke detectors, while a crucial initial step in bolstering safety, has proven to have inherent limitations, necessitating a more sophisticated and integrated approach. Traditional methods of fire and smoke detection often exhibit shortcomings in their ability to promptly and effectively identify the presence of danger unless in close proximity. This limitation poses a significant challenge, hindering the timely response and mitigation necessary for preventing catastrophic outcomes.

As a response to this critical issue, there has been a widespread adoption of cutting-edge solutions that transcend the limitations of traditional systems. The contemporary approach involves the integration of sophisticated sensors, artificial intelligence (AI) algorithms, and real-time monitoring, creating a synergy that significantly enhances the efficiency and reliability of fire and smoke detection systems. This integration allows for a more nuanced and responsive detection mechanism that can identify potential threats even before conventional systems register them. One key component of this advanced approach is the utilization of state-of-the-art sensors capable of detecting subtle changes in the environment. These sensors are designed to pick up on early indicators of fire, such as slight increases in temperature or the presence of trace amounts of smoke. By employing a range of sensors with diverse capabilities, these systems can provide a comprehensive analysis of the surrounding environment, minimizing the risk of false alarms while maximizing the accuracy of threat detection. AI-based algorithms play a pivotal role in processing the vast amounts of data collected by the sensors. These algorithms are trained to recognize patterns associated with fire and smoke, enabling them to distinguish between routine environmental changes and potential threats. The adaptive nature of AI allows these systems to continuously improve their accuracy over time, ensuring a dynamic and evolving defense against fire hazards. Real-time monitoring further amplifies the effectiveness of these advanced systems. Continuous surveillance enables immediate response to any detected anomalies, facilitating swift intervention and mitigating the risk of a developing fire. Moreover, these systems often incorporate connectivity features that enable remote monitoring, providing an additional layer of security and allowing for prompt action even when physical presence is challenging. The implementation of these cutting-edge fire and smoke prevention systems extends beyond buildings to include public transportation vehicles. Recognizing the unique challenges posed by such environments, where rapid evacuation might be more complex, these advanced systems become indispensable. The integration of these systems in public transportation not only enhances passenger safety but also contributes to the overall resilience of urban infrastructure. In conclusion, the escalating trend of fire-related incidents has necessitated a critical

Deep Learning in Action: Image and Video Processing for Practical Use. DOI: https://doi.org/10.1016/B978-0-443-30078-3.00002-0

reassessment of safety measures, driving the adoption of advanced fire and smoke prevention systems. The integration of sophisticated sensors, AI algorithms, and real-time monitoring represents a paradigm shift in enhancing the efficiency and reliability of detection systems. This holistic approach not only addresses the limitations of traditional methods but also ensures a proactive and adaptive defense against the evolving challenges of fire safety in diverse environments. This transformative approach aims not only to enhance the early detection of potential hazards but also to minimize false alarms, a persistent issue with conventional systems. The incorporation of state-of-the-art technologies, such as machine learning and data analytics, enables these advanced systems to analyze complex patterns of heat and smoke, distinguishing between benign incidents and genuine emergencies. Consequently, the deployment of these advanced prevention systems marks a pivotal advancement in mitigating the adverse impacts of fire and smoke incidents on both human lives and economic assets. Moreover, the integration of smart building technologies has further elevated the capabilities of fire and smoke prevention systems. Modern buildings are now equipped with interconnected networks that enable seamless communication between various components of the safety infrastructure. This interconnectedness facilitates a swift and coordinated response in the event of an emergency, allowing for the timely activation of fire suppression systems, evacuation procedures, and communication with emergency services. The synergy between smart building technologies and advanced fire prevention systems exemplifies a holistic approach to enhancing overall safety and minimizing the potential consequences of fire and smoke incidents. Additionally, the implementation of rigorous safety standards and regulations has played a pivotal role in fostering the development and adoption of these advanced technologies. Governments and regulatory bodies worldwide are actively promoting the integration of state-of-the-art fire prevention measures, underscoring the global recognition of the urgency to address the evolving challenges posed by fire and smoke incidents.

The urgency of finding more effective solutions is underscored by alarming statistics, such as the Brazil National Institute for Space Research's report of 80,000 incidents in the Amazon region and the National Fire Protection Association's revelation of 1.3 million fire and smoke accidents annually in the USA (Gibbens, 2019). Numerous methodologies have been explored to mitigate the impact of fire accidents, with a focus on early detection. Advances in computer vision and image processing have paved the way for video-based fire and smoke detection, offering advantages over conventional methods, including broader detection areas and quicker response times. Unlike chemical-photometry or heat-based detectors that require a certain fire threshold for activation, video-based systems offer timely and location-specific alerts. Traditional detectors often experience delays, resulting in significant damage, prompting the development of novel solutions.

Closed-circuit television systems and strategically positioned cameras in diverse settings, such as smart cities and industries, offer a cost-effective method of surveillance. The integration of video processing algorithms and software for fire and smoke detection into existing video systems helps reduce installation costs. An economical alternative involves utilizing distributed video camera nodes equipped with embedded computing capabilities to make real-time decisions on fire and smoke alarms (Gagliardi & Saponara, 2020b). The prevalence of hardware accelerators and high-performance processors has facilitated the rise of AI techniques, particularly deep learning models. Traditional handcrafted visual recognition approaches are gradually being supplanted by deep learning methods, which possess the capability to automatically extract features from raw images (LeCun et al., 2015). This transition has paved the way for more effective and precise fire and smoke detection systems. This chapter introduces an intelligent approach to fire and smoke detection based on two deep learning object detectors: the regional convolutional neural network (R-CNN) and You Only Look Once version II (YOLOv2) network. The primary goals include achieving high detection rates, minimizing false alarm rates, and ensuring real-time performance with minimal memory disk size. The proposed algorithm has undergone testing on various datasets, and the detectors have been successfully implemented on embedded systems such as Raspberry Pi and NVIDIA Jetson Nano for real-time video processing.

The main contributions of this chapter can be encapsulated as follows:

- Jetson Nano deployment

  The deployment of our deep learning model on the Jetson Nano device represents a notable achievement in the realm of edge computing. This compact device enables seamless connectivity through diverse channels, such as Ethernet, Wi-Fi, and wireless interfaces, thereby establishing a versatile link to a remote computer. Our deployed model specializes in robust fire and smoke detection, harnessing the power of AI for enhanced safety protocols within smart cities. Incorporating an Internet of Things (IoT)-based framework, our deployment extends beyond mere on-device processing. This framework facilitates remote visual feedback and real-time alerts, providing a dynamic and responsive layer to our fire and smoke detection system. These alerts are intelligently transmitted to iCloud facilities, underscoring a sophisticated integration of cloud computing capabilities. This not only contributes to the efficiency of our model but also marks a significant advancement in the landscape of smart city safety infrastructure.

  The successful deployment of our deep learning model on the Jetson Nano, with its connectivity options and IoT-based framework, exemplifies a pioneering stride toward comprehensive safety solutions, fostering a secure environment in the context of surveillance application systems.
- Lightweight architectures

  The proposed deep neural network detectors are meticulously crafted with a focus on lightweight architectures, a pivotal facet in optimizing resource utilization. The resultant dimensions of the R-CNN and YOLOv2 stand at a commendable 220 KB and 7.1 MB, respectively. This compactness enhances their applicability for deployment on IoT and low-cost embedded devices, ensuring an integration with constrained computational environments. Such efficiency not only facilitates real-time object detection but also aligns with the exigencies of contemporary technological landscapes, where the demand for nimble yet powerful algorithms is paramount for the successful deployment of intelligent systems across diverse domains.
- Early alerting

  In the field of fire and smoke detection, this study emphasizes the YOLOv2 network's remarkable capacity for early alerting, detecting such incidents within an impressive timeframe of 1–2 seconds. This expeditious response holds profound implications for fire prevention, as it significantly outperforms conventional methods reliant on temperature or chemical sensors. Traditional approaches frequently necessitate several minutes to relay alerts, underscoring the urgency and efficiency YOLOv2 introduces to the domain. The network's swiftness in identifying potential fire and smoke instances positions it as a groundbreaking early alerting system. This research illuminates the paradigm shift from time-intensive methodologies to a rapid and effective surveillance system, marking a pivotal advancement in bolstering safety protocols and mitigating potential hazards.

- Real-time performance on Jetson Nano

  The implementation of YOLOv2 on the Jetson Nano platform exhibits impressive real-time capabilities, achieving smoke and fire detection at an impressive rate of up to 21 frames per second (fps). This level of performance is comparable to human visual cognition, showcasing the potential for our approach to contribute significantly to timely decision-making in emergency situations.

  YOLOv2 represents a significant leap forward in the domain of fire and smoke detection, placing a particular emphasis on the utilization of lightweight deep learning models deployed on edge devices. The innovative approach taken in this research not only addresses the critical need for robust fire detection systems but also opens up new possibilities for real-time safety applications in the context of smart city environments, all made possible through the integration of the IoT.

The deployment of lightweight deep learning models is a key focal point in this pioneering research. Traditionally, deep learning models, with their complex architectures and resource-intensive nature, have posed challenges when it comes to implementation on edge devices with limited computational capabilities. However, the novel lightweight models developed in this study overcome these challenges, offering a scalable and efficient solution for deploying advanced fire and smoke detection capabilities directly on edge devices. The significance of this achievement becomes particularly pronounced in the context of smart cities. As urban areas continue to evolve with an increasing reliance on interconnected technologies, the need for intelligent safety systems becomes paramount. The integration of lightweight deep learning models into edge devices facilitates the creation of real-time, IoT-enabled safety applications tailored for smart city environments. One of the primary advantages of deploying such systems on the edge is the ability to process data locally, minimizing latency and enabling swift responses to potential threats. In the case of fire and smoke detection, a fraction of a second can make a crucial difference. By harnessing the power of edge computing, this research ensures that safety applications can operate in real time, enhancing the overall responsiveness of smart city infrastructures.

Furthermore, the integration of IoT plays a pivotal role in extending the capabilities of these safety applications. Through the seamless connection and communication of various devices, sensors, and systems, the IoT framework enables a holistic approach to safety management. In the context of fire and smoke detection, this translates into a network of intelligent sensors and devices working in unison to detect, analyze, and respond to potential incidents. This interconnected ecosystem not only enhances the accuracy of detection but also provides a comprehensive understanding of the situation, allowing for more informed decision-making in emergency scenarios. The implications of this research extend beyond the realm of fire and smoke detection. The successful deployment of lightweight deep learning models on edge devices, coupled with IoT integration, sets a precedent for the development of sophisticated safety applications across various domains within smart cities. Whether it is air quality monitoring, traffic management, or emergency response systems, the framework established with YOLOv2 offers a versatile and scalable foundation for enhancing the overall safety and efficiency of urban environments.

2.1 State-of-the-art video-based fire/smoke detection

Traditional approaches to video smoke detection have traditionally centered around extracting multidimensional feature vectors from smoke images. These vectors encompass various aspects like color, texture, shape, irregularity, flutter, or frequency (Saponara et al., 2014). The classification of these feature vectors into smoke or nonfire classes has been a common practice. Video-based fire/smoke detection systems, unlike other sensor types, offer quicker detection times in both indoor and outdoor scenarios. Recent efforts to tackle false-negative detections involve exploring different color models for fire and smoke, incorporating statistical analyses, and employing fuzzy logic (Çelik et al., 2007).

Static features, such as two-dimensional wavelet analysis, and dynamic features like smoke disturbance, have been used to capture color and motion (Rafiee et al., 2011). However, challenges persist due to the presence of objects with similar color properties in the background. Techniques like visual background estimation ViBe, similar to those used in the past, have been applied (Vijayalakshmi & Muruganand, 2017). An innovative approach employs a smoke detector that uses a Kalman estimator, color analysis, image segmentation, blob labeling, geometric feature analysis, and an M-out-of-N decider (Gagliardi & Saponara, 2020a). While effective in real-time scenarios with strict deadlines, a drawback remains in the form of manual feature extraction. Other methods focus on detecting geometric properties of flames, categorizing pixels based on color and smoke presence (Toulouse et al., 2016). Enhanced boundary detection operators, such as the Canny edge detector, have also been introduced (Jiang & Wang, 2010), but these are limited to simple and stable fire and flame images. The advent of AI and deep learning has led to a shift toward more automated feature extraction. Some researchers have employed new algorithms based on wave variation to analyze forest fire contours in videos (Zhang et al., 2008). However, it has been noted that these approaches are only suitable under specific conditions. Previous research involved analyzing foreground and background images to detect fires using color pixel statistics. For instance Celik et al. (2007) developed a real-time fire detector that combines colored data with registered foreground and background frames. Various deep learning methods, utilizing popular object detection techniques, have been proposed for fire and smoke detection (Wu & Zhang, 2018). CNN-based fire detection using pretrained architectures like VGG16 and Resnet50 has shown promise (Lestari et al., 2019). The YOLO method has also been utilized for fire and flame detection (Shen et al., 2018). Despite achieving high accuracy, these models often face challenges in cost-effective implementation on embedded platforms due to large disk sizes and the total number of parameters. In response to these challenges, this chapter presents an R-CNN model for fire and smoke detection. The R-CNN model employs a combination of fire and nonfire scenes for training and validation, showcasing effectiveness in real-time tests with a Raspberry Pi camera. The model's ability to automatically extract features from numerous samples suggests promising results in fire and smoke detection. The contemporary landscape of video-based fire and smoke detection has witnessed significant advancements, marked by the integration of cutting-edge technologies and methodologies. The state-of-the-art in this domain revolves around the fusion of computer vision, deep learning, and image processing techniques. Researchers have harnessed the power of CNNs to enhance the accuracy and efficiency of fire and smoke detection algorithms. These CNNs are adept at learning intricate spatial hierarchies within video frames, enabling them to discern subtle patterns indicative of fire or smoke presence. Moreover, the incorporation of recurrent neural networks has facilitated the temporal modeling of video sequences, capturing the dynamic evolution of fire or smoke-related events over time. Transfer learning, leveraging pretrained models on vast datasets, has emerged as a pivotal strategy to mitigate the challenges posed by limited annotated fire and smoke datasets. The advent of two-stream networks, combining spatial and temporal information streams, has further elevated the discriminative capabilities of these systems. Additionally, the integration of thermal imaging, light detection and ranging (LiDAR), and multispectral data has expanded the feature space, enhancing the robustness of detection algorithms in diverse environmental conditions. Real-time processing has become a focal point, with the optimization of algorithms for accelerated inference on edge devices, such as cameras and drones, ensuring swift and effective response to potential fire incidents. Furthermore, the application of explainable AI techniques represents a significant advancement in the field of AI, particularly in addressing concerns surrounding the interpretability of model decisions. As AI systems become increasingly integrated into various aspects of society, from healthcare to finance and beyond, the ability to understand and trust the decisions made by these systems becomes paramount. Explainable AI techniques provide insights into the inner workings of complex algorithms, shedding light on how decisions are reached and allowing users to understand the rationale behind them.

One of the key benefits of explainable AI is its ability to foster trust in automated systems. In domains where AI is utilized to make critical decisions, such as medical diagnosis or autonomous vehicles, trust is essential. Users need to have confidence that the decisions made by AI systems are reliable, fair, and free from bias. By providing explanations for model decisions, explainable AI helps users understand why a particular outcome was predicted or recommended, increasing transparency and accountability.

Despite the significant strides made in the field of explainable AI, challenges persist. One such challenge is the need for large-scale, diverse datasets to train and evaluate these models effectively. Datasets play a crucial role in the performance and generalization ability of AI algorithms, and ensuring that they are representative of the real-world scenarios they aim to address is essential. Additionally, acquiring labeled data that accurately captures the nuances of complex decision-making processes can be challenging, particularly in domains where ground truth labels are subjective or difficult to obtain.

Another challenge facing the field of AI is the potential impact of adversarial attacks on the reliability of detection models. Adversarial attacks involve the deliberate manipulation of input data to deceive AI systems, leading to incorrect or malicious outcomes. In the context of video-based fire and smoke detection, adversarial attacks could have severe consequences, potentially leading to false alarms or failing to detect actual incidents. Mitigating the risk of adversarial attacks requires robust defense mechanisms and ongoing research to stay ahead of evolving threats.

Despite these challenges, ongoing research efforts are focused on refining AI algorithms and addressing the underlying issues. Interdisciplinary approaches that combine expertise from fields, such as computer science, statistics, psychology, and ethics are increasingly being embraced to tackle the complex challenges facing AI. By bringing together diverse perspectives and skill sets, researchers can develop more robust and ethically sound AI systems that meet the needs of society. Furthermore, the integration of emerging technologies, such as 5G connectivity and edge computing, holds promise for advancing video-based fire and smoke detection systems to new levels of efficiency and reliability. 5G networks offer ultra-fast speeds, low latency, and high reliability, enabling real-time transmission of video data from surveillance cameras to AI-powered detection systems. This allows for quicker detection and response to fire and smoke incidents, potentially reducing damage and saving lives. Edge computing, which involves processing data closer to the source of generation, offers additional benefits for video-based fire and smoke detection. By performing AI inference tasks locally on edge devices, such as cameras or sensors, latency is reduced, and bandwidth usage is optimized. This is particularly advantageous in scenarios where real-time decision-making is critical, such as fire detection in remote or resource-constrained environments. Moreover, the combination of 5G connectivity and edge computing enables the deployment of distributed AI systems, where AI models are deployed across a network of edge devices, working collaboratively to analyze video streams and detect fire and smoke. This distributed approach not only improves scalability and reliability but also enhances privacy by minimizing the need to transmit sensitive video data to centralized servers for processing.

2.1.1 Extraction of the regional proposal

In the rapidly evolving landscape of computer vision, the extraction of regional proposals from images has emerged as a critical task, propelled by the transformative capabilities of deep learning. This innovative approach revolutionizes the traditional methods of object detection and localization, offering unprecedented accuracy and efficiency in discerning regions of interest within complex visual data. At the heart of this paradigm shift lies the integration of deep learning models, particularly CNNs, which have proven to be exceptionally adept at capturing intricate patterns and hierarchical features within images. The pursuit of accurate regional proposals is paramount in various applications, ranging from autonomous vehicles and surveillance systems to medical image analysis and augmented reality. This introduction delves into the multifaceted realm of extracting regional proposals using deep learning techniques, unraveling the intricacies of this process, and exploring the diverse applications that benefit from its prowess.

The fundamental challenge addressed by the extraction of regional proposals is the nuanced interpretation of visual content. Traditional computer vision methods often struggled to capture the contextual intricacies inherent in images, leading to limitations in accuracy and robustness. However, with the advent of deep learning, specifically CNNs, the field has witnessed a groundbreaking leap in its ability to automatically learn and extract relevant features from raw visual data. The extraction of regional proposals harnesses the power of these neural networks to identify and delineate potential regions of interest within an image, forming the backbone of subsequent object detection pipelines. This task involves generating a set of candidates bounding boxes, each encapsulating a potential object or region within the image, creating a roadmap for subsequent detailed analysis. One of the key advantages offered by deep learning-based regional proposal extraction is its adaptability to diverse datasets and domains. The hierarchical nature of CNNs enables the model to learn complex representations of objects and scenes, making it versatile across a spectrum of applications. From the rugged terrains encountered by autonomous vehicles to the intricate structures within medical images, the ability to accurately propose regions of interest lays the foundation for robust and context-aware visual understanding. The extraction of regional proposals is not a one-size-fits-all solution but rather a dynamic framework that can be tailored to meet the specific demands of different domains, offering a level of customization and precision previously unattainable with traditional methods. Furthermore, the integration of deep learning in regional proposal extraction has spurred advancements in real-time processing and resource efficiency. The optimization of algorithms and the parallelized nature of neural network computations contribute to faster and more streamlined analyses, paving the way for applications that demand rapid decision-making. This introduction sets the stage for an in-depth exploration of the technical intricacies, innovations, and real-world applications of extracting regional proposals from images using deep learning, underscoring its pivotal role in reshaping the landscape of computer vision and visual understanding.

The proposed detector comprises multiple modules, with the edge boxes algorithm serving as the initial component. This algorithm plays a crucial role in extracting the region of interest (ROI) from the input image by generating suggestions for object bounding boxes, referred to as area suggestions. Its primary purpose is to simplify the image, facilitating the extraction of pertinent information about the object for subsequent analysis by the detector. Moreover, the edges identified by this algorithm can be leveraged to create maps, thereby reducing the set of positions that require further scrutiny to pinpoint the object within the image. The output of the edge boxes algorithm, which includes region suggestions, serves as the input for the second module: the CNN. The feature vector is extracted from each region proposal using an implementation of CNN, as illustrated in the proposed architecture depicted in Fig. 2.1. To create the R-CNN network layers, MATLAB®'s Deep Network Designer tool is employed. The R-CNN object detector is composed of 17 layers, starting with the input image layer that introduces $64 \times 64 \times 3$-sized images.

The subsequent four convolution layers act as a mapping function for the input images, utilizing sliding filters along both vertical and horizontal axes. The first convolution layer is of size 5×5, while the remaining layers are 3×3. Rectified linear units (ReLU) layers are integrated into the architecture to introduce nonlinearity, converting all image values less than zero to zero. Max-pooling and average-pooling layers are employed for downsampling images into rectangular pooling areas, using a 2×2 pooling size and an increment of 2×2 for all pooling layers in the network.

To mitigate overfitting, a dropout layer with a value of 0.6 is incorporated into the architecture. The fully connected layer is then employed to make the final classification decision. The softmax layer, a vital component, computes an input vector of K real numbers, where K represents the number of neurons in the softmax layers. This layer maps the output values of neurons, ranging from 0 to 1, into new values that can be interpreted as the probability of the predicted class, as defined by the softmax function (Eq. 2.1).

$$Softmax\ \sigma(\vec{z})_i = \frac{e^{z_i}}{\sum_{j=1}^{K} e^{z_j}} \tag{2.1}$$

where $Z_i = \log \overline{P}(y = i \mid x)$

The utilization of anchor boxes is instrumental in creating bounding boxes around detected objects in the images. Anchor boxes are predefined rectangular boxes with specified widths and heights. Their purpose is to capture the scale and proportion of certain classes for recognition, typically based on the sizes of objects in the training dataset. K-means clustering is employed to select an optimal set of labeled boxes within the training dataset using MATLAB®. The correct sizes of these bounding boxes, in terms of height and width, are crucial for accurate detection by YOLOv2. The intersection over the union score obtained through K-means clustering determines the required number of bounding boxes for the detector.

An inherent advantage of anchor boxes lies in their ability to prevent overfitting and enhance the performance of the YOLOv2 model by avoiding the use of excessive boxes. YOLOv2 incorporates batch normalization layers in all convolution layers to normalize the distribution of values from one layer to another. This normalization contributes to improved regularization for the

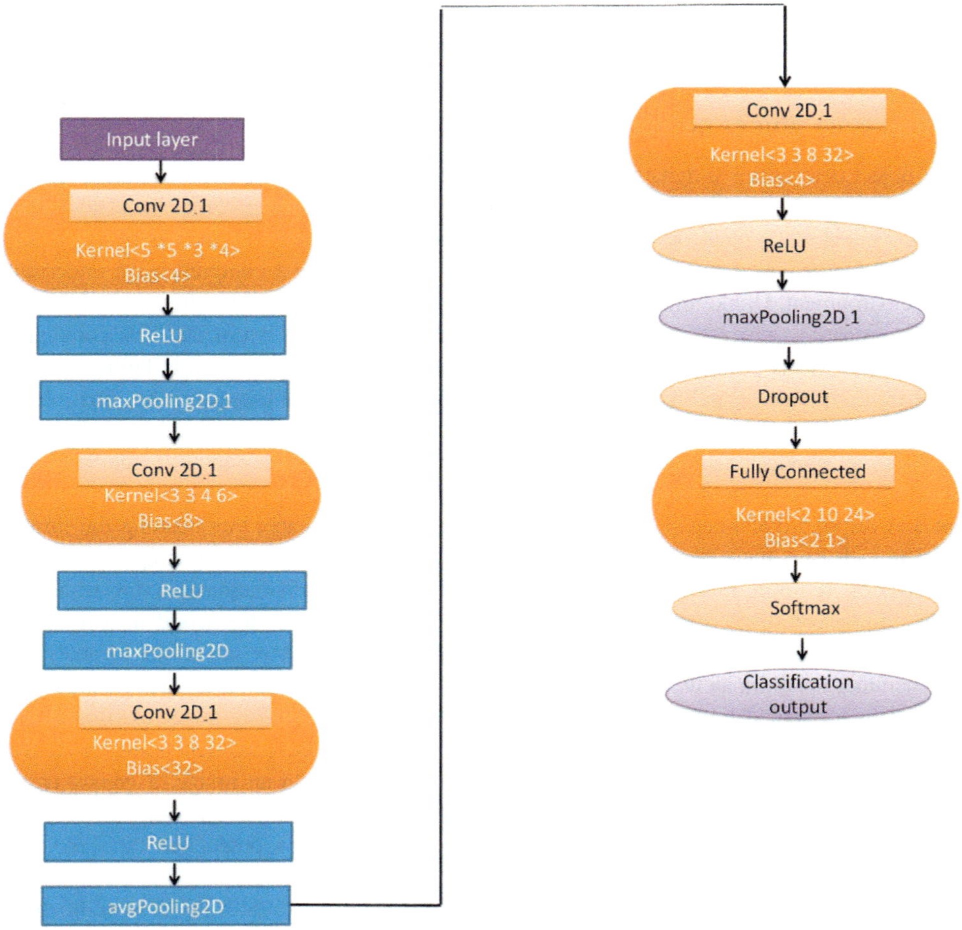

FIGURE 2.1

The proposed architecture of the regional convolutional neural network detector (fire/smoke detection). The figure illustrates the architecture of the regional convolutional neural network detector, showcasing its intricate network design and component interactions, providing a visual understanding of its operational framework. This depiction offers a comprehensive overview, aiding in the comprehension of how the detector processes input data and generates predictions.

YOLOv2 neural network model, reducing the need for a dropout layer to address overfitting concerns. The batch normalization process involves calculating mean and variance values over mini-batches and subsequently normalizing the input, as specified in Eq. (2.2).

$$\hat{x}_i = \sqrt{\frac{xi - \mu_B}{\sigma_B^2 + \epsilon}} \tag{2.2}$$

where ϵ is the epsilon property, which added to the mini-batch variances, specified as a numeric scalar equal to or larger than $1e\text{-}^5$.

2.1.2 Run-time object detection

Run-time object detection is a dynamic and pivotal facet of computer vision that has garnered significant attention and application across various domains, ranging from autonomous vehicles and surveillance systems to augmented reality and robotics. At its core, object detection involves the identification and localization of multiple objects within an image or video stream, providing a comprehensive understanding of the visual environment. Unlike traditional static object detection methods, run-time object detection excels in real-time scenarios, where immediate and accurate decision-making is crucial. This paradigm shift is fueled by advancements in deep learning, particularly CNNs, which have proven to be highly effective in discerning intricate patterns and features from complex visual data. The essence of run-time object detection lies in its ability to process and analyze incoming data on the fly, making split-second decisions that are paramount in applications, such as autonomous navigation, live video analysis, and interactive user interfaces. The seamless integration of object detection into the run-time environment empowers systems to adapt and respond dynamically to the ever-changing visual landscape, transcending the limitations of pretrained models and static analyses. As the demand for real-time decision-making continues to surge across industries, run-time object detection emerges as a linchpin technology, ushering in a new era of intelligent, responsive systems that navigate, interpret, and interact with the world in a manner akin to human perception. During run-time, the detector employs the edge box algorithm to analyze the test image, generating approximately 1000 region suggestions. Subsequently, each suggestion undergoes resizing and is then forwarded to a CNN for feature calculation. The bounding boxes associated with these region suggestions are further refined using a support vector machine classifier, trained with the aid of CNN functions. To optimize the precision of identified regions within an image, a greedy nonmaximal suppression (NMS) is applied independently for each class. This NMS mechanism discards a region if its intersection-over-union overlap with a higher-scored region surpasses a predefined threshold. The schematic representation of the system is illustrated in Fig. 2.2.

For the experimentation phase, a dataset comprising 194 images was utilized to train the R-CNN detector. Notably, regional proposal methods commonly leverage cost-effective features and economical inference schemes. Among these methods, selective search stands out as a popular choice, rearranging superpixels based on low-level engineered features. However, in comparison to efficient recognition networks (Uijlings et al., 2013), selective search exhibits a significantly slower processing time, taking 2 seconds per frame in a central processing unit (CPU) implementation. In contrast, Edge Boxes (Zitnick & Dollár, 2014), with a processing time of 0.2 seconds per frame, strikes a favorable balance between suggestion quality and speed, making it the preferred compromise. Despite this optimization, it is noteworthy that the region suggestion step still accounts for a substantial portion of the overall run-time, similar to the recognition network's computational demands.

2.1.3 Experiment set up and results

In the initial phase of our study, we initiated a preprocessing procedure for the fire and smoke images as a precursor to inputting the data into the proposed model. This initial step aimed to transform raw data into a format compatible with the underlying neural network architecture. The

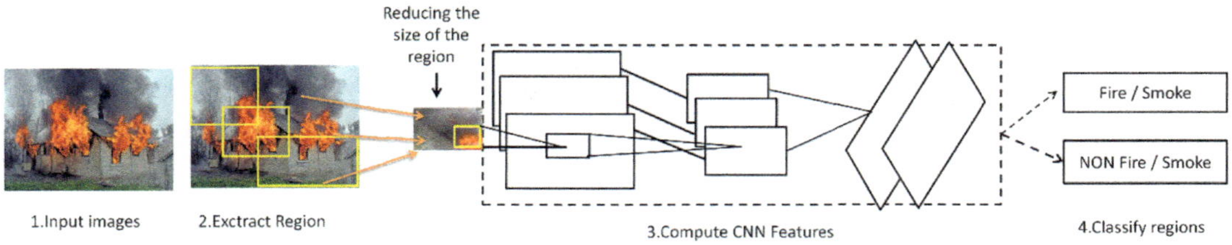

FIGURE 2.2

Regional convolutional neural network fire/smoke detection system overview. The figure provides an overview of the regional convolutional neural network fire/smoke detection system, illustrating its architecture and key components, offering a comprehensive understanding of how it operates to detect and classify fire and smoke events.

images selected for this purpose were derived from diverse realistic scenarios depicting fire and smoke incidents. To execute the preprocessing of the proposed model, the following sequential steps were undertaken:

- Image collection and ground truth labeling:
  Images of fire and smoke were gathered and subsequently uploaded to the Ground Truth Labeler application within the MATLAB® environment. ROIs pertaining to fire and smoke data were delineated using a specialized ground truth algorithm tool. This tool facilitated the labeling of selected features, accommodating variations in sizes. The Ground Truth Labeler application is designed to label data in diverse formats, including videos and image sequences, allowing for simultaneous labeling of multiple classes, such as those derived from camera data. The labeled ground truth data serve as the foundational training data for the proposed deep learning object detector.
- Exporting ground truth data:
  After completing the labeling process, which involves identifying and marking specific features in our data, the resulting ground truth data is transferred or exported to the MATLAB® workspace. This ground truth data includes arrays and coordinates that represent the labeled features we have identified during the labeling process. These labeled features play a crucial role in training a recognition network, which is a system designed to learn and identify patterns or characteristics within the data. Essentially, exporting ground truth data is a necessary step in preparing the information required to teach the recognition network how to accurately identify and categorize features in the data.
- MATLAB® script execution:
  The designed code created specifically for this task is run within the MATLAB® script. This script is responsible for carrying out the teach-in process, which involves training the detector to recognize certain patterns or features. Once this training is successfully completed, the information learned by the detector is saved for future use.
- Fine-tuning using stochastic gradient descent (SGD) with momentum:
  The model fine-tuning process utilized SGD with momentum as the optimization algorithm, with hyperparameter selection guided by considerations outlined in Table 2.1. The mini-batch size of 32 was chosen to balance computational efficiency and pattern diversity within each

Table 2.1 Training hyperparameters for regional convolutional neural network.

Parameter	Method
Training option	sdgm
L2 regularization	0.09
Learning rate drop factor	0.2
Momentum	0.9
Number of epochs	50
Dropout value	0.6
Mini-batch size	32
Learning rate	0.0001

batch. A learning rate of $1e^{-4}$ governed adjustments to model parameters, striking a balance between convergence speed and stability. An impulse (momentum) value of 0.9 expedited training by accumulating gradients from past steps. Training extended over 50 epochs, a decision validated by the satisfactory 93.8% training accuracy. Additional hyperparameters, including L2 regularization (0.09), learning rate drop factor (0.2), and dropout value (0.6), were set in accordance with Table 2.1, contributing to regularization, learning rate control, and stochasticity during training. The chosen hyperparameter values collectively aimed at achieving optimal model performance, as evidenced by the successful capture of meaningful patterns from the training data.

- Importance of initialization weights:

  The significance of initialization weights in neural networks cannot be overstated (Namozov & Cho, 2018). Initialization weights involve the assignment of initial values to the parameters within the neural network, a process critical for optimal performance. This pertains to the careful adjustment of hyperparameters, the settings governing the model's learning process. Through meticulous fine-tuning of these hyperparameters, the model's learning capabilities were substantially improved, resulting in enhanced overall performance. In essence, proper weight initialization and effective hyperparameter tuning constitute pivotal measures in facilitating the neural network's learning process and refining its predictive abilities. The proper initialization of weights addresses the challenge of ensuring that the network starts with values that allow for efficient learning. This is particularly relevant in mitigating issues, such as vanishing or exploding gradients, which can impede the convergence of the neural network during training. Furthermore, the fine-tuning of hyperparameters, including learning rates and regularization terms, contributes to the optimization of the network's performance. The synergy between appropriate weight initialization and judicious hyperparameter tuning forms the cornerstone of creating neural networks that not only learn effectively but also yield accurate and reliable predictions.

- Final model size and embedding capability:

  Upon completing the training process for the R-CNN fire/smoke detector yielded a final model size of approximately 220 KB. This modest size renders the detector highly manageable, akin to a digital file occupying a space of about 220 KB. The compactness of the model is advantageous as it facilitates seamless integration into diminutive devices with restricted storage capacities and processing capabilities. This attribute enhances the detector's versatility, enabling its deployment in diverse real-world scenarios where spatial and computational resources are constrained. The implications of this compact design are profound, particularly for applications in environments where space is at a premium. The detector's diminutive footprint ensures its adaptability to small gadgets or machines, overcoming the limitations imposed by size constraints. In essence, this final model size signifies a practical solution for fire and smoke detection, offering reliability and efficiency while harmonizing with the spatial limitations inherent in modern technologies. Consequently, the R-CNN fire/smoke detector emerges as a pragmatic choice for deployment in various contexts, presenting an innovative paradigm for compact and resource-efficient detection systems. Fig. 2.3 illustrates the mini-batch loss curve for the R-CNN.

The proposed model has undergone validation using a distinct dataset that includes 200 images. Within this dataset, 100 instances showcase the presence of fire or smoke, while an equal number exhibit scenarios devoid of such phenomena. The primary aim of utilizing this dataset was to validate the effectiveness of the R-CNN. The evaluation was performed employing receiver operating characteristic analysis, resulting in an accuracy rate of 91%, as illustrated in Table 2.2. The achieved accuracy of 91% indicates the model's ability to correctly classify instances as either containing fire or smoke or not. This metric is an indicator of overall

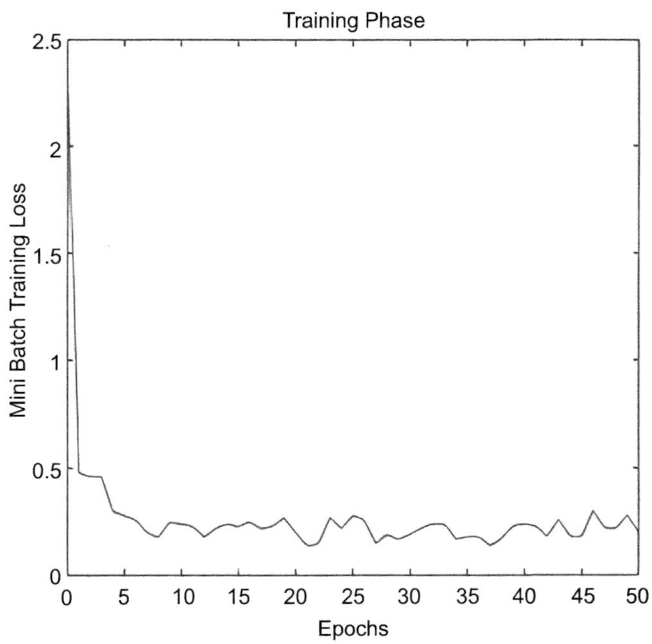

FIGURE 2.3

Mini-batch loss curve for the regional convolutional neural network. The mini-batch loss curve illustrates the fluctuation of loss values during training for the regional convolutional neural network model. It provides insights into the model's learning dynamics and convergence over successive mini-batches.

Table 2.2 Summary of validation results by receiver operating characteristic tool analysis.

Matrices	Validation values
Number of images	200
Accuracy	91%
Sensitivity	99%
Specificity	82%

model performance. Sensitivity, or the true positive rate, measures the model's ability to correctly identify instances with fire or smoke. The high sensitivity of 99% suggests that the model performs exceptionally well in detecting positive instances. Specificity, or the true negative rate, gauges the model's capability to correctly identify instances without fire or smoke. Although specificity is slightly lower at 82%, it is still at a reasonable level, indicating a good balance between identifying positive and negative instances. The resulting accuracy of 91% reflects the model's ability to distinguish between positive and negative instances across different threshold settings. The proposed model demonstrates strong performance across key metrics, especially in terms of accuracy and sensitivity. The specificity, while slightly lower, is still acceptable.

The primary goal of this research is to enhance the utility of a deep learning model tailored for video-based surveillance systems, with a specific emphasis on the identification of fire and smoke. Notably, previous studies, as referenced in Di Lascio et al. (2014) and Chen et al. (2004), predominantly rely on still images rather than video data for their testing procedures. However, these methodologies often lack diversity in simulating a wide range of real-world scenarios involving fire/smoke and normal conditions. In contrast, our proposed approach takes a more comprehensive approach to evaluate the model's performance. We subjected it to an extensive dataset consisting of 287 videos collected from diverse environments, including indoor spaces, outdoor areas, forests, railways, parking lots, and public zones. Within this dataset, 117 videos (with a total of 65,224 frames) represent scenarios without smoke or fire, while 170 videos (with a total of 107,189 frames) depict instances of smoke and fire. To assess the model's effectiveness, we employed performance metrics, such as the false positive rate, false-negative rate, and accuracy. These metrics were calculated using the confusion matrix criteria detailed in Eq. (2.3) and visually represented in Fig. 2.4. By utilizing a more extensive and varied dataset, our approach aims to provide a more robust evaluation of the deep learning model's capability to accurately detect fire and smoke in different real-world scenarios. This not only enhances the reliability of our findings but also contributes to a more comprehensive understanding of the model's practical applicability in video-based surveillance systems.

Our findings highlight the efficacy of the R-CNN in fire and smoke detection, outperforming alternative methods as detailed in Table 2.3, and see Fig. 2.5. The R-CNN achieves an impressive accuracy of 96.5%, surpassing competing approaches represented by Chen et al. (2004), Çelik et al. (2007), Di Lascio et al. (2014), and Wang et al. (2019), which recorded accuracies of 92.86%, 91%, 87.1%, and 83.7%, respectively. This superiority is not only evident in overall accuracy but is further substantiated by the R-CNN's notably low false positive rate, as depicted in the table. The significance of the R-CNN technique in object detection is

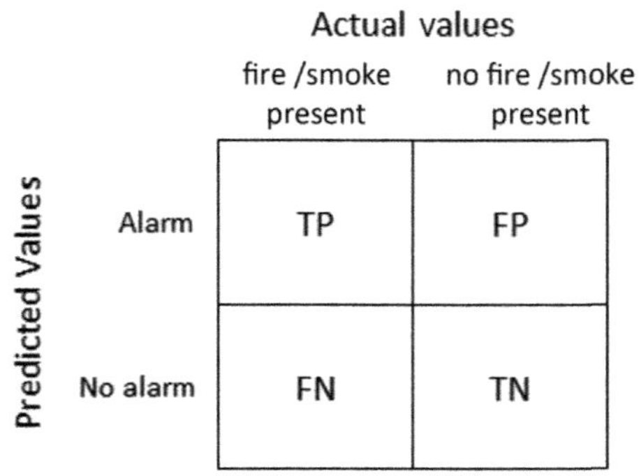

FIGURE 2.4

Confusion matrix. The confusion matrix provides a visual representation of the performance of a classification model, displaying the counts of True Positive, True Negative, False Positive, and False Negative predictions. It serves as a valuable tool for assessing the accuracy and efficacy of machine learning algorithms.

Table 2.3 Performance of the regional convolutional neural network versus other methods.

Method	False Positive %	False Negative %	Accuracy %
Proposed R-CNN	8.5	0	96.5
Di Lascio et al. (2014)	13.3	0	92.86
Wang et al. (2019)	14	8	91
Chen et al. (2004)	11.76	14.29	87.1
Celik et al., (2007)	29.41	0	83.7

R-CCN, *Regional convolutional neural network.*

underscored by these results, establishing it as the mainstream algorithm in the domain of fire and smoke detection. Early detection, a critical factor in minimizing damages and losses from such incidents, is a forte of our proposed methodology utilizing the R-CNN. The algorithm excels in identifying multiple instances of fire and smoke within a frame, demarcated by Bounding Boxes. One distinguishing aspect of our approach is the R-CNN's capability to detect small fire and smoke regions, as evidenced by the smallest recorded Bounding Box dimensions of 39 × 17 pixels. This feature positions the R-CNN as advantageous in delivering early alerts for fire and smoke detection, showcasing its proficiency in identifying minute regions within video data. The quantitative results in Table 2.3 further validate the superiority of the Proposed R-CNN, exhibiting a false positive rate of 8.5%, significantly outperforming the competing methods. This metric is crucial in real-world applications, as a lower false positive rate enhances the reliability of the system, minimizing the chances of false alarms. This study reinforces the prominence of the R-CNN in fire and smoke detection, emphasizing its robustness, accuracy, and ability to detect small regions early on. These findings have practical

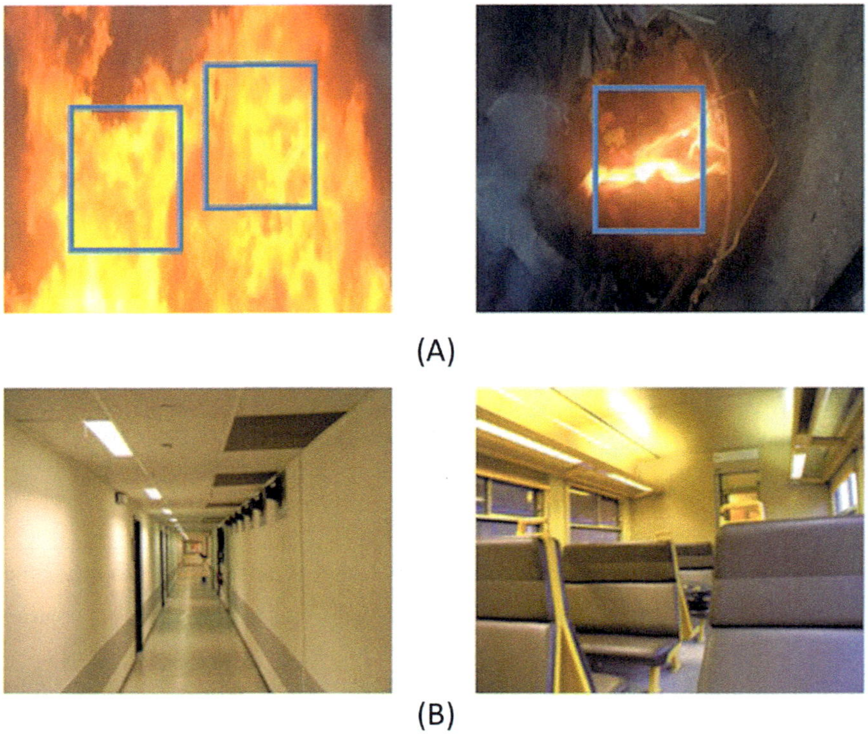

FIGURE 2.5

(A) Images from videos with fire and smoke, (B) images from videos with no fire and smoke.

implications for real-world applications, especially in scenarios where prompt detection and response are imperative.

$$\begin{aligned}
\text{Accuracy} &= \frac{\text{TP} + \text{TN}}{\text{TP} + \text{FN} + \text{TN} + \text{FP}} \\
\text{False} - \text{positive rate} &= \frac{\text{FP}}{\text{FP} + \text{TN}} \\
\text{False} - \text{negativ rate} &= \frac{\text{FN}}{\text{FN} + \text{TP}} \\
1 &= \frac{2 \times \text{precision} \times \text{recall}}{\text{precision} + \text{recall}} \\
\text{Precision} &= \frac{\text{TP}}{(\text{FP} + \text{TP})} \\
\text{Recall} &= \frac{\text{TP}}{(\text{FN} + \text{TP})}
\end{aligned} \tag{2.3}$$

- In the context of video-based fire and smoke detection, the outcomes are systematically classified based on the model's performance. These outcomes are articulated through the terminology of True Positives (TP), False Positives (FP), True Negatives (TN), and False

Negatives (FN). The elucidation of these classifications is paramount in evaluating the efficacy of the detection model. TP represent instances where the model accurately identifies and detects the presence of smoke or fire classes in videos that indeed exhibit these phenomena. On the contrary, FP denote situations where the model erroneously detects smoke or fire classes in videos devoid of such occurrences. TN are indicative of the model's correct discernment in not identifying smoke or fire classes in videos that genuinely lack these elements. Lastly, FN arise when the model fails to detect smoke or fire classes in videos where these elements are, in fact, present.

2.1.4 Size of detected regions

The R-CNN has emerged as a dominant algorithm in the field of object detection, demonstrating its effectiveness in the early identification of fire and smoke incidents. This capability is crucial for timely recognition as it plays a pivotal role in mitigating potential damages and losses. In our proposed methodology, the R-CNN showcases its ability to discern multiple instances of fire and smoke within a given frame, encapsulating each identified object with a Bounding Box. Notably, the R-CNN excels in detecting even minute fire and smoke regions, as evidenced in the table by the smallest recorded region measuring 39×17 pixels (width and height) in image 5, depicted in Fig. 2.6. The experimentation involved extracting minimum values from the detected Bounding Boxes within our testing dataset, revealing the R-CNN's proficiency in identifying diminutive regions. This proficiency serves as a critical early warning indicator for potential fire and smoke occurrences in videos. The significance of this lies in the algorithm's ability to detect small-scale incidents that might be overlooked by traditional methods, thereby enhancing the overall effectiveness of surveillance systems. A distinctive aspect of our approach is the focus on analyzing videos

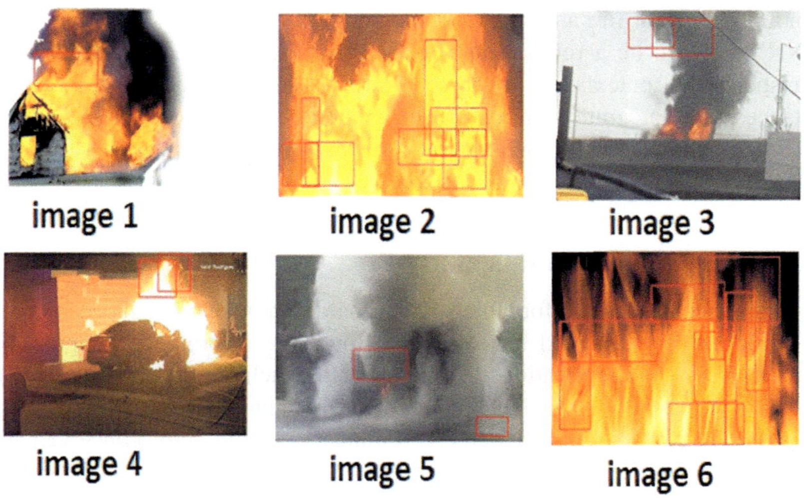

FIGURE 2.6

Bounding boxes of detected regions of fire and smoke from sampled images.

Table 2.4 Size of the minimum detected bounding boxes of smoke and fire.

Images	Minimum size of detected bounding boxes (width, height in pixels)
1	79 × 31
2	44 × 40
3	56 × 22
4	40 × 36
5	39 × 17
6	18 × 74

captured by surveillance cameras integrated into smart cities or smart transportation systems. Unlike a previous study (Habiboğlu et al., 2012) that utilized the fast R-CNN and concentrated on the analysis of expansive areas, such as wildland forests, observed from a considerable distance, our work emphasizes urban and transportation contexts. Surveillance systems in smart cities often cover varying distances, from a few meters to several hundred meters, making it crucial to adapt object detection algorithms to these diverse scenarios. The adaptability and applicability of the R-CNN in different surveillance scenarios are underscored by this distinction. Its effectiveness in detecting fire and smoke in urban environments and transportation systems highlights its versatility. Unlike algorithms tailored for specific environments, the R-CNN can seamlessly transition between different contexts, making it a valuable tool for enhancing public safety in smart city infrastructures. Moreover, the emphasis on surveillance cameras integrated into existing smart systems aligns with the broader trend of leveraging technology to improve urban living. Integrating object detection algorithms into these systems not only enhances safety measures but also contributes to the overall efficiency and responsiveness of smart cities. Table 2.4 illustrates the minimum sizes of the detected bounding boxes for fire and smoke in the images.

The R-CNN proves to be a robust solution for early fire and smoke detection, particularly in urban and transportation contexts. Its ability to identify small-scale incidents, adapt to varying surveillance distances, and integrate seamlessly into existing smart systems positions it as a valuable asset for enhancing public safety in the evolving landscape of smart cities.

2.1.5 Testing the R-CNN with Raspberry Pi

Raspberry Pi is a series of small, affordable, single-board computers developed by the Raspberry Pi Foundation. While initially designed for educational purposes to promote computer science education, Raspberry Pi has found applications in various fields, including deep learning. Raspberry Pi, a groundbreaking series of small, affordable, single-board computers, has emerged as a technological marvel since its inception by the Raspberry Pi Foundation. Originally conceived with a primary focus on advancing computer science education, this versatile platform has transcended its initial purpose and found applications across diverse fields, showcasing its adaptability and ingenuity. With its compact size and cost-effectiveness, Raspberry Pi has become a cornerstone in educational settings, providing students with a tangible and accessible tool to delve into the realms of programming and computer science. However, the capabilities of Raspberry Pi extend far beyond the educational landscape, with one of its most compelling applications lying in the realm of deep learning.

In recent years, the integration of Raspberry Pi into deep learning projects has gained considerable traction, unlocking new possibilities for enthusiasts, hobbyists, and professionals alike. The allure of leveraging this diminutive yet powerful computer for deep learning lies in its ability to balance performance with affordability, making cutting-edge technologies accessible to a broader audience. Raspberry Pi's architecture, featuring a Broadcom system-on-chip and a multitude of connectivity options, provides a robust foundation for building innovative solutions. Its compatibility with various programming languages, including Python, further enhances its appeal as a versatile platform for developing and deploying deep learning models. One of the key advantages of using Raspberry Pi for deep learning is its energy efficiency. The low power consumption of these single-board computers makes them ideal for deployment in edge computing scenarios. In applications where real-time processing and decision-making are crucial, such as in robotics or IoT devices, Raspberry Pi's efficiency becomes a significant asset. The integration of deep learning algorithms on Raspberry Pi enables these devices to perform complex tasks locally, reducing the need for continuous communication with centralized servers and enhancing overall system responsiveness. Raspberry Pi's prowess in computer vision is particularly noteworthy in the context of deep learning. The platform's compatibility with popular deep learning frameworks like TensorFlow and PyTorch facilitates the implementation of CNNs and other sophisticated models. This capability opens up avenues for projects ranging from object recognition and image classification to more advanced applications like facial recognition and gesture detection. As a result, Raspberry Pi serves as a catalyst for innovation in fields such as home automation, surveillance systems, and smart environments. Furthermore, the Raspberry Pi community plays a pivotal role in fostering the platform's growth in the realm of deep learning. Enthusiasts and developers actively contribute to a wealth of resources, tutorials, and projects that showcase the potential of Raspberry Pi in conjunction with deep learning. This collaborative spirit not only accelerates the learning curve for newcomers but also fosters a dynamic ecosystem where ideas flourish and innovations are shared. Despite its commendable capabilities, Raspberry Pi does have its limitations in the context of deep learning. The modest computational power and limited memory of these single-board computers impose constraints on the size and complexity of deep learning models that can be effectively deployed. Nevertheless, ongoing advancements in hardware and software optimization, coupled with the dedication of the Raspberry Pi community, continue to push the boundaries of what can be achieved with this diminutive yet formidable computing platform.

- Affordability and accessibility

  Raspberry Pi boards, renowned for their affordability and accessibility, have emerged as a transformative tool for individuals, students, and hobbyists keen on delving into the realms of deep learning. The cost-effective nature of these boards renders them an attractive option for those seeking to explore the intricacies of machine learning without the financial burden associated with high-end hardware. Their affordability not only democratizes access to technology but also serves as a catalyst for fostering a broader community engagement in the field. This democratization of technology allows aspiring enthusiasts to experiment with and develop innovative projects, thereby promoting a more inclusive and diverse landscape within the realm of deep learning. Consequently, Raspberry Pi contributes significantly to reducing barriers to entry, empowering a wide spectrum of individuals to partake in the dynamic world of AI and machine learning. In doing so, it plays a pivotal role in cultivating a future generation of technologically adept minds.

- Graphics processing unit (GPU) acceleration

  In the realm of GPU acceleration, the Raspberry Pi, despite lacking a dedicated GPU akin to more robust deep learning systems, has avenues to harness enhanced processing capabilities. One notable solution is the integration of external hardware accelerators, such as the Coral USB Accelerator developed by Google. By connecting this accelerator to a Raspberry Pi, users can unlock a tangible hardware acceleration advantage, particularly beneficial for optimizing machine learning workloads. This external device empowers the Raspberry Pi to execute complex computational tasks with greater efficiency, offering a practical workaround for the absence of an inherent GPU. While the Raspberry Pi may not possess built-in graphical processing prowess, the seamless integration of external accelerators exemplifies the adaptability of this versatile single-board computer, expanding its utility and making it a viable option for a spectrum of computational tasks, including those demanding accelerated processing for machine learning applications.

- TensorFlow Lite and PyTorch support

  TensorFlow Lite and PyTorch, two widely utilized deep learning frameworks, seamlessly integrate with the Raspberry Pi, expanding its capabilities in the realm of AI. This compatibility empowers users to deploy pretrained models efficiently, harnessing the power of machine learning directly on the compact Raspberry Pi device. TensorFlow Lite, known for its lightweight and streamlined design, enables the execution of machine learning models with optimized performance on resource-constrained platforms like the Raspberry Pi. Likewise, PyTorch, celebrated for its dynamic computational graph and intuitive syntax, provides a flexible environment for developing and deploying neural networks on this mini-computing marvel. The integration of these frameworks with the Raspberry Pi not only facilitates the deployment of sophisticated AI applications but also opens the door for on-device model training. This means that users can leverage the computing power of the Raspberry Pi to train simpler models without the need for external resources, fostering a decentralized approach to machine learning. In essence, the marriage of TensorFlow Lite and PyTorch with the Raspberry Pi extends the horizons of possibilities, making advanced AI accessible to a broader audience and unlocking the potential for innovative solutions in various domains, ranging from IoT devices to educational projects. As the Raspberry Pi continues to evolve as a versatile computing platform, its compatibility with these prominent deep learning frameworks positions it as a formidable tool for exploring the frontiers of AI at the edge.

- Edge computing

  Edge computing, a paradigm that involves processing data closer to the source rather than relying solely on centralized servers, finds an ideal ally in the form of Raspberry Pi. This credit-card-sized computer is exceptionally well-suited for edge computing applications, showcasing its versatility beyond basic programming exercises. By facilitating the local processing of data directly on the device, Raspberry Pi diminishes the dependency on continuous internet connectivity, providing a solution to scenarios where a stable online connection may not be guaranteed. This proves to be invaluable in real-time applications, such as image recognition and object detection, where rapid and efficient processing is imperative. In such instances, the Raspberry Pi's capability to execute computations at the edge not only minimizes latency but also enhances overall system responsiveness. Moreover, this localized processing approach contributes to a more resilient and fault-tolerant system, as it is less susceptible to disruptions caused by network outages. As the demand for quick and efficient data analysis continues to grow, the Raspberry Pi's role in enabling edge computing emerges as a pivotal factor, offering a cost-effective and compact solution that aligns seamlessly with the evolving landscape of distributed computing.

- Computer vision projects

  Raspberry Pi serves as a versatile platform for computer vision projects by seamlessly integrating with cameras like the Raspberry Pi Camera Module. This compact yet powerful single-board computer enables the creation of sophisticated applications, including facial recognition, surveillance systems, and automated image classification. Through the integration of computer vision technology, Raspberry Pi contributes to enhancing security measures and streamlining visual data analysis. The Raspberry Pi Camera Module, equipped with high-resolution imaging capabilities, facilitates the development of projects that rely on real-time image processing. The cost-effectiveness and accessibility of Raspberry Pi make it an ideal choice for educational institutions, researchers, and hobbyists seeking to delve into the realms of computer vision. This platform not only empowers enthusiasts to explore the fundamentals of image analysis but also serves as a practical tool for developing innovative solutions in various domains, ranging from security and surveillance to automation. The user-friendly nature of Raspberry Pi, coupled with its extensive community support, fosters a collaborative environment for individuals to engage in computer vision projects and explore the vast potential of visual data processing. In essence, Raspberry Pi's compatibility with camera modules facilitates the seamless integration of computer vision into a myriad of applications, thereby democratizing access to this cutting-edge technology and promoting advancements in the field.

- IoT integration

  In the realm of technological innovation, the Raspberry Pi emerges as a versatile tool, seamlessly integrating into the expansive domain of IoT. Specifically designed to be a compact and affordable single-board computer, the Raspberry Pi finds its prowess in its ability to engage with IoT projects that delve into the realm of deep learning. One exemplary application lies in its capacity to scrutinize sensor data with precision, facilitating insightful analyses. Through the employment of deep learning models, this diminutive yet potent device is adept at making accurate predictions based on the intricate patterns discerned from the input data. Moreover, the Raspberry Pi's functionality extends beyond mere analysis, as it becomes an active participant in the decision-making process. By leveraging the outcomes generated by the deep learning model, the Raspberry Pi can autonomously trigger actions, creating a dynamic interplay between data analysis and real-world responses. This integration not only enhances the efficiency of IoT systems but also opens avenues for the seamless implementation of intelligent, data-driven functionalities. As the IoT landscape continues to burgeon with diverse applications, the Raspberry Pi stands as a testament to the democratization of computing power, offering a compact yet potent solution for the fusion of deep learning and sensor-driven IoT projects.

In this research, the R-CNN detector was assessed by deploying it on a Raspberry Pi 3 Model B integrated with a video camera. The R-CNN detection code was executed using MATLAB® on a

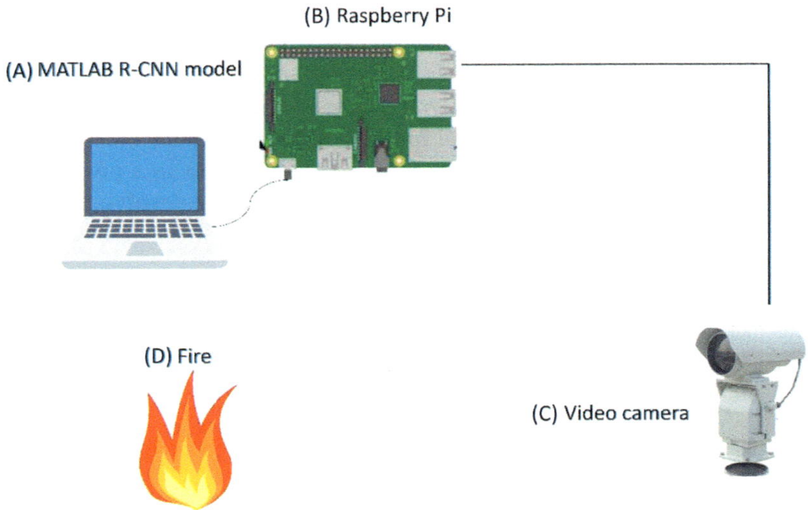

FIGURE 2.7

Testing the regional convolutional neural network detector with a real state of fire and smoke. The hardware setup consists of (A) running the regional convolutional neural network detector with MATLAB® on personal computer (PC), (B) Raspberry Pi, (C) video camera, (D) fire/smoke video simulated from another computer.

personal computer. To emulate diverse scenarios, we generated simulated videos portraying authentic smoke/fire and nonsmoke/fire situations on a separate computer. These videos were then presented to the video camera, as illustrated in Fig. 2.7. The outcomes of our experimentation revealed that the R-CNN model successfully discerned instances of fire and smoke, accurately signaling normal conditions in videos where no fire or smoke was simulated for the camera. It is imperative to note that our investigation represents a preliminary exploration into the applicability of the algorithm within the confines of the presented embedded system. Our future research trajectory involves a comprehensive implementation on an economically viable Raspberry Pi to evaluate both its performance and power consumption during the execution of the R-CNN model. Noteworthy is the observed sluggishness in the fire and smoke detection capability of R-CNN. The primary impediment lies in its protracted processing time, rendering it impractical for real-time image processing scenarios. Specifically, on a conventional deep learning machine, the R-CNN model necessitates an alarming 47 seconds to analyze a single image, rendering it unsuitable for time-sensitive applications. Addressing this computational inefficiency is imperative for the widespread adoption of the R-CNN model in real-world, time-critical settings.

2.2 Real-time fire and smoke detection

In this section, we introduce an advanced approach to real-time fire and smoke detection utilizing the YOLOv2 model, specifically designed for video analysis. Traditionally, many researchers have

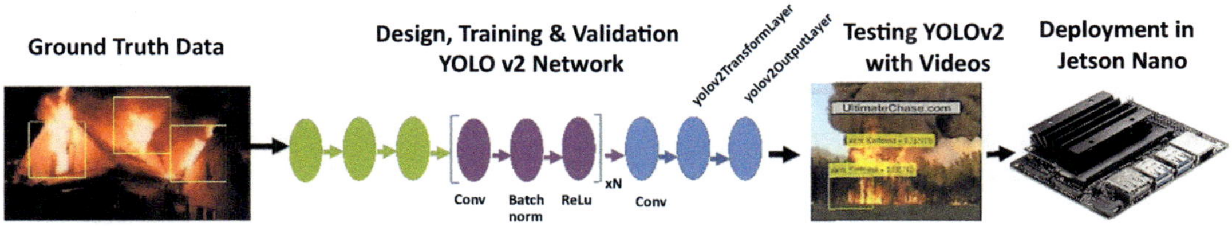

FIGURE 2.8

Workflow for designing the proposed model for fire and smoke detection.

concentrated on employing conventional methods of feature extraction for identifying instances of fire and smoke. However, these methods have encountered a significant challenge due to the considerable time required to perform feature extractions, resulting in suboptimal performance and sluggish real-time detection. Additionally, these techniques often yielded false alarms and errors in background detection.

Motivated by recent advancements in deep learning models, our proposed method leverages the YOLOv2 model for fire and smoke detection through video camera surveillance. This innovative approach facilitates faster image processing, making YOLOv2 an optimal solution for efficiently detecting fire and smoke. The swift detection provided by our model is crucial for firefighters, offering early warnings of potential fire and smoke incidents and enabling timely corrective measures. Fig. 2.8 illustrates the stepwise workflow involved in constructing our fire and smoke detection architecture. The process initiates with the creation of ground truth data through the meticulous labeling of training images. Subsequently, we devised the model using a neural network and integrated YOLOv2 layers for enhanced detection capabilities. Furthermore, rigorous training, validation, and testing procedures were conducted to evaluate the model's performance and accuracy. Finally, the proposed technique is deployed on the target node, specifically the Jetson Nano, allowing it to operate independently as a standalone application within this embedded device.

2.2.1 Methodology and results

In the undertaken project, the significance of employing the Deep Neural Designer tool in the MATLAB® environment became evident. This tool played a crucial role in customizing YOLOv2 layers specifically designed for neural networks. The primary goal was to develop a deep learning model with reduced complexity, tailored to seamlessly integrate with embedded systems. This endeavor resulted in the construction of a CNN comprising a total of 21 layers, as illustrated in Fig. 2.9. Importantly, this lightweight model not only demonstrates proficiency in real-time performance but also proves to be well-suited for deployment on cost-effective IoT devices.

In the outlined approach, the methodology revolves around the amalgamation of distinct layers, specifically, input, middle, and YOLOv2 subnetwork layers. The YOLOv2 object recognition network is a notable component in this framework, distinguished by its dual subnetwork structure. This structure encompasses a feature extraction network followed by a recognition network, both contributing significantly to the overall functionality. The yolov2Layers function plays a pivotal role in this methodology by facilitating the seamless creation of a YOLOv2 object detection

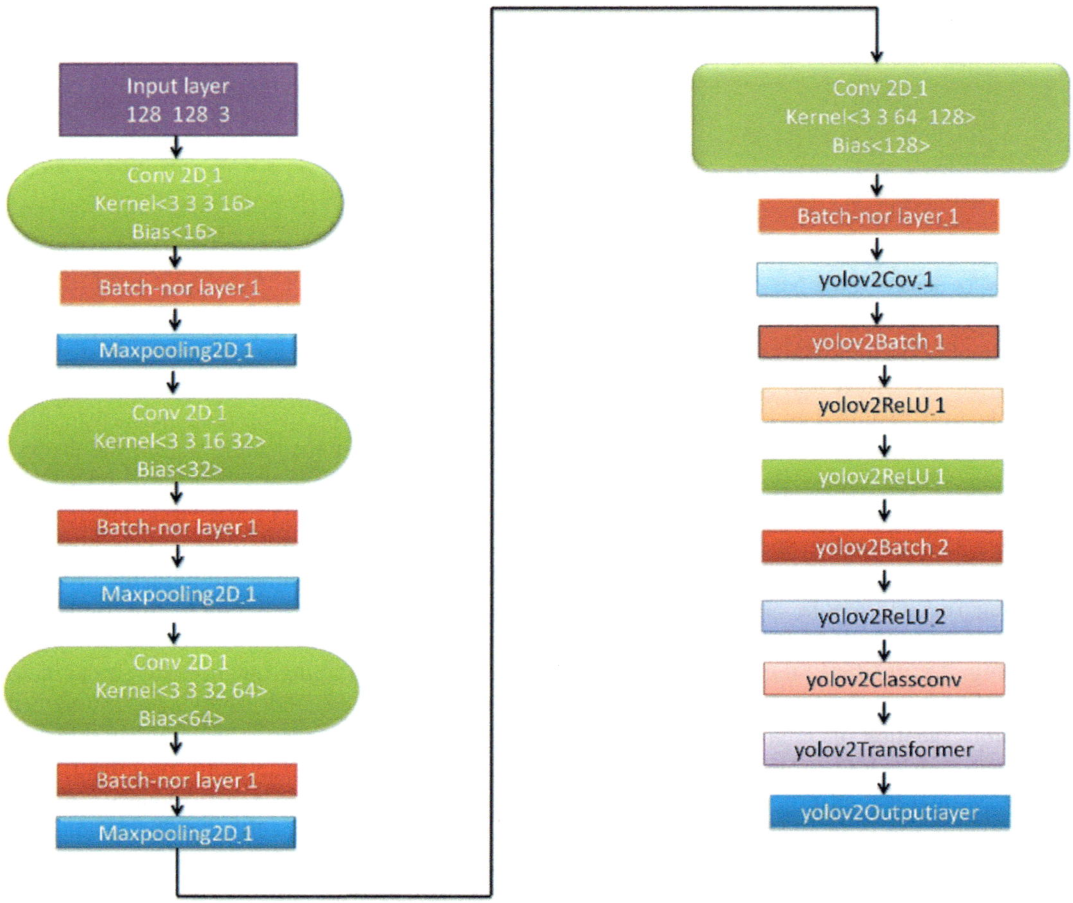

FIGURE 2.9

The proposed approach of You Only Look Once version II model. The proposed approach of the You Only Look Once version II model emphasizes significant enhancements in speed and accuracy, facilitating real-time object detection with improved precision. It introduces batch normalization and a new anchor box optimization technique, vastly increasing the model's ability to generalize across diverse datasets and scenarios.

network. This is achieved through the utilization of custom CNN layers, which are tailored to meet the specific requirements of the YOLOv2 architecture. To instantiate yolov2Layers effectively, certain crucial inputs must be provided. These inputs encompass the network input size, anchor boxes, and specifications related to the feature extraction network. The network input size, in conjunction with the number of classes, stands out as fundamental parameter for this process. The determination of the network input size is influenced by the dimensions of the training images, thereby establishing a connection between the model's configuration and the characteristics of the training dataset.

The computational costs associated with the processing of data of a specified size play a pivotal role in determining the optimal network input size. A deliberate selection was made to closely align the dimensions of the network's input size with that of the training images, intentionally exceeding the size requirement for the network. The initiation of our model involves the establishment of the input image layer, meticulously configured to accommodate a minimum image size of $128 \times 128 \times 3$.

The subsequent layers are structured as a cascade, incorporating a sequence of operations including convolution, batch normalization, ReLU activation, and max-pooling layers. Convolution layers, characterized by a filter size of $[3 \times 3]$, are strategically employed to map features from the input images. Batch normalization layers are integrated to normalize the model, thereby enhancing training efficiency and expediting convergence by mitigating sensitivity to network initialization.

The infusion of ReLU activation functions introduces nonlinearity to the model, contributing to its capacity to capture intricate patterns in the data. Simultaneously, max-pooling layers are strategically placed to facilitate downsampling of images within pooling regions. This is achieved through the utilization of a 2×2 pooling size, consistently applied across all pooling layers in the network, resulting in a reduction in the spatial dimensions of the data. This deliberate downsampling aids in preserving essential features while reducing the computational load and improving the model's overall efficiency.

To develop and assess the effectiveness of the model we propose, a dataset consisting of 600 images depicting instances of fire and smoke was meticulously curated from the Kaggle platform. This dataset was subsequently partitioned into two subsets, with 70% allocated for training purposes and the remaining 30% designated for validation.

The process of labeling the images was streamlined using the Ground Truth application within the MATLAB® environment. The actual training of the detection model was accomplished through the implementation of a MATLAB® script. Upon the culmination of the training phase, the model's parameters were saved, and adjustments were made to the dimensions of the images within the training dataset. Specifically, these dimensions were modified from $416 \times 416 \times 3$ to $128 \times 128 \times 3$ to adhere to the stipulated requirements of YOLOv2. The training regimen employed SGD over 160 epochs, reflecting the number of iterations the model underwent while processing the training dataset. Table 2.5 shows the hyperparameters for training YOLOv2. This deliberate choice of epoch count was made to strike a judicious balance, mitigating the risks associated with overtraining and potential issues like overfitting. Throughout the training process, the learning rate parameter, initially set at $10^{\wedge 2}$, underwent fine-tuning to achieve optimal performance. The final

Table 2.5 Training hyperparameters for You Only Look Once version II model.

Parameter	Method
Training option	sdgm
L2 regularization	0.06
Number of epochs	160
Verbose frequency	50
Mini-batch size	16
Learning rate	0.001

adjustment settled on a learning rate of $10^{\wedge 3}$, which yielded a commendable result of 0.2. An examination of the mini-batch loss curve revealed a trajectory characterized by stability, punctuated by minor fluctuations, as visually depicted in Fig. 2.10.

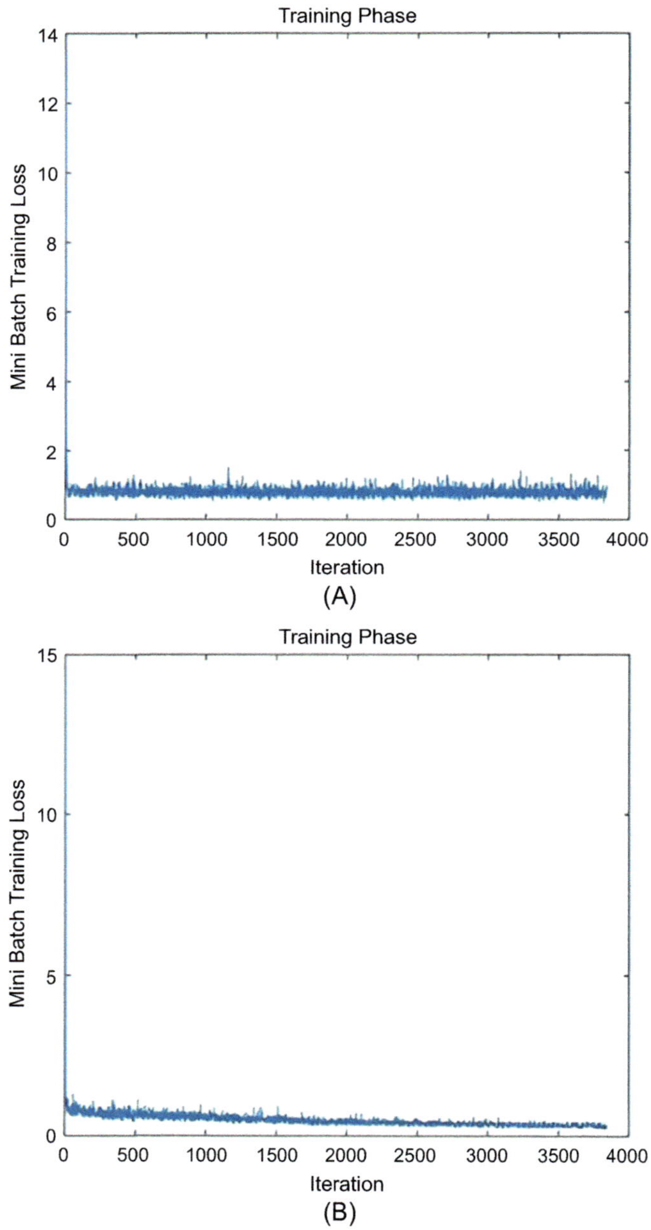

FIGURE 2.10

(A) Mini-batch loss curve before fine-tuning, (B) mini-batch loss curve after fine-tuning.

In the state-of-the-art, it is noteworthy that the prevalent approach to evaluating algorithmic performance leans heavily toward the utilization of static images as opposed to dynamic videos. The assessment methodology elucidated in the citation denoted as Di Lascio et al. (2014) is conspicuously characterized by a dearth of diversity in its incorporation of videos to comprehensively encompass an array of realistic scenarios. Specifically, there is a noticeable oversight in the consideration of dynamic visual inputs portraying scenarios involving fire/smoke dynamics and normal environmental conditions. Furthermore, an analogous limitation is evident in the approach outlined in Wang et al. (2019), wherein the attention is exclusively confined to the monitoring of forest fires. Regrettably, this exclusive focus results in a disregard for the broader spectrum of contexts, both indoor and outdoor, where diverse environmental conditions have been encountered.

In contrast, our model is meticulously tested across a myriad of indoor and outdoor settings. The experimentation process involves a substantial dataset comprising numerous videos. Our investigation incorporates two distinct test datasets, each sourced independently. Dataset v1, serving as our primary test bench, encompasses 287 videos spanning diverse environments such as indoor spaces, outdoor areas, forests, railways, parking lots, and public zones. Of these, 117 videos portray situations devoid of smoke or fire, while 170 videos feature instances of smoke and fire. This deliberately challenging dataset introduces complexity through the inclusion of motion-based and color-based objects, exemplified by the deliberate incorporation of cloud imagery. Dataset v2, drawn from the methodology presented in Jadon et al. (2019), supplements our evaluation process. This dataset, albeit smaller in scale, proves challenging due to the absence of fire/smoke videos during sunset conditions. It aligns with the deep learning approach articulated in Jadon et al. (2019), emphasizing the exclusion of Dataset v2 videos from our model training. Conducting an additional experiment entails creating and training a specialized R-CNN object detector designed specifically for identifying instances of fire and smoke. This detector is then assessed against our proposed model, utilizing the same Dataset v1. To scrutinize diverse aspects and measure the effectiveness of our proposed model, evaluation metrics, such as confusion matrices, are employed. The results of these experiments unveil the commendable classification performance of our method in detecting fire and smoke across both datasets. Notably, our approach surpasses benchmarks established by other methods, namely, Di Lascio et al. (2014), Filonenko et al. (2018), Jadon et al. (2019), Lestari et al. (2019), Wang et al. (2019), and Yuan et al. (2015), as illustrated in Tables 2.6 and 2.7. Furthermore, our proposed methodology demonstrates superior accuracy when juxtaposed with the R-CNN object detector, excelling particularly in the identification of nonfire videos exposed to sunlight. This superiority is evident in the visual representation depicted in Fig. 2.11, where the model effectively predicts nonfire status even in challenging scenarios. The robustness of our model becomes apparent in its ability to outperform existing techniques, showcasing its efficacy in real-world applications for fire and smoke detection. The results substantiate the practical significance of our proposed approach, establishing it as a noteworthy advancement in the domain.

The proposed YOLOv2, which processes the entire image concurrently, reduces false alarm issues associated with fire and smoke detection. Notably, YOLOv2 surpasses the R-CNN object detector by a factor of 25 in real-time object detection, thereby improving the efficiency of our proposed approach and addressing background errors encountered in previous research utilizing a R-CNN. When utilizing an input image size of $128 \times 128 \times 3$, the neural network architecture demonstrates a reduced number of layers. This reduction contributes to an expedited training process for the model. In comparison, the proposed approach not only enhances real-time performance in fire

Table 2.6 Performance of the proposed approach versus state-of-the-art.

Method	False Positive %	False Negative %	Accuracy %
YOLOv2	3.4	2.9	96.82
R-CNN	8.5	0	96.5
Di Lascio et al. (2014)	13.3	0	92.86
Wang et al. (2019)	14	8	91
Lestari et al. (2019)	5	5	90

R-CCN, *Regional convolutional neural network;* YOLOv2, *You Only Look Once version II.*

Table 2.7 The performance of the proposed approach using Dataset v2 versus other methodologies.

Method	Accuracy %	Recall %	F-score %	Precision %
YOLOv2	96.58	97	95.4	97
Jadon et al. (2019)	93.9	94	95	96.9
Filonenko et al. (2018)	85	96	90	85
Yuan et al. (2015)	86	53	65.5	86

YOLOv2, *You Only Look Once version II.*

FIGURE 2.11

Sample examples of Dataset v2, which shows sunset light in nonfire videos. Sample examples of Dataset v2. The figure displays instances from Dataset v2 capturing sunset ambiance in videos unrelated to fire incidents, providing valuable samples for research or analysis in diverse contexts. This dataset offers a unique glimpse into the interplay of natural lighting conditions, contributing to a comprehensive understanding of nonfire video content.

and smoke detection but also surpasses scenarios involving larger $224 \times 224 \times 3$ size images. The key advantage of adopting the proposed approach lies in its capacity to minimize the overall weight of the final deep architecture. Despite this reduction in weight, the model sustains a commendable level of accuracy in detection while ensuring swift processing when deployed in low-cost embedded systems. This design choice involves the utilization of four convolutional layers dedicated specifically to extracting features from fire and smoke images. The accelerated real-time object detection capabilities of YOLOv2 not only contribute to a more efficient approach but also address false alarms more effectively. The significant outperformance of YOLOv2 over the R-CNN object detector underscores the superiority of our chosen methodology. Furthermore, the reduction in layers when employing a $128 \times 128 \times 3$ input image size not only expedites the training process but also showcases the adaptability of our model to different input configurations. Comparatively, the proposed approach's superiority over scenarios involving larger $224 \times 224 \times 3$ size images underscores its efficacy in resource optimization. The strategic incorporation of four dedicated convolutional layers for feature extraction from fire and smoke images emphasizes a focused and efficient architectural design. This nuanced design choice not only enhances real-time performance but also positions the model as a feasible and accurate solution for deployment in low-cost embedded systems, thereby contributing to the practicality and scalability of our proposed methodology.

2.2.2 Execution the protype on NVIDIA Jetson Nano

Jetson Nano, developed by NVIDIA, serves as a cost-effective platform for implementing and evaluating our proposed algorithm. Priced at approximately $100, it functions as a sturdy yet compact embedded computer. Specifically engineered for executing tasks related to neural networks, the Jetson Nano excels in parallel processing, particularly in the context of object recognition. Its suitability is notable in applications dependent on distributed networks. Jetson Nano is equipped with a GPU featuring a 128-core Maxwell architecture, accompanied by a quad-core ARM A57 CPU operating at 1.43 GHz. Its memory configuration comprises 4 GB of 64-bit LPDDR4 RAM, providing a speed of 25.6 GB/second. Notably, the device offers versatile connectivity options with features, such as 4 × USB 3.0 and a USB 2.0 Micro-B port. This combination of features makes the Jetson Nano an ideal choice for a range of applications that require efficient neural network processing within a compact and affordable system. Table 2.8 illustrates the comparison between Jetson Nano, and Raspberry Pi 4 devices.

Jetson Nano has a quad-core ARM Cortex-A57 processor, while Raspberry Pi has a quad-core ARM Cortex-A72 processor. The Jetson Nano's Maxwell GPU with 128 cores provides better parallel processing capabilities, making it suitable for AI and machine learning tasks. Jetson Nano comes with 4 GB of LPDDR4 RAM, providing a performance advantage over Raspberry Pi, which has options for 2 GB, 4 GB, or 8 GB LPDDR4 RAM. Both devices use microSD cards for storage. Jetson Nano offers more USB ports with both USB 3.0 and USB 2.0, providing better connectivity options. Both devices have Gigabit Ethernet, but Jetson Nano also supports Wi-Fi 802.11ac and Bluetooth 4.2. The Jetson Nano's Maxwell GPU is designed for AI and deep learning applications, making it more suitable for tasks like image recognition and neural network processing compared to Raspberry Pi's VideoCore VI GPU. Both devices feature a 40-pin GPIO header for connecting sensors and other peripherals. Jetson Nano's MIPI CSI-2 DPHY lanes offer a dedicated interface for connecting cameras, enhancing its capabilities for computer vision projects. Both devices support HDMI 2.0 for video output. Jetson Nano additionally supports eDP 1.4, providing flexibility for various display options. Jetson Nano runs on an Ubuntu-based Linux distribution, while Raspberry Pi uses Raspbian OS, also a Linux-based distribution. The choice may depend on user

Table 2.8 The comparison between Jetson Nano and Raspberry PI 4.

Feature	Jetson Nano	Raspberry PI 4
Processor	Quad-core ARM Cortex-A57@1.43 GHz	Quad-core ARM Cortex-A72@1.5 GHz
GPU	128-core Maxwell GPU	Broadcom Video Core VI GPU
Memory	4 GB LPDDR4 RAM	Options: 2 GB, 4 GB, or 8 GB LPDDR4 RAM
Storage	microSD card slot	microSD card slot
USB ports	4 × USB 3.0, 4 × USB 2.0	4 × USB 2.0, 2 × USB 3.0
Ethernet	Gigabit Ethernet	Gigabit Ethernet
Wireless Connectivity	Wi-Fi 802.11b/g/n/ac, bluetooth 4.2	Wi-Fi 802.11b/g/n/ac, bluetooth 5.0
GPIO pins	40-pin GPIO header (compatible with Raspberry Pi)	40-pin GPIO header
Camera interface	MIPI CSI-2 DPHY lanes for connecting cameras	MIPI CSI-2 DPHY lanes for connecting cameras
Video output	HDMI 2.0, eDP 1.4	HDMI 2.0, composite video
Operating system	Ubuntu-based Linux	Raspbian OS (Linux-based)
Power supply	5V/4A via micro-USB or GPIO header	5V/3A via USB-C or GPIO header

GPU, *Graphics processing unit.*

preference and compatibility with specific software. Jetson Nano requires a 5V/4A power supply through micro-USB or the GPIO header. Raspberry Pi 4, on the other hand, uses a USB-C power supply with a 5V/3A rating. Jetson Nano excels in AI and deep learning applications due to its powerful GPU, while Raspberry Pi offers a versatile and cost-effective solution for a wide range of projects. The choice depends on the specific requirements of the project and the computational capabilities needed.

For our experimental setup, we utilized a Raspberry Pi Camera Module V2 with an 8-megapixel resolution, capable of capturing images at 1080p and 30 fps. The camera was seamlessly integrated into the Jetson Nano through the Camera Serial Interface CSI connector. The YOLOv2 detector, having been trained beforehand, was deployed to the NVIDIA Jetson Nano and executed as a stand-alone application. To optimize our MATLAB® code for deployment, we employed third-party packages and MATLAB® environments. We were able to harness the power of parallel processing on the NVIDIA GPU, optimizing the performance of our CNN model for real-time object detection.

The GPU Coder tool played a pivotal role in this process by seamlessly converting our MATLAB® code into a highly efficient CUDA code. CUDA, an extension of the C programming language, is tailored for NVIDIA GPUs, allowing us to fully leverage the parallel processing capabilities of the Jetson Nano. This optimization is essential for the rapid execution of complex neural network computations, a crucial aspect of real-time object detection.

Establishing communication between the Jetson Nano and the host computer was achieved through the utilization of an Ethernet cable. This connection is vital for data transfer between the devices, enabling the deployment of the trained CNN model onto the Jetson Nano. Fig. 2.12

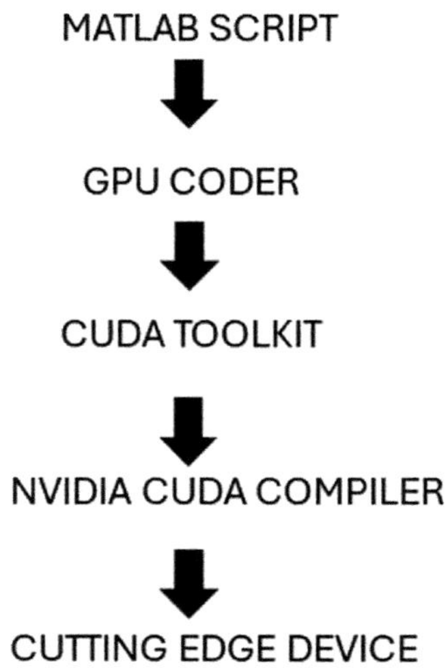

FIGURE 2.12

Diagram for the deployment process of the regional convolutional neural network code. The diagram illustrates the step-by-step deployment process of the regional convolutional neural network code, showcasing the transformation from initial data input to final inference output. It highlights the sequential stages involved, encompassing feature extraction, region proposal, and classification, elucidating the code's operational flow.

illustrates the deployment process, showcasing the integration of various software and hardware components to ensure optimal performance.

The MATLAB® Coder, another key tool in our arsenal, was instrumental in generating C code specifically tailored for the Jetson Nano environment. This step is crucial for compatibility and efficient execution on the embedded platform. Moreover, the Parallel Computing Toolbox played a significant role in addressing computational and data challenges by efficiently utilizing the multicore processors and GPU capabilities. This comprehensive approach ensured a smooth transition from the development phase in MATLAB® to the deployment phase on the Jetson Nano. The real-time object detection system was implemented using the Deep Learning Toolbox, providing a comprehensive framework for executing neural networks with specific algorithms. To adapt the generated code for deployment on the Jetson Nano, we employed the GPU Coder Interface for Deep Learning Libraries. This interface allowed customization through a designated library, ensuring compatibility with the NVIDIA hardware. The GPU Coder Support Package for NVIDIA GPU was then used to generate and deploy CUDA code, enabling seamless communication between MATLAB® and the Jetson Nano. To optimize the code generation process further, we turned to the Embedded Coder, a streamlined tool designed to ensure compatibility with the underlying hardware. Essential variables and applications, such as the JetPack Developer AI tool on the Jetson Nano, were configured to create an environment conducive to efficient code generation. This framework played a crucial role in the deployment of our CNN detector, originating from MATLAB®, onto the Jetson Nano. Microsoft Visual Studio 2019 was installed as a compiler support system for Jetson Nano, enhancing GPU code generation capabilities. Leveraging the CUDA deep neural network libraries, we capitalized on the parallel processing power of the GPU, resulting in a significant boost in the performance of our real-time object detection system. This integration of powerful tools and frameworks not only facilitated the deployment process but also ensured that the final implementation on the Jetson Nano achieved optimal speed and efficiency.

This study showcases a comprehensive approach to deploying a CNN model for real-time object detection on the Jetson Nano. The seamless integration of MATLAB®, GPU Coder, Deep Learning Toolbox, and other supporting tools allowed us to harness the full potential of the NVIDIA GPU, optimizing the performance of our neural network for real-world applications. The deployment process, as illustrated in Fig. 2.12, highlights the successful integration of various hardware and software components, ultimately leading to the creation of an efficient and powerful real-time object detection system on the Jetson Nano platform.

Fig. 2.13 illustrates the execution of the proposed approach for fire and smoke detection on Jetson Nano. We accelerated the processing of deep neural network primitives, contributing to the overall efficiency of our implementation. In practical testing, the deployed detector operated as a standalone application on Jetson Nano, utilizing a Raspberry Pi webcam model V2 for input. The camera was exposed to a computer generating a series of videos containing fire/smoke and negative scenarios. Throughout the execution, our proposed detector recorded various parameters. Notably, the real-time performance achieved was measured at 21 fps, showcasing superior real-time detection capabilities compared to a method documented in a prior study (Habiboğlu et al., 2012). In Fig. 2.14, the real-time detection results for our proposed approach are presented, illustrating its remarkable performance compared to state-of-the-art pretrained deep learning models executed on the Jetson Nano board. This analysis reaffirms the efficacy of our implemented solution in achieving high-quality real-time object detection.

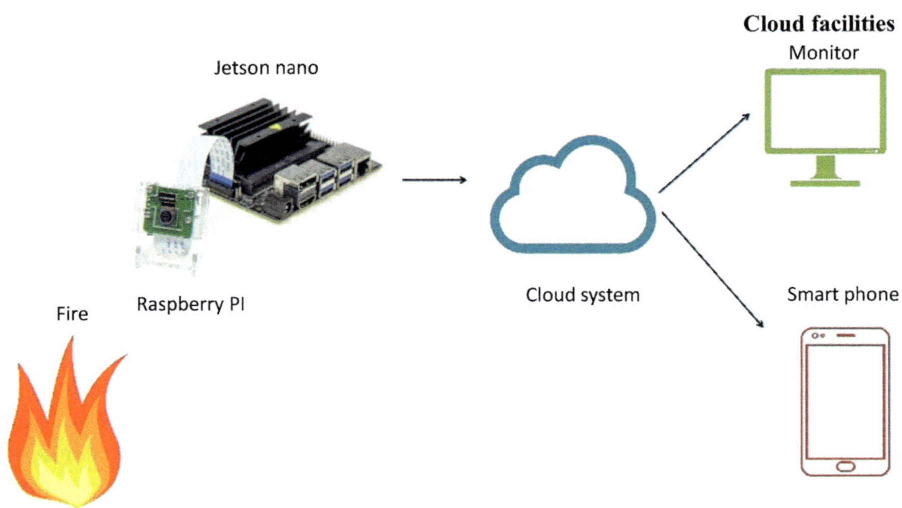

FIGURE 2.13

Testing the proposed detector with a real state of fire and smoke on Jetson Nano.

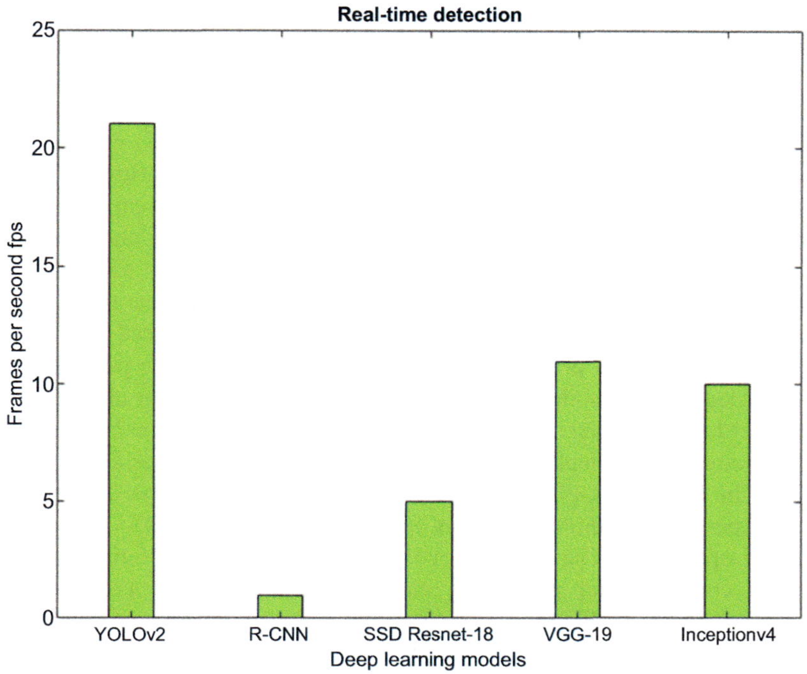

FIGURE 2.14

Real-time detection for the proposed approach versus other pretrained deep learning models, which were executed on Jetson Nano. A comparison of real-time detection performance between our proposed approach and other pretrained deep learning models, all executed on Jetson Nano, showcases the efficiency and effectiveness of our method in real-world applications.

In our investigation, we specifically measured the time delay associated with the identification of fire and smoke. Notably, in the camera's video mode, there is an observable temporal gap lasting 1–2 seconds between the onset of fire or smoke in recorded videos and the initiation of the YOLOv2 detection process. This temporal discrepancy underscores the algorithm's requirement of 1–2 seconds to trigger a smoke or fire alarm. It is crucial to emphasize that our adopted methodology exhibits a notably more proficient temporal decision-making process in the context of fire and smoke detection compared to the methodology proposed by Kim and Lee (2019). The latter suggests the implementation of a R-CNN model, which purportedly facilitates swifter detection. Nevertheless, our approach demonstrates a superior timing mechanism, thereby positioning it as advantageous for achieving early detection of fire and smoke incidents. Additionally, during the course of our experiments, we assessed the power consumption associated with the Jetson Nano. It is pertinent to note that extraneous components, including the keyboard, mouse, and monitor, were deliberately excluded from the Jetson Nano setup for the purpose of this evaluation. This deliberate exclusion allows for a more accurate evaluation of the power consumption specific to the Jetson Nano, contributing valuable insights into the efficiency of our experimental setup. In the evaluation of the Jetson Nano's power consumption, we observed a nominal 1.24 W when the detector was inactive. However, as our method was executed, the power consumption surged to 4.19 W, as documented in Table 2.9, which provides a comprehensive breakdown of power consumption under various scenarios. To contextualize our findings, we extended our inquiry to juxtapose the energy consumption with insights from a comprehensive study (Oh et al., 2017). This study meticulously examined the power consumption implications of numerous CNN algorithms. Notably, the study employed a Jetson TX-1 embedded device running a pretrained Identical GoogLeNet algorithm. The overarching objective of this comparative analysis is to gauge the energy efficiency of deep learning processes across a spectrum of embedded platforms. To this end, Table 2.10 offers a detailed depiction of power consumption specifically when the deep learning algorithm is operational in the Jetson Nano, drawing parallels to the methodology introduced by a prior work (Wang et al., 2014). This juxtaposition provides a nuanced understanding of the power dynamics inherent in diverse embedded platforms during the execution of deep learning algorithms. Notably, the results underscore that the power consumption of is six times higher than our methodology with Jetson Nano. Moreover, an in-depth assessment of resource utilization percentages was conducted, focusing on both the CPU and GPU within the Jetson Nano platform. The CPU plays a crucial role in executing the operating system and various applications, while the GPU is specifically designed to handle graphic operations. The analysis of these components is essential for a comprehensive understanding of computational processing capabilities. To provide a detailed overview, the recorded values for CPU and GPU processors were meticulously documented during the operational phase of our proposed detector in the Jetson Nano. This data is systematically presented in Table 2.11, offering a quantitative representation of the resource utilization distribution. Furthermore, the examination extended to monitoring the temperature variations of the Jetson Nano throughout the processing phase. The findings of this temperature assessment are graphically

Table 2.9 Power consumption measurement in different scenarios.

Method	YOLOv2 status	Power measurement
Jetson Nano without monitor, keyboard, and mouse	Off	1.24 W
Jetson Nano without monitor, keyboard, and mouse	Running	4.19 W
Jetson Nano with monitor, keyboard, and mouse	Off	2.24 W
Jetson Nano with monitor, keyboard, and mouse	Running	5.19 W

YOLOv2, *You Only Look Once version II.*

Table 2.10 Power consumption measurement in Jetson Nano (YOLOv2) versus method (Wang et al., 2013), while deep learning algorithms executed.

Method	Embedded device	Power measurement
YOLOv2	Jetson Nano	4.19 W
Method [31]	Jetson TX-1 embedded device	16.8 W

Table 2.11 % Utilization of the graphics processing unit and central processing unit in Jetson Nano while the proposed algorithm is running on it.

Device	% Utilization
Jetson Nano (GPU)	99%
Jetson Nano (CPU)	53.1%

CPU, *Central processing unit;* GPU, *graphics processing unit.*

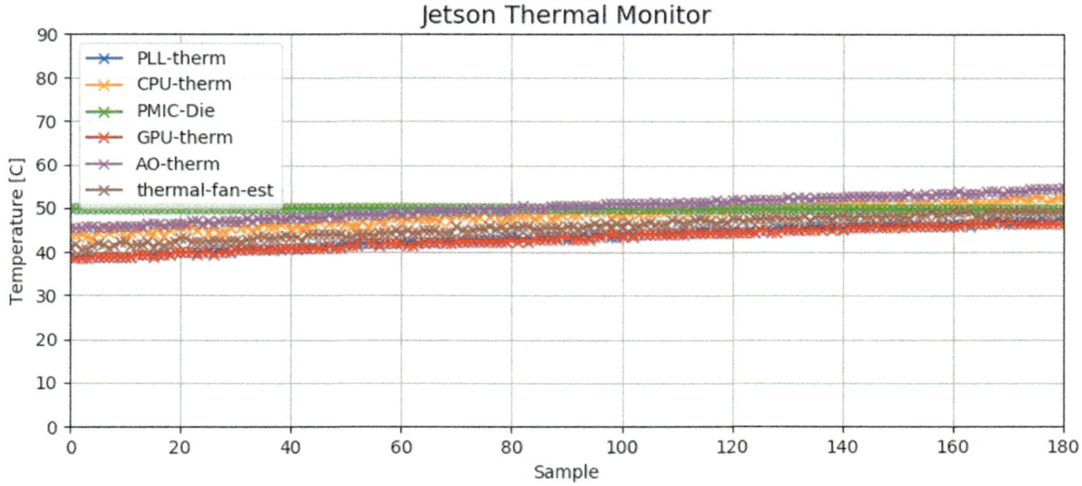

FIGURE 2.15

The temperature measurement for the graphics processing unit and central processing unit in Jetson Nano.

depicted in Fig. 2.15. This comprehensive analysis not only delves into the performance metrics of the CPU and GPU but also takes into account the thermal aspects, ensuring a holistic evaluation of the Jetson Nano's capabilities in handling the proposed detector's computational demands.

References

Celik, T., Demirel, H., Ozkaramanli, H., & Uyguroglu, M. (2007). Fire detection using statistical color model in video sequences. *Journal of Visual Communication and Image Representation*, *18*(2), 176–185. Available from https://doi.org/10.1016/j.jvcir.2006.12.003.

Çelik, T., Özkaramanli, H., Demirel, H. (2007). Fire and smoke detection without sensors: Image processing based approach, European signal processing conference, pp. 1794–1798.

Chen, T. H., Wu P. H., Chiou, Y.C. (2004). An early fire-detection method based on image processing, Proceedings – international conference on image processing, ICIP, pp. 1707–1710. Available from https://doi.org/10.1109/ICIP.2004.1421401.

Di Lascio, R., Greco, A., Saggese, A., & Vento, M. (2014). *Improving fire detection reliability by a combination of videoanalytics* (8814, pp. 477–484). Springer Science and Business Media LLC. Available from https://doi.org/10.1007/978-3-319-11758-4_52.

Filonenko, A., Hernandez, D. C., & Jo, K.-H. (2018). Fast smoke detection for video surveillance using CUDA. *IEEE Transactions on Industrial Informatics, 14*(2), 725–733. Available from https://doi.org/10.1109/tii.2017.2757457.

Gagliardi, A., & Saponara, S. (2020a). AdViSED: Advanced video SmokE detection for real-time measurements in antifire indoor and outdoor systems. *Energies, 13*(8), 2098. Available from https://doi.org/10.3390/en13082098.

Gagliardi, A., & Saponara, S. (2020b). *Distributed video antifire surveillance system based on IoT embedded computing nodes* (627, pp. 405–411). Springer Science and Business Media LLC. Available from http://doi.org/10.1007/978-3-030-37277-4_47.

Gibbens, S. (2019). The amazon is burning at record rates—and deforestation is to blame. *Environment*. Available from https://www.nationalgeographic.com/environment/article/wildfires-in-amazon-caused-by-deforestation.

Habiboğlu, Y. H., Günay, O., & Çetin, A. E. (2012). Covariance matrix-based fire and flame detection method in video. *Machine Vision and Applications, 23*(6), 1103–1113. Available from https://doi.org/10.1007/s00138-011-0369-1.

Jadon, A., Omama, M., Varshney, A., Ansari, M.S., & Sharma, R. (2019). FireNet: A specialized lightweight fire and smoke detection model for real-time IoT applications. arXiv. Available from: https://arxiv.org, https://doi.org/10.48550/arxiv.1905.11922. Accessed 7 Nov 2020.

Jiang, Q., & Wang, Q. (2010). Large space fire image processing of improving Canny edge detector based on adaptive smoothing, CICC-ITOE 2010 – 2010 international conference on innovative computing and communication, 2010 Asia-Pacific conference on information technology and ocean engineering, 264–267. Available from https://doi.org/10.1109/CICC-ITOE.2010.73.

Kim, B., & Lee, J. (2019). A video-based fire detection using deep learning models. *Applied Sciences, 9*(14), 2862. Available from https://doi.org/10.3390/app9142862.

LeCun, Y., Bengio, Y., & Hinton, G. (2015). Deep learning. *Nature, 521*(7553), 436–444. Available from https://doi.org/10.1038/nature14539.

Lestari, D. P., Kosasih, R., Handhika, T., Murni Sari, I., Fahrurozi, A. (2019). Proceedings – 2019 2nd international conference of computer and informatics engineering: Artificial intelligence roles in industrial revolution 4.0, IC2IE 2019. Available from https://doi.org/10.1109/IC2IE47452.2019.8940842. 87–92. Fire hotspots detection system on CCTV videos using you only look once (YOLO) method and tiny YOLO model for high buildings evacuation. http://ieeexplore.ieee.org/xpl/mostRecentIssue.jsp?punumber = 8935454.

Namozov, A., & Cho, Y. I. (2018). An efficient deep learning algorithm for fire and smoke detection with limited data. *Advances in Electrical and Computer Engineering, 18*(4), 121–128. Available from https://doi.org/10.4316/AECE.2018.04015, http://www.aece.ro/displaypdf.php?year = 2018&number = 4&article = 15.

Oh, S., Kim, M., Kim, D., Jeong, M., & Lee, M. (2017). Proceedings of the 2017 4th international conference on computer applications and information processing technology, CAIPT 2017. Available from https://doi.org/10.1109/CAIPT.2017.8320657. 1–4. Investigation on performance and energy efficiency of CNN-based object detection on embedded device

Rafiee, A., Dianat, R., Jamshidi, M., Tavakoli, R., & Abbaspour, S. (2011). ICCRD2011 – 2011 3rd international conference on computer research and development. Available from https://doi.org/10.1109/ICCRD.2011.5764295. 262–265 Fire and smoke detection using wavelet analysis and disorder characteristics.

Saponara, S., Pilato, L., & Fanucci, L. (2014). Proceedings of SPIE – the international society for optical engineering. Early video smoke detection system to improve fire protection in rolling stocks. Available from http://spie.org/x1848.xml9139, https://doi.org/10.1117/12.2052881.

Shen, D., Chen, X., Nguyen, M., Yan, W. Q. (2018). Proceedings – 2018 4th international conference on control, automation and robotics, ICCAR, 416–420. Flame detection using deep learning. Available from https://doi.org/10.1109/ICCAR.2018.8384711, http://ieeexplore.ieee.org/xpl/mostRecentIssue.jsp?punumber58375183.

Toulouse, T., Rossi, L., Celik, T., & Akhloufi, M. (2016). Automatic fire pixel detection using image processing: A comparative analysis of rule-based and machine learning-based methods. *Signal, Image and Video Processing*, *10*(4), 647–654. Available from https://doi.org/10.1007/s11760-015-0789-x.

Uijlings, J. R. R., Van De Sande, K. E. A., Gevers, T., & Smeulders, A. W. M. (2013). Selective search for object recognition. *International Journal of Computer Vision*, *104*(2), 154–171. Available from https://doi.org/10.1007/s11263-013-0620-5.

Vijayalakshmi, S. R. & Muruganand, S. (2017). Proceedings of the 2nd international conference on communication and electronics systems, ICCES 2017, 167–171. Smoke detection in video images using background subtraction method for early fire alarm system. Available from https://doi.org/10.1109/CESYS.2017.8321258.

Wang, G., Zhang, Y., Qu, Y., Chen, Y., & Maqsood, H. (2019). Proceedings of the 31st Chinese control and decision conference, CCDC 2019, 6237–6241. Available from https://doi.org/10.1109/CCDC.2019.8833125. Early forest fire region segmentation based on deep learning, http://ieeexplore.ieee.org/xpl/mostRecentIssue.jsp?punumber = 8822348.

Wang, X., Wang, M., & Li, W. (2014). Scene-specific pedestrian detection for static video surveillance. *IEEE Transactions on Pattern Analysis and Machine Intelligence*, *36*(2), 361–374. Available from https://doi.org/10.1109/TPAMI.2013.124.

Wang, Y., Dang, L., & Ren, J. (2019). Forest fire image recognition based on convolutional neural network. *Journal of Algorithms and Computational Technology*, *13*. Available from https://doi.org/10.1177/1748302619887689.

Wu, S., & Zhang, L. (2018). 11th international symposium on computational intelligence and design, ISCID 2018, 280–284. Using popular object detection methods for real time forest fire detection. Available from http://ieeexplore.ieee.org/xpl/mostRecentIssue.jsp?punumber = 8686041, https://doi.org/10.1109/ISCID.2018.00070.

Yuan, F., Fang, Z., Wu, S., Yang, Y., & Fang, Y. (2015). Real-time image smoke detection using staircase searching-based dual threshold AdaBoost and dynamic analysis. *IET Image Processing*, *9*(10), 849–856. Available from https://doi.org/10.1049/iet-ipr.2014.1032.

Zhang, Z., Zhao, J., Zhang, D., Qu, C., Ke, Y., & Cai, B. (2008). Proceedings – international conference on computer science and software engineering, China, CSSE, 2008, 760–763. Contour based forest fire detection using FFT and wavelet 1. Available from https://doi.org/10.1109/CSSE.2008.837

Zitnick, C. L., & Dollár, P. (2014). *Edge boxes: locating object proposals from edges* (8693, pp. 391–405). Springer Science and Business Media LLC. Available from http://doi.org/10.1007/978-3-319-10602-1_26.

CHAPTER

Enhancing COVID-19 safety measures with AI-powered video analysis

3

3.1 Introduction

COVID-19, short for "Coronavirus Disease 2019," is an infectious respiratory illness caused by the novel coronavirus SARS-CoV-2, which originated in Wuhan, China, in December 2019. The virus quickly spread globally, leading to a pandemic declaration by the World Health Organization (WHO) in March 2020, prompting unprecedented public health measures. Common symptoms of COVID-19 include fever, cough, chills, shortness of breath, body aches, and loss of taste and smell. In severe cases, it can lead to complications and, in many instances, fatalities. The coronavirus responsible for COVID-19 spreads from person to person primarily through respiratory droplets when an infected person coughs, sneezes, or talks. Since its emergence, COVID-19 has rapidly spread across the globe, affecting over 188 countries. As of February 28, 2024, the WHO reported a staggering 703,773,443 confirmed cases of COVID-19 worldwide, with 6,987,925 deaths. The dynamic nature of the virus, coupled with uncertainties surrounding its transmission and behavior, has posed significant challenges in predicting the trajectory and duration of the pandemic. Despite concerted global efforts, including extensive research and public health interventions, a definitive vaccine for COVID-19 remains elusive. Preventive measures play a crucial role in mitigating the spread of COVID-19. These include wearing masks, practicing frequent hand hygiene, and adhering to social distancing guidelines. Individuals who exhibit symptoms of COVID-19, such as fever or chills, are advised to self-isolate to prevent further transmission of the virus. Governments worldwide have implemented various measures, such as temporary business closures, border restrictions, and the suspension of public gatherings, to curb the spread of the disease and alleviate its impact on public health systems. Fever, a common symptom of COVID-19, serves as a vital indicator for identifying potential cases of infection. Studies conducted in China have indicated that a significant proportion of individuals infected with the coronavirus experience elevated body temperatures. Thermal imaging and noncontact infrared thermometers offer noninvasive methods for monitoring individuals' temperatures, thereby aiding in the early detection and containment of COVID-19 outbreaks. Social distancing emerges as a cornerstone strategy in limiting the transmission of COVID-19. This practice entails minimizing physical contact with potentially infected individuals by maintaining a safe distance of approximately 6 ft. Unlike isolation and quarantine, which target individuals confirmed or suspected of having COVID-19, social distancing applies to the general population and aims to reduce opportunities for viral spread in community settings. The integration of technology has emerged as a promising approach to bolstering social distancing efforts and enhancing public health surveillance. Artificial intelligence (AI) offers innovative solutions for monitoring and enforcing social distancing measures in various settings. Computer vision, a branch

Deep Learning in Action: Image and Video Processing for Practical Use. DOI: https://doi.org/10.1016/B978-0-443-30078-3.00003-2

of AI, has gained traction as a robust tool for pedestrian detection and distance measurement in public spaces. Utilizing existing security camera infrastructure, computer vision algorithms can accurately identify and track individuals in real-time, facilitating the enforcement of social distancing protocols. Unlike mobile-based solutions reliant on GPS sensors, computer vision-based approaches offer broader applicability across diverse domains, including intelligent transportation systems (Liu et al., 2021), surveillance (Zheng et al., 2021), and robotics (Zheng et al., 2020). Furthermore, the availability of open-source datasets enables researchers to develop and evaluate pedestrian detection algorithms (Ess et al., 2009), driving advancements in this field. Recent advancements in deep learning have propelled the performance of computer vision systems, enabling them to excel in various tasks, such as image classification (Zheng et al., 2018), object detection (Li et al., 2019), and instance segmentation (Zhang et al., 2017). Deep learning (DL) models leverage vast amounts of data to automatically extract high-level features from images, enabling them to discern complex patterns and make accurate predictions without extensive manual intervention.

In light of the ongoing challenges posed by the COVID-19 pandemic, there is a pressing need to enhance the efficiency of epidemic prevention measures. This project endeavors to address this need by focusing on the development and implementation of advanced technologies for the identification of pedestrians and the monitoring of social distancing practices in public spaces. Central to our approach is the utilization of a novel surveillance system vision-based system designed to recognize any violations of social distancing among individuals while simultaneously screening their body temperature. In this chapter, we delve into the details of our real-time, AI-based video processing system, highlighting its innovative features and contributions to epidemic prevention efforts.

This research presents an advanced method for real-time video processing aimed at enforcing social distancing measures and mitigating the spread of COVID-19. A robust algorithm has been deployed to detect individuals and measure distances, surpassing current methodologies in both velocity and precision. Moreover, a novel technique has been developed to transform camera frames taken from diverse angles into a standardized top–down perspective. This ensures consistency in converting pixels to physical measurements across different viewpoints. The integration of a robust algorithm enhances the efficacy of person detection and distance measurement, vital for enforcing social distancing regulations. By surpassing existing methods in speed and accuracy, this algorithm facilitates real-time monitoring, enabling prompt intervention when violations occur. The novel technique for converting camera frames into a consistent top–down view addresses a crucial challenge in video processing. Varying perspectives in camera placement can distort measurements and hinder accurate analysis. By standardizing the viewpoint to a top–down perspective, this technique ensures uniformity in pixel-to-physical pitch conversion, thus enhancing the reliability of distance measurements. Furthermore, the implementation of this technique contributes to the overall effectiveness of the system in monitoring and enforcing social distancing measures. It enables precise measurement of distances between individuals across different camera angles, facilitating accurate assessment of compliance with safety guidelines. Consequently, this approach enhances the efficiency of COVID-19 mitigation efforts and lays the foundation for future advancements in video processing for public health applications.

Key contributions:-

1. Developed, an advanced algorithm that accurately detects individuals in crowded environments, enabling efficient monitoring of social distancing compliance. Its robust design ensures precise

identification, vital in crowded spaces. Leveraging cutting-edge technology, the algorithm facilitates seamless integration into existing surveillance systems. Enhanced accuracy distinguishes it, surpassing conventional methods. This innovation revolutionizes surveillance capabilities, optimizing crowd management and ensuring public safety. With its implementation, monitoring social distancing adherence becomes streamlined and effective. Its adaptability caters to various settings, from bustling urban centers to crowded events. Overall, this algorithm represents a significant advancement in ensuring public health and safety amidst dense gatherings.

2. Employing sophisticated techniques, the system ensures precise measurement of distances between individuals, crucial for enforcing social distancing protocols. Utilizing Euclidean distance, guarantees accuracy in distance measurement, aiding in the implementation of necessary safety measures. By employing such methodologies, it enables the maintenance of optimal separation between people, contributing to overall public health efforts. Through its precision, it enhances the efficacy of social distancing enforcement, mitigating the risk of transmission in various settings. This system's utilization of intricate methods underscores its commitment to promoting safety and well-being in environments where maintaining distance is paramount.
3. Transforming camera perspectives into a uniform top–down view eliminates distortions and inconsistencies, enhancing the accuracy of distance measurements. This process corrects the visual representation of objects, aligning them with a standardized viewpoint. Through perspective correction, the disparities caused by varying angles and distances are rectified, ensuring that objects appear in their true proportions and positions. This adjustment is particularly crucial in fields like cartography, architecture, and surveying, where precise measurements are imperative. By achieving a consistent perspective, the reliability of data analysis and interpretation is significantly improved. This technique enhances the clarity of visual information. It facilitates more accurate decision-making processes. Perspective correction serves as a fundamental tool in optimizing the usability and effectiveness of imaging systems, contributing to advancements in various domains reliant on precise spatial understanding.
4. Successfully integrated, our system now harmonizes with thermal cameras, repurposing infrastructure for temperature screening and social distancing monitoring. This integration enhances efficiency, optimizing resources for comprehensive surveillance. Thermal cameras, seamlessly integrated, detect elevated temperatures, bolstering safety protocols without additional burdens. By repurposing existing infrastructure, our solution minimizes costs while maximizing effectiveness, ensuring a seamless transition to enhanced surveillance capabilities. This advancement underscores our commitment to innovation, leveraging technology to address evolving needs. The integration with thermal cameras signifies a proactive approach, mitigating risks and safeguarding environments with minimal disruption. This cohesive system empowers stakeholders with actionable insights, enabling informed decision-making for proactive risk management. In essence, our integration with thermal cameras epitomizes adaptability, resilience, and efficacy in navigating contemporary challenges.

The primary motivation behind our research is to mitigate the spread of COVID-19 and minimize its adverse impact on public health and the economy. To achieve this goal, we have developed a state-of-the-art DL model, leveraging You Only Look Once version 2 (YOLOv2) and YOLOv4-tiny architectures, to classify social distancing violations in real-time. By incorporating top–down view, we address camera distortion challenge, ensuring reliable detection and enforcement of social distancing measures. Our algorithms have been deployed on Jetson Nano and Jetson Xavier platforms to evaluate their performance under real-world conditions. The proposed approach represents a significant advancement in the field of epidemic prevention, particularly in the context of COVID-19. By harnessing the power of AI and computer vision technologies, we have developed a comprehensive solution for monitoring social distancing and conducting temperature screenings in public spaces. Our system's ability to operate in real-time, coupled with its high accuracy and efficiency, makes it a valuable tool for mitigating the spread of infectious diseases and safeguarding public health. As we continue to refine and optimize our approach, we remain committed to supporting global efforts to combat epidemics and ensure the well-being of communities worldwide.

3.2 Related work

Social distancing and temperature screening, effective tools in disease prevention, come highly recommended by various organizations, including the WHO. Examining their impact on coronavirus spread, a study by Prem et al. (2020) utilized scientific models of contact patterns to forecast outbreak trajectories using susceptible–exposed–infected–removed methodologies. It was highlighted by the authors that the sudden cessation of social distancing measures could potentially result in heightened contagion and virus transmission among individuals. Nabil Kahale underscored the significance of social distancing measures (Kahalé, 2020). The study aimed to illustrate how the early implementation of social distancing measures could significantly curtail economic losses and the incidence of new infections. As the coronavirus continues its spread within communities, researchers and scientists are actively exploring optimal strategies to combat the pandemic (Sonbhadra et al., 2020; Punn & Agarwal, 2021). Jennifer Berglund (Tracking COVID-19: There's an App for That - IEEE Pulse, 2024) proposed the use of GPS and built-in smartphone applications to track individuals infected with COVID-19. However, this technology faces limitations in tracking individuals without Wi-Fi or cellular signals. Conversely, some authorities utilize drones equipped with video cameras to monitor outdoor gatherings (Robakowska et al., 2017; Harvey & LaPlace, 2019). Such technology proves valuable for surveillance during the coronavirus outbreak.

Advancements in computer vision and deep learning have facilitated the development of solutions addressing various complex tasks such as neural style transmission, segmentation, tracking, and object recognition (Pitts & McCulloch, 1947). Computer vision, akin to human visual processing, relies heavily on object recognition and operates as a sophisticated neural network (Zhao et al., 2019). Initially conceived in the 1940s to tackle learning problems efficiently, neural networks have evolved, with convolutional neural networks (CNNs) emerging as a popular choice for object detection in DL models. CNNs assign learnable weights and biases to different classes in an image, enabling effective object differentiation (Wang et al., 2017). Several DL models like region-based (R) CNN, single shot detector (SSD), and YOLO are employed across diverse object detection applications, particularly in motion estimation within video scenes. For instance, Kajabad and Ivanov (2019) proposed a method combining background subtraction, Gaussian mixing, and deep learning for human detection in videos, achieving high performance across multiple datasets. Similarly, Hosang et al. (2015) and Kim et al. (2019) developed pedestrian detection approaches that outperform existing methods in various benchmarks. Zhang et al. (2014) introduced a pedestrian detector leveraging common knowledge, demonstrating superior performance with minimal computational resources. Walk et al. (2010) demonstrated the efficacy of motion features derived from optical flow in improving image sequence recognition, along with introducing a novel self-similarity feature enhancing recognition across different datasets. Furthermore, they highlighted the importance of evaluating detector complexity for accurate assessment.

To quantify social distancing violations (Ahmed, Ahmad, Rodrigues, et al., 2021), researchers approximated physical distances between individuals using pixel distances and set a threshold. This framework, employing YOLOv3, effectively identifies instances of proximity, indicating violations of social distancing guidelines. Ahamad et al. (2020) measured distances between individuals based on segmented tracking, issuing alarms for unsafe distances. Hou et al. (2020) utilized deep learning to evaluate interindividual distances, transforming video frames into a top–down view for accurate assessment.

3.3 Social distancing using YOLOv2

Utilizing thermal imaging, a deep learning system is introduced for detecting social distancing, employing the YOLOv2 method for developing a novel detection technique to identify and track individuals both indoors and outdoors. An algorithm is incorporated to measure and categorize distances between individuals, automatically evaluating adherence to distancing guidelines, with the primary objective being the reduction of COVID-19 transmission through the assessment of social distancing compliance. Application of the method involves thermal imaging camera images, thereby creating a comprehensive AI system for tracking individuals, categorizing social distancing, and monitoring body temperature. The training process utilizes two datasets sourced from various thermal imaging cameras, with the labeling of individuals facilitated by the Ground Truth Labeler app. Notably, this technique is implemented on a cost-effective embedded system equipped with a stationary camera.

3.3.1 Social distancing workflow

In this subsection, we will delve into the essential steps required to craft a sequence design aimed at determining and verifying compliance with social distancing rules through the analysis of thermal imaging videos, as depicted in Fig. 3.1.

3.3.1.1 Preparation of thermal images or video streaming

Obtaining thermal images or streaming video footage captured by a thermal camera initiates the process. These visuals should represent areas where people frequent, like public spaces, workplaces, or event venues. Quality and clarity of the thermal data become paramount for precise analysis. Evaluating these visuals forms the foundation for subsequent steps in the process. Without clear and reliable thermal imagery, the accuracy of any ensuing analysis could be compromised. Therefore meticulous attention is paid to the acquisition of these images or video streams. Their fidelity ensures that any insights derived from the analysis are robust and dependable. In essence,

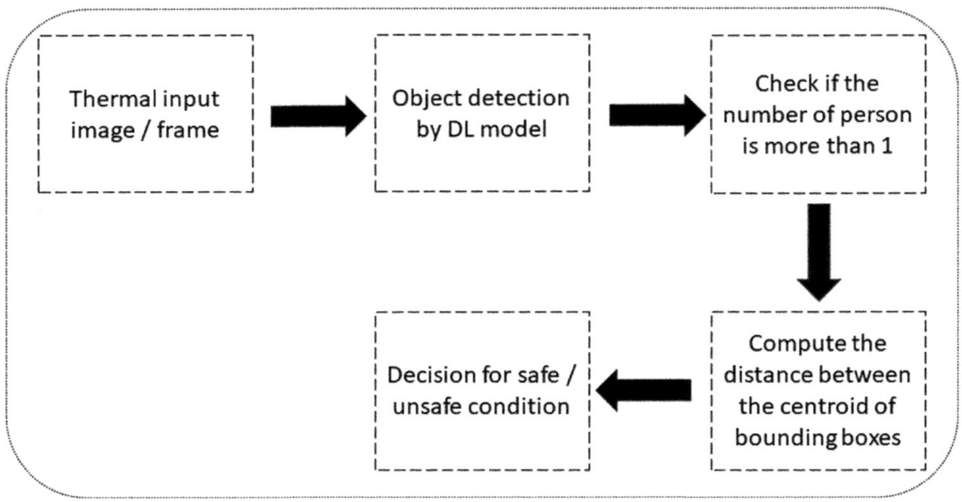

FIGURE 3.1

The steps for identifying individuals and maintaining social distancing in thermal images.

the integrity of the thermal datasets the stage for effective decision-making and action planning in various domains, ranging from security to health monitoring.

3.3.1.2 Application of deep learning object detector

After data acquisition, employing a deep learning object detection model specialized in recognizing human figures within thermal imagery is essential. This model must be trained to distinguish human shapes and features in thermal data, considering variations in body temperature and environmental conditions. The object detector scans thermal images or video frames, identifying and delineating individuals present within the scene. By utilizing this model, accurate detection of humans in thermal imagery is facilitated, enabling various applications such as surveillance, search and rescue operations, and monitoring of human activity in diverse environments. The robustness of the model ensures reliable performance even in challenging conditions, contributing to enhanced security and safety measures across different domains.

3.3.1.3 Verification of people count

Following the completion of the object detection process, verification of the count of individuals detected within the thermal imagery or video stream is conducted. This ensures an accurate assessment of crowd density, essential for analyzing social distancing compliance. The accuracy of people counting is pivotal, laying the groundwork for evaluating the effectiveness of distancing measures in any environment. By meticulously verifying the number of individuals identified, the system enables precise monitoring and evaluation of adherence to social distancing protocols. This meticulous process underscores the importance of reliable data in assessing and improving strategies for maintaining public health and safety.

3.3.1.4 Calculation of interpersonal distances

Establishing the count of individuals, the system proceeds to compute distances between centroids of bounding boxes surrounding detected people. This computation reveals insights into spatial distribution and facilitates the evaluation of interpersonal distances within the monitored area. Quantifying separation between individuals, the system acquires a nuanced understanding of adherence to social distancing guidelines. This analysis aids in assessing the effectiveness of implemented measures and identifying areas where adjustments can be necessary to ensure compliance with safety protocols. Additionally, it enables real-time monitoring and intervention to address potential breaches of social distancing, contributing to overall public health and safety efforts.

3.3.1.5 Algorithmic decision-making

The final stage involves algorithmic decision-making based on the gathered data. The algorithm considers both the number of individuals present and the measured distances between them to determine whether social distancing protocols are being observed. By analyzing these parameters, the system classifies the observed scenario as either safe or unsafe in terms of compliance with established distancing norms.

By following this systematic approach, organizations and authorities can effectively utilize thermal imaging technology to monitor and enforce social distancing measures. The integration of deep learning algorithms enables real-time analysis of crowd dynamics, facilitating initiative-taking interventions to mitigate the spread of contagious diseases. Additionally, the reliance on thermal imaging enhances the nonintrusive nature of surveillance, respecting privacy while ensuring public health and safety. Moreover, advancements in object detection and machine learning techniques continue to refine the accuracy and efficiency of such systems, empowering stakeholders with actionable insights for optimizing spatial planning and resource allocation. As part of a comprehensive public health strategy, the deployment of thermal-based social distancing monitoring holds promise in safeguarding communities against infectious threats while fostering a culture of responsible behavior and collective well-being.

3.3.2 YOLOv2 architecture

In MATLAB, the creation of Deep Neural Network (DNN) applications is a pivotal step in modern machine learning and computer vision tasks. One of the widely used architectures for object detection tasks is YOLOv2. In this context, developers often design and optimize DNN models in MATLAB before deploying them onto embedded platforms for real-world applications, such as the NVIDIA Jetson Nano, which offers high computational power in a compact form factor. The specific DNN model discussed here is a 29-layer CNN, as illustrated in Fig. 3.2. The primary objective behind designing this CNN is to create a lightweight yet efficient model capable of real-time inference, even on resource-constrained embedded platforms like those found in Internet of Things (IoT) nodes. Let's delve deeper into the architecture and functionality of this DNN.

The neural network comprises various layers, each serving a specific purpose in the object detection pipeline. These layers can be categorized into three main groups: the input layer, middle layers, and subnetworks of YOLOv2 layers.

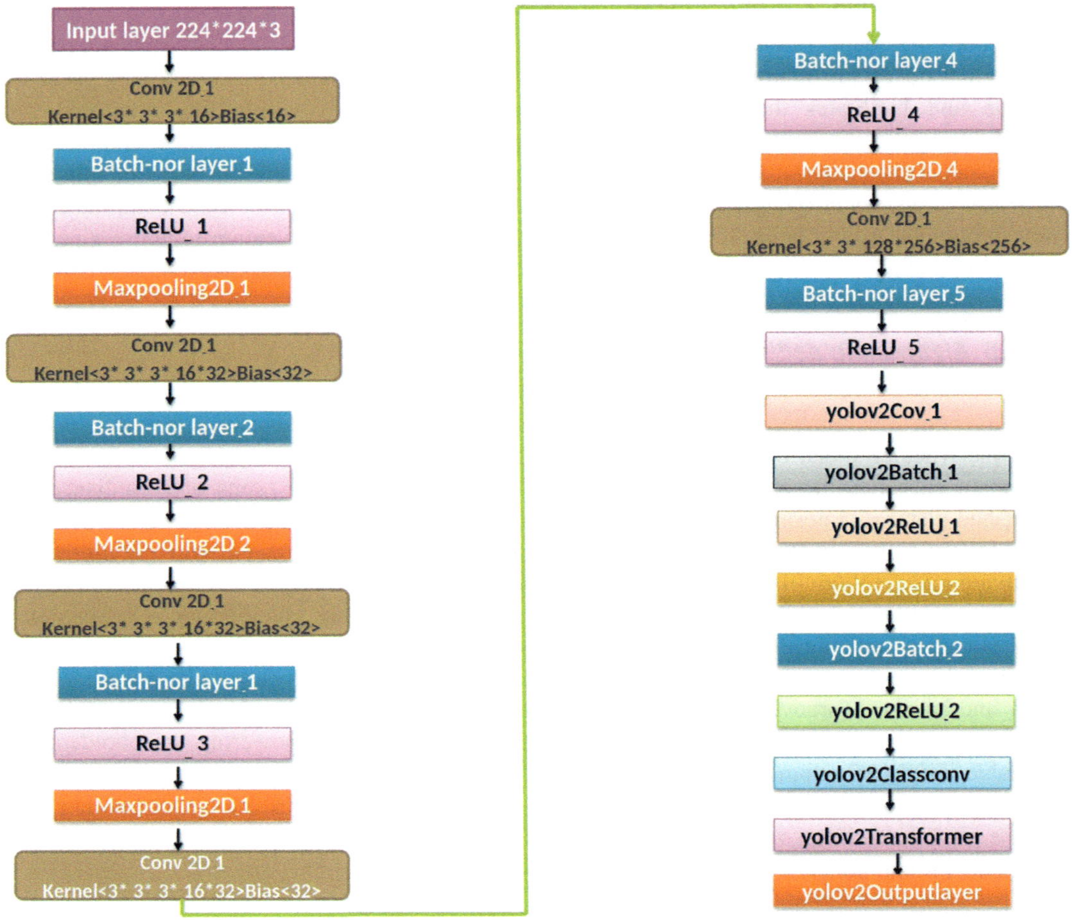

FIGURE 3.2

The proposed design of the YOLOv2 framework.

3.3.2.1 Input layer

The input layer introduces the image data into the neural network. For this model, images of size $224 \times 224 \times 3$ are utilized, representing height, width, and color channels (RGB), respectively.

3.3.2.2 Middle layers

The middle layers of the CNN consist of batch normalization, convolution, max pooling, and rectified linear unit (ReLU) layers.

- Convolution layers: These layers are responsible for extracting features from the input images. A filter size of 3×3 is employed, determining the height and width of the receptive fields.

- Batch normalization layers: These layers aid in regularizing the neural network architecture and mitigate overfitting issues.
- ReLU activation functions: Applied after convolution layers, ReLU introduces nonlinearity into the model, enhancing its capacity to learn complex patterns.
- Max pooling layers: Utilized for downsampling the feature maps obtained from convolution layers. A pooling size of 2 × 2 with a stride of 2 × 2 is employed, reducing the spatial dimensions while preserving essential features.

3.3.2.3 Feature extraction layer

ReLU_5 serves as a dedicated feature extraction layer, extracting pertinent features from the preceding neural network layers to feed into the subsequent YOLOv2 subnetwork layers.

3.3.2.4 YOLOv2 subnetwork layers

The YOLOv2 model comprises a series of specialized layers tailored for object detection tasks.

- Convolution (yolov2cov) layers: These layers extract higher-level features from the feature maps obtained from previous layers.
- Stack normalization (yolov2Batch) layers: Similar to batch normalization in the middle layers, these layers normalize the activations within the YOLOv2 subnetwork.
- ReLU (yolov2ReLU) layers: Introduce nonlinearity into the YOLOv2 subnetwork, enhancing its expressive power.
- Transform and output layers: The transformation layer plays a crucial role in stabilizing the object localization network, transforming raw CNN outputs into a suitable format for generating object detections. The output layer defines the bounding box positions for detected objects.

3.3.3 Experimental setup

The experiments were conducted utilizing a computer equipped with an Intel Core TM I3−6006U central processing unit (CPU) @ 2 GHz. MATLAB2020a served as the primary platform, leveraging its suite of integrated tools such as *Neural Network Designer, and Ground Truth Labeler*. This setup provided a robust environment for designing, training, and evaluating the neural network models. The designed neural network underwent training using two distinct sets of thermal images. Dataset I comprised 775 thermal images featuring individuals engaged in various activities such as running, walking, or sneaking. These images captured individuals in diverse body positions and movement speeds, thereby creating a rich and realistic dataset mimicking surveillance scenarios. Sourced from diverse online platforms, these images offered a broad spectrum of scenarios for detecting individuals within surveillance environments. On the other hand, Dataset II encompassed 800 infrared images specifically generated by FLIR for thermal imaging cameras (FLIR, 2017). These images, specifically tailored for thermal imaging purposes, provided a standardized dataset for comparative analysis and validation of the developed model. To facilitate the training process, the Ground Truth Labeler application within MATLAB was employed to annotate individuals within the thermal images accurately. This step was crucial for providing the neural network with ground truth data, enabling it to learn and discern features associated with human presence effectively. To ensure robustness and reliability, the dataset was partitioned into three subsets: 70% for training, 20% for validation, and 10% for testing. This partitioning strategy helped prevent overfitting and provided a balanced distribution of data for training and evaluation purposes. For training the neural network, stochastic gradient descent (SGD) was utilized as the optimization algorithm. SGD is a widely used optimization technique known for its efficiency in training large-scale neural networks. Learning rate was tuned to regulate the rate at which the model adjusted its parameters in response to the training error. Table 3.1 presents the training hyperparameters employed for training the proposed neural network. These hyperparameters, including the learning rate, batch size, and number of epochs, play a crucial role in shaping the training process and ultimately determining the performance of the trained model. Expanding further on the training process, it's worth highlighting the significance of each hyperparameter. The learning rate parameter controls the step size during optimization, influencing the convergence speed and stability of the training process. A carefully chosen learning rate ensures efficient learning without overshooting or getting stuck in local minima. Moreover, the batch size parameter determines the number of samples processed in each iteration of the training process. Larger batch sizes can lead to faster convergence and require more memory, while smaller batch sizes offer better generalization and slower convergence. Finding the right balance is essential for optimizing training efficiency and model performance. Additionally, the number of epochs specifies the number of times the entire training dataset is passed forward and backward through the neural network during training. Increasing the number of epochs allows the model to learn from the data more comprehensively, potentially improving its performance. However, excessive epochs can lead to overfitting, where the model memorizes the training data without generalizing well to unseen data. The training process involved meticulous parameter tuning and dataset preparation to ensure the development of a robust and effective neural network model for detecting individuals in thermal images. By leveraging state-of-the-art tools and methodologies within MATLAB, coupled with carefully curated datasets, the experiments aimed to push the boundaries of surveillance technology and enhance the capabilities of thermal imaging systems in various real-world applications.

3.3.4 Euclidean formula for measuring the distance

In this project, we have implemented MATLAB code tailored to analyze bounding boxes of individuals detected within thermal images. The primary objective of this code is to classify and determine whether individuals within the image are maintaining a safe distance from one another. This

Table 3.1 Setting of the hyperparameters for YOLOv2.

Parameter	Setting
Training option	sdgm
Verbose frequency	50
Learning rate	0.001
L2 parameter	0.06
Epochs	80
Size of minibatch	16

crucial functionality is indicated visually by coloring the bounding boxes; a green color is assigned to denote safe social distancing, while a red hue indicates unsafe proximity.

Initially, the algorithm identifies the number of individuals present in the thermal images. Upon detection of a single individual, their bounding box is assigned a green color, signifying adherence to safe social distancing practices. However, when the algorithm detects two or more individuals, a more intricate process ensues.

The key function involved in this decision-making process is "findColor()". This function undertakes two primary tasks: determining the appropriate color for the bounding boxes and calculating the distance between the centroid of bounding boxes

To calculate the center points $C(X, Y)$ of the bounding boxes, we utilize Eq. (3.1):

$$C(X, Y) = \frac{X_{min} + X_{max}}{2}, \frac{Y_{min} + Y_{max}}{2} \tag{3.1}$$

At the center of the bounding box lies C. X_{min} and X_{max} denote the minimum and maximum values for the width of the bounding box, respectively. As for the height of the bounding box, Y_{min} and Y_{max} signify the lowest and highest values, respectively.

Following the determination of the center points, the next crucial step involves calculating between $C1$ (X_{max} − X_{min}) and $C2$ (Y_{max} − Y_{min}) the distance between these points. This is achieved using the Euclidean distance formula, as depicted in Eq. (3.2):

$$D(C_1C_2) = \sqrt{(X_{max} - X_{min})^2 + (Y_{max} - Y_{min})^2} \tag{3.2}$$

D represents the distance between the center of these bounding boxes.

The calculated distance is then compared against a predetermined threshold value. If the function identifies two bounding boxes with a distance smaller than the specified threshold, indicating unsafe proximity, the bounding boxes are colored red. Conversely, if the distance exceeds the threshold, denoting a safe distance between individuals, the bounding boxes are colored green.

In Fig. 3.3 D represents the distance measured from the centroid of one bounding box to another.

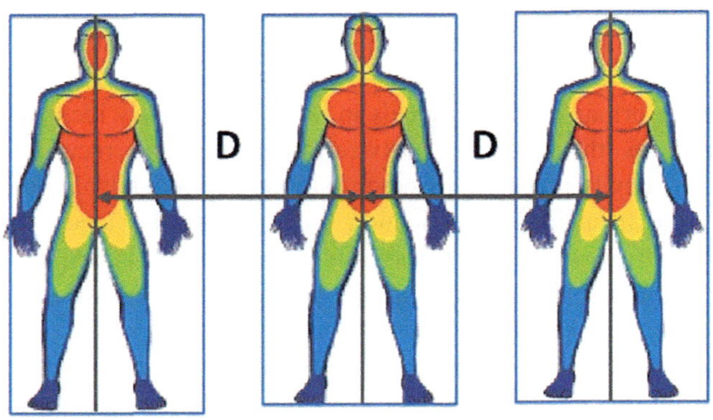

FIGURE 3.3

A visual representation of the measured distances between the centroid of the bounding box for the detected individuals.

Implemented MATLAB code effectively processes thermal images, identifying individuals and assessing their spatial proximity to ensure adherence to safe social distancing measures. Strategic use of bounding box coloring and distance calculations in the algorithm provides a valuable tool for monitoring and enforcing public health guidelines in various environments. This technology plays a crucial role in safeguarding public health, especially in densely populated areas where maintaining safe distances is challenging. By automating the process of identifying and analyzing thermal data, it streamlines the enforcement of social distancing protocols, reducing the burden on human resources. Additionally, its versatility allows its application in diverse settings such as transportation hubs, workplaces, and public events, contributing to the overall effort to mitigate the spread of contagious diseases. The algorithm's accuracy and efficiency make it an indispensable asset in the arsenal of tools utilized by authorities and organizations to safeguard public health and promote community well-being.

3.3.5 Results and discussion

The technique discussed in the previous subsection has undergone evaluation using two distinct sets of test data to assess its capability in detecting and locating individuals within thermal images. These datasets were deliberately crafted to present challenging scenarios mirroring real-world conditions, achieved by capturing the actual body temperatures of individuals using thermal imaging cameras. The rationale behind selecting these datasets for our experiments stems from the desire to conduct assessments under conditions that closely resemble practical applications. The thermal images were processed, in our evaluation, employing YOLOv2 and distance classification algorithms. Utilizing YOLOv2, an advanced object detection model, facilitated the recognition of individuals and the provision of bounding box information demarcating their locations within the images. Following person detection, the Euclidean distance between each pair of detected centroids was computed, employing the bounding box and centroid information derived from the dimensions (x, y) of each bounding box.

Furthermore, R-CNN and fast R-CNN models were devised and trained for person recognition, utilizing the same training datasets. These models were then juxtaposed against the technique proposed in the previous subsection using identical test datasets of thermal images. To assess the effectiveness of the proposed approach, the three architectures were evaluated based on parameters such as accuracy, precision, and recall values, utilizing the confusion matrix criteria. These metrics provide insights into the performance of the models in terms of correctly identifying positive and negative instances, as well as the trade-offs between precision and recall. Upon analysis of the experimental results, the newly proposed detector exhibited commendable performance in both people detection and social distancing classification within thermal images across both datasets, as illustrated in Fig. 3.4. In the evaluation process, understanding the intricacies of each step involved, starting from data collection to model training and performance evaluation, is crucial. The realism of the datasets plays a significant role in ensuring that the evaluation accurately reflects the model's performance in practical scenarios. By capturing body temperatures with real thermal imaging cameras, the datasets used in this evaluation effectively simulate real-world conditions, thus enhancing the relevance and applicability of the findings. The utilization of YOLOv2 for person detection showcases the effectiveness of state-of-the-art object detection techniques in identifying individuals within thermal images. The bounding box information provided by YOLOv2 enables precise localization of individuals within the images, laying the foundation for subsequent analysis. The

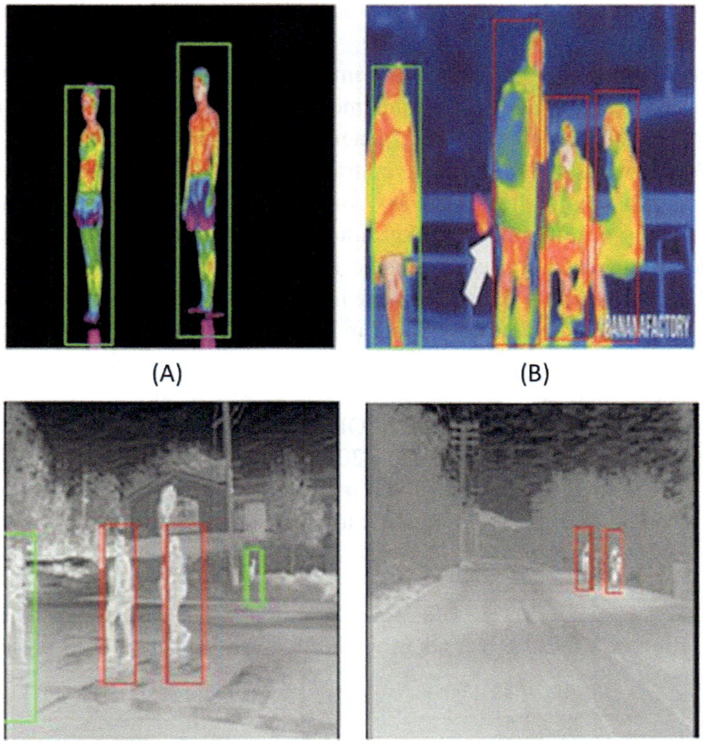

(A) (B)

(C) (D)

FIGURE 3.4

The samples from dataset I (A and B) and dataset II (C and D).

computation of Euclidean distances between detected centroids adds another layer of analysis, allowing for the assessment of spatial relationships between individuals within the thermal images. This information is instrumental in tasks such as social distancing classification, where understanding the proximity between individuals is crucial for ensuring compliance with safety measures. The inclusion of R-CNN and fast R-CNN models in the evaluation expands the scope of analysis, providing insights into the performance of different architectures for person recognition tasks. These models, which are specifically designed for object detection and recognition, offer alternative approaches to addressing the challenges posed by thermal images. Comparing the performance of these models against the proposed technique allows for a comprehensive evaluation of the proposed approach's efficacy. By assessing metrics such as accuracy, precision, and recall, we gain a nuanced understanding of how well the proposed technique performs relative to established methodologies. The results depicted in Fig. 3.4 serve as a visual representation of the experimental findings, providing a concise summary of the performance of the proposed technique across both datasets. Visualizations play a crucial role in conveying complex information in a comprehensible manner, enabling stakeholders to grasp key insights at a glance.

Significant results were achieved with two datasets, outperforming R-CNN, and fast R-CNN detectors, see Tables 3.2 and 3.3.

YOLOv2 neural network, a pivotal advancement in object detection methodology, revolutionizes image analysis by restructuring the fundamental approach. Unlike preceding models like R-CNN and fast R-CNN, which depend on the generation of region proposals followed by individual region analysis, YOLOv2 adopts a distinctive strategy. It processes the entire image in a singular pass, thus obtaining a comprehensive view of the image's contents. This approach yields notable benefits, notably in minimizing background errors and refining object localization accuracy. This improvement is particularly conspicuous in the identification of people within images. Consequently, YOLOv2 marks a paradigm shift in object detection, harnessing a holistic perspective to enhance the efficacy and precision of image analysis. By considering the entire image at once, YOLOv2 streamlines the detection process, leading to more precise localization of objects. In comparison to methods like R-CNN and fast R-CNN, which struggle with precisely localizing objects due to their region-based approach, YOLOv2 offers superior accuracy, as evidenced by empirical comparisons (Keniya & Mehendale, 2020; Sener & Ikizler-Cinbis, 2015; Yadav, 2020) (refer to Table 3.4). The method outlined in the previous subsection demonstrates promising results specifically for individual detection and classification of social distancing within the images.

Table 3.2 Evaluation of YOLOv2 versus other models with utilization of dataset I.

Methodologies	Accuracy (%)	Precision (%)	Recall (%)
YOLOv2	95.6	95	96
R-CNN	88.5	87	90
Fast R-CNN	91.2	92	90

Table 3.3 Evaluation of YOLOv2 versus other models with utilization of dataset II.

Methodologies	Accuracy(%)	Precision (%)	Recall (%)
YOLOv2	94.5	94	95
R-CNN	86.5	86	96
Fast R-CNN	90.5	91	90

Table 3.4 Evaluation of the YOLOv2 versus other approaches.

Methodologies	Accuracy(%)
YOLOv2 (dataset I)	95.7
YOLOv2 (dataset II)	94.6
Sener and Ikizler-Cinbis (2015)	93.3
Keniya and Mehendale (2020)	92.8
Yadav (2020)	91

The primary objective of this research is to enable real-time detection and recognition of people. This necessitates continuous monitoring and tracking of individuals' movements through video surveillance. Deep learning, particularly the advancements in CNNs, has revolutionized object detection methodologies, making them more efficient and accurate. Deep learning technologies have found extensive applications across various domains, including surveillance, where they excel in identifying and locating objects within images, offering encouraging results for real-time detection scenarios (Shubham, 2019). To gain a deeper understanding and validate the effectiveness of the proposed approach, rigorous experiments were conducted to compare it against established DL models such as R-CNN, and fast R-CNN. These experiments were conducted using MATLAB, leveraging a dedicated test bench equipped with a thermal imaging camera for capturing video footage. The comparison involved running the three models simultaneously and measuring the frames per second (fps) performance for each model.

The experimental results unequivocally demonstrate the superiority of the neural network proposed in this work in terms of speed and real-time detection capabilities when compared to both fast R-CNN and R-CNN. Notably, the proposed method exhibits significantly higher fps rates, underscoring its suitability for real-time applications. This performance advantage is particularly striking when contrasted with R-CNN and fast R-CNN, which exhibit comparatively lower fps rates, rendering them less viable for real-time deployment. In essence, the findings illustrate the marked efficacy of the proposed neural network model over its counterparts, namely, fast R-CNN and R-CNN, in facilitating rapid detection tasks without compromising accuracy. Such findings are pivotal for advancing the field of computer vision, as they provide concrete evidence of the practical utility of novel neural network architectures in enhancing real-time detection capabilities. Consequently, these results carry substantial implications for various domains reliant on timely and precise object detection, including autonomous vehicles, surveillance systems, and industrial automation.

It is essential to highlight that the performance of the proposed method is competitive and comparable to more recent advancements, such as the YOLOv3 detector proposed in Punn et al. (2020). The comparative analysis, as depicted in Fig. 3.5, illustrates the real-time detection capabilities of the proposed approach vis-à-vis other deep-learning object detectors. This visual representation reinforces the empirical findings, showcasing the efficiency and effectiveness of the proposed method in real-world scenarios.

YOLOv2 neural network represents a significant leap forward in object detection, offering improved accuracy and real-time performance compared to traditional methods like R-CNN and fast R-CNN. Through comprehensive experimentation and empirical comparisons, the proposed method has demonstrated its efficacy in detecting and recognizing people in real-time, particularly in the context of thermal imaging. With its superior speed and accuracy, the proposed approach holds promise for various applications requiring efficient and reliable object detection capabilities.

In addition to evaluating the performance metrics, an integral aspect of our experimentation involved measuring the power consumption of the Jetson Nano. To ensure precise measurements, we meticulously removed all peripheral accessories commonly associated with the device, including the mouse, monitor, and keyboard. By isolating the Jetson Nano, we aimed to accurately its power requirements under specific operational conditions. During the execution of the distance classification algorithm, a fundamental component of our study, the Jetson

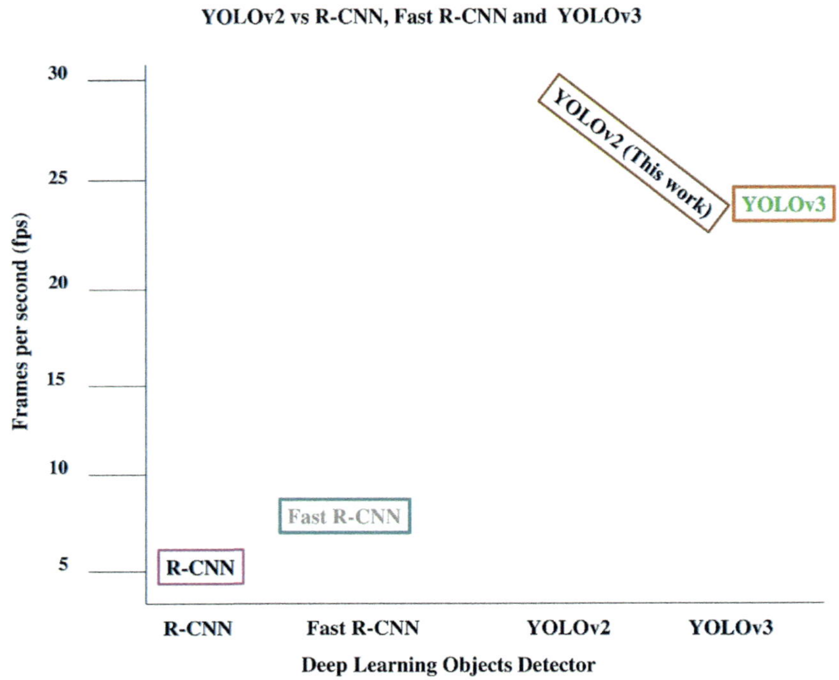

FIGURE 3.5

The performance of this method with other deep learning model of object detection in terms of real-time detection performance.

Nano exhibited a power consumption of 4.4 W. This measurement underscores the device's efficiency in handling computational tasks while maintaining relatively low power utilization. Such insights into power consumption are invaluable for understanding the operational characteristics of the Jetson Nano and optimizing its performance in various applications. Our investigation into power consumption extended beyond a singular scenario, encompassing a range of conditions to provide a comprehensive understanding of the device's energy requirements. Table 3.5 presents a detailed breakdown of the power measurements obtained across different usage scenarios. From idle states to peak processing loads, each scenario offers valuable insights into how the Jetson Nano responds to varying levels of computational demand. By meticulously documenting the power consumption across diverse operational scenarios, we empower researchers, developers, and end-users with critical information for designing and deploying applications on the Jetson Nano platform. These findings facilitate informed decision-making regarding power management strategies and contribute to the development of energy-efficient algorithms and systems tailored to the capabilities of the Jetson Nano. The exploration of power consumption enriches our understanding of the Jetson Nano's operational dynamics and serves as a valuable resource for optimizing its performance in real-world applications.

Table 3.5 Power consumption for the proposed approach across various scenarios.

Method	YOLOv2	Power consumption (W)
Jetson Nano without accessories	Off	1.24
Jetson Nano without accessories	On	4.40
Jetson Nano with accessories	Off	2.24
Jetson Nano with accessories	On	5.40

3.4 Social distancing with YOLOv4-tiny

Exploring advancements built upon previous research, Section 3.3 discusses real-time AI platform design for people detection and social distancing classification using thermal imaging cameras with YOLOv2. Leveraging YOLOv4-tiny, a deep learning object detector known for simplicity and compatibility with low-cost embedded devices (Jiang et al., 2020), surpasses alternative real-time detection methods in effectiveness. Incorporating an algorithm for monitoring social distancing from a bird's-eye perspective, the approach applies to thermal imaging camera recordings for comprehensive people detection, social distancing analysis, and simultaneous measurement of skin temperatures. To refine the model for individual detection, extensive training using thermal imaging across various indoor and outdoor settings employs a larger dataset than previous work in Section 3.3 with YOLOv2, significantly enhancing the performance of the DL model. Furthermore, the algorithm autonomously assesses adherence to safe conditions based on both the number of individuals within the thermal video and the measured distances between the centroids of their bounding boxes. Establishing three distinct levels of violation, each with corresponding thresholds for the measured distances between bounding box centers, enhances the precision and granularity of the analysis.

3.4.1 The proposed approach

Utilizing YOLOv4-tiny for people detection in thermal videos corresponds to employing the YOLOv4 model. This variant leverages several modifications from the original YOLOv4 network to ensure swift execution on a low-cost embedded system. The YOLOv4-tiny architecture adopts the cross-stage partial (CSP) Darknet53-tiny network as its backbone instead of the CSPDarknet53 network employed in the YOLOv4 approach. In contrast to YOLOv4, YOLOv4-tiny utilizes the CSPBlock module within the CSPDarknet53-tiny network instead of the ResBlock module. Furthermore, YOLOv4-tiny employs the LeakyReLU function as its activation function within the CSPDarknet53-tiny network, eschewing the Mish activation function used in YOLOv4. Fig. 3.6 illustrates the proposed architecture of YOLOv4-tiny.

In the design of YOLOv4-tiny, two consecutive 3×3 convolutions are utilized to achieve 5×5 receptive fields for extracting global features. Additionally, both channel attention and spatial attention mechanisms are employed to extract more effective information. The CSPBlock module divides the feature map into two parts and integrates them via residual edges across the stages. This facilitates gradient flow propagation along two different network paths, enhancing the correlation difference of gradient information. A 37-layer CNN is constructed for YOLOv4-tiny. The primary

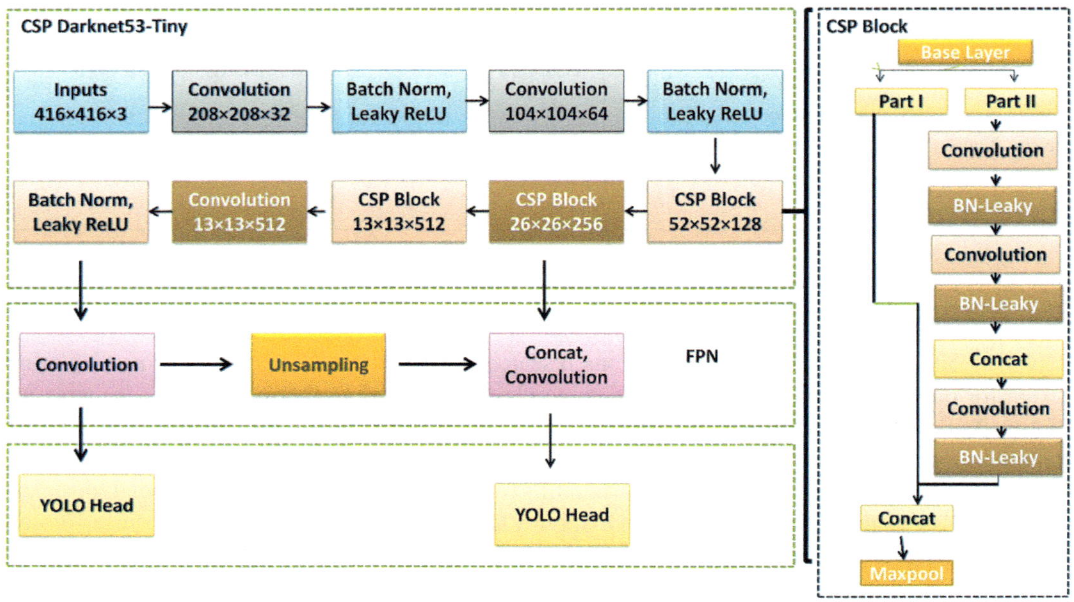

FIGURE 3.6

The architecture of YOLOv4-tiny. This figure depicting the modular structure of YOLOv4-tiny, highlighting its three main components: CSPDarknet53 Tiny for primary feature extraction, Feature Pyramid Network (FPN) for semantic and geometric data fusion, and YOLO Head for dense prediction generation. This architecture is tailored for real-time people detection in thermal videos, optimized for low-cost embedded systems.

objective of this research is to devise a lightweight model to meet the real-time application demands of CNNs in low-cost embedded systems like IoT devices. This endeavor entails reducing the total weight of the final deep-learning model. Principally, compression is applied to the number of convolutional layers in the CSP backbone. Additionally, the number of YOLO layers is reduced to two from three, and the number of anchor boxes for prediction is minimized. YOLOv4-tiny comprises three main modules: CSPDarknet53 Tiny, feature pyramid network (FPN), and YOLO head. CSPDarknet53-tiny is employed for primary feature extraction, comprising convolutional block and CSPBlock. Convolution layers feature stack normalization and activation functions, with batch normalization utilized for model regularization. Dropout layers are replaced with batch normalization to mitigate overfitting issues, enhancing input normalization by defining variance values. The activation functions employed are LeakyReLu, aligned with the systematic characteristics of CSPNet. The CSPBlock in CSPDarknet53-tiny divides the base layer model into two parts. One part serves as a residual edge, while the other part is merged with the first to yield the final output post a series of convolution operations. The FPN structure amalgamates the characteristics of different network layers, preserving both semantic and geometric data. This consolidation enhances feature extraction capabilities. YOLO Head serves as the final module, generating output results. In the case of a single-stage detector, the YOLO head is tasked with density prediction, yielding a final vector comprising the coordinates of predicted bounding boxes (height, width, center), labels, and confidence values. Eq. (3.3) encapsulates this, where P_{w} and P_{h} denote the width and height of bounding boxes, while (C_{x}, C_{y}) represents the coordinates of the top-left corner of the image.

$$\begin{aligned} bx &= \sigma(t_x) + Cx \\ bx &= \sigma(t_y) + Cy \\ b_{\mathrm{w}} &= P_{\mathrm{w}} \times e^{tw} \\ b_{\mathrm{h}} &= P_{\mathrm{h}} \times e^{th} \end{aligned} \tag{3.3}$$

3.4.2 Violation threshold

During this phase of the work, the Euclidean formula is utilized to estimate the distance between each detected centroid pair, incorporating the enclosed bounding boxes and their centroid data. The distance calculation integrates a scaling factor for translating measurements into real-world metrics, specifically around 6 ft (or 180 cm). Predefined rules dictate the minimum social distance violations, based on distance assumptions, with two thresholds for identification: one denoted by yellow and the other by red for detected bounding boxes. Crossing the first threshold triggers an alert, marked by a yellow indication while surpassing the second threshold is categorized as a risk, indicated by a red marker. Initially, bounding box color is set to green, assuming a distance greater than 6 ft between detections. If the distance falls below or equals 6 ft but exceeds 5 ft (the threshold for the first alert), the bounding box color switches to yellow. Additionally, if the distance equals or falls below 5 ft (the threshold for the second risk), bounding box color changes to red, signifying failure to maintain social distancing. This system operates seamlessly, continually monitoring distances and adjusting visual cues accordingly, ensuring adherence to safety protocols without interruption.

3.4.3 Bird's-eye view transformation

In the previous Section 3.3 conducted on thermal imaging for people detection and distance measurement, it was observed that the accuracy of bounding boxes identifying individuals varied depending on their proximity. Bounding boxes for nearby individuals tended to be larger, while those for distant individuals were less precise due to the perspective distortion inherent in such imaging methods. This distortion complicates the direct calculation of distances between individuals based solely on pixel measurements. To address this limitation, the current study proposes a novel approach involving the conversion of the perspective view to a bird's-eye view. By adopting this strategy, the distances between individuals can be accurately determined using a pixel/meter scale.

The key innovation of this method lies in its utilization of computer vision techniques from an overhead perspective, thereby enhancing the scalability of people surveillance systems. Unlike conventional approaches that require specific camera configurations, our method allows for more flexible deployment. Central to the implementation of the bird's-eye view transformation is the calculation of matrices necessary for the process, a technique known as reverse perspective mapping (RPM). RPM involves converting a frontal view of the scene into a top–down perspective by applying homograph transformations. Fig. 3.7 illustrates the transition from a perspective view to a bird's-eye view, where the spatial dimensions in the image correspond accurately to real-world

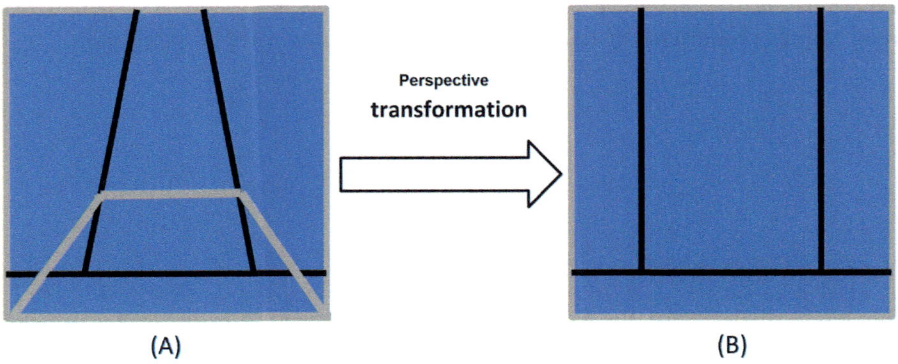

FIGURE 3.7

The process of transforming a perspective view into a bird's-eye view: (A) Original image. (B) Transformation to bird's-eye view.

measurements (Ivan & Kholopov, 2017). To compute the transformation matrix (TM), we utilize the "*getPerspectiveTransform*" function available in the OpenCV Library, as depicted in Eq. (3.4):

$$\begin{bmatrix} t_i x_i' \\ t_i y_i' \\ t_i \end{bmatrix} = TM \times \begin{bmatrix} x_i \\ y_i \\ 1 \end{bmatrix} \tag{3.4}$$

The calculation process involves prompting the user to identify source and destination points within the captured image. Subsequently, the TM is computed based on these points. Additionally, the bird's-eye view matrix is generated by applying the War perspective function from the OpenCV library to each element matrix of the source image, as shown in Eq. (3.5):

$$\mathrm{St}(x,y) = \mathrm{src}\left(\frac{TM_{11}x, TM_{12}y, TM_{13}}{TM_{31}x, TM_{32}y, TM_{33}}, \frac{TM_{21}x, TM_{22}y, TM_{23}}{TM_{31}x, TM_{32}y, TM_{38}}\right) \tag{3.5}$$

In this equation, St(x, y) represents the transformed image, while src denotes the source image. The transformation is performed using the elements of the TM matrix, which are calculated based on the identified source and destination points. This process facilitates the conversion of the perspective view to a top–down view, enabling accurate distance measurements between individuals in the scene. Furthermore, the prototype of our system involves the user in predicting the coordinate points of individuals within the captured image. By engaging the user in this manner, we ensure that the transformation accurately reflects the spatial relationships between individuals in the real-world environment. This user-assisted approach enhances the robustness and adaptability of our method across various surveillance scenarios. This research presents a novel approach to people detection and distance measurement using thermal imaging. By transitioning from a perspective view to a bird's-eye view, we overcome the limitations associated with perspective distortion, thus enabling accurate distance calculations between individuals. The implementation of RPM and the utilization of computer vision techniques contribute to the scalability and flexibility of our system, making it suitable for diverse surveillance applications. Moreover, the involvement of the user in predicting coordinate points enhances the accuracy and reliability of our method, ensuring its effectiveness in real-world settings.

3.4.4 Experiment setup and results

The YOLOv4-tiny model underwent training utilizing two distinct thermal datasets, akin to the YOLOv2 approach delineated in the preceding segment. Noteworthy is the augmentation of image volumes within both datasets to enhance data richness. Dataset I, comprising 1000 images, and dataset II, comprising 950 images, encompassed a variety of scenarios depicting individuals engaging in activities such as sneaking, walking, running, and assuming diverse body postures. The training system employed the Tesla K80 graphics processing unit (GPU) hosted on a cloud service platform, specifically configured for training YOLOv4 architectures tailored for tasks related to object detection and image classification. The training loss curves for both datasets are depicted in Fig. 3.8, encapsulating the trajectory of loss reduction throughout the training iterations.

An assorted array of experiments was conducted to assess the efficacy of the proposed methodology. To this end, the algorithm was executed on test thermal images extracted from both datasets, each comprising realistic depictions captured by different thermal imaging cameras across indoor and outdoor environments. The selection of thermal imagery stems from the inherent capability of thermal cameras to swiftly and securely capture radiated energy emanating from human skin, rendering them apt for the intended experiments. Furthermore, the YOLOv4-tiny model, in conjunction with the proposed technique, was applied to large-scale thermal videos, facilitating bird's-eye view social distancing measurements. These videos, scalable for monitoring human movement, leverage thermal imaging to measure skin temperature, thereby enabling comprehensive analysis of population dynamics within various settings.

In addition to the primary investigation, a comparative analysis ensued, evaluating detectors such as fast R-CNN and YOLOv2 against each other for person detection tasks. Utilizing identical thermal images found within the training datasets, this analysis sought to discern the most effective architecture. The experimental findings unequivocally favored the YOLOv4-tiny framework, demonstrating superior performance metrics across both test datasets and the thermal video repository. This superiority is visually depicted in Fig. 3.9. Noteworthy is its outperformance of counterparts like fast R-CNN and YOLOv2, as corroborated by the evidence presented in Fig. 3.10. To aid in the interpretation of the results, a bird's-eye view visualization was employed, appearing in a distinct window. This visualization method served to augment the comprehensibility of the findings by portraying the efficacy of the YOLOv4-tiny model in distinguishing between safe and risky scenarios. Each scenario is delineated by distinct color-coded representations, providing a clear delineation of safety levels.

The success attained by the YOLOv4-tiny model finds its roots in the innovative design elements imbued within its framework. Notably, a modified path aggregation network and spatial sub-pyramid pooling mechanisms play pivotal roles in bolstering the accuracy of object detection. Complementing these features is the integration of CSPDarknet53 as the foundational neural network, which introduces further enhancements. CSPDarknet53, an evolved iteration of the Darknet53 architecture, incorporates CSPNet within sizable residual blocks, facilitating the mapping of features derived from input images. These feature mappings undergo successive

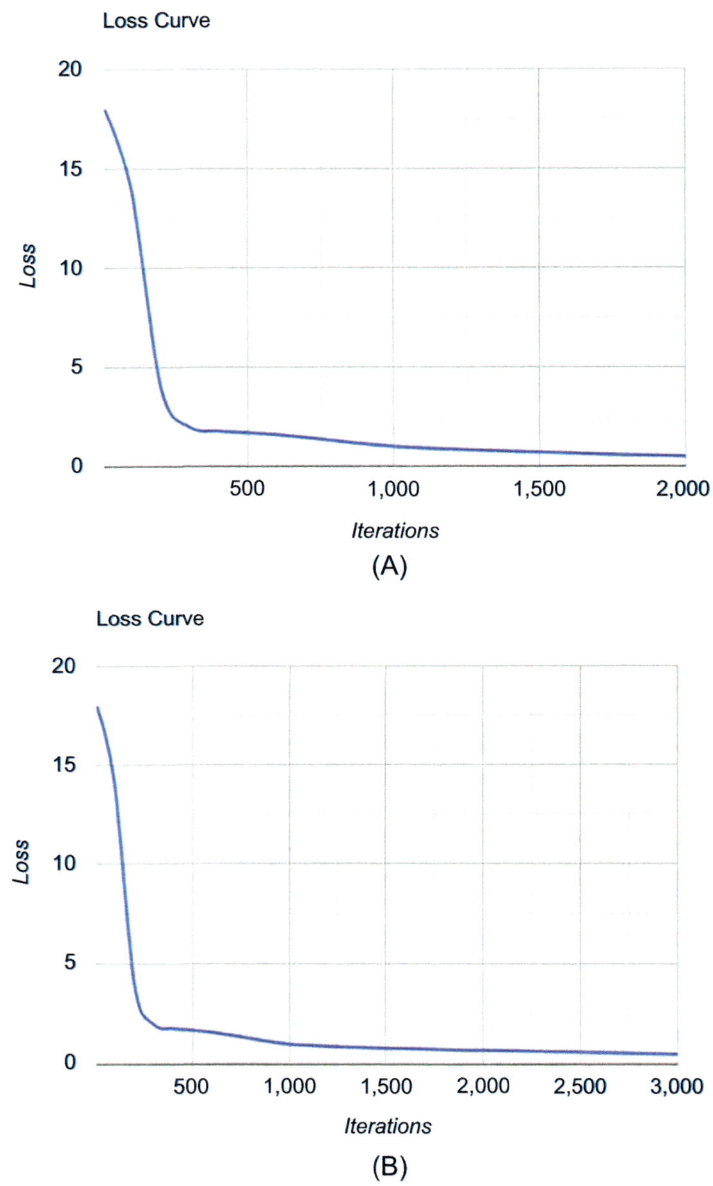

FIGURE 3.8

(A) The training loss progression for dataset I. (B) The training loss evolution for dataset II.

convolutional operations, resulting in a refined representation that amplifies the learning potential of convolutional layers. Moreover, this refinement process operates to curtail computational burdens, thus furnishing the network with augmented detection capabilities.

(A) (B)

FIGURE 3.9

In this depiction, the proposed approach reveals the social distancing compliance, indicating two individuals breaching the recommended distance threshold, while five others maintain safe distances. (A) Transformation of human detection points to a bird's-eye view perspective. (B) Detection of people using enclosed bounding boxes in thermal video footage.

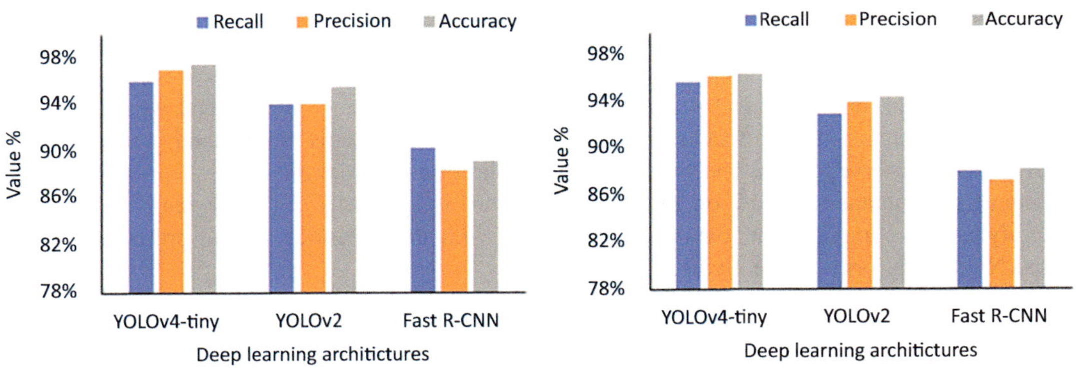

(A) (B)

FIGURE 3.10

(A) Comparison of YOLOv4-tiny's performance against other object models using Dataset I. (B) Evaluating YOLOv4-tiny's performance in comparison to other object detectors using Dataset II.

The proposed DL model exhibits proficiency in detecting individuals and furnishing corresponding rectangle box information. Following detection, the Euclidean distances between centroids of detected objects are computed using bounding box coordinates and centroid information, encapsulating dimensions denoted by (x, y) for each bounding box. However, delineating precise distances between pedestrians within a 2-dimensional scene, as captured by conventional cameras, poses a formidable challenge. Addressing this challenge necessitates specialized cameras equipped with calibration features capable of approximating 3-dimensional dimensions, incorporating parameters denoted by (x, y, z). Consequently, the present research advocates for the utilization of bird's-eye view solutions, wherein the detection center of bounding boxes approximates the centroid of pedestrians. This approach effectively mitigates perspective distortions inherent in 2-dimensional representations, facilitating the perception of uniform distribution of distances across the entire image while obviating the influence of perspective effects.

3.5 Algorithms implementation on the embedded system

Utilizing Nvidia platforms, the proposed technique is implemented to assess its efficacy. The aim is to evaluate the performance of the proposed methodologies across different hardware configurations. To achieve this objective, a series of targeted tests are conducted to scrutinize the computational costs incurred by the proposed technique when deployed on varying hardware setups. The utilization of Jetson Nano and Jetson AGX Xavier serves a dual purpose in this endeavor. Firstly, these platforms represent distinct tiers of computational capability, with Jetson Nano catering to resource-constrained environments and Jetson AGX Xavier offering substantially greater computational prowess. By deploying the proposed technique across these platforms, the comparative performance across different computational resources can be effectively assessed. The evaluation process entails a meticulous examination of the computational demands imposed by the proposed technique on each hardware configuration. Specifically, attention is directed toward delineating the computational cost incurred during key stages of the technique's execution, such as preprocessing, feature extraction, inference, and postprocessing. By dissecting the computational workload across these stages, insights into the technique's resource utilization patterns are gleaned, elucidating any discrepancies observed across the tested hardware platforms. Furthermore, the dependency of the technique's computational cost on the target hardware is systematically analyzed. This involves quantifying the computational overheads associated with the execution of the prototype on proposed Nvidia platforms, respectively.

3.5.1 Social distancing on NVIDIA devices

Employing a V2 Raspberry Pi Camera, the algorithm interfaced with an additional computing unit, exhibiting a sequence of videos sourced from thermal imaging cameras. Through meticulous testing, the utmost attainable fps were assessed, juxtaposing the outcomes against alternative methodologies. The comparative analysis is tabulated in Table 3.6.

From the experimental findings, the NVIDIA Jetson Xavier emerged as the superior performer in fps, achieving a noteworthy 23 fps. Conversely, real-time processing on the NVIDIA Jetson Nano yielded a mere 11 fps. This discerns a twofold disparity in speed, with the Xavier board manifesting twice the rapidity of its Nano counterpart in this setup. The deployment of the algorithm as standalone applications on distinct NVIDIA devices was executed smoothly. The V2 Raspberry Pi Camera played a pivotal role in facilitating seamless interfacing with the additional computing unit.

Table 3.6 Comparison of real-time detection between the proposed approach and alternative methods.

Method	Real time in frames per second (fps)
YOLOv4-tiny on Xavier AGX	23
Ahmed, Ahmad, and Jeon (2021)	20
YOLOv4-tiny on Jetson Nano	11
AbdulRahman and Zhu (2020)	11
Pouw et al. (2020)	10

Videos sourced from thermal imaging cameras were effectively exhibited, showcasing the algorithm's functionality. The testing process was conducted meticulously, ensuring accurate measurements of fps. The outcomes were then meticulously compared with alternative methodologies to provide comprehensive insights. The tabulated results in Table 3.6 offer a clear overview of the performance disparities among the different setups. The experimental setup showcased the prowess of the NVIDIA Jetson Xavier, highlighting its superior performance in handling the algorithm's processing tasks. Conversely, the NVIDIA Jetson Nano lagged significantly in terms of fps, emphasizing the importance of selecting appropriate hardware for such applications.

Table 3.7 presents the utilization percentages of both the GPU and CPU on NVIDIA devices, specifically the Jetson Nano and Xavier, during the execution of our proposed prototype. These percentages are indicative of the workload each component bears while running AI algorithms. The GPU, responsible for handling intensive computational tasks, exhibits a higher utilization rate compared to the CPU, which primarily manages general-purpose tasks. In the case of the Jetson Nano, the GPU demonstrates a substantial utilization rate of 98%, indicating its significant involvement in executing AI algorithms. Meanwhile, the CPU's utilization stands at 71.2%, suggesting a considerable but lesser workload compared to the GPU. Similarly, on the Jetson Xavier, the GPU registers a utilization rate of 86%, showcasing its integral role in processing AI tasks. However, the CPU utilization is notably lower at 50%, implying that the CPU is less burdened relative to the GPU in executing the proposed technique. These utilization percentages provide valuable insights into the distribution of computational workload between the GPU and CPU on NVIDIA devices, aiding in the evaluation of their performance capabilities for running AI algorithms.

This research aims to contrast the proposed method with current leading pretrained neural network architectures. The proposed techniques exhibit a notable advantage in compact disk storage size. YOLOv4, for instance, requires only 21 MB, while YOLOv2 utilizes a modest 14 MB. This advantage in storage size is significant for various applications where resource constraints are a concern, such as deployment on edge devices or mobile platforms. The smaller storage footprint enables more efficient deployment and utilization of these models in real-world scenarios. Moreover, this advantage suggests potential cost savings in storage infrastructure for organizations employing these models at scale. Consequently, the compact size of the proposed techniques enhances their practicality and accessibility in diverse computational environments, fostering broader adoption and integration into various applications. Consequently, these architectures entail a relatively limited number of trainable parameters, rendering them highly suitable for deployment on low-cost IoT devices. In contrast, alternative methods often rely on expansive CNN layers, resulting

Table 3.7 Percent of GPU and CPU utilization on Jetson Nano and Jetson Xavier while the proposed method is running.

NVIDIA platform	Percent utilization
Jetson Nano (GPU)	98
Jetson Nano (CPU)	71.2
Jetson Xavier (GPU)	86
Jetson Xavier (CPU)	50

in larger storage requirements, exemplified by the Resnet50 model approach. Furthermore, these pretrained architectures typically exhibit suboptimal performance when deployed on low-cost IoT devices, thereby hindering real-time object detection, and impeding human visual perception in tracking objects. Fig. 3.11 provides a visual representation of the disk memory size comparison between YOLOv4-tiny and other pretrained neural network models.

Investigations reveal varying power consumption levels between the Jetson Nano and Jetson Xavier across diverse scenarios. Each NVIDIA device underwent scrutiny autonomously, devoid of external peripherals such as monitors, mice, or keyboards. During algorithmic execution, the Jetson Nano exhibited a power draw of 3.21 W, meticulously documented. Conversely, the Jetson Xavier's power utilization was monitored with precision, yielding a measurement of 17 W, as delineated in Table 3.8. Comparatively, the Jetson Nano demonstrates significantly lower power consumption than its counterpart, the Jetson Xavier. This discrepancy suggests potential differences in computational efficiency and hardware specifications between the two devices. The Jetson Nano's modest power draw of 3.21 W hints at its suitability for low-power applications or scenarios where energy efficiency is paramount. Conversely, the Jetson Xavier's higher power consumption of 17 W indicates its capacity for more intensive computational tasks, likely due to superior processing capabilities and additional hardware features.

These findings underscore the importance of considering power consumption when selecting between the Jetson Nano and Jetson Xavier for specific use cases. Applications with stringent power constraints or those emphasizing energy efficiency could favor the Jetson Nano, leveraging its lower power draw to prolong battery life or minimize operational costs. Conversely, tasks requiring robust computational power could necessitate the utilization of the Jetson Xavier, despite its higher power consumption, to ensure optimal performance and throughput.

Table 3.8 presents a comprehensive overview of the power consumption associated with YOLOv4-tiny across different configurations. The analysis encompasses the status of the NVIDIA devices in two distinct scenarios: one without any accessories and the other with additional peripherals connected. For the Jetson Nano, the power draw without accessories amounted to 3.21 W, while with accessories, it increased to 5.5 W. In contrast, the Jetson Xavier exhibited a higher baseline power consumption of 17 W without peripherals, which slightly escalated to 18.3 W when accessories were integrated. These findings underscore the significance of considering various factors that could influence power consumption in computational devices. The inclusion of external peripherals evidently impacts the overall energy utilization of both the Jetson Nano and Jetson Xavier. Moreover, the discernible contrast in power consumption between the two devices highlights the variance in energy efficiency inherent in their respective architectures. Such insights are

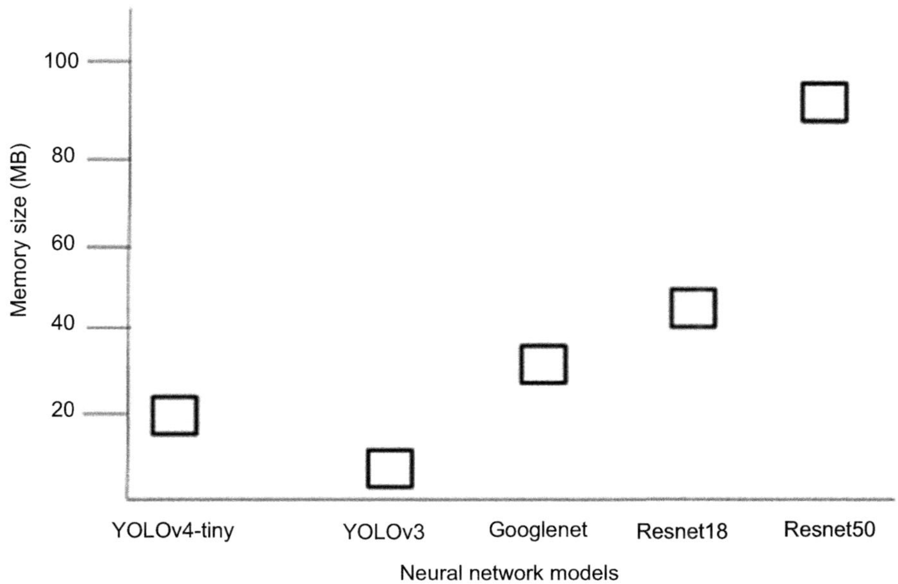

FIGURE 3.11

A comparison between our suggested method and alternative pretrained neural network models regarding memory usage.

Table 3.8 Power consumption of YOLOv4-tiny across various scenarios.

NVIDIA platforms	Power measurement (W)
Jetson Xavier without accessories	17
Jetson Xavier with accessories	18.3
Jetson Nano without accessories	3.21
Jetson Nano with accessories	5.5

invaluable for optimizing power management strategies and enhancing the overall performance of NVIDIA devices in computational tasks.

3.5.2 Distributed video infrastructure for social distancing

Video surveillance cameras serve as an effective tool for authorities to monitor and ensure compliance with social distancing measures. This study introduces a distributed surveillance camera system built upon NVIDIA technology. The system architecture comprises multiple Jetson Nano devices, each equipped with a camera, functioning as intelligent nodes. These nodes are integrated with Wi-Fi capabilities for internet connectivity. Through a router with a static IP address, all devices are interconnected, enabling the transmission of video streams to a centralized computer system, as depicted in Fig. 3.12.

Facilitating communication between the centralized surveillance management system, operating on Windows, and the Nvidia Jetson Nano nodes, the MobaXterm application serves as the intermediary. Employing OpenSSH, a remote data communication protocol, connections are established with the designated IP addresses of each device. Within the MobaXterm application, multiple OpenSSH sessions are initiated to interact with the Jetson Nano nodes individually. The latency between the centralized computer and NVIDIA boards is assessed at 0.3 ms. This minimal latency ensures swift communication, crucial for real-time surveillance operations. The proposed method is tailored for a distributed surveillance infrastructure capable of detecting individuals and classifying social distancing adherence in thermal videos captured by multiple Jetson Nano nodes. The utilization of Jetson Nano devices enhances the scalability and flexibility of the surveillance system. By distributing the computational load across multiple nodes, the system can handle a large volume of video streams while maintaining efficient performance. Additionally, the integration of thermal imaging technology enables the detection of individuals even in challenging lighting conditions, further enhancing the system's effectiveness. The adoption of a centralized surveillance computer management system streamlines the monitoring process. By consolidating data from multiple nodes onto a single platform, authorities can gain comprehensive insights into compliance levels across

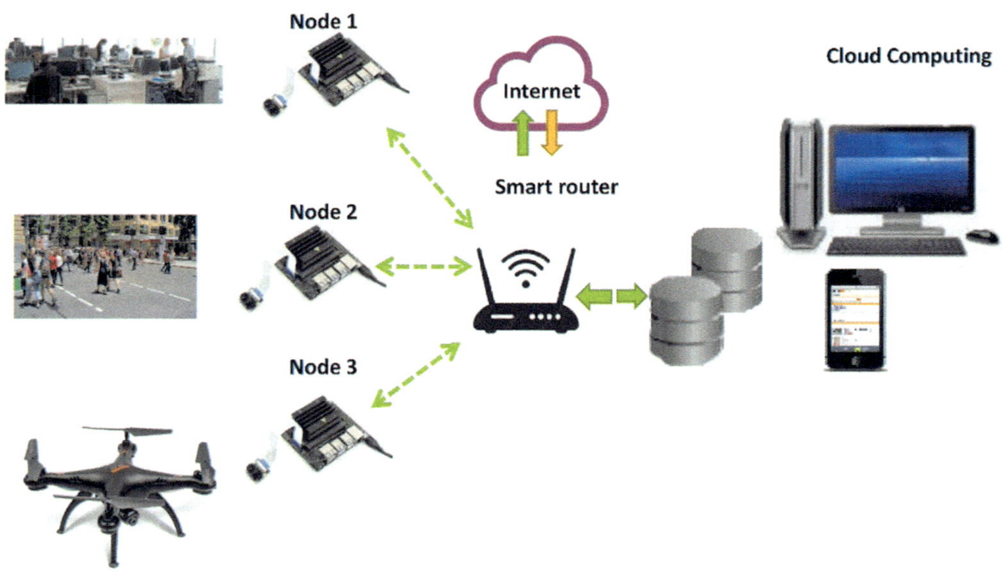

FIGURE 3.12

Cutting-edge smart surveillance technology utilizes a distributed video system to effectively classify social distancing practices. This advanced system employs sophisticated algorithms to analyze video feeds and identify instances where individuals maintain safe distances from each other, contributing to the promotion of public health and safety. By leveraging state-of-the-art technology, it provides real-time insights into adherence to social distancing guidelines, enabling proactive measures to be taken when necessary.

different locations. Furthermore, the real-time nature of the system allows for prompt intervention in case of noncompliance, contributing to the overall effectiveness of social distancing enforcement efforts. The reliance on OpenSSH for communication ensures secure data transfer between the centralized computer and Jetson Nano nodes. This protocol encrypts the transmitted data, mitigating the risk of unauthorized access or tampering. As a result, sensitive information captured by the surveillance system remains protected, maintaining the integrity and trustworthiness of the data collected. The use of thermal imaging technology adds an additional layer of sophistication to the surveillance system. By capturing thermal signatures, the system can detect individuals even in environments with poor lighting conditions or obstructed visibility. This capability enhances the system's reliability and accuracy, ensuring that no individuals go unnoticed during the monitoring process. The proposed distributed surveillance camera system represents a significant advancement in the field of social distancing enforcement. By leveraging state-of-the-art technology, authorities can effectively monitor and enforce compliance with social distancing measures, thereby contributing to the containment of infectious diseases and the protection of public health.

3.6 Integrated approach for monitoring social distancing, face mask, and facial temperature measurement

The research endeavors to enhance the COVID-19 prevention system through the integration of an AI-enabled algorithm with existing methodologies, aiming to minimize lockdown phases by implementing surveillance, detection, and monitoring systems utilizing DL models and IoT-embedded devices. This approach seeks to address the ongoing pandemic by simultaneously monitoring social distancing, detecting face masks, and measuring facial temperature in real-time, fusion of three distinct YOLOv4-tiny object detectors facilitated, highlighting superiority in object detection, and tracking speed over other DL models while maintaining high accuracy despite compact size. Implementation on NVIDIA boards like Jetson Nano and Xavier AGX highlights scalability and efficiency, suitable for diverse real-world scenarios with varying trade-offs between cost and performance. Notably, the deployment of a single thermal camera enables the development of thermal screening systems capable of measuring facial temperature for multiple individuals concurrently while monitoring social distancing among pedestrians. Integrating YOLOv4-tiny aims to detect objects within video frames, processing input frames via CNNs to generate bounding box predictions and class probabilities. Integration of three YOLOv4-tiny object detectors, each designated for distinct tasks—social distancing monitoring, mask detection, and facial temperature measurement—underscores versatility. Models trained on diverse datasets ensure robustness and accuracy across different contexts, enriching efficacy in combating the spread of COVID-19. Fig. 3.13 represents a complete solution designed to combine the detection of face masks, monitoring of social distancing, and accurate measurement of facial temperature using video analysis.

The proposed method's implementation involves various tasks. These tasks include monitoring social distancing protocols, measuring facial temperature, and detecting face masks using sophisticated algorithms. This comprehensive approach plays a crucial role in establishing an automated surveillance system. The system aims to assist authorities in enforcing compliance with social distancing directives. Additionally, it evaluates individuals' adherence to face mask mandates. This dual function is essential for reducing the spread of contagious pathogens. By combining these

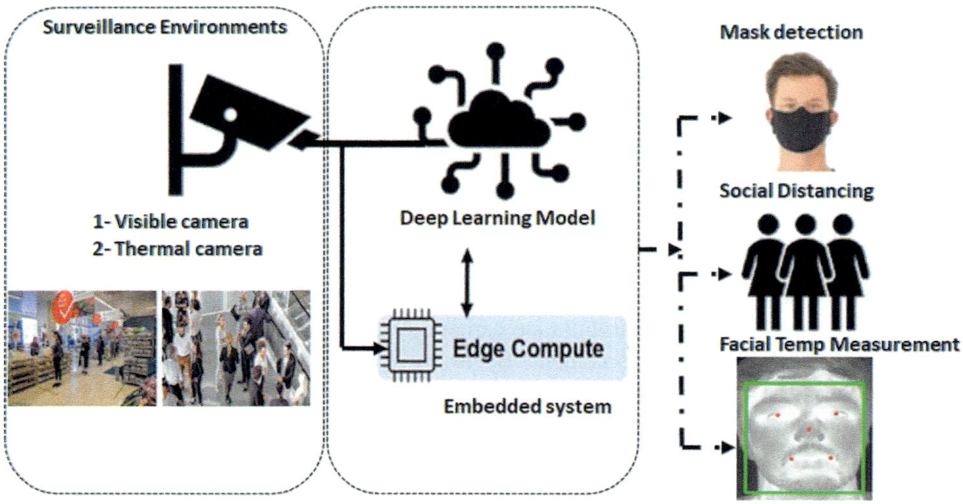

FIGURE 3.13

This framework represents a complete solution designed to combine the detection of face masks, monitoring social distancing, and accurate measurement of facial temperature using video analysis.

tasks, the method provides a holistic solution to the challenges posed by the current health crisis. Moreover, it enables efficient monitoring and enforcement without relying solely on manual interventions. Thus it enhances public safety measures by integrating technology with health protocols. This integrated approach is integral to effectively managing public health crises and safeguarding community well-being. The operational framework revolves around the utilization of three distinct models of YOLOv4-tiny, meticulously calibrated to address the aforementioned tasks with precision. Commencing with the meticulous curation of datasets pertinent to the threefold objectives, our methodology proceeds to the rigorous training and subsequent evaluation of the YOLOv4-tiny models, a pivotal step in gauging their efficacy and resilience in real-world scenarios. The culminating prototype is seamlessly integrated into embedded systems such as Jetson Nano or Xavier AGX, affording autonomous functionality within these devices. Central to the system's efficacy is the synchronous operation of both visible and thermal cameras, strategically deployed to facilitate face mask detection and social distancing classification, alongside the precise measurement of facial temperature. These cameras are adeptly harnessed within NVIDIA devices, underscoring the technological sophistication underpinning our approach. Fig. 3.1 visually encapsulates the integrated framework, illustrating the seamless synergy between face mask detection, social distancing surveillance, and facial temperature assessment, thus underscoring the holistic nature of our methodological paradigm.

3.6.1 Dataset and annotation of face masks

Collected from various sources across the internet, the images presented in this study encompass a diverse array of individuals, spanning different age groups, captured in both indoor and outdoor public settings. A total of 900 images were meticulously curated to represent a broad spectrum of scenarios, featuring solitary visages as well as densely populated gatherings, each offering a unique perspective on the subject matter. Within this assortment, an assortment of masks, distinguished by their varying hues and designs, were carefully selected, and documented, as depicted in Fig. 3.14. Central to the efficacy of our model is the process of data annotation, which assumes a pivotal role in ensuring the accuracy and reliability of our analyses. The taxonomy of data annotations encompasses various modalities, including image and video annotations, key-point annotations, and polygonal segmentation annotations, each playing a distinct role in elucidating the underlying patterns within the dataset. In the context of our study, the tool LabelImg emerged as an indispensable resource for facilitating the image annotation process, offering a versatile platform capable of accommodating a range of annotation formats compatible with ImageNet. Moreover, this tool seamlessly integrates with YOLO algorithms, further enhancing its utility in the realm of object detection and classification. Through the adept utilization of LabelImg, we meticulously delineated the pertinent facial features within the images, demarcating them with precise bounding boxes to facilitate subsequent analyses and model training. This meticulous annotation process serves as the bedrock upon which our analytical framework is constructed, furnishing the requisite foundation for the robust interpretation and classification of facial attributes within the dataset.

3.6.2 Dataset and annotation of facial temperature

Utilizing data from Kuzdeuov et al. (2022) (refer to Fig. 3.15), facial images sourced from various indoor and outdoor environments constitute the primary dataset. These images encapsulate diverse scenarios, capturing individuals in varied positions of the body and facial expressions through thermal camera recordings, totaling 9982 images for analysis. To enhance visibility, a preprocessing step involves inverting the thermal images to obtain negative representations, followed by gamma correction to optimize brightness, thus accentuating facial features. The system operates through the computation of facial mean temperatures, employing pixel interpolation within image frames. The process begins by iterating through bounding boxes encompassing facial regions within the frame, extracting corresponding region of interests (ROIs). The *get_person_temperature* function sequentially processes bounding boxes and the input image frame, extracting ROIs assuming facial inclusion. Utilizing Python and relevant libraries such as OpenCV or PyTorch, the system accesses image data and extracts pixel information. By analyzing pixels within ROIs, the average temperature is derived and mapped to a predefined temperature range of 36°C–38°C using a custom

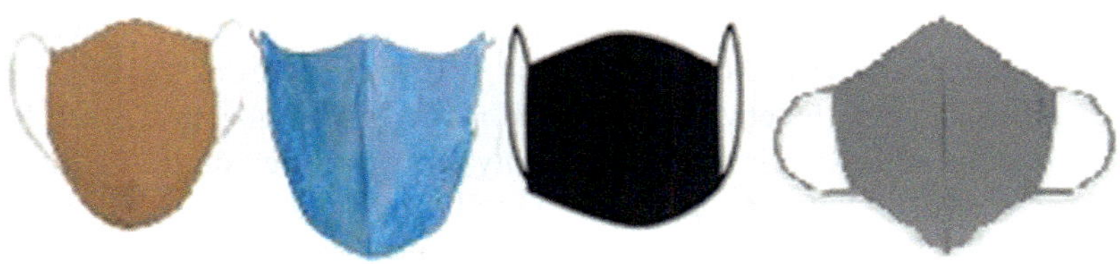

FIGURE 3.14

Different types of masks.

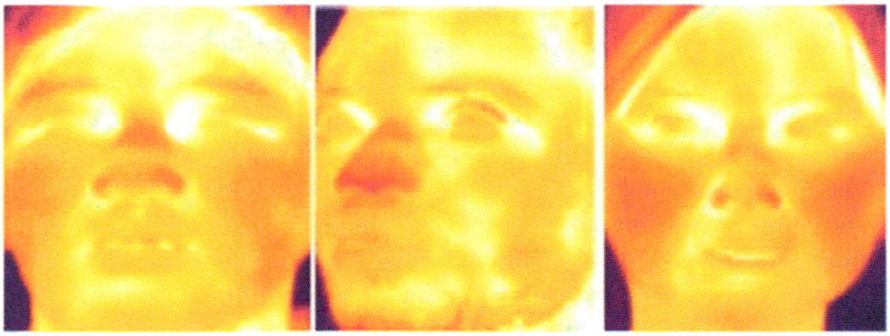

FIGURE 3.15

Sampled images taken for facial temperature measurement are drawn from a sample (Kuzdeuov et al., 2022).

mapping function. This mapping step is crucial for converting temperature values into a more interpretable and visually representative format. Finally, raw pixel values are discretized into integers to ensure compatibility with subsequent computational processes.

3.6.3 Experimental setup and results

The dataset of images undergoes meticulous partitioning into 70% for training, 20% for validation, and 10% for testing. This division strategy ensures a substantial amount of data for training and mitigates the risk of overfitting, thereby fostering the model's capacity to generalize well to unseen instances. The allocation of a distinct testing set is indispensable as it serves as the litmus test for the model's efficacy on previously unseen data, ultimately culminating in the final evaluation of its performance. Employing a graphical image labeling tool facilitates the annotation of bounding boxes delineating the target classes, while the determination of anchor box sizes hinges upon the inherent aspect ratios and scales of objects prevalent within the dataset. Although Table 3.3 furnishes a rudimentary example delineating anchor box sizes for various tasks, the practical determination of these dimensions necessitates a nuanced approach involving iterative experimentation and fine-tuning, tailored to optimize performance vis-à-vis the specific dataset and model architecture under scrutiny. The fine-tuning process for the YOLOv4-tiny model entails meticulous adjustment of several hyperparameters, meticulously referenced in Table 3.9. Opting for the "sdgm" training methodology, the model undergoes a rigorous training regimen spanning 80 epochs, thereby affording it ample opportunities to traverse the dataset iteratively, thus honing its predictive prowess over time. L2 regularization, characterized by a coefficient of 0.05, emerges as a pivotal tool in forestalling overfitting during training, thereby bolstering the model's generalization capabilities on unseen data. This regularization technique leverages a penalty term premised on the L2 norm of the model's weights, thereby incentivizing the optimizer to minimize weight values, curbing their influence on the final predictions. By fostering the cultivation of leaner weight parameters, L2 regularization engenders a parsimonious model architecture, inherently less prone to overfitting and endowed with superior generalization aptitude. Set at 16, the batch size orchestrates the concurrent processing of samples during each iteration of the training process, meticulous calibration occurs for the

Table 3.9 Hyperparameters settings for YOLOv4-tiny.

Hyperparameter	Setting
Training option	sdgm
Number of epochs	80
L2 norm	0.05
Lr	0.001
Size of minibatch	16

learning rate via iterative experimentation, predicated upon the model's responsiveness to training error. Guided by performance benchmarks on the validation set, a learning rate of 0.001 is adjudged optimal, striking a delicate equilibrium between stable convergence and heightened performance efficacy for the designated task. Tailored optimization of the YOLOv4-tiny model underscores a concerted endeavor toward enhancing its performance and accuracy vis-à-vis the designated task or dataset. The discerning selection of hyperparameters assumes a pivotal role in shaping the model's acumen for object detection and the generation of meaningful predictions during inference. The training curves depicted in Fig. 3.16 illustrate the three YOLOv4-tiny models across different tasks, each iteration meticulously conducted within the ambit of Google Colab, powered by the NVIDIA Tesla K80 GPU system.

The proposed system operates autonomously to enforce social distancing measures, detect face masks, and measure facial temperatures. Extensive simulations have been conducted using a diverse testing dataset comprising images captured in various real-world scenarios, spanning both indoor and outdoor environments. Complementing these efforts, a suite of DL models has been meticulously crafted, encompassing iterations such as YOLOv2, YOLOv3-tiny, YOLO, and faster R-CNN. This multipronged approach aims to comprehensively evaluate the efficacy of YOLOv4-tiny architecture vis-à-vis its counterparts, utilizing identical training and testing datasets across all object detection frameworks. Notably, empirical findings, as illustrated in Fig. 3.17 unequivocally demonstrate the superior performance of YOLOv4-tiny across all three core tasks: mask detection, person detection, and facial temperature estimation. Particularly noteworthy is the successful deployment of the initial YOLOv4-tiny architecture for person detection in thermal videos, exhibiting promising results in tandem with the social distancing classification algorithm. However, a pivotal challenge lies in accurately gauging the spatial separation between identified individuals within thermal video feeds. Mitigating this challenge necessitates the adoption of a top–down view approach, wherein video frames are processed to transition from a conventional 2-D perspective to top–down view. This transformation enables the localization of bounding box centroids from the input image onto the top–down view, facilitating the subsequent classification of social distancing adherence. Moreover, the system employs a predefined threshold to delineate violations of social distancing norms, visually accentuated through distinct bounding box colors corresponding to individual subjects. Concurrently, the secondary YOLOv4-tiny model is leveraged for facial detection, enabling precise temperature measurements. By mapping average pixel values from enclosed bounding boxes encompassing facial regions, denoted by a distinctive blue hue, numerical temperature readings are generated, as depicted in Fig. 3.18.

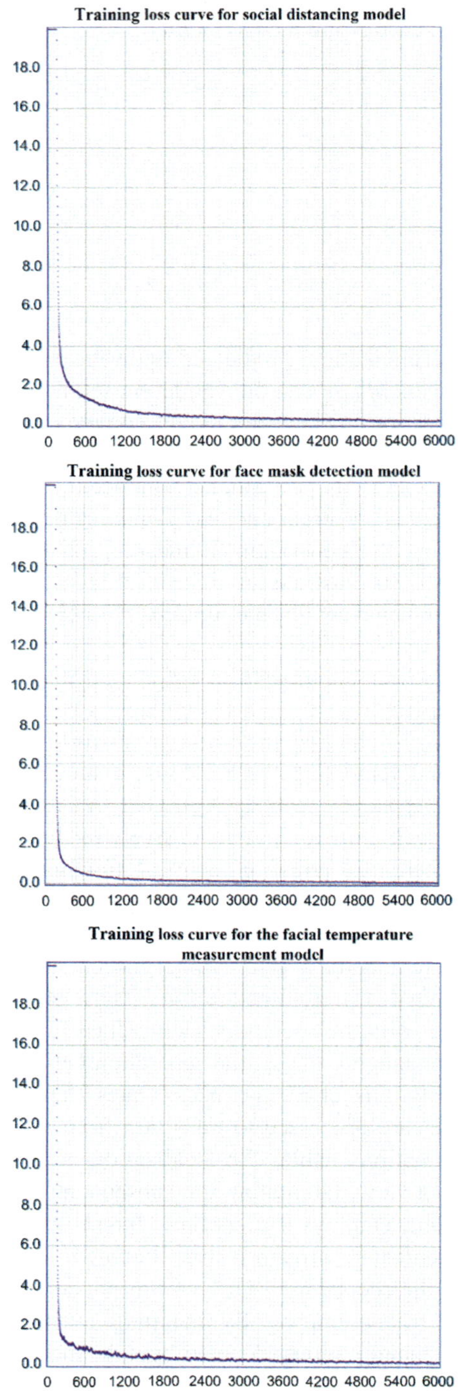

FIGURE 3.16

Loss functions from the training phase of the three YOLOv4-tiny models.

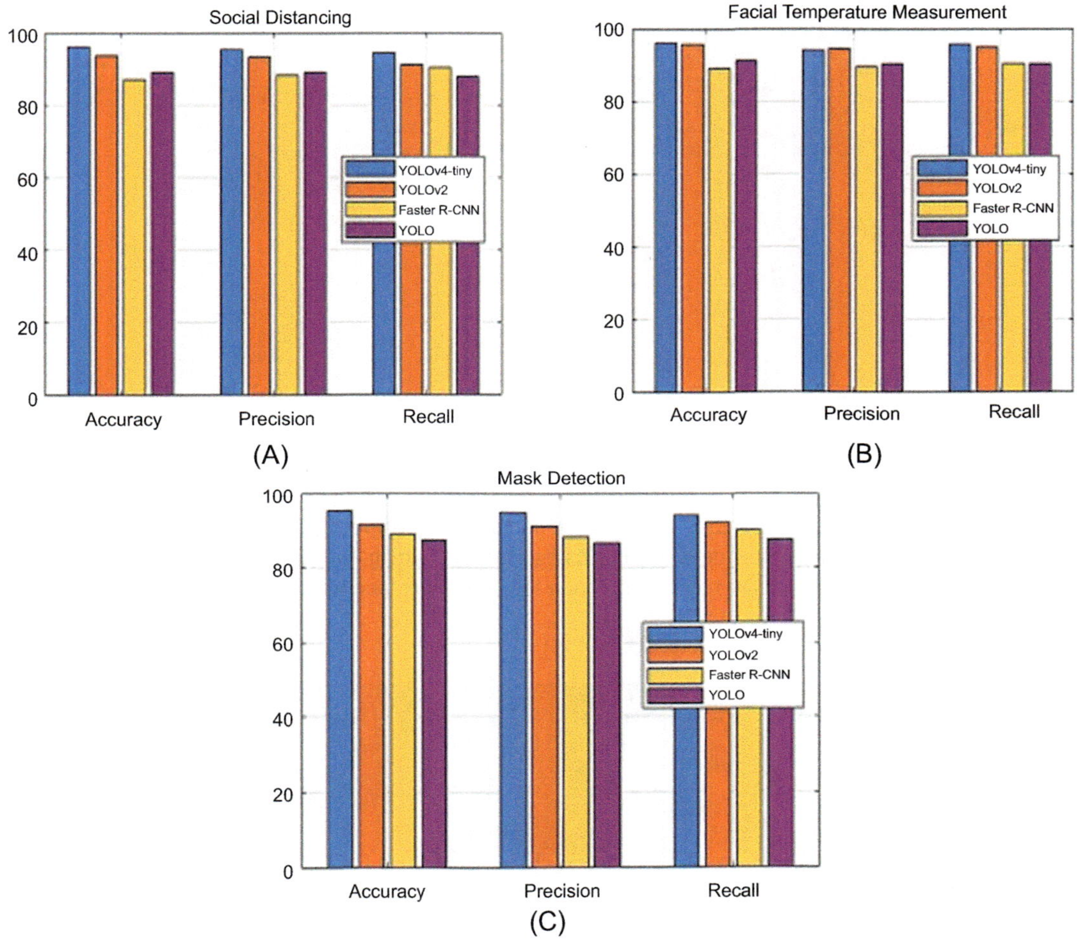

FIGURE 3.17

YOLOv4-tiny's performance: (A) ensuring social distancing, (B) measuring facial temperature, and (C) detecting masks.

Examining the third YOLOv4-tiny model for the detection of individuals wearing respirator face masks, we observed that a green color signifies individuals adhering to mask-wearing protocols, while red denotes those not wearing masks. Fig. 3.19 showcases the assignment of labels "Mask" or "No Mask" atop each detected bounding box, although instances of false negatives and positives were observed in the experiment. Despite these discrepancies, promising outcomes were demonstrated in real-time interaction detection among individuals by the proposed model. In contrast to a method utilizing two datasets of thermal images and employing a customized YOLOv2 lightweight architecture for object detection, superior results were yielded by the proposed social distancing approach. The adoption of YOLOv4-tiny signifies a notable advancement over YOLOv2, characterized by a more potent

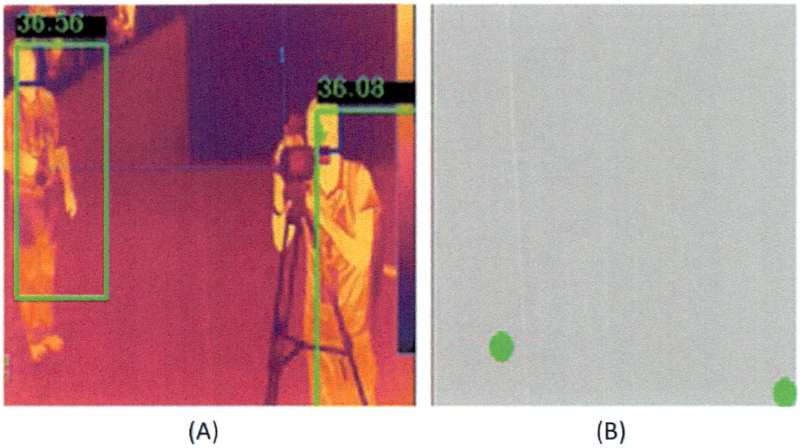

FIGURE 3.18

(A) The initial YOLOv4-tiny architecture identifies social distancing, displaying a green bounding box for safe conditions, while the second model detects faces using a blue bounding box for temperature measurement. (B) Detection of individuals indicated by points from a top–down perspective.

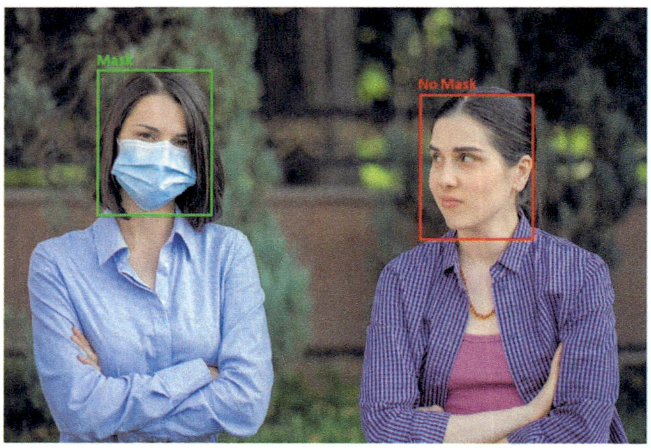

FIGURE 3.19

Experiment results for no mask/mask recognition.

backbone network employing CSPDarknet53, thereby facilitating enhanced feature extraction and superior object detection performance. Comparative analysis with other methodologies for social distance measurement and face mask detection, assessed based on accuracy, reveals that distinct datasets were employed compared to these methodologies. Demonstrating an accuracy of 96.2% for social distance measurement, 95.1% for face mask detection, and 96% for facial temperature measurement, the proposed approach underscores its efficacy. Moreover, YOLOv4-tiny's utilization of anchor boxes for object detection across varied scales and aspect ratios enables swifter and more precise detection compared to MobileNet SSD utilized in a previous method. Noteworthy is YOLOv4-tiny's heightened robustness to occlusion and small objects, which surpasses the capabilities of the CV and IoT algorithm utilized in another method, owing to its superior feature extractor capturing detailed object features from images. While MobileNetv2 is leveraged for face mask detection, renowned for its lightweight and efficient design suitable for mobile and embedded devices, the architecture presents limitations such as the absence of residual connections found in other DL models like ResNet in YOLOv4-tiny. These connections facilitate information flow between layers, addressing challenges like the vanishing gradient problem, potentially encountered in models lacking such connections, thereby easing training. Model accuracy in comparison with alternative social distancing and mask detection methods is exhibited in Tables 3.10 and 3.11, emphasizing YOLOv4-tiny's pivotal role in detecting COVID-19 pandemic adherence concerning social distancing, face mask usage, and facial temperature measurement among individuals.

3.6.4 Implementation of the integrated algorithms on NVIDIA platforms

Successfully accomplishing the execution of the final prototype in real-time on NVIDIA platforms was crucial. It was imperative to leverage Jetson Xavier and Jetson Nano for executing the proposed architectures. Table 3.12 provides a comprehensive comparison of the NVIDIA platforms utilized in this study, highlighting the distinctive features of Jetson Nano and Jetson Xavier.

Jetson Nano delivers a noteworthy 472 GFLOPs of AI performance, equipped with a 128-core Maxwell GPU and a Quad-core ARM A57 CPU. Its hardware includes 4 GB of 64-bit LPDDR4

Table 3.10 YOLOv4-tiny compared with alternative approaches for social distancing.

Methodologies	Accuracy (%)
YOLOv4-tiny for social distancing	96.2
Saponara et al. (2021)	95.6
Giuliano et al. (2022)	95.2
Ahamad et al. (2020)	95.8
Gopal and Ganesan (2022)	94.1

Table 3.11 YOLOv4-tiny compared with alternative approaches for face masks/no mask detection methods.

Methodologies	Accuracy (%)
YOLOv4-tiny for mask/no mask detection	95.1
Nagrath et al. (2021)	92.64
Teboulbi et al. (2022)	93.3
Li et al. (2021)	92.61

Table 3.12 The specification for the proposed NVIDIA platforms (Jetson Nano and Jetson Xavier).

Feature	Jetson Nano	Jetson Xavier
GPU	128-core Maxwell	512-core
CPU	Quad-core ARM A57	8-core ARMv8.2
AI performance	472 GFLOPs	30 TOPs
RAM	4 GB 64-bit LPDDR4	16 GB 256-bit LPDDR4x
Storage	MicroSD card slot	16 GB eMMC flash
Max resolution	4 K @ 30 fps	2 × 4 K @ 30 fps
AI frameworks	TensorFlow, PyTorch, Caffe,	TensorFlow, PyTorch, Caffe, cuDNN, CUDA, etc.
Power consumption	5–10 W	10–30 W

RAM and a MicroSD card slot for storage, supporting resolutions up to 4 K at 30 fps. Supported AI tools include PyTorch and Caffe. On the other hand, Jetson Xavier boasts a robust 512-core GPU and an 8-core ARMv8.2 CPU, providing a remarkable 30 TOPs of AI performance. It features 16 GB of 256-bit LPDDR4 × RAM and 16 GB eMMC flash storage, capable of handling 2 × 4 K resolutions at 30 fps. Additionally, it supports a wide array of AI frameworks such as cuDNN, PyTorch, CUDA, TensorFlow, and Caffe. However, it is noteworthy that Jetson Xavier consumes comparatively more power, ranging from 10 to 30 W, while Jetson Nano operates within the 5–10 W range.

Seamlessly integrating face mask recognition with social distancing and facial temperature estimation was the focus of this research initiative. Multiple DL models were executed concurrently on a single NVIDIA board. Visible face mask detection utilized various cameras including Raspberry Pi model 2.1 and See2CAM camera, while social distancing and facial temperature measurement employed Lepton 3.5 and FLIR BOSON cameras. The cameras were connected with Jetson Nano and Jetson Xavier AGX accordingly. The thermal cameras provided radiometric measurements, enabling the extraction of temperature values for each pixel in the image. The integration of temperature data for analysis was facilitated by converting the color map in the image into an array. OpenCV and its supported libraries allowed adjustments to the height and width of the frame for each camera output, standardized to 416 × 416 dimensions. The proposed technique was successfully deployed on Jetson Nano and Jetson Xavier AGX platforms. Experiment results demonstrated simultaneous detection of masked faces, facial temperature measurement, and social distancing classification by the two cameras, feeding data into a centralized monitoring system as depicted in Fig. 3.20.

Comparing the performance of various techniques for social distancing, mask detection, and facial temperature estimation across both Edge's NVIDIA platforms reveals intriguing insights, as outlined in Tables 3.13 and 3.14. One notable observation is the decline in real-time detection performance when all three models are executed concurrently, attributable to heightened computation costs. This decrease underscores the challenge of managing simultaneous tasks, particularly in resource-constrained environments.

Moreover, an interesting phenomenon emerges concerning temperature differentials between Jetson Nano and Jetson Xavier during the simultaneous execution of the proposed approach for the

(A) (B) (C)

FIGURE 3.20

(A) Identification of pedestrians with points displayed in a top–down perspective. (B) Employment of a thermal camera to detect social distancing, displaying green bounding boxes, and measuring facial temperature, represented by blue bounding boxes. (C) Utilization of a visible camera to detect masks.

Table 3.13 The performance of real-time on Jetson Nano.

Method	Thermal camera (fps)	Visible camera (fps)	Power consumption (W)
Social distancing + mask detection + facial temp	5.5	21	6.7
Social distancing + facial temp	7.24	–	5.2
Mask detection	–	29	4.2

Table 3.14 The performance of real-time on Jetson Xavier AGX.

Method	Thermal camera (fps)	Visible camera (fps)	Power consumption (W)
Social distancing + mask detection + facial temp	18	62	22.6
Social distancing + facial temp	23	–	18
Mask detection	–	68	13

three tasks, as depicted in Fig. 3.21A and B. Specifically, the temperature of Jetson Nano surpasses that of Jetson Xavier, triggering temperature alarms and potentially compromising Jetson Nano's performance. This discrepancy stems from Jetson Nano grappling with the increased workload,

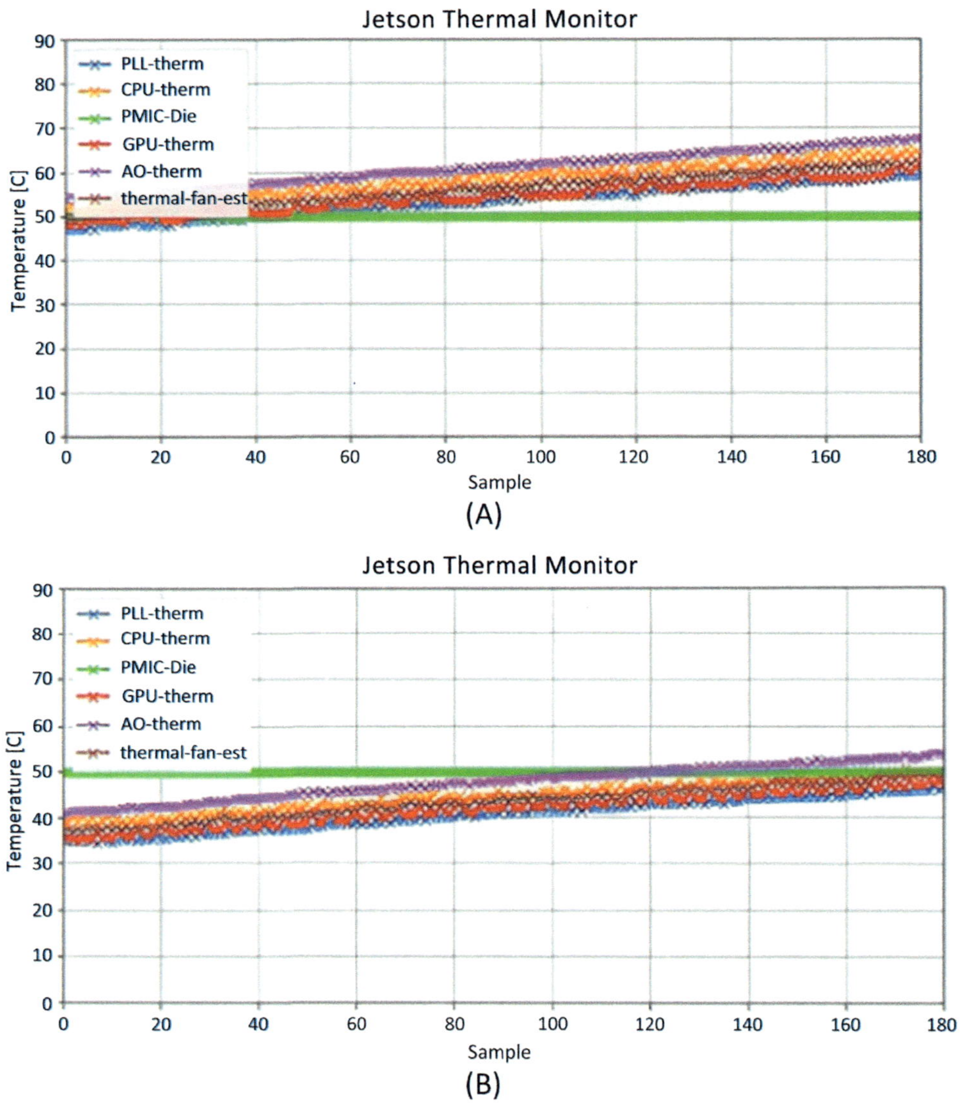

FIGURE 3.21

Temperature monitoring comparison between (A) Jetson Nano and (B) Jetson Xavier AGXReferences.

resulting in elevated heat generation and consequent performance degradation. Delving deeper into the performance metrics, Tables 3.6 and 3.7 provide insights into real-time detection rates across different algorithm scenarios and camera configurations for both Jetson Nano and Jetson Xavier AGX. For instance, the proposed method yields varying frame rates and power consumption levels based on the algorithm scenario and camera type.

Expanding the scope of comparison, this research contrasts the proposed approach with alternative methodologies, including those employing pretrained neural network models. Notably, the integrated techniques boast compact disk storage sizes for YOLOv4-tiny models dedicated to social distancing, facial temperature measurement, and mask detection tasks. This compactness, with file sizes ranging from 22.8 MB to 23 MB, facilitates execution on low-cost IoT devices, rendering them highly accessible.

In contrast, competing methodologies relying on pretrained CNN layers exhibit larger disk storage requirements, such as the ResNet50 model. Beyond storage considerations, these pretrained models struggle to deliver satisfactory real-time performance on the embedded platforms, hampering the efficacy of deep learning architecture in analyzing images and videos. The proposed approach for the three tasks prioritizes lightweight and efficient architecture tailored for resource-constrained environments. Leveraging techniques like model quantization, pruning, and knowledge distillation, these algorithms minimize the computational cost while preserving performance to the extent possible. Notably, NVIDIA boards (Jetson Nano and Jetson Xavier) with GPUs optimized for matrix operations and deep learning tasks. This hardware optimization significantly accelerates AI processing, while parallel computing techniques enable concurrent processing of multiple features across multiple cores or threads, enhancing overall efficiency and throughput. The comparative analysis underscores the nuanced performance dynamics and trade-offs inherent in deploying deep learning techniques for edge computing tasks. It underscores the importance of tailored algorithm design and hardware optimization to maximize performance and efficiency in resource-constrained environments.

References

AbdulRahman, B., & Zhu Z. (2020). Measuring and visualizing social distancing using deep learning and 3D computer vision. In *CEUR Workshop Proceedings*. Vol. 2884. United States: CEUR-WS. Available from http://ceur-ws.org/.

Ahamad, A.H., Zaini, N., & Latip, M.F. A. (2020). Person detection for social distancing and safety violation alert based on segmented ROI. In *Proceedings—10th IEEE International Conference on Control System, Computing and Engineering, ICCSCE* (pp. 113–18). Malaysia: Institute of Electrical and Electronics Engineers Inc. Available from http://ieeexplore.ieee.org/xpl/mostRecentIssue.jsp?punumber = 9203789, https://doi.org/10.1109/ICCSCE50387.2020.9204934.

Ahmed, I., Ahmad, M., & Jeon, G. (2021). Social distance monitoring framework using deep learning architecture to control infection transmission of COVID-19 pandemic. *Sustainable Cities and Society*, *69*, 102777. Available from https://doi.org/10.1016/j.scs.2021.102777.

Ahmed, I., Ahmad, M., Rodrigues, J. J. P. C., Jeon, G., & Din, S. (2021). A deep learning-based social distance monitoring framework for COVID-19. *Sustainable Cities and Society*, *65*, 102571. Available from https://doi.org/10.1016/j.scs.2020.102571.

Ess, A., Leibe, B., Schindler, K., & Van Gool, L. (2009). Moving obstacle detection in highly dynamic scenes. In *Proceedings—IEEE International Conference on Robotics and Automation* (pp. 56–63). Switzerland: Institute of Electrical and Electronics Engineers Inc. https://doi.org/10.1109/ROBOT.2009.5152884.

FLIR (2017). *Free Teledyne FLIR Thermal Dataset for Algorithm Training*. Teledyne FLIR No. 282.

Giuliano, R., Innocenti, E., Mazzenga, F., Vegni, A. M., & Vizzarri, A. (2022). Impersonal: An IoT-aided computer vision framework for social distancing for health safety. *IEEE Internet of Things Journal*, *9*(10),

7261–7272. Available from https://doi.org/10.1109/JIOT.2021.3097590, http://ieeexplore.ieee.org/servlet/opac?punumber = 6488907.

Gopal, B., & Ganesan, A. (2022). Real time deep learning framework to monitor social distancing using improved single shot detector based on overhead position. *Earth Science Informatics*, *15*(1), 585–602. Available from https://doi.org/10.1007/s12145-021-00758-4, http://www.springer.com/geosciences/computer + %26 + mathematical + applications/journal/12145.

Harvey, A., & LaPlace, J. (2019). Megapixels: Origins, ethics, and privacy implications of publicly available face recognition image datasets. *Megapixels*, *1*(2).

Hosang, J., Omran, M., Benenson, R., & Schiele, B. (2015). Taking a deeper look at pedestrians. In *Proceedings of the IEEE Computer Society Conference on Computer Vision and Pattern Recognition* (pp. 4073–82). Germany: IEEE Computer Society. Available fromhttps://doi.org/10.1109/CVPR.2015.7299034.

Hou, Y.C., Baharuddin, M.Z., Yussof, S., & Dzulkifly, S. (2020). Social distancing detection with deep learning model. In *8th International Conference on Information Technology and Multimedia, ICIMU 2020* (pp. 334–38). Malaysia: Institute of Electrical and Electronics Engineers Inc. Available from http://ieeexplore.ieee.org/xpl/mostRecentIssue.jsp?punumber = 9243083, https://doi.org/10.1109/ICIMU49871.2020.9243478.

Kholopov, I. S. (2017). Bird's eye view transformation technique in photogrammetric problem of object size measuring at low-altitude photography. *Advances in Engineering Research.*

Jiang, Z., Zhao, L., Li, S., & Jia, Y. (2020). Real-time object detection method based on improved YOLOv4-tiny. *arXiv*. Available from https://doi.org/10.48550/arXiv.2011.04244, https://arxiv.org.

Kahalé, N. (2020). On the economic impact of social distancing measures. *SSRN*. Available from https://doi.org/10.2139/ssrn.3578415, https://www.ssrn.com/index.cfm/en/.

Kajabad, E. N., & Ivanov, S. V. (2019). People detection and finding attractive areas by the use of movement detection analysis and deep learning approach. *Procedia Computer Science*, *156*, 327–337. Available from https://doi.org/10.1016/j.procs.2019.08.209.

Keniya, R., & Mehendale, N. (2020). Real-time social distancing detector using socialdistancingnet-19 deep learning network. *SSRN*. Available from https://doi.org/10.2139/ssrn.3669311, https://www.ssrn.com/index.cfm/en/.

Kim, S., Kwak, S., & Ko, B. C. (2019). Fast pedestrian detection in surveillance video based on soft target training of shallow random forest. *IEEE Access*, *7*, 12415–12426. Available from https://doi.org/10.1109/access.2019.2892425.

Kuzdeuov, A., Aubakirova, D., Koishigarina, D., & Varol, H. A. (2022). TFW: Annotated thermal faces in the wild dataset. *IEEE Transactions on Information Forensics and Security*, *17*, 2084–2094. Available from https://doi.org/10.1109/TIFS.2022.3177949.

Li, G., Gan, Y., Wu, H., Xiao, N., & Lin, L. (2019). Cross-modal attentional context learning for RGB-D object detection. *IEEE Transactions on Image Processing*, *28*(4), 1591–1601. Available from https://doi.org/10.1109/tip.2018.2878956.

Li, Y., Guo, K., Lu, Y., & Liu, L. (2021). Cropping and attention based approach for masked face recognition. *Applied Intelligence*, *51*(5), 3012–3025. Available from https://doi.org/10.1007/s10489-020-02100-9.

Liu, T., Du, S., Liang, C., Zhang, B., & Feng, R. (2021). A novel multi-sensor fusion based object detection and recognition algorithm for intelligent assisted driving. *IEEE Access*, *9*, 81564–81574. Available from https://doi.org/10.1109/access.2021.3083503.

Nagrath, P., Jain, R., Madan, A., Arora, R., Kataria, P., & Hemanth, J. (2021). SSDMNV2: A real time DNN-based face mask detection system using single shot multibox detector and MobileNetV2. *Sustainable Cities and Society*, *66*, 102692. Available from https://doi.org/10.1016/j.scs.2020.102692.

Pitts, W., & McCulloch, W. S. (1947). How we know universals the perception of auditory and visual forms? *The Bulletin of Mathematical Biophysics*, *9*(3), 127–147. Available from https://doi.org/10.1007/bf02478291.

Pouw, C. A. S., Toschi, F., van Schadewijk, F., Corbetta, A., & Chialvo, D. R. (2020). Monitoring physical distancing for crowd management: Real-time trajectory and group analysis. *PLoS One*, *15*(10), e0240963. Available from https://doi.org/10.1371/journal.pone.0240963.

Prem, K., Liu, Y., Russell, T. W., Kucharski, A. J., Eggo, R. M., Davies, N., Jit, M., Klepac, P., Flasche, S., Clifford, S., Pearson, C. A. B., Munday, J. D., Abbott, S., Gibbs, H., Rosello, A., Quilty, B. J., Jombart, T., Sun, F., Diamond, C., ... Hellewell, J. (2020). The effect of control strategies to reduce social mixing on outcomes of the COVID-19 epidemic in Wuhan, China: A modelling study. *The Lancet Public Health*, *5*(5), e261. Available from https://doi.org/10.1016/s2468-2667(20)30073-6.

Punn, N. S., & Agarwal, S. (2021). Automated diagnosis of COVID-19 with limited posteroanterior chest X-ray images using fine-tuned deep neural networks. *Applied Intelligence*, *51*(5), 2689–2702. Available from https://doi.org/10.1007/s10489-020-01900-3.

Punn, N. S., Sonbhadra, S. K., Agarwal, S., & Rai, G. (2020). Monitoring COVID-19 social distancing with person detection and tracking via fine-tuned YOLO v3 and Deepsort techniques. *ArXiv*. Available from https://doi.org/10.48550/arxiv.2005.01385, https://arxiv.org.

Robakowska, M., Tyranska-Fobke, A., Nowak, J., Slezak, D., Zuratynski, P., Robakowski, P., Nadolny, K., & Ładny, J. R. (2017). The use of drones during mass events. *Disaster and Emergency Medicine Journal*, *2* (3), 129–134. Available from https://doi.org/10.5603/demj.2017.0028.

Saponara, S., Elhanashi, A., & Gagliardi, A. (2021). Implementing a real-time, AI-based, people detection and social distancing measuring system for Covid-19. *Journal of Real-Time Image Processing*, *18*(6), 1937–1947. Available from https://doi.org/10.1007/s11554-021-01070-6, http://www.springer.com/sgw/cda/frontpage/0,11855,1-40392-70-112907049-0,00.html?changeHeader = true\.

Sener, F., & Ikizler-Cinbis, N. (2015). Two-person interaction recognition via spatial multiple instance embedding. *Journal of Visual Communication and Image Representation*, *32*, 63–73. Available from https://doi.org/10.1016/j.jvcir.2015.07.016.

Shubham, P. (2019). Real-time object detection using deep learning: A survey. *International Journal of Engineering Research and Technology*, *6*(10), 2395.

Sonbhadra, S. K., Agarwal, S., & Nagabhushan, P. (2020). Target specific mining of COVID-19 scholarly articles using one-class approach. *Chaos, Solitons & Fractals*, *140*, 110155. Available from https://doi.org/10.1016/j.chaos.2020.110155.

Teboulbi, S., Messaoud, S., Hajjaji, M. A., & Mtibaa, A. (2022). Real-time implementation of AI-based face mask detection and social distancing measuring system for COVID-19 prevention. *Scientific Programming*, *2021*, 1–21.

Tracking COVID-19: There's an App for That (2024). IEEE pulse. Available from https://www.embs.org/pulse/articles/tracking-covid-19-theres-an-app-for-that/.

Walk, S., Majer, N., Schindler, K., & Schiele, B. (2010). New features and insights for pedestrian detection. In *Proceedings of the IEEE Computer Society Conference on Computer Vision and Pattern Recognition* (pp. 1030–37). Germany. https://doi.org/10.1109/CVPR.2010.5540102.

Wang, X., Ng, H.W., & Liang, J. (2017). Lapped convolutional neural networks for embedded systems. In *IEEE Global Conference on Signal and Information Processing, Global SIP 2017—Proceedings* (pp. 1135–39). Canada: Institute of Electrical and Electronics Engineers Inc. https://doi.org/10.1109/GlobalSIP.2017.8309138.

Yadav, S. (2020). Deep learning based safe social distancing and face mask detection in public areas for COVID-19 safety guidelines adherence. *International Journal for Research in Applied Science and Engineering Technology*, *8*(7), 1368–1375. Available from https://doi.org/10.22214/ijraset.2020.30560.

Zhang, Q., Yang, M., Zheng, Q., & Zhang, X. (2017). Segmentation of hand gesture based on dark channel prior in projector-camera system. In *IEEE/CIC International Conference on Communications in China,*

ICCC 2017 (pp. 1–6). China: Institute of Electrical and Electronics Engineers Inc. https://doi.org/10.1109/ICCChina.2017.8330336.

Zhang, S., Bauckhage, C., & Cremers, A.B. 2014 Informed haar-like features improve pedestrian detection. In *Proceedings of the IEEE Computer Society Conference on Computer Vision and Pattern Recognition* (pp. 947–54). Germany: IEEE Computer Society. Available from https://doi.org/10.1109/CVPR.2014.126.

Zhao, Z.-Q., Zheng, P., Xu, S.-T., & Wu, X. (2019). Object detection with deep learning: A review. *IEEE Transactions on Neural Networks and Learning Systems*, *30*(11), 3212–3232. Available from https://doi.org/10.1109/tnnls.2018.2876865.

Zheng, Q., Yang, M., Tian, X., Jiang, N., & Wang, D. (2020). A full stage data augmentation method in deep convolutional neural network for natural image classification. *Discrete Dynamics in Nature and Society*, *2020*, 1–11. Available from https://doi.org/10.1155/2020/4706576.

Zheng, Q., Yang, M., Yang, J., Zhang, Q., & Zhang, X. (2018). Improvement of generalization ability of deep cnn via implicit regularization in two-stage training process. *IEEE Access*, *6*, 15844–15869. Available from https://doi.org/10.1109/access.2018.2810849.

Zheng, Q., Zhao, P., Zhang, D., & Wang, H. (2021). MR-DCAE: Manifold regularization-based deep convolutional autoencoder for unauthorized broadcasting identification. *International Journal of Intelligent Systems*, *36*(12), 7204–7238. Available from https://doi.org/10.1002/int.22586.

CHAPTER

Deep learning approaches for fingerprint image restoration

4

4.1 Background on biometric identification

In the modern era, biometric systems have become an integral part of various authentication technologies utilized across industrial and daily life scenarios. These applications range from electronic payment systems (Conti et al., 2009), access control mechanisms (Alshehri et al., 2019), the infrastructure of smart cities (Jin et al., 2020), to banking operations. Such systems, capable of recognizing individuals are crafted leveraging unique physical (e.g., fingerprints [Sang et al., 2018], retina [Figueiredo et al., 2016]) or behavioral traits (such as voice and walking patterns [Luo et al., 2020]). Among these, fingerprint recognition stands out as the preferred choice due to its distinctiveness, permanence, and enhanced security features. The critical aspects of fingerprint analysis hinge on minutiae, which represent the core elements of fingerprint patterns, as depicted in Fig. 4.1. The process of fingerprint registration is noted for its user-friendliness, propelling the widespread adoption of this technology in various embedded systems.

Advancements in chip fabrication and related technologies have led to the miniaturization of the fingerprint scanning area, subsequently shrinking the size of captured fingerprint images. This reduction often results in compromised image quality due to factors of physical damage to fingerprints such as (dirt, scars, blood, etc.) or issues with the scanning devices themselves (contaminated sensor surfaces, low resolution, and signal noise). The practical application of fingerprint recognition thus encounters obstacles such as degraded image quality, obscured patterns, nonlinear distortions, matching algorithm inefficiencies, and the absence of comprehensive public fingerprint databases (Ezhilmaran & Adhiyaman, 2017). Ensuring high computational performance (Dospinescu & Lîsîi, 2016; Shaheed et al., 2018) is crucial, especially when integrating fingerprint-based methods into mobile devices. Moreover, intricate overlapping fingerprint patterns further deteriorate image quality, significantly impairing the efficacy of fingerprint identification systems (Yoon & Jain, 2015). Specifically, low-quality fingerprint images can precipitate several critical issues:

- The emergence of numerous false feature points, profoundly impacting the accuracy of the recognition system.
- The omission of genuine feature points, which disrupts the structural integrity of the recognition framework.
- Variations in perspective and pose across different captures can lead to erroneous estimations of feature points' positions and trajectories, culminating in significant deviations from true outcomes.

These challenges underscore the necessity for ongoing research and development to enhance the reliability and performance of fingerprint-based biometric systems, ensuring that they can effectively meet the demands of various applications.

Deep Learning in Action: Image and Video Processing for Practical Use. DOI: https://doi.org/10.1016/B978-0-443-30078-3.00004-4

FIGURE 4.1

Anatomy of a fingerprint.

In the realm of fingerprint recognition, various models have been explored, each focusing on the distinct minutiae features present in fingerprint images (Cao & Jain, 2019; Wang et al., 2021). These minute details within small areas of the fingerprint are pivotal, yet they do not always aid the algorithm in accurately identifying matches. Consequently, enhancing the quality of low-resolution fingerprint images emerges as a critical challenge within the fingerprint recognition and matching process. In recent times, extensive research efforts have been devoted to the development of technologies aimed at fingerprint image enhancement or restoration. The methods for restoring fingerprint images can be broadly classified into two main categories: enhancements in the spatial domain and improvements in the frequency domain.

Enhancement techniques within the spatial domain encompass methods such as directional filtering (Park et al., 2004), Gabor filtering (Mei et al., 2014), and filtering based on partial differential equations (Tang et al., 2012). On the other hand, frequency domain enhancements primarily include techniques such as Fourier domain improvement (Chikkerur et al., 2005), short-time Fourier transform (STFT) enhancement (Ghafoor et al., 2016), wavelet transform enhancement (Bidishaw & Nalini, 2014), and discrete cosine transform enhancement (Liu et al., 2014), among others. Fingerprint images are characterized by their unique textural features. While median filters or low-pass filters are commonly employed in image processing to mitigate noise and distortion, their effectiveness is often suboptimal due to their uniform application across all pixels. The essence of Gabor filtering lies in accurately and swiftly capturing the ridge period; failing which, the resultant fingerprint image may appear devoid of details (Ding et al., 2017). An efficient fingerprint restoration algorithm, therefore leverages local frequency and ridge direction information to enhance the ridge and valley structures, thereby improving differentiation between these features. Currently, deep learning methodologies find extensive application across various domains, including image processing, due to their remarkable ability to adapt to and learn from vast amounts of data. These models excel at understanding the structural distribution and intrinsic properties of data. However, applying conventional deep learning frameworks directly to the task of image reconstruction, particularly for fingerprints which require capturing high levels of detail, poses significant challenges. Such models often struggle with generalization across diverse conditions and may not meet the real-time processing needs of practical applications. This underscores the importance of designing lightweight neural network models specifically tailored to efficiently capture fingerprint features while addressing the aforementioned limitations.

The realm of fingerprint recognition technology faces challenges in individual identification, primarily due to the nuances of quality and accuracy in the data input. The technique of fingerprint reconstruction has gained prominence within automated fingerprint systems for its consistent performance over time. Over recent decades, the evolution of algorithms and methodologies has been swift, marking significant advancements and diversification in commercial fingerprinting applications. A notable method (Cao & Jain, 2015) employs ridge information prediction, leveraging the orientation map of patterns to diminish the disparity between extracted data and its verifiable counterparts. Such strategies aim to forecast ridge data, disregarding the image quality of fingerprints. In an innovative approach, Chakraborty and Rao (2012) introduced a fingerprint image enhancement technique utilizing frequency domain adaptive filtering, where the process of histogram equalization is applied post-Gabor filtering to enhance the original image significantly.

The computational demands of the Gabor filter prompted Mei et al. (2014) to propose a simplification by decomposing the two-dimensional Gabor filter into a one-dimensional bandpass and a low-pass Gabor filter. Furthering this, Tang et al. (2012) refined the oriented second-order partial differential equation model for fingerprint image recovery. This enhancement connects broken ridges, fills image gaps, smoothens ridges, and eradicates minor imperfections. Chikkerur et al. (2005) suggested utilizing the curve area transform within the Fourier domain to design a filter that recovers fingerprint images from frequency images of curve areas. (Ghafoor et al., 2016) introduced a technique focusing on eliminating frequency distortion and enhancement via STFT analysis combined with local adaptive context filtering, validating their method's efficacy through extensive experimentation. Despite the inherent limitations in STFT's spatial and temporal resolution, solutions such as wavelet transforms offer promise. Additionally, the potential for performance gains through hyperparametric optimization of STFT parameters warrants further exploration. Addressing common issues such as cracks, scars, and low contrast in poor-quality fingerprint images, Bidishaw and Nalini (2014) developed an effective two-stage block enhancement framework that operates in both spatial and frequency domains. Liu et al. (2014) crafted a method for reconstructing fingerprint orientation fields using weighted discrete cosine transforms, while Ding et al. (2017) improved fingerprint imaging through classification dictionary learning and spectral diffusion. Despite the plethora of filter-based recovery schemes, achieving both high accuracy and efficiency remains a challenge. Cao and Jain (2019) introduced a method to compare potential fingerprints with reference databases, generating a shortlist of candidates through the alignment of unfolding branches. The development of an end-to-end deep learning model, FingerNet (Li et al., 2018), signifies a leap forward in fingerprinting enhancement. To further advance fingerprint matching technology, Manickam et al. (2019) recommended the use of Scale Invariant Feature Transform for fingerprint enhancement and matching. Cao et al. (2020) proposed a comprehensive latent fingerprint search system that integrates automatic region of interest cropping, latent image preprocessing, feature extraction, and comparison to yield a candidate list. This study showcases the advantages of convolutional neural network (CNN) autoencoders over traditional filtering methods, particularly in adapting to complex scenarios without prior knowledge, a testament to the power of deep learning methods fueled by extensive data and the inherent capability for self-organization during training phases.

This study presents a significant contribution and motivation through:

- The implementation and evaluation of two distinct autoencoder models, specifically sparse and CNN architectures, for the classification of fingerprints. This investigation aims to assess their effectiveness in extracting intricate contextual features that may enhance the accuracy of fingerprint recognition systems.
- A comprehensive series of experiments utilizing extensive fingerprint dataset volumes was undertaken. The objective was to delve into the performance nuances of the introduced autoencoders across various datasets, each exhibiting unique fingerprint traits.
- The facilitation of fingerprint recognition processes utilizing the aforementioned models, which are noted for their reduced computational demands when compared to conventional pretrained neural network frameworks.
- The assessment of newly proposed, efficient architectural designs, encompassing sparse and CNN models, in accurately duplicating complex fingerprint patterns. This comparison extends to existing methodologies, highlighting the proposed models' relative performance and efficiency.
- The development of compact deep learning structures, specifically designed to be lightweight in memory requirements—0.155 MB for the Sparse autoencoder (SAE) and 1.257 MB for the Convolutional autoencoder. Such specifications render these architectures particularly suitable for integration within low-cost embedded systems.
- Enhancements in image preprocessing techniques, including cropping and tiling, have been shown to significantly improve the training efficiency and Mean Squared Error (MSE) performance of SAEs. Notably, optimal MSE values were achieved with tile sizes of 10×10 pixels, underscoring the critical role of preprocessing in model optimization.

This chapter delves into the realm of lightweight deep learning architectures, with a specific focus on sparse and convolutional autoencoders, to adeptly replicate intricate features from fingerprint images. The core objective is to assess the efficacy of these models by juxtaposing them with other prevalent deep learning approaches and cutting-edge methods currently dominating the field. In doing so, the chapter meticulously outlines the construction of these autoencoders and explicates their goal, which is to learn functions that can accurately map input data derived from images to output data that represents those images faithfully.

Fingerprint recognition stands as a pivotal application within the broader spectrum of image recognition and security systems, owing to its critical role in identity verification and forensic investigations. Thus the ability of sparse and convolutional autoencoders to capture the detailed features of fingerprint images for the overall pattern and the minutiae such as ridges, bifurcations, and ending points—is of paramount importance. These lightweight architectures, by virtue of their design, promise to enhance the accuracy of feature replication and to offer computational efficiency, making them well-suited for real-world applications where resources may be limited. The chapter further explores the principle behind the functioning of these autoencoders. SAEs, for instance, are designed to learn efficient representations by introducing sparsity in the activations of the hidden layers, thereby encouraging the model to identify and utilize the most salient features of the data. On the other hand, convolutional autoencoders leverage the CNN architecture to efficiently handle spatial hierarchies in images, making them exceptionally good at recognizing patterns that are spatially invariant. By conducting a comparative analysis with other deep learning models and state-of-the-art methods, this research highlights the superior performance of sparse and convolutional autoencoders in terms of efficiency and accuracy and also their potential in revolutionizing the field of fingerprint recognition. This comparison serves a dual purpose: it underscores the capabilities of lightweight architectures in managing complex image data and contributes valuable insights to the ongoing discourse in image recognition and security technologies. Moreover, the chapter sheds light on the broader implications of employing such lightweight deep learning models in real-world scenarios, where the balance between accuracy and computational efficiency is critical. In environments where processing power and memory are constrained, the adoption of sparse and convolutional autoencoders can lead to significant improvements in the speed and accuracy of fingerprint feature replication, thereby enhancing the overall performance of security systems. This exploration into the application and effectiveness of lightweight deep learning architectures, particularly sparse and convolutional autoencoders, provides a comprehensive understanding of their operation and significant potential in improving the precision of fingerprint feature replication. This research contributes to the field of deep learning and image recognition and paves the way for future advancements in security systems, where these models can be applied to ensure more reliable and efficient identity verification processes.

4.1.1 Deep learning related work for fingerprint

In the realm of biometric identification, the accuracy of fingerprint recognition holds paramount importance. Wang et al. (2017) made significant strides in this area by introducing an improved fingerprint recognition method. Their approach leverages the capabilities of deep CNNs enhanced with point feature analysis. The effectiveness of this method was clearly demonstrated through comparative analysis, showcasing its superiority over traditional methods such as kernel principal component analysis and the k-nearest neighbor algorithm. This breakthrough addresses several critical challenges in fingerprint recognition, including rotation, scaling, and corruption, by presenting a robust method that excels in speed and resistance to abnormal degradation.

Further contributions to this field include the development of a deep learning-based unique affine Fourier moment matching method (Su et al., 2017). This innovative approach focuses on integrating scores from three distinct fingerprint features to mitigate local and global linear biases effectively. Pandya et al. (2018) introduced a new architectural framework for deep learning in fingerprint recognition, achieving an impressive 98.21% classification accuracy with minimal loss. Similarly, Li (2021) provided empirical evidence supporting the enhanced efficiency of the CNN-based recognition method, which demonstrated a reduction in both the number of iterations during training and the overall training loss. This method notably reduced false detection and rejection rates when identifying unknown fingerprints, highlighting the advanced capability of deep CNNs in learning distinguishing features directly from original fingerprint images without the need for explicit feature extraction.

The utility of deep CNNs extends beyond feature extraction to improving identification efficiency through the reduction of false positives, as evidenced by the work of Zia et al. (2019). Their research employed the uncertainty principles of a Bayesian model, showcasing an innovative approach to enhancing fingerprint identification. The integration of deep CNN models with batch normalization technology (Jeon & Rhee, 2017) marked a significant advancement in the quality improvement processes for fingerprint images. Peralta et al. (2018) proposed a hybrid method that combines image processing techniques with a CNN classifier, eliminating the necessity for explicit feature extraction and thereby streamlining the identification process. An approach focusing on local fingerprint recognition was developed (Zeng et al., 2019), which, by refining the CNN structure and optimizing two loss functions, significantly improved fingerprint image recognition performance.

Despite the remarkable advancements brought forth by deep learning in pattern recognition and fingerprint identification, several challenges remain. A critical concern is the generalization capability of models to effectively interpret and classify scenes or patterns not encountered during training (Zheng, Zhao, et al., 2021). Moreover, the efficient utilization of small and multimodal data sets (Mohammed Ali & Farhan, 2020; Zheng, Tian, et al., 2021) presents an ongoing obstacle. Additionally, the process of data transmission and its impact on the integrity and quality of data necessitates further investigation. These challenges highlight the need for continued research and development in deep learning applications for fingerprint recognition, aiming to enhance accuracy, efficiency, and adaptability in biometric identification technologies. The contributions of researchers in this field are instrumental in pushing the boundaries of what is possible, setting new standards for security and identification methodologies.

4.2 Feature extraction

The advent of deep learning technologies has indeed marked a watershed moment in the field of data analysis and interpretation, particularly through the lens of automatic feature extraction. This leap in technology offers a robust framework for handling and analyzing the colossal volumes of data that define the digital age. At the heart of this, revolution is the development of sophisticated methods designed to distill the rich information contained within images into a more digestible, lower-dimensional form. This process is meticulously engineered to preserve the integrity and the nuanced details of the original data, ensuring that the essence of the information is not lost in translation.

Deep learning's core strength lies in its unparalleled ability to extract meaningful features from complex datasets. This capability is merely about reducing data volume and understanding and interpreting the data in fundamentally new ways. By leveraging layers of artificial neural networks, deep learning algorithms learn to identify and prioritize the most informative features of the data without explicit programming. This automatic feature extraction is a radical departure from traditional methods, where manual feature selection often led to oversight and bias, limiting the scope and accuracy of data analysis. This paradigm shift has propelled significant achievements across various domains, particularly in the field of computer vision. Computer vision aims to mimic the human visual system, enabling machines to see, interpret, and understand the visual world. Deep learning has been instrumental in advancing this field, transforming theoretical possibilities into practical applications. One of the most compelling applications of deep learning within computer vision is facial recognition technology. Facial recognition represents a complex challenge that involves the accurate identification and analysis of facial features from images. This task requires distinguishing between different faces recognizing the same face under various conditions such as changes in lighting, expression, and angle.

Deep learning algorithms approach this challenge by learning a rich representation of facial features. Through training on vast datasets of faces, these algorithms learn to identify and encode distinctive features, such as the distance between the eyes, the shape of the jawline, and the contour of the cheekbones. This encoding process generates a unique digital "signature" for each face, which can then be used to match or recognize faces across different images. The success of deep learning in facial recognition is evident in its widespread adoption across numerous sectors. In security, facial recognition systems are deployed to enhance surveillance and access control. In mobile technology, they provide convenient and secure authentication methods. Furthermore, facial recognition has significant implications for personalized advertising and social media, offering new ways to engage with users. However, the proliferation of facial recognition technology also raises important ethical and privacy concerns. The ability to identify and track individuals without their consent poses a significant challenge to personal privacy. As such, the deployment of this technology must be balanced with stringent ethical guidelines and privacy safeguards to ensure that the benefits do not come at the expense of fundamental rights. The work of Sun et al. (2014) highlights a sophisticated approach that leverages CNNs for this purpose. By applying deep learning techniques to CNNs, it is possible to reduce the dimensionality of specific regions within input images, thus extracting a set of deep learning identifiers. These identifiers can then be amalgamated to enhance the facial recognition process. This methodology underscores the flexibility of deep learning models, which can be employed in both supervised and unsupervised manners to perform end-to-end regression and classification tasks. Deep learning's capability extends beyond the realm of facial recognition. It serves as a foundational technology for feature extraction across various applications. By leveraging deep learning models, it becomes feasible to efficiently process complex input data. This efficiency is crucial, as it eliminates the need for the labor-intensive and often low-quality feature extraction methods previously employed. Through the integration of deep learning with traditional machine learning techniques, a synergistic effect is achieved, allowing for the sophisticated analysis of input data. This combination harnesses the strengths of both methodologies: the intuitive feature recognition and extraction capabilities of deep learning, coupled with the nuanced data processing and analysis provided by machine learning. The significance of recent advancements in computer vision technology extends far beyond the surface, heralding a new era in the way we process, analyze, and interpret visual information. These innovations have carved out fresh avenues for exploration and development in the field, allowing for the creation of tools that are more precise vastly more reliable and efficient than ever before. One of the most groundbreaking aspects of these advancements is the ability to automatically compress data within images to a lower dimension while preserving the essence of the information they contain. This process, often referred to as dimensionality reduction, is crucial because it tackles one of the most persistent challenges in computer vision and data analysis: managing the sheer volume of data contained in images without losing important information.

In practical terms, dimensionality reduction enables computers and algorithms to focus on the most relevant features of an image, discarding redundant or unnecessary information. This efficiency is not just about saving storage space; it's about enhancing the speed at which images can be processed and analyzed. Faster processing times mean that applications relying on computer vision can operate more smoothly and swiftly, which is essential for real-time applications such as autonomous driving systems, surveillance, and interactive gaming. Moreover, the improved accuracy and reliability of these tools have profound implications for various sectors. In healthcare, for example, enhanced image analysis can aid in early diagnosis and more accurate monitoring of diseases, potentially saving lives. In environmental monitoring, it can help in tracking changes in ecosystems, deforestation, and urban expansion with greater precision, contributing to more effective conservation efforts. The efficiency gained through these technological advancements also means that devices with limited processing power, such as smartphones and small robots, can now perform complex visual tasks they couldn't handle before. This democratization of technology paves the way for innovative applications across different fields, making advanced computer vision capabilities accessible to a broader audience. Furthermore, the ability to analyze visual data more effectively opens up new research opportunities. Scientists and researchers can uncover patterns and insights that were previously obscured by the sheer volume and complexity of the data. This can accelerate advancements in various scientific fields, from astrophysics to biology, by enabling more comprehensive and detailed studies than were previously possible. The recent advancements in computer vision represent a significant leap forward in our ability to handle and interpret visual information. By making data analysis processes more accurate, reliable, and efficient, these innovations enhance the capabilities of existing applications and unlock the potential for new discoveries and technologies that could transform our world. As we continue to explore and expand the boundaries of what computer vision can achieve, the implications of these advancements are likely to reverberate across industries and disciplines for years to come.

4.3 Fingerprint dataset

The exploration of fingerprint image datasets involves a comprehensive analysis through the lens of autoencoder technology. These datasets, originating from diverse sources provide a rich ground for evaluating the performance of autoencoders in reproducing fingerprint images with high fidelity. To uphold the highest standards of privacy and confidentiality, all fingerprint images included in these datasets were thoroughly anonymized. This step ensured that there was no possibility of tracing back any fingerprint to its original owner, thus safeguarding individual identities. The anonymization process is crucial, considering the sensitive nature of biometric data and the ethical implications of its handling. The datasets were compiled using a variety of collection methods, which included the use of different scanners and sensors, as well as traditional ink-based techniques. This diversity in collection methods contributed to the richness and variability of the datasets, making them ideal for a robust evaluation of autoencoder performance. Each method brought its own set of challenges and peculiarities, from the resolution and clarity of the captured images to the nuances of patterns captured by different technologies. Further detailing the unique aspects of each dataset, it becomes evident that they encompass a wide range of complexities. Some datasets might feature high-resolution images captured under controlled conditions, offering clear and detailed fingerprint patterns. Others could include lower-quality images, perhaps due to the limitations of the capturing technology or conditions, presenting additional challenges in accurately reproducing the intricate details of fingerprint ridges and valleys. By dissecting these datasets and their inherent characteristics, the study aims to assess the adaptability and efficiency of autoencoders across varying degrees of data quality and complexity. This analysis contributes to the understanding of autoencoder technology in the specific context of fingerprint image reproduction also sets the stage for further innovations in biometric data processing and privacy-preserving methodologies.

4.3.1 Dataset I

This dataset consists of 250 images, each measuring 200 × 200 pixels. These images were acquired through the utilization of the Digital Persona Model (4500) Reader, a device specifically designed for fingerprint capture. The subjects contributing to this dataset include both students and faculty staff from Yeshwantrao Chavan College of Engineering (YCCE) College, as referenced in source number Fingerprint Color Image Database.v1 (2019).

This particular dataset serves as a valuable resource for a variety of research purposes, including but not limited to biometric authentication studies, pattern recognition, and security system enhancements. The use of the Digital Persona Model (4500) Reader ensures high-quality image capture, crucial for detailed analysis and accurate recognition in subsequent applications. The inclusion of fingerprints from a diverse group of individuals, such as students and faculty staff, enriches the dataset, providing a wide range of fingerprint patterns. This diversity is instrumental in developing more robust and inclusive biometric systems that can cater to a broader user base.

Furthermore, the specificity of the image size (200 × 200 pixels) is noteworthy, as it provides a balance between ensuring sufficient detail for analysis and maintaining manageable file sizes for processing. This aspect is particularly important when dealing with large datasets, as it impacts the efficiency of data handling and processing algorithms. The contribution of such a dataset by YCCE College highlights the collaborative effort between academic institutions and technological research, fostering advancements in the field of biometrics. It also underscores the importance of real-world data in enhancing the reliability and applicability of theoretical research findings. Through careful compilation and ethical sourcing, the dataset adheres to the required scientific standards contributes significantly to the ongoing developments in digital identity verification methods.

4.3.2 Dataset II

The dataset under discussion contains a total of 250 images, each having dimensions of 153 × 185 pixels. The collection process for these images involved the use of a specific type of fingerprint device, known as the Digital Persona Model (4500) Reader. This equipment was instrumental in capturing the fingerprint images from a variety of individuals, all of whom were associated with the YCCE College. The significance of this dataset lies in its homogeneous nature regarding the method of collection and the technology used, ensuring consistency across all the images. In the realm of biometric analysis, the quality and consistency of data play a crucial role in the accuracy of the results obtained. By utilizing a single type of fingerprint reader, the dataset achieves a level of uniformity that is essential for conducting reliable research. This approach mitigates the potential variability that could arise from using different devices or methodologies, allowing for a more focused analysis of the fingerprints themselves, rather than the nuances of varying collection techniques.

Furthermore, the choice of the Digital Persona Model (4500) Reader for this task underscores the importance of employing industry-standard technology in the collection of biometric data. Such devices are designed to capture high-resolution images that are critical for detailed analysis, ensuring that the minutiae of each fingerprint are clearly visible and can be accurately assessed. The dataset's association with YCCE College also adds an academic dimension to the research, providing a valuable resource for students and faculty members engaged in biometric studies. The involvement of a specific educational institution in the dataset's creation facilitates a practical learning experience and contributes to the body of knowledge within the academic community regarding biometric data collection and analysis (Fingerprint Grayscale Image Database v2, 2019).

4.3.3 Dataset III

This dataset encompasses a comprehensive collection obtained from the Sokoto Coventry Fingerprint Dataset (SOCOFing) database, specifically tailored for research within scientific domains. This extensive dataset features a total of 6000 fingerprint records sourced from 600 African individuals. It encapsulates detailed attributes and features that cover a wide spectrum, including distinctions across genders, specific hand, and finger identifications, alongside synthetically altered versions. These modifications are meticulously crafted across three distinct alteration intensities – namely- central rotation, obliteration, and z-cut – employing the innovative STRANGE framework.

The STRANGE Toolbox emerges as a groundbreaking methodology in the realm of fingerprint imaging, facilitating the creation of realistic synthetic alterations. To achieve this, the toolbox operates across three different parameter settings labeled as simple, medium, and advanced, thereby ensuring a wide range of modification intensities. These alterations are executed on high-resolution images exceeding 500 dots per inch (dbi), with each image maintaining a resolution of 96×103 pixels. The acquisition process of these fingerprints involved the use of a high-precision scanner, specifically the Hamster Plus (HSDU03PTM), ensuring the capture of high-quality fingerprint images. The dataset is methodically organized into three categories based on the level of difficulty associated with the changes: mild, moderate, and severe. This categorization aids in the nuanced study of fingerprints under varying conditions of alteration, providing a rich resource for in-depth analysis in biometric research and related scientific investigations. Through this structured and detailed compilation, Dataset III serves as a pivotal tool for researchers aiming to explore and understand the complexities and variabilities inherent in fingerprint biometrics (Shehu et al., 2018).

4.3.4 Dataset IV

The dataset under examination encompasses a total of 320 images, each varying in size. These images originate from the Competitive Fingerprint Verification Database, known as FVC2004. Within FVC2004, there exist four distinct databases labeled DB1, DB2, DB3, and DB4. The classification of these databases is based on the specific type of scanner utilized for capturing the fingerprints as well as the dimensions of the images. A notable characteristic of this dataset is its comparatively lower quality in terms of fingerprint pattern features when juxtaposed against other datasets. Despite this, the FVC2004 dataset is heralded as the pinnacle of sophistication among databases of its kind. This acclaim is attributed to the dataset's incorporation of cluttered and complex contextual features within the fingerprint images, setting a high standard for complexity and detail in such databases.

The creation of comprehensive datasets, particularly those comprising fingerprint images is fundamental to advancing the capabilities of deep learning models in pattern recognition tasks. These tasks are pivotal in various applications, including security systems, identity verification, and access control mechanisms. The essence of using fingerprints lies in their uniqueness to every individual, making them an ideal candidate for developing highly secure and reliable biometric authentication systems. The primary goal behind assembling such image datasets is to provide a rich resource that helps in training, testing, and evaluating the performance of algorithms designed to recognize and differentiate between intricate patterns unique to each fingerprint.

In the context of these endeavors, Fig. 4.2 illustrates fingerprint images harvested from different databases. Each image in this figure is carefully selected to represent the wide array of patterns, ridges, and whorls that are characteristic of human fingerprints. This diversity underlines the complexity of the task at hand and illuminates the myriad challenges that researchers and developers face when attempting to design algorithms that are capable of accurately interpreting such patterns. Deep learning models, at their core, are adept at identifying and learning from patterns in data. By exposing these models to a vast and varied collection of fingerprint images, they gradually learn to discern the subtle differences and similarities between them. This learning process is crucial for the development of algorithms that can reliably authenticate individuals based on their fingerprints. It involves a continuous cycle of training, where the model is fed data, and evaluation, where its ability to accurately identify or verify fingerprints is tested. The significance of having access to extensive and diverse datasets cannot be overstated. These datasets serve as the foundation for training deep learning models provide the benchmark for evaluating their performance. By comparing the model's predictions against known outcomes within the dataset, researchers can gauge the model's accuracy, efficiency, and reliability. This process is instrumental in identifying areas where the

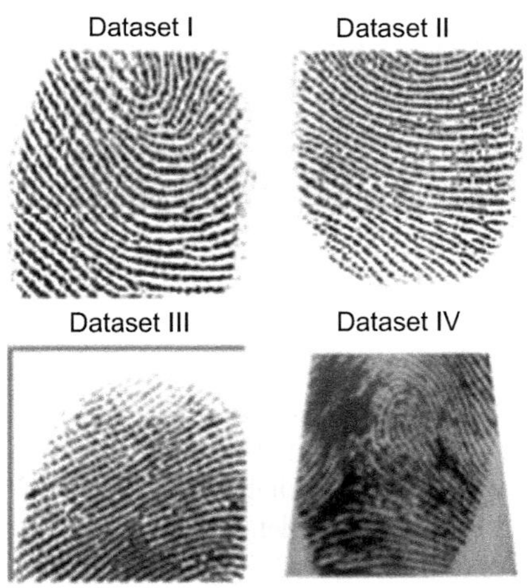

FIGURE 4.2

Samples for fingerprint images from four datasets.

model excels, as well as those requiring further refinement. Furthermore, the advancement of biometric authentication technology hinges on the continuous improvement of these pattern recognition systems. As the algorithms become more sophisticated, the potential applications of biometric authentication expand, offering more secure and convenient solutions for identity verification. This enhances security measures across various domains and paves the way for innovative applications of biometric technology in everyday life. The development and dissemination of fingerprint image datasets are critical for the progress of deep learning research in pattern recognition. It illustrates the diversity and complexity of fingerprints, underscoring the challenges involved in developing algorithms capable of accurate and efficient pattern recognition. Through diligent research, development, and evaluation, the field of biometric authentication continues to advance, driven by the goal of creating more secure, reliable, and user-friendly systems for identity verification (Maio et al., 2004).

4.4 Sparse autoencoder for image reconstruction

This study delves into the innovative use of a SAE algorithm specifically tailored for the challenging task of reconstructing fingerprint images. SAEs belong to an advanced class of deep learning algorithms designed with the primary goal of faithfully reproducing their input data at their output. This unique characteristic of SAEs, combined with their inherent ability to extract and leverage the most critical features of the input data, renders them particularly effective for complex applications like image reconstruction. The architecture of the SAE deployed in this research has been thoughtfully designed to tackle the nuanced task of fingerprint image reconstruction. This study embarks on a comprehensive exploration, employing four meticulously curated datasets comprised of fingerprint images. Each dataset is subjected to a rigorous preprocessing regimen aimed at ensuring the images are in an optimal state for processing by the model. This preprocessing stage is pivotal, as it significantly enhances the model's training efficiency and the fidelity of the reconstructed images. Key steps in the preprocessing phase include normalization and noise reduction. Normalization involves scaling the pixel values of the images to a common range, which facilitates faster and more stable convergence of the deep learning model during training. Noise reduction, on the other hand, seeks to eliminate irrelevant or superfluous information that could potentially detract from the model's ability to learn the essential patterns within the fingerprints. These preprocessing techniques are critical for refining the input data, thereby setting the stage for a successful reconstruction process. The core of this study provides an in-depth analysis of the SAE's architecture, shedding light on the rationale behind specific design decisions made to capture the intricate details inherent in fingerprint images. This includes the selection of an appropriate number of layers, the choice of activation functions, and the implementation of sparsity constraints. These architectural elements are crucial for ensuring that the model learns the general shape and patterns of the fingerprints accurately captures the fine details that are essential for individual identification. Moreover, the preprocessing techniques applied to the fingerprint images prior to model training are discussed in greater detail. This section elucidates how normalization and noise reduction contribute to enhancing the model's performance. By improving the quality of the input data, these preprocessing steps help in mitigating the challenges associated with learning from complex and highly variable images such as fingerprints. This study represents a significant step forward in the field of image reconstruction, demonstrating the potential of SAEs to tackle the intricate task of fingerprint reconstruction. Through a combination of careful architectural design and strategic preprocessing of the input data, this research showcases the effectiveness of SAEs in capturing the nuanced details of fingerprint images, thereby offering promising avenues for further advancements in biometric identification and security technologies.

The experimental setup is thoroughly described, outlining the procedures followed to evaluate the performance of the SAE. This includes the criteria for selecting the datasets, the training process, and the metrics used to assess the quality of the reconstructed images. Results from these experiments are presented and analyzed, offering a comprehensive view of the model's effectiveness in reproducing fingerprint images with high fidelity.

4.4.1 Sparse autoencoder model

The SAE operates as an unsupervised deep learning framework, distinguished by its incorporation of individual hidden layers, as noted in the referenced study Kang et al. (2017). Characterized by a structure that integrates a sparsity penalty into its training regimen, SAE stands out for its simplicity in construction compared to other autoencoder models. This model is specifically designed with a higher number of hidden nodes compared to its input nodes, a configuration aimed at enhancing the extraction of significant features from the provided data. One of the pivotal aspects of the SAE is the implementation of a sparsity constraint within its hidden layers. This approach is deliberately chosen to prevent the model's output layers from merely replicating the input information, thus ensuring that the learning process focuses on meaningful data representation. The model's loss function incorporates a penalty for the activation of hidden layers, specifically targeting scenarios where only a limited number of nodes are activated in response to a single input pattern. This design choice facilitates the model's ability to encode relevant features from unlabeled input data effectively. Fig. 4.3 illustrates the structure of SAE.

Through the utilization of hidden layers, the SAE is adept at approximating the minimum mean square error, thereby achieving an optimal expression of features extracted from the data. The architecture sets a minimal threshold for the activation value in the hidden layers to adhere to the sparsity constraint, denoted by the parameter p. A penalty function is subsequently applied to discourage any significant deviation from the preset value of p, ensuring adherence to the model's sparsity requirements.

The Kullback-Leibler divergence serves as the penalty's cost function as shown in Eq. (4.1), a mathematical formulation that quantifies the difference between the actual distribution of activated nodes and the desired sparse distribution. This approach underlines the model's capacity to learn from unlabeled data to refine its feature representation capabilities, making it a valuable tool in the field of deep learning for tasks that require efficient and effective data interpretation.

$$KL(\rho \| l\rho j) = \rho \ln \underbrace{\rho}_{m*} + (1-\rho) \ln \frac{1-\varrho}{1-ei} \tag{4.1}$$

When pj matches the parameter p, the Kullback-Leibler value is zero. If pj differs from p, the Kullback-Leibler value grows as the difference increases.

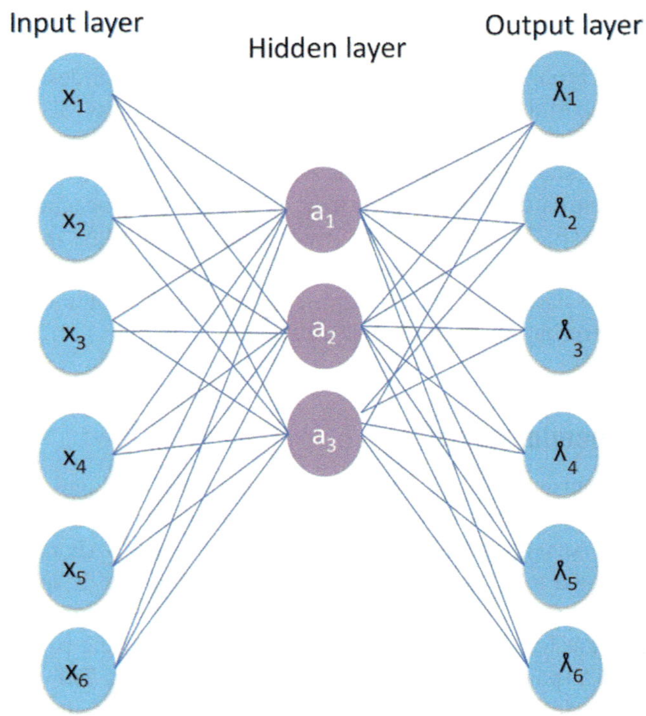

FIGURE 4.3

Structure of the sparse autoencoder.

4.4.2 Preprocessing the image

The initiation of the experiments focused on utilizing a SAE paired with preprocessing activities. For each dataset involved, images were allocated, with 80% designated for training and the remaining 20% for testing purposes. This division was applied across both the training and test data for every dataset under consideration. Preprocessing involved standardizing the dimension of each image to a uniform size of 100 × 100 pixels (both width and height). Additionally, any extraneous white space surrounding fingerprint images was meticulously removed. This step was crucial for ensuring a consistent number of sections when proceeding with the cropping of fingerprint images. To further refine the analysis of SAE models in understanding structural aspects, a variety of filters were applied to the images.

The transformation of images to grayscale was another pivotal step, where the distinctive features of fingerprints were delineated in black against a white background. The objective behind this conversion was to generate a binary representation of the images, facilitating more effective feature extraction. This approach significantly reduces distortion and variability within the fingerprint images. It aids in the extraction of pertinent data while also introducing specific artifacts that could potentially influence the preprocessing phase. Given the model's requirements for processing small images, a meticulous cropping process was undertaken. This involved segmenting each image into smaller tiles before

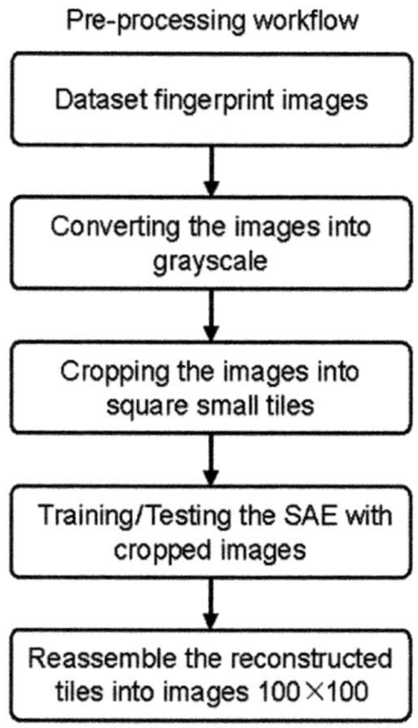

FIGURE 4.4

The preprocessing workflow to prepare the fingerprint images to be trained and tested with the sparse autoencoder.

reassembling them into a reconstructed image. The cropping was executed on individual images, generating tiles of various dimensions (50×50, 25×25, 20×20, and 10×10 pixels). This procedure was aimed at evaluating the SAE architecture under multiple scenarios, thereby enriching the understanding and application of this model. The preprocessing task was facilitated by the use of an image processing toolbox, which played a crucial role in preparing the fingerprint images for both training and testing phases within the SAE framework. The methodology adopted for image preprocessing, including resizing, whitespace elimination, grayscale conversion, and cropping, was instrumental in standardizing the input data. This standardization is essential for minimizing inconsistencies and ensuring that the SAE model operates under optimal conditions for feature extraction and analysis. By dividing the images into smaller segments, the experiment sought to enhance the model's ability to learn from and reconstruct the fingerprint images effectively. This approach allows for a comprehensive exploration of the SAE's capabilities paves the way for a deeper understanding of its application in processing and analyzing fingerprint data. The preprocessing workflow, as depicted in the designated figure within the study, outlines the systematic process undertaken to prepare the images, highlighting the critical steps and considerations involved in the preprocessing stage. Fig. 4.4 illustrates the preprocessing workflow for fingerprint images.

4.4.3 Algorithm description

In the process of initiating the training phase for a SAE, the function designated as "trainAutoencoder" is employed, targeting the input dataset labeled "X" alongside the component known as Hidden Layers. The initialization phase involves setting up the weight matrix, denoted as 'W', and the base vector, represented by 'h', in conjunction with the hidden layers. The introduction of a sparsity regularizer into the cost function serves a dual purpose: it aligns with prior expectations regarding the structure of input variables and fosters a condition of sparsity within the network. This is achieved by incorporating sparsity regularization into the model that is subject to optimization. To address potential issues of overfitting within the proposed architectural framework, L2 regularization is integrated. This form of regularization acts as a countermeasure to prevent the model from fitting too closely to the training data, thereby enhancing its generalizability to new, unseen data. Fig. 4.5 shows the proposed algorithm methodology for recreating fingerprint images by SAE.

The methodology underpinning the proposed algorithm, particularly in the context of reconstructing fingerprint images through the use of a SAE, is visually depicted in Fig. 4.6. This representation offers a schematic overview of the steps and components involved in the algorithm's operation, providing insights into how the SAE is applied to the task of image reconstruction. The essence of employing a SAE lies in its ability to learn significant features from the input data in an unsupervised manner. By enforcing sparsity, the network is encouraged to discover a small number of active neurons for each input sample, thereby capturing the most salient characteristics of the data. The weight matrix 'W' plays a critical role in this process, as it determines the strength of connections between neurons in the network. The base vector 'h', on the other hand, is pivotal in adjusting the activation threshold of neurons, thereby influencing the overall sparsity of the network.

Sparsity regularization plays a crucial role in the field of deep learning, especially in the context of autoencoders, which are types of artificial neural networks designed for tasks such as image reconstruction. When sparsity regularization is added to the cost function of these networks, it fundamentally influences how the network operates. The core idea behind this technique is to apply a constraint to the network that limits the number of neurons that can be active at any one time. This concept is not without reason. It is based on the observation that many forms of data in the real world, including images like fingerprints, can be described, or represented using a relatively small

Algorithm 1 Proposed methodology for sparse autoencoder

Input:

Train set x

Process:

```
Start
Initialize h,g,w, w', b,b'.
Obtain the reconstruction error function E.
Add sparsity regularizer to the cost function
Add L2 regularization to the cost function
Train networks.
End.
```

Output:

Reconstructed fingerprint images x'.

FIGURE 4.5

The proposed algorithm methodology for recreating fingerprint images by sparse autoencoder.

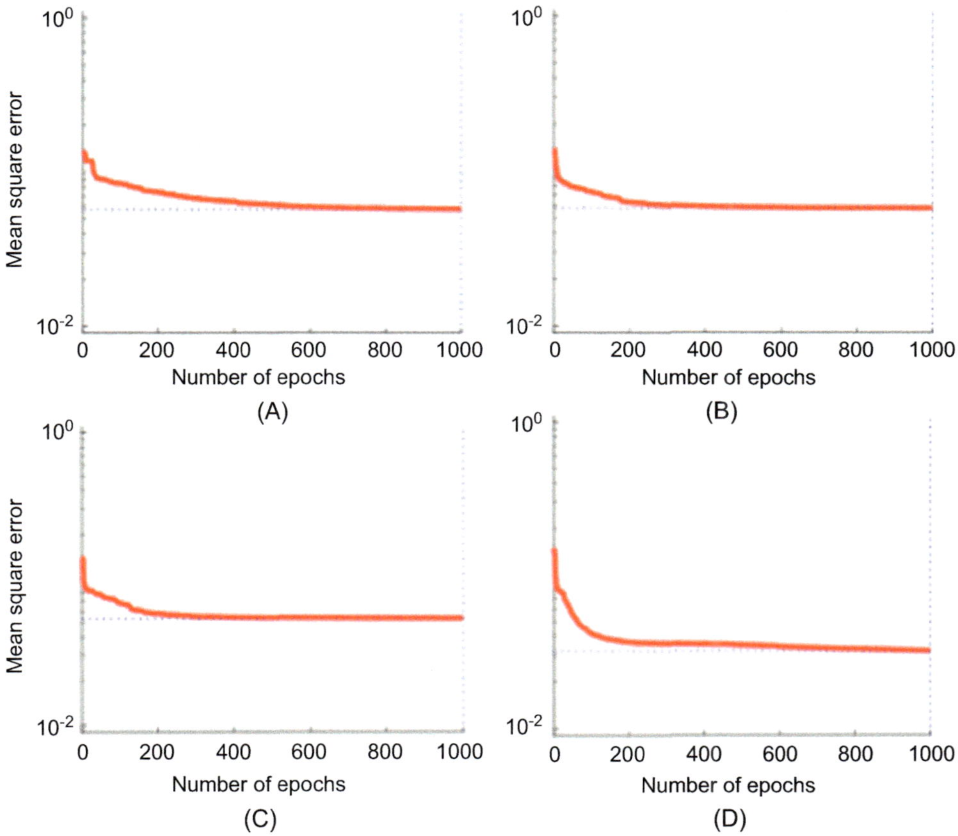

FIGURE 4.6

Training performance for the sparse autoencoder with different sizes for cropped tiles of fingerprint images: (A) Tile size (50 × 50), (B) Tile size (25 × 25), (C) Tile size (20 × 20), and (D) Tile size (10 × 10).

number of features compared to the total number of possible features. For instance, in a fingerprint image, only certain patterns or lines are crucial for identifying an individual, while the rest of the image may not carry unique information. Incorporating sparsity into the network through regularization forces the network to identify and focus on these critical features. As a result, a SAE, which is a specific type of autoencoder that includes sparsity regularization, is optimized to find and use these essential patterns in the data. The sparse representation it learns is then used to reconstruct the input image with a focus on these key features. This approach improves the efficiency of the network by reducing the number of active neurons, thereby saving computational resources, and enhances the network's ability to capture and represent the underlying structure of the data more effectively. Through the process of learning to identify and reconstruct these essential features from sparse representations, the SAE becomes a powerful tool for tasks like image reconstruction, achieving high performance by focusing on the most meaningful aspects of the data. The challenge of overfitting is a common hurdle in the development of machine learning models, particularly in complex architectures such as autoencoders. Overfitting occurs when a model learns the training data too well, capturing noise and anomalies as if they were significant features. This results in poor performance on new, unseen data. The integration of L2 regularization into the model's architecture is a strategic response to this challenge. L2 regularization works by adding a penalty term to the cost function, which is proportional to the square of the magnitude of the model's weights. This penalty encourages the model to maintain smaller weights, leading to a simpler and more generalizable model.

The training of a SAE involves a series of meticulously designed steps, starting from the initialization of the model's parameters to the integration of specific regularization techniques aimed at promoting sparsity and preventing overfitting. The algorithm's methodology, particularly in the context of fingerprint image reconstruction, illustrates the application of these principles in a practical setting. By adhering to these strategies, the SAE is poised to learn efficient representations of the input data, facilitating the accurate reconstruction of fingerprint images. This approach highlights the potential of SAEs in image processing tasks and underscores the importance of regularization techniques in enhancing the performance and reliability of machine learning models.

4.4.4 Experiment setup

The SAE architecture is intricately designed to comprise three main components: an input layer known as the encoder, an output layer referred to as the decoder, and the latent representation which houses the hidden units. In our specific configuration, we have decided to equip the latent representation with a total of 50 neurons. This decision was informed by the need to achieve a balance between complexity and performance, allowing the model to capture essential features without becoming overly intricate. For this particular architecture, careful consideration was given to the selection of transfer functions for both the encoder and decoder components, as these functions play a pivotal role in the transformation of data through the network. Specifically, for the encoder, we opted for the linear Satlin function. The choice of Satlin, a linear rectifier, was motivated by its ability to introduce nonlinearity in a controlled manner, enabling the encoder to efficiently compress input data into a lower-dimensional space. On the other hand, for the decoder part of the architecture, the linear function Purlin was selected. Purlin, being linear, is particularly suited for the reconstruction phase, where the goal is to accurately reconstruct the original input from the compressed data representation with minimal loss. In our pursuit of optimizing the SAE's performance, a comprehensive search was conducted to identify the best hyperparameters for the training phase. The culmination of this meticulous process is presented in Table 4.1, where we detail the hyperparameters that were ultimately selected. These parameters were chosen based on their ability to enhance the model's learning efficiency and accuracy, thereby ensuring that the SAE achieves its intended purpose of effectively capturing and reconstructing the input data. Through this careful configuration and optimization of both the architecture and its hyperparameters, we have endeavored to create a model that is both robust and efficient, capable of tackling complex data representation tasks. Fig. 4.6 illustrates Training performance for the SAE (SAE) with different sizes for cropped tiles of fingerprint images: (A) Tile size (50×50), (B) Tile size (25×25), (C) Tile size (20×20) and (D) Tile size (10×10).

Table 4.1 Training hyperparameters for sparse autoencoder.

Parameter	Method
Number of epochs	1000
L2 regularization	0.007
Number of neurons	50
Decoder transfer function	Purline
Encoder transfer function	Satlin
Sparsity regularization	0.05

L2 regularization is a critical technique used in machine learning to address the challenge of overfitting, ensuring that models generalize well to unseen data. This method was applied to train a SAE architecture, focusing on extracting and learning the latent representations of fingerprint features from images. The training was conducted using four distinct datasets, each composed of cropped images in tiles of varying pixel sizes: 50×50, 25×25, 20×20, and 10×10. This variation in tile sizes was deliberate, aimed at exploring and assessing how the size of input data affects the performance of the SAE, particularly in terms of its loss function.

The primary objective was to achieve the most accurate latent representation of the input features, which could then be used for various applications, including but not limited to, security systems and biometric identification. To quantify the performance of the SAE model, the mean square error (MSE) was employed. MSE is a measure of the difference between the original and predicted values, providing a clear metric for the accuracy of the model. It is pivotal in machine learning as it directly correlates to the effectiveness of the model in predicting or reconstructing data accurately. Through rigorous training and evaluation, it was observed that the size of the cropped image tiles had a significant impact on the learning curve of the SAE. Specifically, as the size of the tiles was reduced, the learning curve improved markedly, indicating better model performance. This phenomenon was most pronounced with the smallest tile size of 10×10 pixels, where the SAE achieved the best learning curve. Furthermore, the analysis of mean square error values across different tile sizes revealed that the lowest MSE, and thus the highest accuracy, was obtained when the model was trained with the 10×10 pixel tile size. This finding underscores the importance of input data size in the training of neural networks, particularly in tasks involving feature extraction and representation learning. It suggests that smaller input sizes may facilitate more precise learning of features, leading to more accurate models. This research contributes to the understanding of how data size affects machine learning model performance and highlights the effectiveness of L2 regularization in combating overfitting, ensuring that models are robust and reliable. Table 4.2 shows The measured values for mean square error (MSE) for SAE with different sizes of cropped tiles during the training process.

4.4.5 Efficiency and parameter sensitivity

In this research, we embarked on an in-depth analysis of the SAE's capabilities in reconstructing fingerprint images. Fingerprint recognition is a pivotal component in biometric security, and its accuracy hinges on the quality of image reconstruction. To quantitatively evaluate the performance

Table 4.2 The measured values for mean square error for sparse autoencoder with different sizes of cropped tiles during the training process.

Image size	Size of each cropped image (Tile)	mseError
100 × 100	50 × 50	0.069
100 × 100	25 × 25	0.061
100 × 100	20 × 20	0.053
100 × 100	10 × 10	0.028

of our model, we employed loss as a metric, which serves as a barometer for the fidelity of image recovery. The principle behind this is straightforward: the lower the loss, the closer the reconstructed image is to the original, indicating a higher degree of accuracy in the reconstruction process. Our experimental setup involved manipulating two primary variables within the SAE architecture: the number of hidden units and the iteration count during the training phase. This approach allowed us to systematically explore the model's responsiveness to changes in its internal configuration and to refine our understanding of how these factors influence the quality of the reconstructed images. One of the key observations from our experiments was the impact of the hidden layer's dimensionality on the reconstruction outcome. Specifically, we discovered that an autoencoder with a hidden layer size of 50 units was capable of restoring high-dimensional fingerprint images with remarkable clarity after approximately 500 iterations. This was a notable finding, as determining the optimal iteration count for achieving clear image recovery can be challenging, particularly when dealing with high-dimensional data. Furthermore, our experiments revealed that the choice of the hidden layer's dimension and the number of training iterations play a crucial role in enhancing the model's efficiency. In scenarios where the hidden layer was comprised of fewer units, we noticed that even after a substantial number of iterations, the clarity of the reconstructed images did not significantly improve. This underscores the importance of carefully selecting the model's parameters to achieve a substantial reduction in loss, thereby enhancing the quality of image reconstruction. Illustrative of our findings, Fig. 4.7 in our study showcases the remarkable improvement in image quality that can be attained through judicious parameter selection. It serves as a compelling visual confirmation of our analytical results, highlighting the SAE's potential in effectively reconstructing fingerprint images. Through this work, we aim to contribute to the ongoing advancements in biometric technology, offering insights that could pave the way for more secure and reliable fingerprint recognition systems.

As shown in Fig. 4.7, the number of hidden layers on the vertical axis and the number of epochs on the horizontal axis. Epochs are iterations of training where the entire dataset is passed forward and backward through the neural network once.

The first row with 10 hidden layers shows very poor reconstruction even after 1000 epochs, indicating that too few hidden units cannot capture the complexity of the fingerprints. As we move down the rows, increasing the number of hidden layers, the quality of the fingerprint reconstruction improves. At 50 hidden layers, the fingerprints are distinguishable from the background and have clear ridge patterns after around 500 epochs. The columns represent the progression of training over time (as represented by the number of epochs). The images in the early columns (100 and 200 epochs) are mostly black, indicating that the autoencoder has not learned to reconstruct the

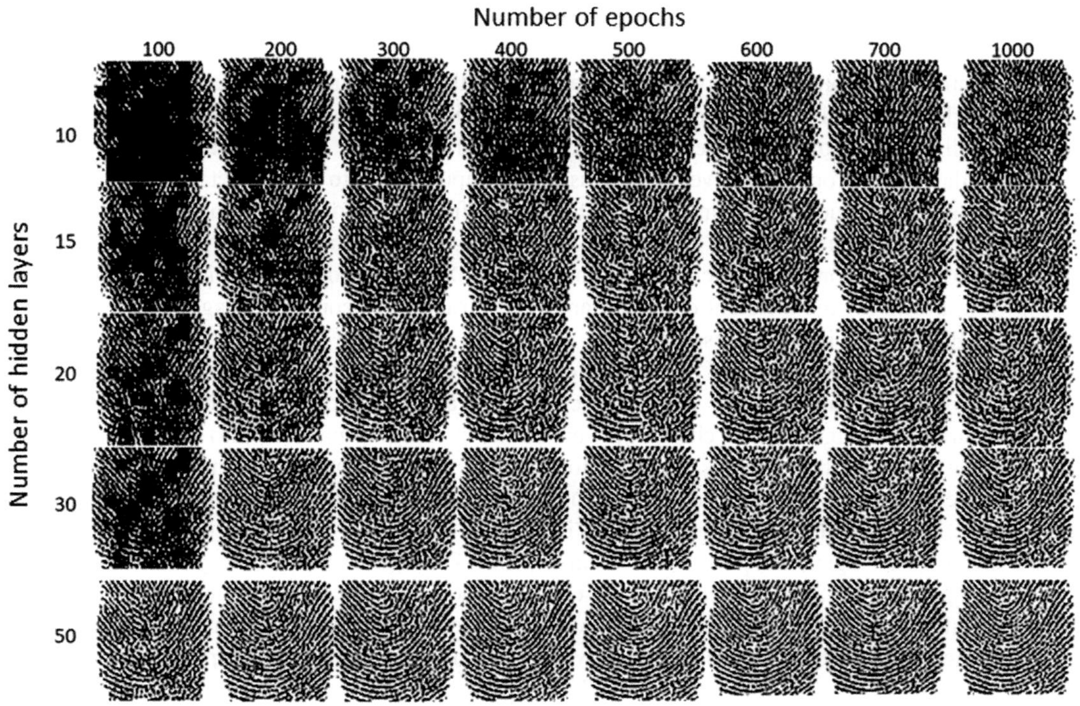

FIGURE 4.7

Output of different hidden layer units and different iterations to show the reconstruction results.

fingerprints yet. As we move to the right along the columns, representing more epochs, the images become clearer. This suggests that the autoencoder needs to be trained for a sufficient number of epochs to learn an accurate reconstruction of the fingerprints. The clearest images are in the bottom right corner of the grid, where the autoencoder has 50 hidden layers and has been trained for 1000 epochs. Here, the reconstructed fingerprints are the most detailed and closest to what one would expect a fingerprint to look like. This figure effectively illustrates the importance of both the architecture of the neural network (number of hidden units) and the extent of training (number of epochs) in the quality of image reconstruction. It seems that there is a threshold number of hidden units below which the quality of reconstruction does not significantly improve regardless of the number of training epochs. Moreover, even with a sufficient number of hidden units, a certain minimum number of epochs is required for the network to learn effectively.

4.5 Recreating fingerprint images by convolutional neural network

In the contemporary realm of biometric technology, the reconstruction of fingerprint images through the application of CNN autoencoders represents a significant advancement. A CNN is a sophisticated architecture within the broader family of neural networks, characterized by its utilization of multiple convolutional layers specifically designed for processing images. Convolutional layers function by applying a convolution operation to the input data, which effectively filters the input to highlight certain features or patterns within the image. An autoencoder, on the other hand, is a specialized form of neural network devised to learn efficient representations (encodings) of unlabeled data. The process involves compressing the input data into a compact, latent-space representation, and subsequently, reconstructing the output from this condensed form. The essence of this technique lies in its ability to distill and capture the most salient features of the data, facilitating a form of dimensionality reduction. The integration of convolutional layers into the autoencoder framework allows for the efficient encoding and reconstruction of complex image data, such as fingerprints. Fingerprint images present unique challenges due to the variations and distortions that can occur from different states of the finger (e.g., dryness, wetness) or imperfections in the sensor technology used for capturing the prints. By employing a CNN autoencoder, the proposed method adeptly learns to navigate these challenges, encoding the fingerprint data into a latent space that encapsulates the essential features required for accurate reconstruction. The model developed for this purpose comprises two concurrent streams: one dedicated to the reconstruction of the fingerprint image itself and the other to the restoration of the orientation field, which is critical for capturing the unique ridges and patterns of a fingerprint. Through experimental evaluation, utilizing the well-regarded FVC2004 fingerprint dataset as a benchmark, the effectiveness of this approach has been substantiated. The results demonstrate a notable enhancement in the quality of the reconstructed fingerprint images, as well as improvements in the accuracy of fingerprint matching. This advancement underscores the potential of CNN autoencoders in the domain of fingerprint reconstruction but also opens up new avenues for enhancing the reliability and performance of biometric identification systems.

4.5.1 Convolution neural network for image reconstruction

Image reconstruction, or the process of image recovery, is a critical area within computer vision and digital image processing that aims at retrieving the original, uncorrupted version of an image from a degraded version. The degradation can arise due to several factors such as motion blur, low resolution, and more prominently, noise, which is the main focus of this paper. Noise introduces random variations in the color and brightness of images, deviating from their ideal representation. These disturbances typically stem from environmental conditions, affecting the image's clarity and quality. With technological advancements, CNNs have emerged as fundamental tools in addressing various challenges in computer vision, such as segmentation, denoising, and object recognition. CNNs utilize their feature extraction capabilities and in-depth analysis to enhance image fidelity. Their versatility is demonstrated across a range of tasks, including their remarkable performance in competitions like the ChaLearn contest, which highlights the development of deep learning algorithms for image restoration from corrupted inputs. CNNs are known for their relatively fewer trainable parameters compared to deeper, more complex neural networks. This characteristic makes them more efficient for learning from smaller datasets. Deep convolutional networks, such as autoencoders, are particularly interesting as they can be understood within the context of discrete dynamics. This perspective aids in comprehending the mechanisms of deep neural networks facilitates the design of highly efficient networks suitable for diverse applications in fields like machine learning, computer vision, inverse problems, and natural language processing. Recent research has delved into the connections between deep convolutional networks and the multigrid method, a sophisticated approach for solving differential equations. This exploration has unveiled new interpretations of deep learning models, leading to more effective and precise methods for image reconstruction. These innovations are paving the way toward resolving the intricate issue of image noise and degradation, thereby enabling the generation of clearer and more accurate visual representations of the world around us. Through such advancements, the domain of image reconstruction continues to evolve, offering promising solutions to enhance image quality and the reliability of visual information.

4.5.2 Convolutional neural network algorithm design

In this section, we delve into the methodology used to reconstruct fingerprint images through the application of a CNN autoencoder. The process begins with the preprocessing of fingerprint images sourced from four distinct datasets. Each image within these datasets possesses pixel values that fall within a 0–255 range. To prepare these images for the CNN autoencoder, we scaled them to a uniform size of 224×224 pixels. Subsequently, these resized images were transformed into matrices of equivalent dimensions (224×224), a necessary step to facilitate their integration into the input layer of the CNN. A critical aspect of our approach is the partitioning of data. This step is crucial for enhancing the model's ability to generalize and significantly mitigates the risk of overfitting, ensuring the model's robustness and reliability. Our proposed CNN architecture is composed of several convolutional and max-pooling layers, which are depicted in Fig. 4.8 for reference. The architecture itself is comprised of 11 layers, designed to be lightweight to accommodate the constraints related to power consumption and memory usage that are often associated with

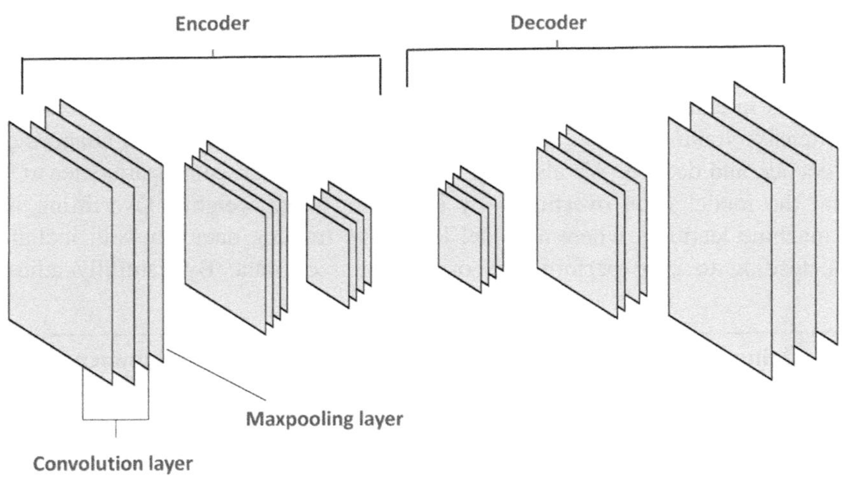

FIGURE 4.8

Structure of convolutional neural network autoencoder.

Internet of Things (IoT) devices and low-cost embedded systems. The convolutional layers within our model serve a vital function; they are responsible for extracting and mapping the features from the input images. We opted for a filter size of [3 × 3] for these layers, a choice informed by common practices in CNN model design. The dimensions of these filters directly influence the height and width of the input regions to which the neural network is connected. Furthermore, we incorporated max-pooling layers to downsample the images into smaller, more manageable regions, using a stride filter size of [2 × 2].

The architecture of the CNN autoencoder is bifurcated into two primary components: the encoder and the decoder. The encoder section is equipped with three layers; the initial layer contains 32 filters, followed by a second layer with 64 filters. This structure is meticulously designed to compress the input image into a condensed representation, capturing the essence of the data while minimizing information loss. This compressed data is then passed to the decoder, which works to reconstruct the image from this condensed form, aiming to replicate the original image as closely as possible. Through this process, we aim to demonstrate the effectiveness of the CNN autoencoder in accurately recovering fingerprint images, highlighting its potential applications in enhancing security measures and identification systems.

4.5.3 Training and validation

In the process of developing a CNN autoencoder for image processing, we meticulously divided the images into distinct sets for the purpose of training, validation, and testing. Specifically, 70% of the images were allocated for training, 20% for validation, and the remaining 10% for testing across each dataset. This strategic partitioning is crucial for effectively teaching the model to understand and process images, validating its performance on unseen data, and finally testing its overall generalization capability. To ensure the CNN autoencoder was trained optimally, we meticulously configured various hyperparameters, as detailed in Table 4.3. Among these, we set the number of epochs—a full iteration over the entire training dataset—to 1000 for each dataset. The choice of 1000 epochs was made to provide ample opportunity for the model to learn from the data, adjusting its internal parameters to minimize the error between its predictions and the actual data. This extensive training period is essential for the model to capture the nuances of the data it is meant to encode and decode. We also fine-tuned the L2 regularization parameter to 0.005, which helps prevent the model from overfitting by penalizing large weights. Overfitting is a common problem in machine learning, where a model learns the training data too well, including its noise and outliers, leading to poor performance on new, unseen data. By carefully adjusting the L2

Table 4.3 Training hyperparameters for convolutional neural network autoencoder.

Parameter	Method
Number of epochs	1000
Batch size	128
L2 regularization	0.005
Number of channels	1

regularization, we aimed to strike a balance between learning the training data's patterns and maintaining the model's ability to generalize to new data.

Furthermore, we adjusted the batch size to 128. The batch size determines how many samples the model sees before it updates its internal parameters. A batch size of 128 a balance between computational efficiency and the granularity of the update steps, allowing for a smoother and more stable training process. Fig. 4.9 provides a visual representation of the training and validation loss curves for the CNN autoencoder across all four datasets. These curves are instrumental in understanding how the model learns over time. The training loss curve indicates how well the model fits the training data, decreasing as the model learns. The validation loss curve, on the other hand, shows how well the model performs on data it has not seen during training, providing insights into

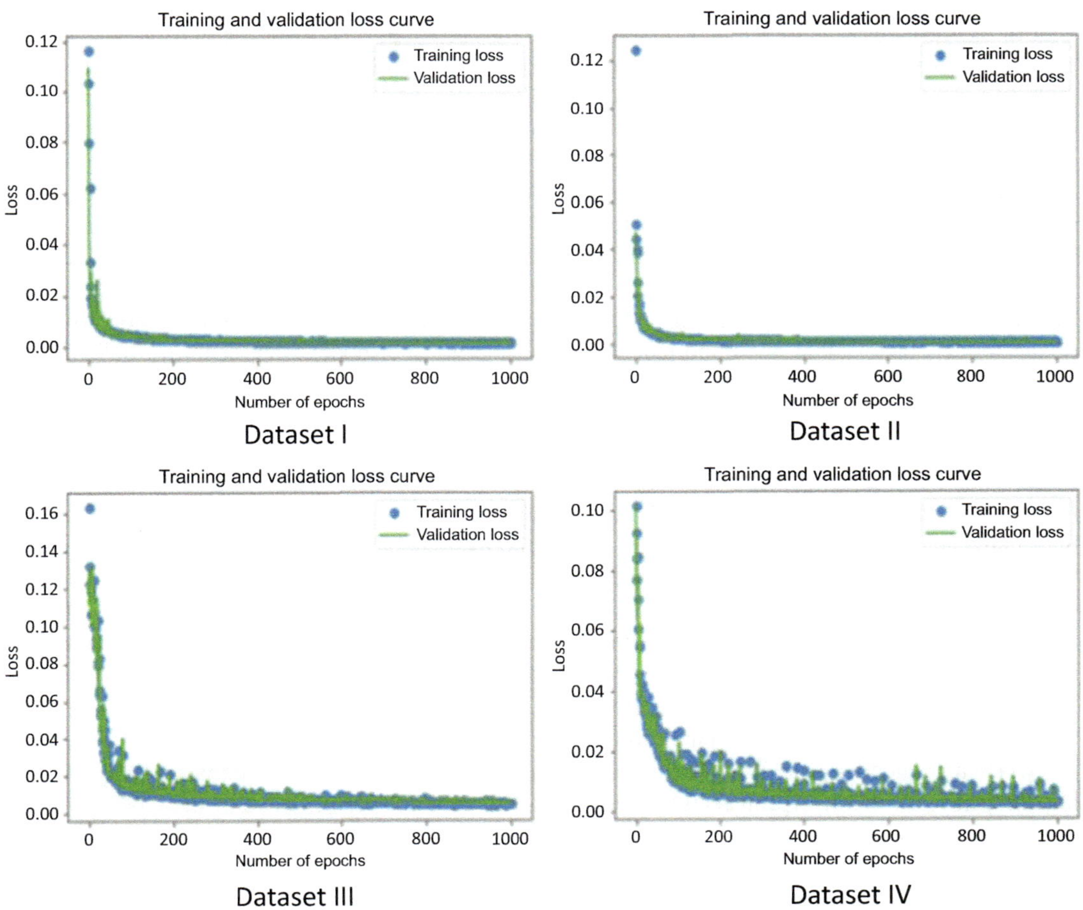

FIGURE 4.9

Training and validation loose curves for a convolutional neural network autoencoder throughout all four datasets of fingerprint images.

the model's generalization ability. Ideally, both curves should show a downward trend, converging to a point where further training does not significantly improve the model's performance. This convergence is a sign that the model has learned to capture the underlying patterns in the data effectively, making it ready for testing and eventual deployment in real-world applications.

4.6 Experiment results and discussion

In this study, we explored the effectiveness of using autoencoders, specifically a SAE and a CNN autoencoder, for predicting fingerprint features across four distinct test datasets. Autoencoders are a type of artificial neural network used to learn efficient data coding in an unsupervised manner. The goal of our research was to evaluate which architecture provides a superior method for image restoration and feature prediction in fingerprints. The CNN autoencoder architecture we proposed includes several key components: the number of filters, the size of these filters, the size of the training patch, and the step size for the skip connection within the network. Through our experiments, we observed that the CNN autoencoder tends to outperform the SAE in terms of image restoration quality. This can be attributed to the design of its architecture, which is optimized for capturing and reconstructing the intricate patterns found in fingerprint images. To provide a detailed understanding of the CNN autoencoder's structure, we examined the number of parameters, including weights and biases, present in each layer, as well as the total parameters involved in the model. This analysis is crucial as it helps in understanding the complexity and the computational demand of the model, factors that are important when considering the model's applicability in real-world scenarios.

Our evaluation of the two architectures' performance was systematic. We considered different types of classifications and databases to ensure a comprehensive assessment. To quantify the error between the estimated fingerprint features by our models and the original features, we employed the mean square error (MSE). The MSE is a widely used metric in image processing for measuring the quality of reconstructed images. It calculates the average squared difference between the pixel values of the original and estimated images, providing a clear measure of accuracy for the autoencoders. The performance comparison between the CNN autoencoder and the SAE across all datasets revealed a significant difference in their effectiveness. As illustrated in our results, the CNN autoencoder consistently achieved lower MSE values across all datasets, indicating a higher accuracy in feature prediction and image restoration. For instance, in Dataset I, the CNN autoencoder recorded an MSE of 0.0013, compared to the SAE's 0.023. This pattern of superior performance by the CNN autoencoder was consistent across all datasets, underscoring its enhanced capability in handling the task of fingerprint feature prediction. The superior performance of the CNN autoencoder can be attributed to its architecture, which is specifically designed to capture the spatial hierarchies in images. The use of multiple layers and the incorporation of filter and skip connections allow the CNN autoencoder to effectively learn and reproduce the complex patterns found in fingerprints. This makes it a promising tool for applications in biometric identification and security systems, where accurate fingerprint feature prediction is crucial.

This study demonstrates the advantages of utilizing a CNN autoencoder over a SAE for the task of fingerprint feature prediction. The design and structure of the CNN autoencoder make it a more effective tool for image restoration and feature extraction, as evidenced by its superior performance across various datasets. This research contributes to the ongoing development of more accurate and efficient methods for biometric feature prediction, with potential applications in enhancing security and identification processes.

$$MSE = \frac{1}{n}\sum_{i=1}^{n}\left(Y_i - \hat{Y}\right)^2 \tag{4.2}$$

In the equation represented as Eq. (4.2), the term MSE is used to denote the mean square error. This statistical measure is critical in the field of machine learning and signal processing, as it quantifies the difference between the observed values (represented as Y_i) and the predicted values (denoted as Y) across n data points, where n stands for the total number of observations in the dataset. The calculation of MSE is pivotal in evaluating the performance of predictive models, providing insights into the accuracy of predictions made by the model in question.

During the course of experiments conducted on various test datasets, a notable observation was made regarding the performance of SAEs. It was found that the mean square error (MSE) associated with these autoencoders showed significant improvement when the fingerprint images underwent manual enhancement as part of the preprocessing activities. Specifically, the act of cropping images before feeding them into the SAEs emerged as a beneficial strategy. This preprocessing step facilitated a faster training time by simplifying the input data and enhanced the learning capability of the SAEs, thereby leading to an overall improvement in the model's performance. Furthermore, CNN autoencoders were explored for their ability to replicate fingerprint features accurately. The algorithm developed in this study showcased superior performance in capturing the intricate patterns of fingerprints when compared to the SAE, as evidenced by the results presented in Table 4.4 and Fig. 4.10. It was particularly noted that fingerprints with complex patterns yielded the best latent representations in the images recreated by the CNN model, effectively minimizing the MSE error. However, despite the promising outcomes achieved with CNN architectures, certain limitations were identified. These included a poor generalization capacity, the necessity for a large training dataset to achieve satisfactory results, and a lack of stability. To address the issue of low generalization capacity, the study increased the size of the training dataset, allowing the network to learn from a broader array of samples and thereby enhance its ability to generalize across different data points. The performance of the CNN was found to be heavily dependent on the quality of the fingerprint images. The challenge of network stability was attributed to the diverse types of finger scanners utilized for capturing fingerprints, including optical and thermal scanning sensors. Overcoming the hurdle of ensuring good classification performance across such a variety of data

Table 4.4 Performance of the convolutional neural network autoencoder versus sparse autoencoder among all datasets.

Model	Dataset I	Dataset II	Dataset III	Dataset IV
CNN autoencoder	0.0013	0.0015	0.0045	0.0048
Sparse autoencoder	0.023	0.026	0.033	0.07

CNN, *Convolutional neural network.*

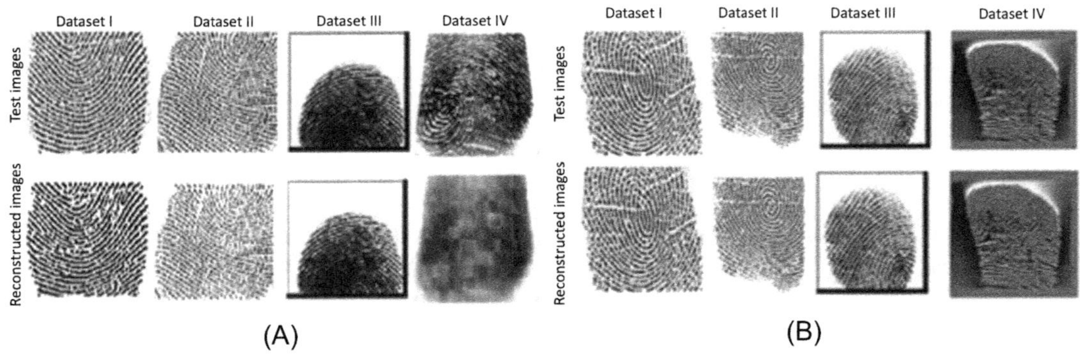

FIGURE 4.10

Reconstructed images by using (A) Sparse autoencoder. (B) Convolutional neural network autoencoder on the testing sets for four datasets.

sources was a significant challenge faced during the study. To mitigate these issues, the approach adopted in this research included the integration of training and validation monitoring. By setting the number of epochs to 3000, a form of regularization was introduced, and learning curve plots were utilized to determine model convergence. This strategy effectively addressed overfitting concerns and potential data leakage in the reconstructed images, showcasing the importance of careful model training and validation practices in achieving reliable and accurate predictive performance. Fig. 4.11 illustrates number of parameters (weights and biases) in each layer and also the total parameters in the CNN autoencoder.

4.6.1 Evaluation

After conducting our initial investigation into the efficiency of fingerprint matching algorithms, we proceeded to perform a series of validation experiments. These experiments were crucial in assessing the performance of the newly proposed model, CNN-based nonlinear autoencoder, and comparing it with the performance of a traditional SAE. To ensure a comprehensive evaluation, we selected four distinct test datasets as the basis for our experiments.

CMC stands for Cumulative Match Characteristics. It is a metric used in biometric systems to assess the accuracy of identification algorithms. Specifically, Cumulative Match Characteristics calculates the probability that the correct match for a given query appears within the top N matches suggested by the system. This makes it a valuable tool for evaluating the precision of algorithms in matching biometric data, such as fingerprints, by providing a clear measure of how effectively the system can identify a correct match from a set of possible matches. The primary objective of these experiments was to measure and compare the fingerprint matching capabilities of both models. To achieve this, we employed the CMC as our performance metric. CMC is widely recognized in the field of biometrics for its effectiveness in evaluating the accuracy of matching algorithms. Essentially, CMC calculates the probability that the correct match for a given query is within the top N matches provided by the system, offering a clear indicator of the algorithm's precision.

```
Layer (type)                  Output Shape               Param #
=================================================================
input_1 (InputLayer)          [(None, 224, 224, 1)]      0
_________________________________________________________________
conv2d (Conv2D)               (None, 224, 224, 32)       320
_________________________________________________________________
max_pooling2d (MaxPooling2D)  (None, 112, 112, 32)       0
_________________________________________________________________
conv2d_1 (Conv2D)             (None, 112, 112, 64)       18,496
_________________________________________________________________
max_pooling2d_1 (MaxPooling2D) None, 56, 56, 64)         0
_________________________________________________________________
conv2d_2 (Conv2D)             (None, 56, 56, 128)        73,856
_________________________________________________________________
conv2d_3 (Conv2D)             (None, 56, 56, 128)        147,584
_________________________________________________________________
up_sampling2d (UpSampling2D)  (None, 112, 112, 128)      0
_________________________________________________________________
conv2d_4 (Conv2D)             (None, 112, 112, 64)       73,792
_________________________________________________________________
up_sampling2d_1 (UpSampling2D)(None, 224, 224, 64)       0
_________________________________________________________________
conv2d_5 (Conv2D)             (None, 224, 224, 1)        577
=================================================================
Total params: 314,625
Trainable params: 314,625
Non-trainable params: 0
```

FIGURE 4.11

Number of parameters (weights and biases) in each layer and also the total parameters in the convolutional neural network autoencoder.

4.6.2 Comparative analysis

The evaluation of fingerprint identification technologies has seen significant advancements over the years, leading to the development of more sophisticated and accurate systems for identifying individuals based on their fingerprints. Among these advancements, the introduction of deep learning techniques, particularly CNNs, has played a crucial role in enhancing the performance of fingerprint identification systems. A comparative analysis was conducted to assess the performance of a newly proposed CNN autoencoder approach against existing state-of-the-art methods, including SAEs and other traditional algorithms. This analysis was aimed at determining which methodology offers the highest identification accuracy, a critical factor for the practical application of fingerprint identification in areas such as law enforcement, security, and access control systems. The study utilized datasets collected from the Fingerprint Verification Competition (FVC2004), a well-regarded source in the field, to test the various algorithms. This provided a standardized basis for comparing the effectiveness of each method under the same conditions, ensuring the reliability of the results obtained. Table 4.5 shows The performance of the proposed approach versus state-of-the-art methods by using fingerprint images from FVC2004 database.

Table 4.5 Performance of the proposed approach versus state-of-the-art methods by using fingerprint images from FVC2004 database.

Author	Algorithm	Accuracy %
Proposed approach	CNN autoencoder	95.02
Gowthami and Mamatha (2015)	Neural network	94.24
Gowthami and Mamatha (2015)	Euclidean distance	92.79
Deshpande et al. (2020)	CNNAI	80

CNN, *Convolutional neural network.*

The findings from this analysis revealed that the proposed CNN autoencoder approach significantly outperformed the existing methods in terms of identification accuracy across multiple datasets. The superiority of the CNN autoencoder method can be attributed to its ability to learn more complex and discriminative features from the fingerprint images, which is crucial for accurately distinguishing between different individuals' fingerprints. The effectiveness of different methodologies in real-world scenarios was further underscored by the practical implications of these results. With the increasing need for reliable and efficient identification systems, the demonstrated improvements in identification accuracy highlight the potential of CNN autoencoders to meet these demands. Consequently, this research contributes to the ongoing development of fingerprint identification technologies and provides valuable insights for the implementation of more accurate and reliable systems in various applications.

The proposed CNN autoencoder approach demonstrated promising identification rates, achieving 98.1% for dataset I, 97% for dataset II, 95.9% for dataset III, and 95.02% for dataset IV. These results notably surpassed those achieved by the SAE, which recorded identification accuracies of 92.3% for dataset I, 90.01% for dataset II, 87.5% for dataset III, and 70% for dataset IV. Such a comparison underscores the superiority of the proposed CNN model in handling fingerprint identification tasks across various datasets. Further comparative analysis with other state-of-the-art methods using the same fingerprint images from the FVC2004 database reveals the CNN autoencoder's superior performance. The proposed approach achieved an accuracy rate of 95.02%, outperforming the Neural Network algorithm by Gowthami and Mamatha (2015) with 94.24%, the Euclidean distance algorithm also by Gowthami and Mamatha (2015) with 92.79%, and the Combination of Nearest Neighbor Arrangement Indexing (CNNAI) method by Deshpande et al. (2020) with 80%. This comparison highlights the proposed CNN autoencoder's effectiveness in reconstructing and identifying fingerprint features more accurately than other advanced algorithms. The effectiveness of the CNN autoencoder in real-world image identification suggests its potential applicability in various application areas. Fingerprint identification technologies are crucial for security systems, personal identification, and access control, among other uses. The proposed model's high accuracy and reliability could significantly enhance the performance of systems relying on fingerprint identification, providing a more secure and efficient means of verifying individuals' identities. Moreover, the comparative analysis of the proposed approach with SAEs and other methods indicates a broader trend in the field towards utilizing deep learning and neural network-based solutions for biometric identification tasks. The ability of CNNs to extract and learn complex features from fingerprint images, combined with autoencoder architectures for efficient data encoding and reconstruction, represents a powerful toolset for improving identification accuracy and reliability. Fig. 4.12 illustrates Cumulative match characteristics (CMC) curves display fingerprint matching results. (A) CMC results by the proposed approach (CNN autoencoder). (B) CMC results by SAE.

The proposed CNN autoencoder approach demonstrates superior identification accuracy across multiple datasets and signifies a step forward in the application of advanced neural network technologies for biometric identification. Its success compared to traditional methods and other state-of-the-art approaches highlights the potential for further research and development in this area, aiming to refine and adapt such technologies for broader application in security, personal identification, and beyond. The continuous evolution of machine learning and neural network models promises further improvements in identification technologies, offering more secure, reliable, and efficient solutions for various real-world applications.

In the realm of deep learning, especially when discussing the deployment of neural network models on embedded systems and IoT devices, the size of the model becomes a critical factor. This is because such devices typically have limited storage and processing capabilities. In this context, the comparison of different neural network architectures, focusing particularly on their memory size, becomes highly relevant. The proposed architecture and a SAE, with memory sizes of 1.257 and 0.155 MB respectively, serve as focal points for this discussion. This comparative analysis aims to shed light on why these architectures might be more suitable for deployment on constrained devices compared to other pretrained models such as SqueezeNet, AlexNet, ResNet50, and ShuffleNet.

Before delving into the comparative analysis, it's essential to understand why model size is such a crucial factor. In environments where computational resources are limited, such as embedded systems or IoT devices, the available memory and processing power are much lower

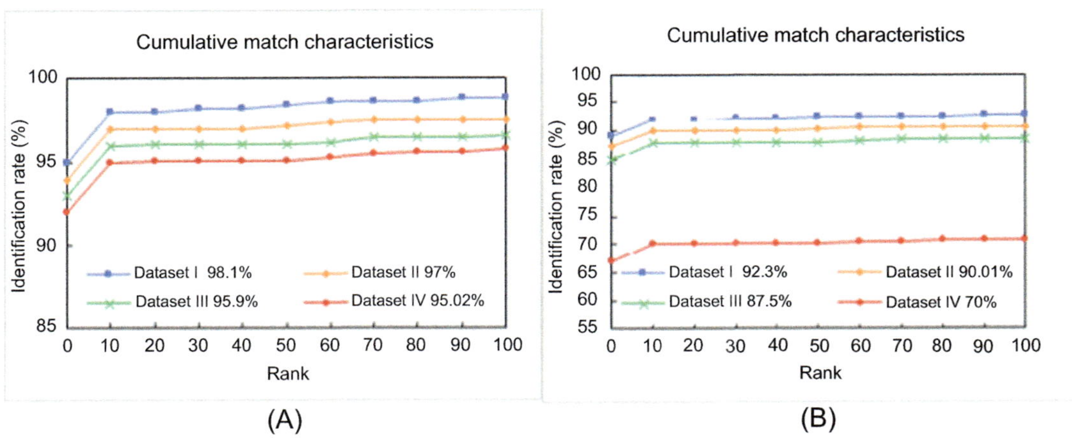

FIGURE 4.12

Cumulative match characteristics curves display fingerprint matching results. (A) Cumulative match characteristics results by the proposed approach (convolutional neural network autoencoder). (B) Cumulative match characteristics results by sparse autoencoder.

than what you'd find in standard computing environments. Deploying large models on such devices could lead to inefficiencies, including slower inference times and increased power consumption, which is often a critical constraint in battery-operated devices. The proposed architecture, with a memory size of 1.257 MB, and the SAE, at 0.155 MB, represent two approaches to designing neural networks that are lightweight yet effective. The stark difference in their sizes can be attributed to the inherent design choices made during their development. SAEs, for example, are designed to learn compressed, sparse representations of input data, which inherently leads to models that require less memory. This is particularly useful in applications where the input data dimensionality is high, but the underlying patterns are represented in a lower-dimensional space.

When comparing these models to larger, pretrained architectures such as SqueezeNet, AlexNet, ResNet50, and ShuffleNet, several points come to light. These well-known models have been foundational in advancing deep learning applications, offering high accuracy rates on various tasks. However, their design did not prioritize memory efficiency to the same extent as newer architectures tailored for deployment in resource-constrained environments.

1. **SqueezeNet** was an early attempt to create a more efficient neural network architecture, with a focus on reducing the model size while maintaining accuracy. Despite its innovations, such as the use of fire modules, it is still considerably larger than the proposed architecture or the SAE.
2. **AlexNet** is often considered the model that reignited interest in neural networks for computer vision. However, its architecture, featuring millions of parameters, makes it a poor fit for memory-constrained devices.
3. **ResNet50** introduced the concept of residual learning to enable the training of very deep networks. While it marked a significant advancement in terms of accuracy, its size, due to the depth and complexity of the network, is a limiting factor for deployment on embedded systems.
4. **ShuffleNet** is another model designed with efficiency in mind, utilizing pointwise group convolution and channel shuffle to reduce computational cost. While it represents a step forward in creating compact models, it still falls short in comparison to the ultra-lightweight nature of the proposed architecture and the SAE.

The memory size directly impacts the feasibility of deploying these models on embedded systems and IoT devices. The larger the model, the more storage is required, which increases the cost on very low-end devices. Additionally, larger models require more computational resources to run, which can lead to slower inference times and greater power consumption. In contrast, models with smaller memory footprints, such as the proposed architecture and SAE, are much more suitable for real-time applications on devices with limited resources. Fig. 4.13 shows Comparison of the proposed approach (CNN autoencoder), and SAE versus other pretrained models in terms of memory usage.

This analysis of the memory sizes of different neural network architectures highlights the importance of considering model efficiency for deployment on embedded systems and IoT devices. The proposed architecture and SAE, with their significantly smaller memory sizes, offer compelling advantages over larger, more traditional models such as SqueezeNet, AlexNet, ResNet50, and ShuffleNet. As the field of deep learning continues to evolve, the trend towards developing more efficient, lightweight models is likely to gain further momentum, driven by the growing need to bring AI capabilities to a wider range of devices and applications.

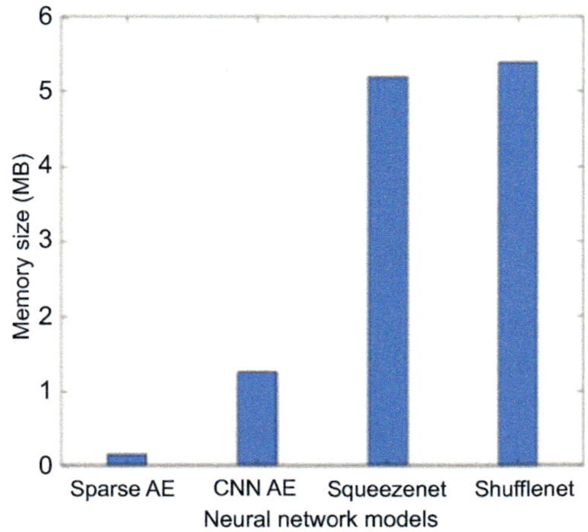

FIGURE 4.13

Comparison of the proposed approach (convolutional neural network autoencoder), and sparse autoencoder versus other pretrained models in terms of memory usage.

References

Alshehri, H., Hussain, M., Aboalsamh, H. A., Emad-Ul-Haq, Q., AlZuair, M., & Azmi, A. M. (2019). Alignment-free cross-sensor fingerprint matching based on the co-occurrence of ridge orientations and Gabor-HoG descriptor. *IEEE Access*, *7*, 86436–86452. Available from https://doi.org/10.1109/access.2019.2924127.

Bidishaw., & Nalini. (2014). Two stage block-wise fingerprint enhancement using discrete wavelet transform. *International Journal of Computer Science and Information Technology*, *5*(3), 2837–2846.

Cao, K. Jain, A. K. (2015). Latent orientation field estimation via convolutional neural network Proceedings of 2015 international conference on biometrics, ICB 2015 9781479978243 349 356. Institute of Electrical and Electronics Engineers Inc., United States. Available from https://doi.org/10.1109/ICB.2015.7139060

Cao, K., & Jain, A. K. (2019). Automated latent fingerprint recognition. *IEEE Transactions on Pattern Analysis and Machine Intelligence*, *41*(4), 788–800. Available from https://doi.org/10.1109/tpami.2018.2818162.

Cao, K., Nguyen, D.-L., Tymoszek, C., & Jain, A. K. (2020). End-to-end latent fingerprint search. *IEEE Transactions on Information Forensics and Security*, *15*, 880–894. Available from https://doi.org/10.1109/tifs.2019.2930487.

Chakraborty, S., & Rao. K. R. (2012). Fingerprint enhancement by directional filtering 9th international conference on electrical engineering/electronics, computer, telecommunications and information technology, ECTI-CON 2012 United States. Available from https://doi.org/10.1109/ECTICon.2012.6254113.

Chikkerur, S., Govindaraju, V., & Cartwright, A. N. (2005). *Fingerprint image enhancement using STFT analysis* (3687, pp. 20–29). Springer Science and Business Media LLC. Available from https://doi.org/10.1007/11552499_3.

Conti, V., Militello, C., Sorbello, F., & Vitabile, S. (2009). A multimodal technique for an embedded fingerprint recognizer in mobile payment systems. *Mobile Information Systems*, *5*(2), 105–124. Available from https://doi.org/10.1155/2009/284124, http://www.hindawi.com/journals/misy/contents/.

Deshpande, U. U., Malemath, V. S., Patil, S. M., & Chaugule, S. V. (2020). CNNAI: A convolution neural network-based latent fingerprint matching using the combination of nearest neighbor arrangement indexing. *Frontiers in Robotics and AI*, *7*. Available from https://doi.org/10.3389/frobt.2020.00113.

Ding, S., Bian, W., Liao, H., Sun, T., & Xue, Y. (2017). Combining Gabor filtering and classification dictionaries learning for fingerprint enhancement. *IET Biometrics*, *6*(6), 438–447. Available from https://doi.org/10.1049/iet-bmt.2016.0161.

Dospinescu, O., & Lîsîi, I. (2016). The recognition of fingerprints on mobile applications—An android case study. *Journal of Eastern Europe Research in Business and Economics*, 1–11. Available from https://doi.org/10.5171/2016.813264.

Ezhilmaran, D., & Adhiyaman, M. (2017). A review study on latent fingerprint recognition techniques. *Journal of Information and Optimization Sciences*, *38*(3-4), 501–516. Available from https://doi.org/10.1080/02522667.2016.1224468.

Figueiredo, I. N., Moura, S., Neves, J. S., Pinto, L., Kumar, S., Oliveira, C. M., & Ramos, J. D. (2016). Automated retina identification based on multiscale elastic registration. *Computers in Biology and Medicine*, *79*, 130–143. Available from https://doi.org/10.1016/j.compbiomed.2016.09.019.

Fingerprint Color Image Database.v1. 2019 2024 3 25. <https://it.mathworks.com/matlabcentral/fileexchange/52507-fingerprint-color-image-database-v1/>.

Fingerprint Grayscale Image Database v2. 2019 2024 3 29. https://it.mathworks.com/matlabcentral/fileexchange/52508-fingerprint-grayscale-image-database-v2.

Ghafoor, M., Taj, I. A., & Jafri, M. N. (2016). Fingerprint frequency normalisation and enhancement using two-dimensional short-time Fourier transform analysis. *IET Computer Vision*, *10*(8), 806–816. Available from https://doi.org/10.1049/iet-cvi.2016.0005.

Gowthami, A. T., & Mamatha, H. R. (2015). Fingerprint recognition using zone based linear binary patte. *Procedia Computer Science*, *58*, 552–557. Available from https://doi.org/10.1016/j.procs.2015.08.072, http://www.sciencedirect.com/science/journal/18770509.

Jeon, W.-S., & Rhee, S.-Y. (2017). Fingerprint pattern classification using convolution neural network. *International Journal of Fuzzy Logic and Intelligent Systems*, *17*(3), 170–176.

Jin, B., Cruz, L., & Gonçalves, N. (2020). Deep facial diagnosis: Deep transfer learning from face recognition to facial diagnosis. *IEEE Access*, *8*, 123649–123661. Available from https://doi.org/10.1109/access.2020.3005687.

Kang, M., Ji, K., Leng, X., Xing, X., & Zou, H. (2017). Synthetic aperture radar target recognition with feature fusion based on a stacked autoencoder. *Sensors*, *17*(12), 192. Available from https://doi.org/10.3390/s17010192.

Li, H. (2021). Feature extraction, recognition, and matching of damaged fingerprint: Application of deep learning network. *Concurrency and Computation: Practice and Experience*, *33*(6), e6057. Available from https://doi.org/10.1002/cpe.6057.

Li, J., Feng, J., & Jay Kuo, C.-C. (2018). Deep convolutional neural network for latent fingerprint enhancement. *Signal Processing: Image Communication*, *60*, 52–63. Available from https://doi.org/10.1016/j.image.2017.08.010.

Liu, M., Liu, S., & Zhao, Q. (2014). Fingerprint orientation field reconstruction by weighted discrete cosine transform. *Information Sciences*, *268*, 65–77. Available from https://doi.org/10.1016/j.ins.2013.08.022.

Luo, C., Wu, J., Li, J., Wang, J., Xu, W., Ming, Z., Wei, B., Li, W., & Zomaya, A. Y. (2020). Gait recognition as a service for unobtrusive user identification in smart spaces. *ACM Transactions on Internet of Things*, *1* (1), 1–21. Available from https://doi.org/10.1145/3375799.

Maio, D., Maltoni, D., Cappelli, R., Wayman, J. L., & Jain, A. K. (2004). *FVC2004: Third fingerprint verification competition* (3072, pp. 1–7). Springer Science and Business Media LLC. Available from https://doi.org/10.1007/978-3-540-25948-0_1.

Manickam, A., Devarasan, E., Manogaran, G., Priyan, M. K., Varatharajan, R., Hsu, C. H., & Krishnamoorthi, R. (2019). Score level based latent fingerprint enhancement and matching using SIFT feature. *Multimedia Tools and Applications*, *78*(3), 3065−3085. Available from https://doi.org/10.1007/s11042-018-5633-1, https://www.springer.com/journal/11042.

Mei, Y., Zhao, B., Zhou, Y., & Chen, S. (2014). Orthogonal curved-line Gabor filter for fast fingerprint enhancement. *Electronics Letters*, *50*(3), 175−177. Available from https://doi.org/10.1049/el.2013.2619.

Mohammed Ali, A., & Farhan, A. K. (2020). A novel improvement with an effective expansion to enhance the MD5 hash function for verification of a secure e-document. *IEEE Access*, *8*, 80290−80304. Available from https://doi.org/10.1109/access.2020.2989050.

Pandya, B., Cosma, G., Alani, A. A., Taherkhani, A., Bharadi, V., McGinnity, T. M. (2018). Fingerprint classification using a deep convolutional neural network 4th international conference on information management, ICIM 2018 9781538661451 86 91. Institute of Electrical and Electronics Engineers Inc. United Kingdom. Available from http://ieeexplore.ieee.org/xpl/mostRecentIssue.jsp?punumber = 8386603, https://doi.org/10.1109/INFOMAN.2018.8392815.

Park, C.-H., Lee, J.-J., Smith, M. J. T., Park, S.-I., & Park, K.-H. (2004). Directional filter bank-based fingerprint feature extraction and matching. *IEEE Transactions on Circuits and Systems for Video Technology*, *14*(1), 74−85. Available from https://doi.org/10.1109/TCSVT.2003.818355.

Peralta, D., Triguero, I., García, S., Saeys, Y., Benitez, J. M., & Herrera, F. (2018). On the use of convolutional neural networks for robust classification of multiple fingerprint captures. *International Journal of Intelligent Systems*, *33*(1), 213−230. Available from https://doi.org/10.1002/int.21948.

Sang, J., Wang, H., Qian, Q., Wu, H., & Chen, Y. (2018). An efficient fingerprint identification algorithm based on minutiae and invariant moment. *Personal and Ubiquitous Computing*, *22*(1), 71−80. Available from https://doi.org/10.1007/s00779-017-1094-1.

Shaheed, K., Liu, H., Yang, G., Qureshi, I., Gou, J., & Yin, Y. (2018). A systematic review of finger vein recognition techniques. *Information*, *9*(9), 213. Available from https://doi.org/10.3390/info9090213.

Shehu, Y. I., Ruiz-Garcia, A., Palade, V., & James, A. (2018). arXiv*Sokoto coventry fingerprint dataset*. United Kingdom: arXiv. Available from https://arxiv.org, https://doi.org/10.48550/arxiv.1807.10609.

Su, H. R., Chen, K. Y., Wong, W. J., & Lai, S. H. (2017). A deep learning approach towards pore extraction for high-resolution fingerprint recognition ICASSP, IEEE international conference on acoustics, speech and signal processing - proceedings 9781509041176 2057 2061. Institute of Electrical and Electronics Engineers Inc. Taiwan. Available from https://doi.org/10.1109/ICASSP.2017.7952518.

Sun, Y., Wang, X., & Tang, X. (2014). Deep learning face representation from predicting 10,000 classes. Proceedings of the IEEE computer society conference on computer vision and pattern recognition. IEEE Computer Society Hong Kong. Available from https://doi.org/10.1109/CVPR.2014.244.

Tang, C., Yang, N., & Mi, Q. (2012). Fingerprint enhancement using the second-order oriented partial differential equation 5th International congress on image and signal processing, CISP 2012 307 311 China https://doi.org/10.1109/CISP.2012.6469988

Wang, T., Zheng, Z., Bashir, A. K., Jolfaei, A., & Xu, Y. (2021). FinPrivacy: A privacy-preserving mechanism for fingerprint identification. *ACM Transactions on Internet Technology*, *21*(3), 1−15. Available from https://doi.org/10.1145/3387130.

Wang, Y., Wu, Z., Zhang, J. (2017). Damaged fingerprint classification by deep learning with fuzzy feature points Proceedings - 2016 9th international congress on image and signal processing, biomedical engineering and informatics, CISP-BMEI 2016 9781509037100 280 285. Institute of Electrical and Electronics Engineers Inc., China https://doi.org/10.1109/CISP-BMEI.2016.7852722

Yoon, S., & Jain, A. K. (2015). Longitudinal study of fingerprint recognition. *Proceedings of the National Academy of Sciences*, *112*(28), 8555−8560. Available from https://doi.org/10.1073/pnas.1410272112.

Zeng, F., Hu, S., & Xiao, K. (2019). Research on partial fingerprint recognition algorithm based on deep learning. *Neural Computing and Applications*, *31*(9), 4789–4798. Available from https://doi.org/10.1007/s00521-018-3609-8.

Zheng, Q., Tian, X., Yang, M., & Su, H. (2021). CLMIP: Cross-layer manifold invariance based pruning method of deep convolutional neural network for real-time road type recognition. *Multidimensional Systems and Signal Processing*, *32*(1), 239–262. Available from https://doi.org/10.1007/s11045-020-00736-x.

Zheng, Q., Zhao, P., Li, Y., Wang, H., & Yang, Y. (2021). Spectrum interference-based two-level data augmentation method in deep learning for automatic modulation classification. *Neural Computing and Applications*, *33*(13), 7723–7745. Available from https://doi.org/10.1007/s00521-020-05514-1.

Zia, T., Ghafoor, M., Tariq, S. A., & Taj, I. A. (2019). Robust fingerprint classification with Bayesian convolutional networks. *IET Image Processing*, *13*(8), 1280–1288. Available from https://doi.org/10.1049/iet-ipr.2018.5466.

CHAPTER

Deep learning for classification and localization of multiple abnormalities on chest X-ray images

5

5.1 Overview of diagnosis on medical images

The diagnosis of diseases through medical imaging has transformed the field of medicine, offering a noninvasive means to explore the human body and detect conditions at their earliest stages. This process involves various imaging techniques, such as X-rays, CT scans, MRI, PET scans, and ultrasound, each with its unique advantages and applications, tailored to capture detailed aspects of the body's internal structures. Radiologists and medical specialists interpret these images, relying on their extensive training and experience to identify abnormalities that may indicate the presence of diseases or injuries. The evolution of digital imaging and the advent of artificial intelligence (AI) and machine learning (ML) have further enhanced diagnostic capabilities, enabling the analysis of images with unprecedented precision and speed. These technologies can detect patterns invisible to the human eye, assisting in the diagnosis of complex conditions, and often predicting the onset of diseases before symptoms manifest. The integration of AI in medical imaging has also streamlined workflow processes, reducing the burden on healthcare professionals and improving patient outcomes. Despite these advancements, the interpretation of medical images remains a challenging task that requires a nuanced understanding of human anatomy, disease processes, and the potential limitations and artifacts inherent in each imaging modality. Challenges such as variability in image quality, patient movement, and the presence of implants or other foreign bodies can complicate the diagnostic process. Furthermore, the ethical implications of AI in healthcare, including concerns about privacy, data security, and the potential for bias in algorithmic decision-making, are critical considerations that must be addressed. As medical imaging technology continues to evolve, ongoing research, interdisciplinary collaboration, and rigorous training programs are essential to harness its full potential in improving diagnostic accuracy, enhancing patient care, and advancing the overall field of medicine. AI methods are pivotal in diagnosing novel coronavirus pneumonia, as highlighted in significant studies (Zhang et al., 2020; Li et al., 2021). In the realm of clinical diagnosis, tests like sputum and throat swabs, alongside lower respiratory tract secretions analyzed through reverse transcription-polymerase chain reaction (PCR) and gene sequencing, are considered the benchmark for COVID-19 diagnosis, with nucleic acid tests playing a crucial role in determining patient discharge criteria. Nevertheless, given the rapid escalation of COVID-19 cases and the challenges posed by nucleic acid testing—including delays in results, the risk of false negatives, and shortages in testing materials—chest X-ray (CXR) imaging emerges as a crucial supplementary diagnostic tool. Common radiological signs in COVID-19 patients, such as ground-glass opacities, multifocal patchy consolidation, and peripheral interstitial changes, underscore the utility of CXR images for swift patient classification pending definitive test outcomes, enhancing diagnostic accuracy and disease management. The dire consequences of COVID-19, particularly severe

Deep Learning in Action: Image and Video Processing for Practical Use. DOI: https://doi.org/10.1016/B978-0-443-30078-3.00005-6

pneumonia and potential asphyxiation due to oxygen loss, are under investigation, with limited vaccines or treatments available. Amidst the ongoing pandemic and the emergence of virus variants, the unpredictability of vaccine efficacy against new strains underscores the importance of early detection and individual precautionary measures in the face of symptoms like coughing, sneezing, or fever.

The research proposes the following key contributions:

1. The introduction of two novel deep learning (DL) methods for analyzing CXR images represents a significant advancement in medical imaging technology. These methods are designed to address the challenges of multiclassification and object detection of various abnormalities in the chest region. Each technique is tailored to a specific function and utilizes separate, specialized datasets to optimize performance. The first method employs convolutional neural networks (CNNs) to perform multiclassification tasks. By leveraging DL architectures, this method efficiently learns from vast amounts of imaging data, automatically extracting and processing relevant features. This capability enables it to distinguish between different types of pulmonary abnormalities with high accuracy, an essential factor in diagnosing conditions such as pneumonia, tuberculosis, or lung cancer. The second method focuses on the object detection aspect, where the goal is to localize and identify abnormalities within the complex anatomical structures visible in CXRs. This method also uses CNNs but is fine-tuned to recognize and outline specific abnormalities, such as tumors or cysts, within the images. By doing so, it provides valuable insights that assist radiologists in assessing the exact location and potential severity of each detected anomaly. Together, these methods offer a comprehensive toolset for enhancing diagnostic accuracy and efficiency in the field of chest radiology, paving the way for more precise and timely medical interventions.
2. The multiclassification method is a significant advancement in medical imaging, particularly in analyzing CXR images. This technique effectively categorizes these images into four distinct classes: COVID-19, normal, lung opacity, and viral pneumonia. Each category represents a specific diagnostic criterion that aids clinicians in accurately distinguishing between various respiratory conditions and healthy lung states. This classification is crucial because it allows for rapid and precise identification of COVID-19, which is essential for timely treatment and isolation measures. Additionally, distinguishing between other serious respiratory illnesses like lung opacity and viral pneumonia is vital, as these conditions require different management strategies. For instance, lung opacity could indicate fluid in the lungs or fibrosis, while viral pneumonia often requires antiviral treatments. The ability to identify "normal" or healthy lung conditions also helps in reducing unnecessary medical interventions and focusing healthcare resources where they are most needed. By implementing such a multiclassification system, healthcare providers can not only improve diagnostic accuracy but also enhance patient outcomes through more tailored treatment plans. Moreover, this method leverages advanced algorithms and ML techniques to ensure high precision and reliability in classification. It significantly contributes to the field of radiology by providing a robust tool for early disease detection and monitoring, thereby supporting effective clinical decision-making in fast-paced medical environments.
3. An innovative ensemble model approach that integrates the outputs of three leading object detection models—EfficientNet, YOLOv7, and Faster R-CNN—utilizes weighted box fusion techniques to enhance performance significantly. This method leverages the strengths of each

model to create a robust system. EfficientNet is known for its efficiency and scalability, optimizing both accuracy and computational resource usage. YOLOv7 excels in real-time object detection, offering exceptional speed and precision. Faster R-CNN, on the other hand, is distinguished for its accuracy in detecting and classifying objects. By applying a weighted box fusion strategy, the ensemble model strategically combines the bounding boxes from each individual detector, weighted by their confidence scores. This not only increases the mean average precision—a critical metric in evaluating object detection models—but also mitigates the risk of overfitting. Overfitting is a common challenge where models perform well on training data but poorly on unseen data. The ensemble method effectively addresses this by pooling diverse detection capabilities, thus ensuring more generalizable and reliable predictions. Consequently, this approach enhances detection accuracy across a variety of scenarios and object classes, making it a versatile tool in both academic research and practical applications.

4. Advanced image preprocessing techniques play a crucial role in enhancing the quality and consistency of CXR images, making them more useful for diagnostic purposes. These techniques include augmentation, cropping, rotation, and normalization, each serving a specific purpose in improving image analysis. Image augmentation is particularly valuable as it increases the diversity of available data for training ML models without the need for additional images. By artificially creating variations through adjustments in lighting, scaling, and flipping, augmentation helps models become robust against different imaging conditions. Cropping is used to focus on relevant areas of an X-ray, eliminating unnecessary background and highlighting areas of interest, which improves the clarity and detail visibility crucial for accurate diagnoses. Rotation adjusts images to a standard orientation, compensating for patient positioning variations during X-ray procedures. This standardization is essential for automated systems to consistently recognize and analyze anatomical structures. Lastly, normalization standardizes the intensity values of pixels across different images, enhancing contrast and making it easier for models to process and compare images. These preprocessing steps are vital for developing reliable diagnostic tools and achieving high accuracy in medical image analysis, ultimately supporting better patient outcomes.

The impetus behind the conducted research resides in the exploration and application of two distinct methodologies: multiclassification and localization, aiming at the advancement of medical diagnostics and the enrichment of patient care. The crux of this initiative involves the crafting of precise algorithms that empower healthcare practitioners to adeptly classify and pinpoint a spectrum of abnormalities, including but not limited to pneumonia, negative results, and various lung diseases, within CXRs. The core objective is to harness the capabilities of early diagnosis coupled with accurate localization to pave the way for prompt intervention, thereby enhancing patient outcomes and diminishing healthcare expenses. This study is dedicated to the utilization of DL techniques, striving to bolster the efficacy and precision in the identification of chest-related health conditions. Fig. 5.1 illustrates suggested framework encompasses identifying various abnormalities on CXR images through both multiclassification and object detection techniques.

In the realm of medical imaging, the utility of CXRs stands as a cornerstone, offering vital insights into the pulmonary system's health status. However, the intricate nature of these images necessitates advanced analytical tools for a comprehensive evaluation. DL, a subset of AI, emerges as a formidable solution, equipped with the potential to transform raw data into actionable

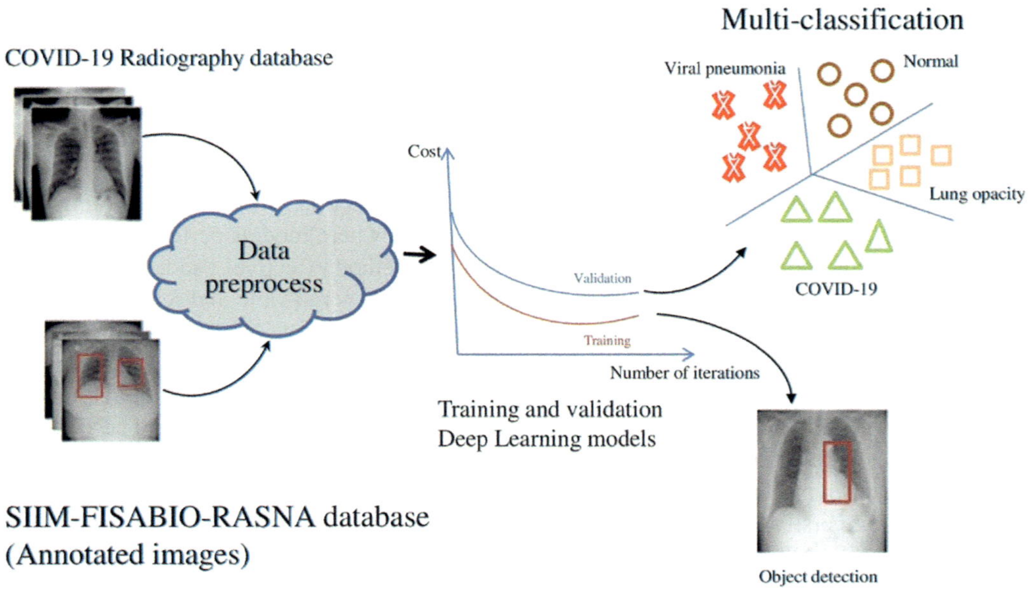

FIGURE 5.1

The proposed framework encompasses identifying various abnormalities on chest X-ray images through both multiclassification and object detection techniques. The process involves utilizing two distinct databases, preprocessing them, and then inputting them into the deep learning models for training and validation. Ultimately, we analyze the results obtained from each method to determine the outcomes.

knowledge. Through the application of CNNs and other sophisticated models, DL algorithms can learn to recognize patterns and anomalies within vast datasets of X-ray images with remarkable accuracy. The dual strategy of multiclassification and localization addresses the challenges of medical imaging from two fronts. Multiclassification involves categorizing X-ray images into multiple predefined classes based on the detected abnormalities, such as distinguishing between pneumonia, normal findings, and other lung diseases. This process is instrumental in streamlining patient triage, guiding healthcare providers toward appropriate diagnostic pathways. On the other hand, localization goes a step further by not only identifying the presence of an abnormality but also pinpointing its exact location within the X-ray image. This precision is critical in assessing the severity of a condition and formulating a targeted treatment strategy. Advancements in DL methodologies have unlocked new horizons in medical diagnostics. By feeding extensive collections of annotated CXR images into these algorithms, they gradually refine their predictive capabilities through a process known as "training." Over time, these models achieve an exceptional level of accuracy, rivaling, and sometimes surpassing, the diagnostic acumen of experienced radiologists. The incorporation of such technology into clinical settings promises to augment the diagnostic process, facilitating the detection of subtle signs of disease that may elude the human eye.

The integration of these advanced diagnostic tools into healthcare workflows holds the promise of revolutionizing patient care. Early and precise diagnosis is the linchpin of effective medical intervention, dramatically influencing the patient's prognosis. By identifying diseases at their nascent stages, healthcare professionals can initiate treatment regimens that are both timely and tailored to the individual's specific condition. This proactive approach not only improves the quality of life for patients but also contributes to the overall efficiency of healthcare systems by preventing the escalation of treatable conditions into more serious, costly health crises. Furthermore, the economic implications of implementing DL in medical diagnostics cannot be overstated. The reduction in healthcare costs is multifaceted, stemming from decreased hospital stays, lower rates of advanced disease complications, and more efficient utilization of medical resources. In addition, the ability to automate part of the diagnostic process alleviates the workload on radiologists, allowing them to focus their expertise on more complex cases where human judgment is indispensable.

5.2 Literature review

CXRs and CT scans are affordable and straightforward procedures widely accessible, facilitating the detection of coronavirus in numerous countries. According to Hou and Gao (2021), the employment of three distinct CNN models—ResNet50, InceptionV3, and Inception-ResNetV2—proved effective in diagnosing coronavirus pneumonia through X-ray images, as mentioned by Narin et al. (n.d.). The widespread utilization of CXR tools underscores their critical role in offering swift diagnoses in healthcare settings. A considerable amount of research (Aslan et al., 2022; Tang et al., 2021; Bhowal et al., 2021; Attallah, 2022; Minaee et al., 2020; Chen et al., 2022) has been devoted to leveraging DL algorithms for the accurate identification of medical conditions, thereby enabling the efficient screening of individuals for abnormalities. Medical imaging plays a pivotal role in the early detection of such abnormalities, aiding in curbing disease spread. Specifically, X-ray, CXR, and CT imaging techniques are vital in the coronavirus diagnostic process. The exploration of image diagnostic systems has incorporated diverse methodologies, including feature learning, to enhance disease detection capabilities. Among these, CNNs stand out as a significant and effective method for analyzing digital images to detect illnesses. Recent studies (Dong et al., 2021; Shi et al., 2021) underscore the pivotal contributions of CNNs in identifying coronavirus. Notably, an inception network-based CNN was deployed by Wang et al. (2020) for pinpointing COVID-19 anomalies in CT scans, while a tailored ResNet50 model was utilized by Ying et al. (2020) for detecting COVID-19 and bacterial pneumonia from CT images. Further, Sethy et al. (2020) detailed the use of CXR in conjunction with a CNN adapted from various ImageNet architecture deep neural networks (DNN) to extract relevant features from X-ray images, which were subsequently analyzed using a support vector machine (SVM) to diagnose COVID-19. An approach involving five AI models for coronavirus detection via blood cell counts was introduced by Reis and Oliveira-Esquerre (n.d.), where Bayesian optimization was applied for algorithmic hyperparameter tuning, facilitating clear result interpretation for medical professionals. Lastly, Karim et al. (2020) implemented a DNN model to detect coronavirus in CXR images, employing class activation maps for gradient and relevance propagation to delineate class-specific regions, thereby offering an explanatory analysis to assist clinicians in understanding AI model decision-making processes. Geetha et al. (2022) introduced a method for automatically identifying COVID-19 in CT scans using deep convolutional neural network (DCNN) models. This method leverages transfer learning to achieve optimal accuracy with specific inputs. To enhance understanding and interpretation of the model's forecasts, visualization techniques were utilized. Basu et al. (2020) detail a strategy employing DL to examine lung X-rays, integrating pretrained models through domain extension transfer learning (DETL) aimed specifically at detecting COVID-19 instances in these images. In Sethi et al. (2020), the implementation of a CNN was reported for the detection of COVID-19. This approach was tested with a small dataset of CXRs, particularly those from patients confirmed to have COVID-19, highlighting a challenge with class imbalance previously encountered in related research. Furthermore, these investigations predominantly relied on CNNs for the classification and segmentation of COVID-19 (Elhanashi et al., 2022), offering a rapid analysis of CXRs. Despite CT scans providing more detailed insights, their higher cost and reduced availability make them less accessible in lower-income regions. Conversely, X-ray–based lung disease diagnosis is more feasible in such areas, although less informative in the early stages of the disease compared to CT scans, as noted by Jiang et al. (2021) and Jaiswal et al. (2021) applied deep transfer learning using DenseNet201 for categorizing CT images of COVID-19 patients, demonstrating the high efficiency and promising results of CNNs in COVID-19 identification. The mask R-CNN (Cao et al., 2019; Lin et al., 2020) is highlighted as a sophisticated model for object detection, serving as a crucial tool in AI for various applications including lung nodule identification (Liu et al., 2018), liver (Mulay et al., 2019) and multiorgan segmentation (Shu et al., 2020), facial and hand segmentation (Nguyen et al., 2018), gastric cancer segmentation (Shibata et al., 2020; Cao et al., 2019), and breast tumor classification (Chiao et al., 2019). It surpasses other models in object detection and segmentation capabilities.

5.3 Computer vision for medical image processing

Computer vision (CV) has been a transformative force in enabling computers to interpret and understand visual information, similar to the way humans do. This field encompasses a broad spectrum of capabilities, from basic tasks like edge detection to complex scene understanding. The remarkable progress witnessed in CV over the last decade can be attributed to several key developments. Firstly, the evolution of DL—a subset of ML—has facilitated the end-to-end learning of intricate functions directly from raw data. This was made possible by the advent of powerful graphical processing units (GPUs), which significantly boosted localized computing capabilities. Furthermore, the accessibility of vast, labeled datasets has played a crucial role in training these sophisticated algorithms. The synergy between CV and the surge in digital data across various scientific domains has catalyzed numerous advances, especially in medicine. DL's ability to learn from diverse data sources has led to breakthroughs in medical diagnostics and scene analysis, achieving near-physician-level accuracy in tasks such as object classification and localization. This entails not only identifying objects within images but also understanding their context within the scene. Fig. 5.2 illustrates CV for medical image processing.

CV, a branch of AI facilitating computers and systems in extracting significant insights from digital images, videos, and visual data, has increasingly become a cornerstone in the medical field, particularly in the analysis and interpretation of X-ray images. The utilization of CV in this domain enhances diagnostic accuracy, improves patient outcomes, and increases the efficiency of healthcare services.

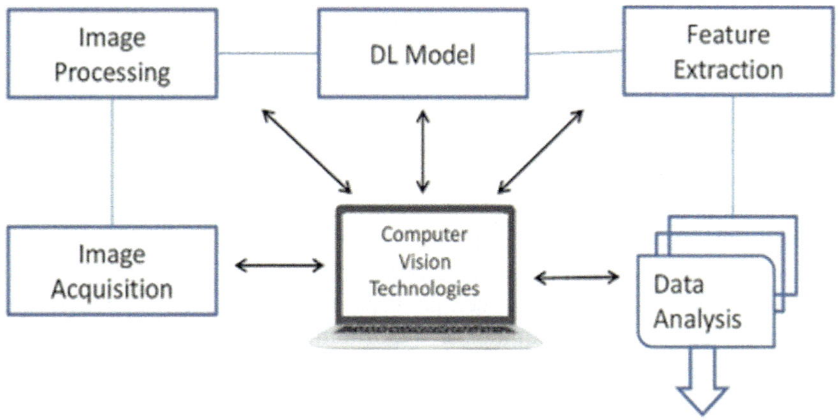

FIGURE 5.2

Computer vision for medical image processing.

A comprehensive examination of its utility reveals a myriad of applications, which can be categorized as follows:

5.3.1 Disease detection and diagnosis

Disease detection and diagnosis represent pivotal aspects of modern healthcare, where advancements in technology have significantly augmented traditional methods. Among these advancements, CV algorithms stand out for their capacity to revolutionize early disease detection. Through the examination of medical imagery like X-rays, these algorithms possess the capability to detect nuanced variations that could signal the existence of conditions such as cancer, tuberculosis, and osteoporosis. A significant advantage of CV algorithms is their adeptness in identifying patterns and irregularities that might go unnoticed by human observers. This is particularly crucial in the context of early disease detection, where the manifestations of illnesses can be subtle and easily overlooked. Through the analysis of extensive datasets annotated with diagnostic information, these algorithms are trained to recognize various pathological conditions with a high degree of accuracy. As a result, they offer a powerful tool for clinicians to expedite diagnosis and initiate timely interventions. The superiority of CV algorithms in disease detection can be attributed to several factors. Firstly, these algorithms are not subject to the limitations of human cognition, such as fatigue or cognitive biases, which can affect the accuracy and consistency of diagnoses. Moreover, they can process vast amounts of medical data rapidly, enabling healthcare providers to analyze images more efficiently and allocate resources effectively. Additionally, the scalability of these algorithms allows for widespread implementation across healthcare systems, thereby democratizing access to advanced diagnostic capabilities. Furthermore, CV algorithms have demonstrated the potential to outperform human radiologists in certain diagnostic tasks. Studies have shown that these algorithms can achieve levels of accuracy and sensitivity that surpass those of experienced medical professionals. This does not imply a replacement of human expertise but rather signifies a synergistic relationship wherein algorithms augment the capabilities of clinicians, providing them with valuable insights and assisting in decision-making processes. Despite their significant advantages, CV algorithms also pose challenges and limitations in the realm of disease detection and diagnosis. One notable concern is the interpretability of algorithmic decisions, commonly referred to as the "black box" problem. Unlike human diagnosticians, whose reasoning processes can often be elucidated, the inner workings of DL models remain opaque, making it difficult to understand the rationale behind their predictions. This lack of interpretability raises ethical and regulatory considerations regarding the trustworthiness and accountability of algorithmic diagnoses. Moreover, the reliance on large datasets for training these algorithms raises issues related to data quality, bias, and privacy. Biases inherent in the data, such as disparities in disease prevalence among different demographic groups, can lead to inequities in algorithmic performance and exacerbate existing healthcare disparities. Additionally, concerns about patient privacy and data security must be addressed to ensure the responsible and ethical use of medical data in algorithm development and deployment. CV algorithms have emerged as powerful tools in disease detection and diagnosis, offering unprecedented capabilities for early detection and improved patient outcomes. However, their widespread adoption must be accompanied by rigorous evaluation, transparency, and ethical considerations to maximize their potential benefits while mitigating potential risks. By addressing these challenges, CV algorithms have the potential to revolutionize healthcare delivery and transform the landscape of medical diagnostics.

5.3.2 Anomaly identification

Algorithms harnessing the power of CV have revolutionized medical diagnostics by offering unparalleled capabilities in anomaly identification. From detecting fractures in bones to spotting lung nodules and pinpointing cardiac irregularities, these algorithms sift through vast amounts of medical imagery with precision and speed that surpass human capability. This prowess is particularly crucial in high-pressure situations like emergency rooms, where every second counts in delivering life-saving interventions.

In the realm of emergency medicine, swift and accurate diagnosis is paramount. CV algorithms shine in this aspect, swiftly identifying anomalies in medical images and alerting clinicians to potential issues that might have been missed in manual examinations. This not only expedites the diagnostic process but also ensures that critical conditions are addressed promptly, potentially saving lives in the process. However, the value of CV in medical diagnostics extends beyond mere identification. These algorithms offer a level of analysis that goes far deeper than what the human eye can perceive. For example, in cases of pneumonia or COVID-19, CV can provide insights into the extent of lung damage, allowing clinicians to gauge the severity of the condition more accurately. This nuanced assessment is invaluable in treatment planning, as it enables healthcare providers to tailor interventions based on the specific characteristics of each case. Moreover, the ability of CV algorithms to track the progression of medical conditions over time adds another layer of utility. By analyzing changes in medical images obtained during follow-up examinations, these algorithms can provide clinicians with valuable information about how a condition is evolving and whether current treatments are proving effective. This real-time feedback loop enhances decision-making and allows for adjustments to treatment plans as needed, leading to better patient outcomes. Furthermore, CV algorithms hold promise in predictive analytics, where they can forecast the likelihood of certain medical events based on patterns identified in medical images. For example, in cardiology, these algorithms can analyze cardiac images to predict the risk of future heart attacks or other cardiovascular events. This proactive approach to healthcare enables early intervention and preventive measures, ultimately reducing the burden on healthcare systems and improving patient quality of life. However, despite their immense potential, CV algorithms are not without limitations and challenges. One significant hurdle is the need for large and diverse datasets for training these algorithms effectively. Additionally, ensuring the accuracy and reliability of algorithmic diagnoses remains a constant concern, especially when it comes to complex and rare medical conditions. CV algorithms represent a game-changer in medical diagnostics, offering unprecedented capabilities in anomaly identification and analysis. From expediting emergency diagnoses to providing nuanced insights into disease progression, these algorithms have the potential to revolutionize healthcare delivery and improve patient outcomes. However, addressing challenges such as dataset quality and algorithmic accuracy is crucial to unlocking the full potential of this technology in the medical field.

5.3.3 Automated radiological measurements

Automated radiological measurements powered by CV technology represent a significant advancement in the field of healthcare, particularly in radiology and medical imaging. The integration of sophisticated algorithms with medical imaging modalities has revolutionized the way clinicians diagnose, treat, and monitor various medical conditions. This technology offers unparalleled precision in measuring anatomical structures and pathological features, providing invaluable assistance in surgical planning, treatment evaluation, and disease monitoring. One of the key advantages of automated radiological measurements is the enhancement of measurement precision. Traditional manual measurements in radiology are susceptible to human error and subjectivity, leading to inconsistencies in results. CV algorithms, on the other hand, can precisely identify and measure critical anatomical landmarks with high accuracy and reproducibility. This not only improves the reliability of radiological assessments but also reduces the potential for interpretation discrepancies among radiologists. Moreover, automated measurements facilitate progress monitoring in patients undergoing treatment or disease management. For instance, in oncology, CV systems can accurately measure tumor size and assess tumor response to therapy by analyzing longitudinal imaging studies such as X-rays or CT scans. This capability enables clinicians to track disease progression or regression over time objectively. By providing quantifiable data on treatment efficacy, automated radiological measurements assist clinicians in making informed decisions regarding treatment modifications or adjustments. Furthermore, CV technology enables the identification and measurement of subtle changes in anatomical structures that may be indicative of disease progression or treatment response. In orthopedics, for example, automated measurements can detect and quantify bone displacement in fractures with greater sensitivity than manual methods. This capability is particularly valuable in assessing the healing process and guiding decisions regarding the timing of surgical intervention or the implementation of alternative treatment approaches. The longitudinal analysis of radiological images facilitated by CV systems offers a comprehensive view of disease dynamics and treatment outcomes over time. By comparing current imaging findings with baseline measurements, clinicians can identify trends, detect early signs of complications, and tailor patient management strategies accordingly. This proactive approach to monitoring enables timely intervention and optimization of patient care, ultimately improving clinical outcomes and patient satisfaction. Moreover, the integration of AI algorithms with radiological measurements holds promise for predictive modeling and personalized medicine. Through the analysis of extensive imaging data and patient records, AI-driven systems can detect patterns, foresee disease progression, and suggest tailored treatment plans based on individual patient traits and responses. This predictive analytics capacity stands to transform healthcare delivery by streamlining resource allocation, enhancing treatment effectiveness, and enriching patient care. Automated radiological measurements empowered by CV signify a groundbreaking advancement in healthcare. By refining measurement accuracy, facilitating ongoing monitoring, and enabling personalized treatment, these innovations have the potential to revolutionize clinical practices and enhance patient outcomes across various medical domains. Embracing these technologies and fully leveraging their capabilities will undoubtedly shape the future landscape of radiology and medical imaging.

5.3.4 Image enhancement and reconstruction

Image enhancement and reconstruction techniques represent a critical facet of modern medical imaging, particularly in refining X-ray images to improve interpretability for radiologists. These techniques encompass a range of methods such as denoising, contrast enhancement, and superresolution, each tailored to address specific challenges encountered in X-ray imaging. Denoising algorithms are designed to reduce noise artifacts present in X-ray images, which can obscure important anatomical details and hamper diagnostic accuracy. By employing sophisticated mathematical models and statistical methods, denoising techniques effectively distinguish between signal and noise, enabling the preservation of essential image features while suppressing unwanted distortions. This enhancement not only enhances image clarity but also contributes to more precise diagnostic assessments. Contrast enhancement plays a crucial role in highlighting subtle variations in tissue density within X-ray images, thereby improving the visibility of structures of interest. Through the manipulation of pixel intensities, contrast enhancement algorithms accentuate the boundaries between different anatomical elements, making them more discernible to radiologists. This enhancement is particularly valuable in scenarios where certain structures exhibit low inherent contrast, allowing for better differentiation and characterization of abnormalities or pathologies. Superresolution techniques represent an advanced approach to image enhancement, aiming to increase the spatial resolution of X-ray images beyond the limits imposed by the imaging system. By extrapolating high-frequency information from multiple low-resolution images, superresolution algorithms generate a single high-resolution image with enhanced detail and clarity. This capability is especially beneficial in scenarios where fine anatomical structures or subtle abnormalities need to be visualized with greater precision, facilitating more accurate diagnoses and treatment planning. Moreover, the integration of CV algorithms has revolutionized the process of 3D reconstruction from sequences of 2D X-ray images. Through sophisticated image processing techniques and mathematical algorithms, these algorithms construct detailed 3D models of anatomical structures, offering a comprehensive spatial representation for diagnostic analysis. This advancement not only enables radiologists to explore internal structures from multiple perspectives but also provides valuable insights into spatial relationships and anatomical variations. The implications of these advancements extend beyond clinical practice, with significant implications for medical education and training. Enhanced visualization and understanding of complex anatomical features afforded by 3D reconstruction contribute to more effective teaching methodologies and improved anatomical comprehension among medical students and healthcare professionals. Interactive 3D models facilitate immersive learning experiences, allowing learners to explore anatomical structures in unprecedented detail and gain insights into their spatial relationships and functional relevance. Furthermore, these techniques hold promise for advancing surgical planning and simulation, where accurate anatomical models are indispensable for preoperative assessment and intraoperative guidance. By providing surgeons with detailed 3D reconstructions of patient-specific anatomy, these tools enable more precise surgical interventions, reduced operative times, and improved patient outcomes. Image enhancement and reconstruction techniques represent indispensable tools in modern medical imaging, offering enhanced diagnostic capabilities, educational opportunities, and therapeutic advancements. Continued research and innovation in this field are poised to further revolutionize medical practice, empowering healthcare professionals with unprecedented insights into the human body's intricacies and pathologies.

5.3.5 Workflow optimization

Workflow optimization in healthcare has become increasingly reliant on CV systems, particularly in the realm of medical imaging. These systems not only expedite the process of triaging X-ray images but also prioritize cases based on the severity of detected conditions. By doing so, they ensure that urgent cases receive timely attention, potentially saving lives in critical situations. This aspect highlights the crucial role played by CV in enhancing the efficiency of healthcare delivery. Moreover, the integration of CV systems with electronic health records (EHRs) has revolutionized documentation processes in healthcare settings. Automated interpretation and annotation of X-ray images streamline the workflow of healthcare providers by providing easy access to relevant information. This seamless integration empowers healthcare professionals with comprehensive data, enabling informed decision-making and improving overall patient care outcomes. The ongoing advancements in CV technology, coupled with the increasing collaboration between AI researchers and healthcare professionals, continue to expand the horizons of its application in medical imaging. This synergy fosters innovation and drives progress, promising significant improvements in both patient care and healthcare efficiency. By leveraging the capabilities of CV, healthcare providers can optimize their workflows and deliver more effective treatments to patients. The vibrant community of DL researchers has played a pivotal role in shaping the evolution of CV techniques. This community thrives on both competition and collaboration, pushing the boundaries of innovation in the field. In the context of healthcare, the application of these cutting-edge technologies is particularly noteworthy. DL algorithms assist in all stages of medical imaging, from data acquisition and processing to feature extraction. CV and AI tools are invaluable in analyzing and segmenting medical images, offering substantial advancements in disease detection and classification. Notably, these technologies have demonstrated their effectiveness in identifying conditions such as COVID-19 in X-ray images, underscoring their potential in revolutionizing medical diagnostics. By providing accurate and efficient analysis of medical images, CV systems contribute to the early detection and treatment planning of various diseases, thereby paving the way for precision medicine. Moreover, the combination of CV with emerging technologies like augmented reality and wearable devices offers great promise for the future of healthcare. These collaborations facilitate instant visualization of medical data and improve clinical decision-making. As these technologies advance and become more accessible, they could revolutionize healthcare delivery, making it more tailored, efficient, and impactful. CV plays an increasingly crucial role in optimizing workflows in healthcare, using advanced algorithms and seamless integration with existing infrastructure to streamline processes, enhance decision-making, and ultimately improve patient outcomes. With ongoing technological evolution and interdisciplinary partnerships, the possibilities for innovation in medical imaging and healthcare delivery are limitless.

5.3.6 Convolutional neural network for feature extraction for medical images

Medical imaging plays a pivotal role in the diagnosis and treatment of various diseases, offering clinicians invaluable insights into the human body's internal structures. As the field of medical imaging continues to evolve, there is an increasing demand for advanced feature extraction techniques to improve the accuracy and efficiency of image analysis. Feature extraction refers to the process of identifying and extracting relevant information or features from raw data, enabling the characterization and interpretation of medical images. In recent years, significant advancements have been made in this field, driven by innovations in AI, ML, and DL algorithms. These techniques have revolutionized medical image analysis by automating tasks that were once performed manually, enhancing diagnostic accuracy, and expediting treatment planning. One of the key challenges in medical image analysis is the extraction of meaningful features from complex and heterogeneous data. Traditional feature extraction methods often rely on handcrafted features designed by domain experts, which may be limited in capturing the full complexity of medical images. However, with the advent of DL approaches, such as CNNs, feature extraction has become more data-driven and adaptive, enabling the extraction of hierarchical and abstract features directly from raw images. CNNs have demonstrated remarkable success in various medical imaging tasks, including disease classification, segmentation, and detection, by automatically learning discriminative features from large-scale datasets. Moreover, transfer learning, a technique that leverages pretrained CNN models on large generic image datasets, has shown promise in medical image analysis by fine-tuning these models on smaller medical image datasets, thereby enhancing their performance on specific tasks.

Furthermore, the integration of CNNs with attention mechanisms has facilitated the extraction of salient features, enabling the model to focus on relevant regions within the medical images while suppressing noise and irrelevant information. Attention mechanisms enable the model to dynamically weigh the importance of different image regions based on their contribution to the task at hand, thereby improving the model's interpretability and robustness. Additionally, recurrent neural networks (RNNs) and their variants, such as long short-term memory (LSTM) networks, have been employed for sequential feature extraction in medical imaging tasks involving time-series data or sequential patterns. These models excel in capturing temporal dependencies and contextual information, making them well-suited for tasks such as cardiac image analysis, where the temporal evolution of anatomical structures is crucial for accurate diagnosis. Moreover, the fusion of multimodal imaging data, such as combining MRI, CT, and PET scans, has become increasingly prevalent in clinical practice, offering complementary information for more comprehensive analysis. Feature fusion techniques, including early fusion, late fusion, and attention-based fusion, have been proposed to effectively integrate information from multiple modalities, thereby enhancing the discriminative power and robustness of the models.

In addition to deep learning-based approaches, traditional feature extraction methods, such as texture analysis, shape analysis, and intensity-based features, remain valuable tools in medical image analysis, particularly in scenarios with limited training data or specific imaging modalities. Texture analysis quantifies spatial patterns and variations in pixel intensities within an image, providing valuable insights into tissue characteristics and pathological changes. Shape analysis focuses on extracting geometric properties and contours of anatomical structures, facilitating tasks such as tumor detection and organ segmentation. Intensity-based features capture statistical properties of pixel intensities, such as mean, variance, and skewness, which are indicative of underlying tissue properties and pathology. While these traditional methods may lack the discriminative power of DL approaches, they remain relevant in certain clinical contexts and can be combined with DL models to leverage their respective strengths.

Moreover, the emergence of generative adversarial networks (GANs) has opened new avenues for feature extraction and synthesis in medical imaging. GANs consist of two neural networks, a generator and a discriminator, which are trained simultaneously in a competitive fashion. The generator learns to generate synthetic images that are indistinguishable from real medical images, while the discriminator learns to differentiate between real and synthetic images. This adversarial training process results in the generation of high-fidelity synthetic images that capture the underlying statistical distribution of the training data. GANs have been applied to various tasks in medical image analysis, including data augmentation, image denoising, and image synthesis, thereby addressing challenges associated with limited annotated data and image quality issues. Additionally, GAN-based approaches have been utilized for domain adaptation, where models trained on data from a source domain are adapted to perform well on data from a different target domain, such as transferring knowledge from one imaging modality to another.

Despite the remarkable progress in feature extraction techniques for medical image analysis, several challenges and limitations persist. One of the major challenges is the interpretability of DL models, particularly CNNs, which are often regarded as "black box" models due to their complex architectures and large number of parameters. Interpretable AI techniques, such as attention mechanisms, gradient-based attribution methods, and model distillation, aim to enhance the transparency and interpretability of DL models, enabling clinicians to understand the rationale behind the model's predictions and decisions. Another challenge is the lack of annotated data for training DL models, especially in medical imaging domains where expert annotation is time-consuming and expensive. Weakly supervised learning, semisupervised learning, and self-supervised learning techniques have been proposed to mitigate the need for large amounts of annotated data by leveraging weak or incomplete labels, auxiliary tasks, and data augmentation strategies. Moreover, ensuring the robustness and generalizability of DL models across different populations, imaging protocols, and acquisition settings remains a significant challenge in medical image analysis. Feature extraction plays a crucial role in medical image analysis, enabling clinicians to extract meaningful information from raw image data for accurate diagnosis, treatment planning, and disease monitoring. With the advent of DL techniques, such as CNNs, RNNs, and GANs, significant advancements have been made in feature extraction, offering more automated, adaptive, and data-driven approaches to medical image analysis. However, challenges such as interpretability, data scarcity, and generalizability continue to pose significant hurdles in the field. Addressing these challenges requires interdisciplinary collaboration between computer scientists, clinicians, and medical imaging experts to develop robust, interpretable, and generalizable feature extraction techniques that can translate into improved clinical outcomes and patient care.

5.3.7 Role of deep learning in medical imaging

The role of DL in medical imaging has significantly evolved, revolutionizing diagnostic processes, treatment planning, and patient care. DL algorithms, a subset of AI, have demonstrated remarkable capabilities in analyzing complex medical images, such as CT scans, and ultrasounds, with unprecedented accuracy and efficiency. One of the primary advantages of DL in medical imaging lies in its ability to extract intricate patterns and features from vast amounts of image data, surpassing human performance in certain tasks. CNNs, a type of DL architecture, have emerged as a cornerstone in medical image analysis, enabling automated detection, segmentation, and classification of abnormalities, including tumors, fractures, and lesions. By leveraging large datasets annotated by expert radiologists, DL models can learn intricate representations, enabling them to generalize across diverse patient populations and imaging modalities. Moreover, DL techniques facilitate the integration of multimodal imaging data, enhancing diagnostic accuracy and enabling a more comprehensive understanding of disease pathology. The deployment of DL algorithms in medical imaging holds immense promise for improving clinical workflows, streamlining diagnosis, and ultimately enhancing patient outcomes. For instance, DL-based computer-aided diagnosis (CAD) systems can assist radiologists by providing rapid and accurate interpretations of medical images, reducing interpretation time and minimizing diagnostic errors. Furthermore, DL algorithms can aid in personalized medicine by analyzing imaging data to predict treatment responses, optimize therapy strategies, and stratify patient risk profiles. The integration of DL with radiomics, a field that extracts quantitative features from medical images, enables the development of robust predictive models for disease prognosis and therapeutic response assessment. Additionally, DL-driven image reconstruction techniques represent a significant leap forward in medical imaging, promising to revolutionize patient care by addressing several critical issues. One of the primary advantages of these techniques lies in their ability to enhance image quality while simultaneously reducing radiation exposure. This dual benefit is particularly crucial in fields like radiology, where clinicians rely heavily on imaging modalities such as X-rays, CT scans, and MRIs to diagnose and monitor various medical conditions. By producing higher-quality images with lower radiation doses, DL algorithms can mitigate the risks associated with repeated exposure to ionizing radiation, especially in vulnerable populations such as children and pregnant women. Moreover, the accelerated imaging protocols enabled by DL can have profound implications for patient safety and comfort. Shorter scan times not only minimize patient discomfort but also reduce the likelihood of motion artifacts, which can compromise image quality and diagnostic accuracy. This aspect is particularly relevant in scenarios where patient cooperation is limited, such as pediatric imaging or emergency situations. By streamlining imaging protocols, DL algorithms can improve workflow efficiency and alleviate strain on healthcare resources, ultimately enhanced patient experiences and outcomes.

Furthermore, the integration of DL into medical imaging extends beyond image reconstruction to encompass image-guided interventions and surgical planning. By leveraging advanced computational techniques, clinicians can precisely target pathological tissues while minimizing damage to surrounding healthy structures. This level of precision is especially critical in procedures such as tumor resections, where the margin between diseased and healthy tissue can be minimal. DL algorithms provide clinicians with valuable insights and predictive capabilities, enabling them to make informed decisions and optimize treatment strategies for individual patients. Despite the transformative potential of DL in medical imaging, several challenges must be addressed before widespread clinical adoption can be achieved. One of the most significant hurdles is the interpretability of DL models. Unlike traditional image processing algorithms, which operate based on explicit rules and logic, DL models often function as black boxes, making it challenging to understand their decision-making process. This lack of interpretability raises concerns regarding the reliability and trustworthiness of AI-driven diagnostic systems, especially in high-stakes medical scenarios. Additionally, ensuring the robustness and generalizability of DL models across diverse patient populations and imaging settings is paramount. Variability in patient demographics, disease presentations, and imaging equipment can significantly impact algorithm performance, necessitating robust validation and evaluation frameworks. Interdisciplinary collaboration between computer scientists, radiologists, clinicians, and regulatory bodies is essential to address these challenges effectively. By pooling expertise from multiple disciplines, stakeholders can develop standardized protocols for model validation, evaluation, and clinical integration, thereby facilitating the seamless translation of DL technologies from research laboratories to clinical practice. Moreover, efforts to enhance the transparency and explainability of DL models are underway. By making AI-driven decision support systems more interpretable, clinicians can gain insights into the rationale behind model predictions, empowering clinicians with enhanced transparency in AI systems enables them to make better-informed clinical decisions. This transparency not only builds trust in AI but also equips clinicians to fully utilize DL technologies in patient care. As DL advances, its integration into medical imaging workflows offers great promise for radiology's future. By providing clinicians with robust tools for early detection, precise diagnosis, and personalized treatment planning, DL stands to revolutionize radiology practice, enhancing patient care and outcomes globally. However, achieving this vision demands concerted efforts to tackle technical, regulatory, and ethical hurdles, highlighting the significance of interdisciplinary collaboration and continual innovation in medical imaging.

5.4 Dataset description

This chapter utilized two separate sets of data to train and evaluate the effectiveness of the proposed models. The first dataset utilized is the COVID-19 Radiography database, primarily intended for tasks involving multiple classifications. In addition to this, the second dataset employed is the SIIM-FISABIO-RSNA database, specifically tailored for localizing and detecting abnormalities within X-ray images of the lungs. These datasets serve a dual purpose, enabling evaluation of both multiclassification and localization tasks, thus offering a comprehensive assessment of the proposed models' strength. Furthermore, these datasets were chosen for their relevance and suitability in evaluating the proposed models' ability to identify abnormalities in chest X-ray images. Derived from real cases, these datasets encompass individuals who have tested both positive and negative for the virus, ensuring the realism and applicability of the models trained on them to real-world scenarios. Below, we offer a concise description of each dataset to enhance comprehension. The COVID-19 Radiography database, published in 2020, consists of 21,165 X-ray images, each with a resolution of 299×299 pixels and in PNG format. This database does not include annotations for the images. On the other hand, the SIIM-FISABIO-RSNA database, which was released a year later in 2021, contains a smaller collection of 6334 images. These images are not only X-rays but also include CT scans and have a higher resolution of 512 × 512 pixels. They are stored in the digital imaging and communications in medicine (DICOM) format and come with annotations, providing additional data for analysis and study.

5.4.1 COVID-19 radiography database

The COVID-19 pandemic has prompted an unprecedented global effort to leverage technology and data to combat the spread of the virus. One such endeavor is the creation of specialized datasets for training and validating ML models aimed at detecting COVID-19 from medical imaging. Among these, the COVID-19 Radiography database stands out as a significant resource, offering a rich collection of X-ray images specifically curated for COVID-19 detection. This dataset, accessible through Kaggle, has been meticulously compiled by medical professionals, researchers, and scientists affiliated with Qatar University and Dhaka, ensuring its quality and relevance to the medical community (Chowdhury et al., 2020; Rahman et al., 2020). In this regard, this dataset consists of 21,165 CXR images, meticulously categorized into various classes crucial for COVID-19 detection. These categories include 3616 cases of COVID-19, 6012 instances of lung opacity (often indicative of viral infection), 10,192 normal cases, and 1345 cases of viral pneumonia. The distribution of these classes is visually depicted in Fig. 5.3, offering a clear overview of the dataset's composition. Such comprehensive categorization is essential for training and evaluating ML algorithms, enabling them to differentiate between normal and abnormal lung conditions with a high degree of accuracy. Each image in the COVID-19 Radiography database is stored in PNG format, ensuring compatibility with a wide range of image processing and ML libraries. Moreover, the images boast a resolution of 299 × 299 pixels, striking a balance between image quality and computational efficiency. This resolution is particularly suitable for training DL models, which often require large volumes of data to achieve optimal performance. One of the most notable strengths of the COVID-19 Radiography database is its size, making it an ideal resource for developing and evaluating DL models. The sheer volume of data allows researchers to train models on a diverse range of cases, thereby improving their generalization performance. Furthermore, the dataset encompasses images capturing various degrees of COVID-19 severity, ranging from mild to severe cases. This diversity is crucial for training robust models capable of accurately diagnosing COVID-19 across a spectrum of presentations. Another advantage of the COVID-19 Radiography database is its compatibility with pretrained CNNs, such as ResNet50, VGG19, VGG16, and Xception. These CNN architectures, originally trained on CXR images, can be fine-tuned using the COVID-19 Radiography dataset to achieve state-of-the-art performance in COVID-19 detection. Leveraging pretrained models not only accelerates the development process but also ensures that the resulting models benefit from the wealth of knowledge encoded in the pretrained weights. Despite its strengths, the COVID-19 Radiography database has limitations that researchers must consider. One significant limitation is the absence of patient-specific information, such as age and sex, associated with each image. While the dataset provides a rich source of imaging data, the lack of accompanying clinical information hampers the ability to contextualize findings and tailor diagnostic algorithms to individual patient profiles. Incorporating such metadata could significantly enhance the utility of the dataset and improve the accuracy of diagnostic models. The COVID-19 Radiography database represents a valuable resource for researchers and practitioners engaged in the development of ML models for COVID-19 detection. Its comprehensive collection of X-ray images, coupled with its compatibility with pretrained CNN architectures, makes it an invaluable asset in the fight against the pandemic.

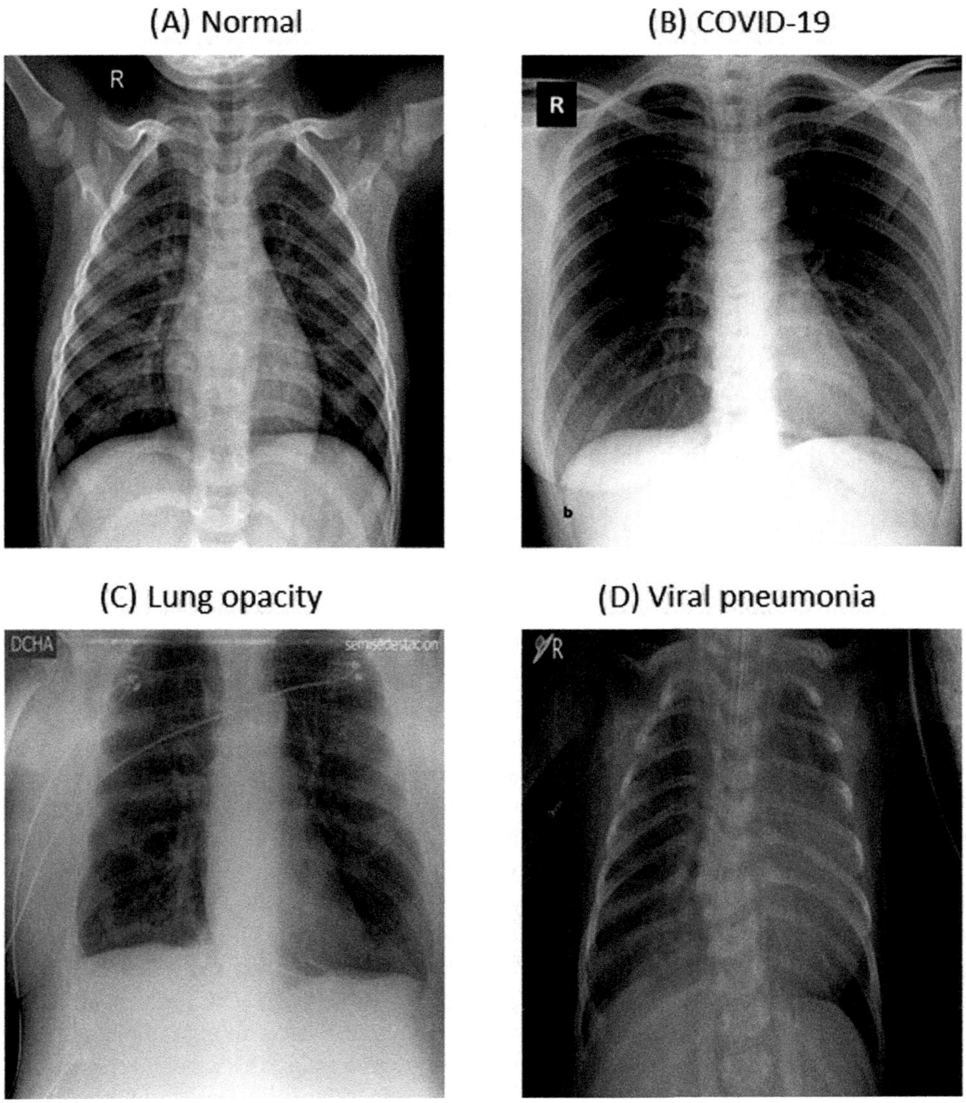

FIGURE 5.3

The radiography database is categorized into four classes, namely: (A) healthy, (B) COVID-19 positive, (C) lung opacity detected, and (D) viral pneumonia identified.

However, addressing the dataset's limitations, particularly the absence of patient-specific information, will be essential for realizing its full potential in clinical practice. As the field of medical imaging continues to evolve, datasets like the COVID-19 Radiography database will play a crucial role in advancing our understanding and management of COVID-19 and other respiratory diseases.

5.4.2 COVID-19 SIIM-FISABIO-RSNA COVID-19 dataset

The effort led by the Society for Imaging Informatics in Medicine (SIIM) to compile a thorough dataset containing X-ray and chest CT scans, along with relevant patient information, represents a major advancement in the field of DL algorithms for identifying and diagnosing diseases. This database includes 6334 de-identified images stored in the commonly used DICOM format, obtained from patients of different ages with a range of respiratory ailments, including COVID-19. It serves as a crucial resource for both researchers and developers in this field. At its core, the dataset serves as fertile ground for refining DL algorithms aimed at parsing medical imagery for pathological indicators. The meticulous annotations provided by expert radiologists further elevate the dataset's utility by facilitating the identification of subtle abnormalities. This meticulous curation not only enhances the accuracy of DL models but also underscores the importance of human expertise in training algorithms effectively. As DL algorithms continue to evolve, the availability of such meticulously annotated datasets becomes increasingly vital in ensuring their efficacy in clinical settings. One of the most notable aspects of this dataset is its inclusivity, encompassing a diverse range of respiratory conditions beyond COVID-19. By incorporating a variety of pathologies, the dataset reflects the complexity of real-world medical scenarios, thereby better preparing DL algorithms for the challenges encountered in clinical practice. This diversity not only enhances the generalizability of algorithms but also fosters a deeper understanding of the nuances inherent in different disease presentations. Furthermore, the dataset's organization is divided into four distinct classes, which include atypical, indeterminate, atypical, and negative images. By delineating between various manifestations of pulmonary pathology, clinicians gain nuanced insights into chest image patterns, which can significantly aid in the diagnosis and management of conditions such as COVID-19 and pneumonia. This classification scheme not only facilitates more accurate diagnoses but also helps streamline healthcare workflows by enabling clinicians to prioritize cases based on severity and urgency. The implications of advancements in DL algorithms for medical imaging extend far beyond the realm of diagnosis. By enabling early and accurate detection of abnormalities, these algorithms have the potential to vastly improve patient outcomes. Timely identification of respiratory conditions, such as pneumonia or COVID-19, can facilitate prompt initiation of treatment, thereby reducing morbidity and mortality rates. Additionally, by automating the analysis of medical images, DL algorithms can help alleviate the burden on healthcare providers, allowing them to focus their time and expertise on patient care. However, despite the immense promise offered by DL algorithms, several challenges remain. Chief among these is the need for robust validation and testing to ensure the reliability and safety of algorithmic outputs. While the SIIM-curated dataset represents a crucial step toward addressing this challenge, ongoing efforts are required to continuously refine and validate DL algorithms in real-world clinical settings. Additionally, issues related to data bias and generalizability must be addressed to confirm the effective deployment of these technologies across diverse patient populations. The SIIM-curated dataset of chest CT images, accompanied by relevant clinical data, stands as a testament to the transformative potential of DL algorithms in medical imaging. By providing researchers and developers with a rich and diverse resource for algorithmic refinement, this initiative holds promise for accelerating progress in disease detection and diagnosis. As DL algorithms continue to evolve, fueled by datasets of this caliber, the future of medical imaging looks increasingly bright, with the potential to revolutionize patient care and healthcare delivery on a global scale. Fig. 5.4 shows four categories within the suggested dataset aimed at identifying and pinpointing irregularities in X-ray images.

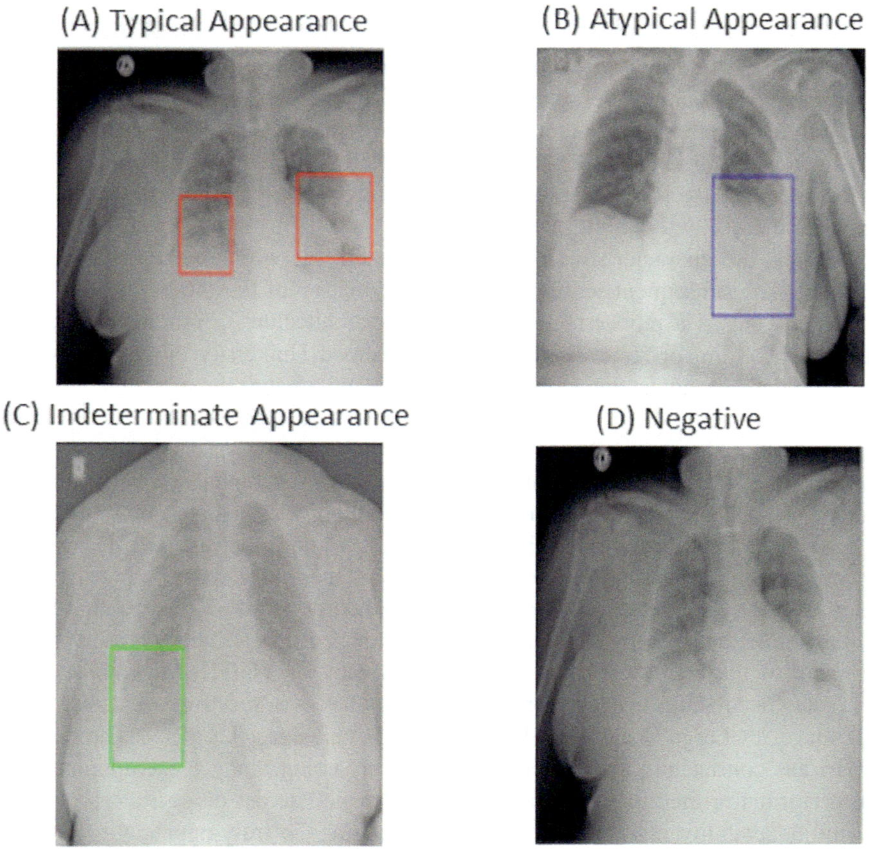

FIGURE 5.4

Four categories within the suggested dataset aimed at identifying and pinpointing irregularities in X-ray images.

5.5 Method

The progress in medical imaging has led to a growing need for quick and precise disease diagnosis. DL techniques show great potential in detecting abnormalities in medical images. This research aims to explore the use of multiclassification and object detection algorithms to classify and identify coronavirus infections and other issues in CXRs. Multiclassification models will categorize images into different groups like COVID-19, pneumonia, or normal, making it easier to identify coronavirus cases while also detecting other chest irregularities. On the other hand, object detection models are designed to spot abnormalities in images, allowing for the identification of specific patterns indicative of issues and highlighting them, thus offering a more accurate diagnosis by pinpointing the affected areas in the chest caused by COVID-19.

5.5.1 Multiclassification of abnormalities on chest X-ray images

Fig. 5.5 illustrates the multiclassification technique, comprised of various analysis blocks encompassing image preprocessing, leveraging proposed CNN models, model training, and fine-tuning parameter configuration. This study endeavors to investigate diverse CNN architectures applied to medical CXR images for COVID-19 identification. Four efficient pretrained CNN model, which includes VGG16, VGG19, ResNet50, and Xception—are employed to achieve the multiclassification objective of disease detection in these images.

Fig. 5.6 details the characteristics of these four neural networks, encompassing their size and parameter count. The subsequent section provides information of these CNN models.

VGG16 stands tall as a pioneering neural network architecture, a product of meticulous craftsmanship by a consortium of researchers from the esteemed University of Oxford. With its genesis rooted in the pursuit of advancing object recognition and image classification tasks, VGG16 has emerged as a stalwart in the field of DL. At its core, this architecture boasts 16 convolutional layers, strategically orchestrated to unravel the complexities inherent in visual data. One of the hallmarks of VGG16 lies in its strategic utilization of multiple 3×3 convolutional layers in tandem with max-pooling filters. This design choice is not arbitrary; rather, it is a calculated maneuver aimed at enhancing the model's ability to discern intricate features within input images. By employing a series of smaller convolutional filters, VGG16 effectively scours the image space, capturing nuanced details that might otherwise evade detection. Furthermore, the incorporation of max-pooling layers facilitates dimensionality reduction, thereby mitigating computational overhead while preserving crucial information pertinent to the classification process. The efficacy of VGG16 transcends mere theoretical conjecture; it has been subjected to rigorous evaluation across a spectrum of datasets, including the prestigious ImageNet Large Scale Visual Recognition Challenge (ILSVRC). Through these evaluations, VGG16 has consistently showcased its mettle, surpassing many contemporaneous DL models in terms of performance metrics. Its ability to generalize well across diverse datasets underscores the robustness and adaptability ingrained within its architecture. To truly appreciate VGG16 prowess, it is imperative to delve into the nuances of its convolutional layers. Each layer serves as a hierarchical extractor of features, progressively abstracting information from raw pixel data to high-level representations. This hierarchical feature extraction is pivotal in enabling VGG16 to discern complex patterns with remarkable precision. Moreover, the modular nature of its architecture facilitates ease of interpretation and transferability, making it an invaluable asset in various CV applications. Despite its resounding success, VGG16 is not without its limitations. Chief among these is its computational inefficiency, owing largely to the sheer depth and complexity of its architecture. The proliferation of parameters necessitates substantial computational resources during both training and inference phases. Furthermore, adherence to 3×3 convolutional filters, though proficient at capturing nearby features, might constrain the model's capacity to comprehend deeper contextual nuances within the image. This model exemplifies the creativity and persistence of its developers. Its remarkable proficiency in recognizing objects and classifying images emphasizes its importance in the domain of DL. Nevertheless, as the field progresses, VGG16 must evolve to confront new challenges and capitalize on emerging prospects. With continuous enhancement and inventive strides, VGG16 stands ready to make a lasting impact on the fields of CV and AI.

VGG19, a significant iteration in the VGG (visual geometry group) series, represents a remarkable advancement over its predecessor, VGG16, by integrating a total of 19 layers into its

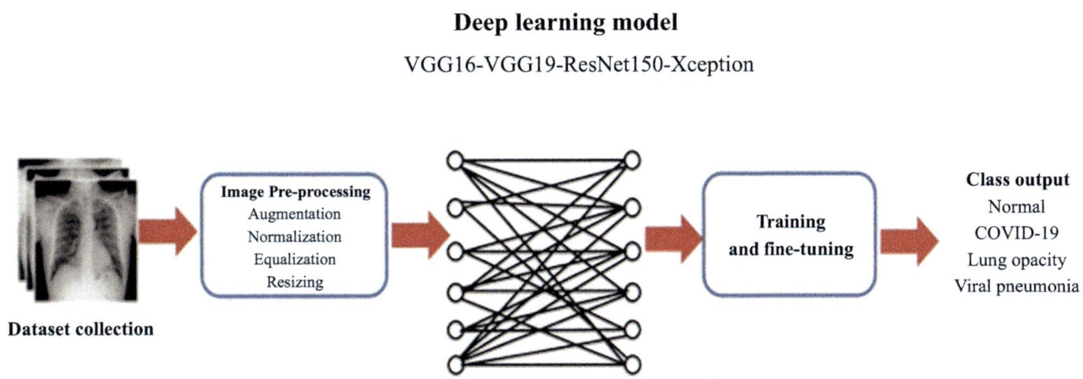

FIGURE 5.5

The proposed method for multiclassification, comprises data gathering, image preprocessing, and training of deep learning models.

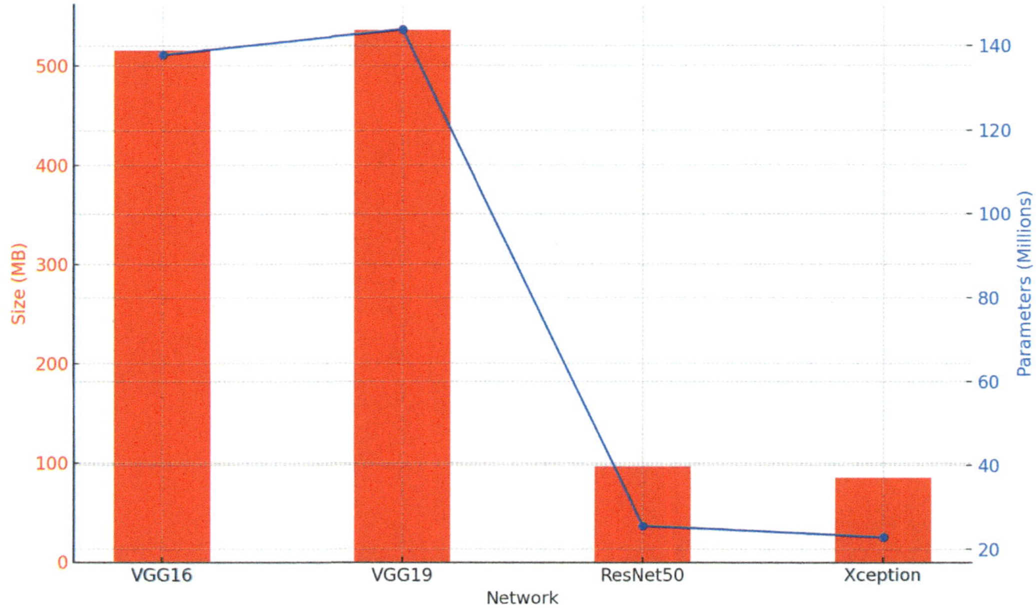

FIGURE 5.6

This graph displays the comparison of model sizes in megabytes (MB) and the number of parameters in millions for four different neural networks. The red bars represent the storage size of each network, while the blue line with markers shows the count of parameters.

architecture. This increase in depth allows for a more nuanced understanding of image features, leading to improved performance across various CV tasks. One of the defining characteristics of VGG19 is its reliance on compact 3×3 convolutional filters. These filters are adept at capturing intricate details within images, making them highly effective in feature extraction. By utilizing such filters, VGG19 is able to enhance the number of channels in feature maps while simultaneously reducing their spatial dimensions. This architectural refinement not only contributes to superior feature representation but also aids in mitigating overfitting, thus enhancing the model's generalization capabilities. Comparing VGG19 to VGG16, the primary difference lies in their depth and complexity. While VGG16 consists of 16 layers, VGG19 incorporates three additional layers, allowing for a more comprehensive analysis of image data. This deeper architecture enables VGG19 to capture increasingly abstract features, leading to enhanced discriminative power and performance. However, it is essential to note that this increase in depth also comes with a trade-off in terms of computational complexity and resource requirements. In practical applications, VGG19 has demonstrated its effectiveness across different tasks, which includes image recognition, object detection, and style transfer. Its ability to meticulously extract and categorize image features has made it a popular choice for both research and practical implementations in the field of CV. For instance, in image recognition tasks, VGG19 deep architecture allows it to discern subtle patterns and variations within images, leading to more accurate classification results. Moreover, VGG19 versatility extends beyond conventional CV tasks into domains such as medical imaging. Here, the model has proven instrumental in aiding diagnoses by identifying subtle biomarkers and abnormalities indicative of various diseases. Its ability to analyze medical images with precision and reliability has led to improved diagnostic accuracy and patient outcomes. Furthermore, in the realm of artistic expression, VGG19 capabilities shine through in facilitating style transfer techniques. By leveraging its deep understanding of image features, VGG19 enables the creation of visually captivating compositions that blend multiple artistic styles seamlessly. This has sparked creativity and innovation in digital art, allowing artists to explore new avenues of expression and produce captivating visual content. VGG19 represents a significant advancement in CNN architecture, offering enhanced depth and feature extraction capabilities compared to its predecessor, VGG16. Its compact 3×3 convolutional filters and deep architecture make it a versatile and powerful tool across various domains, from traditional CV tasks to medical imaging and artistic expression through style transfer.

ResNet50, a product of the innovative minds at Microsoft Research Group, stands tall as a beacon of advancement in the realm of image classification and recognition. Featuring a robust architecture comprising 50 layers, ResNet50 introduces a groundbreaking approach to DL with its implementation of residual learning techniques. These techniques, which harness skip connections, mark a departure from traditional neural network designs by allowing information to bypass certain layers. This strategic bypassing serves to alleviate the vanishing gradient problem, a notorious obstacle encountered in training deep networks, thereby enabling more efficient and effective learning. The impact of ResNet50 novel architecture reverberates throughout the fields of CV and AI. By facilitating the training of significantly deeper networks, ResNet50 has unlocked new frontiers in image analysis tasks. From object detection to facial recognition, ResNet50 consistently demonstrates unparalleled accuracy and reliability, setting a new standard for performance in image-centric endeavors. Its versatility and robustness have earned it widespread recognition and adoption, cementing its status as a cornerstone in both academic research and industrial applications. Beyond its immediate applications, ResNet50 influence extends far and wide, catalyzing advancements in diverse areas of technology. Its success has spurred further exploration into the possibilities of DL architectures, inspiring researchers to push the boundaries of what is achievable in visual understanding. Moreover, ResNet50 open-source availability has democratized access to state-of-the-art image recognition capabilities, empowering developers and enthusiasts worldwide to leverage its power for a myriad of applications. The significance of ResNet50 transcends its individual components; it symbolizes a paradigm shift in the approach to DNN design. By prioritizing not only depth but also the flow of information through the network, ResNet50 exemplifies a more holistic and nuanced understanding of the challenges inherent in training deep models. Its enduring legacy serves as a testament to the power of innovation and collaboration in driving progress within the fields of AI and ML.

XCEPTION, a formidable advancement stemming from the Inception architecture, represents a significant leap forward in the domain of DL. It revolutionizes model efficiency through the implementation of depth-wise separable convolutions, a technique that divides the convolution operation into two distinct stages: depth-wise convolutions and pointwise convolutions. This decomposition dramatically reduces the number of parameters, thereby streamlining the network architecture while preserving accuracy. The elegance of XCEPTION lies in its adeptness at navigating the intricate trade-off between model complexity and computational cost.

By embracing depth-wise separable convolutions, XCEPTION achieves unparalleled efficiency without compromising on performance. This makes it particularly well-suited for resource-constrained environments where computational resources are limited. Despite its leaner profile, XCEPTION delivers exceptional results in tasks such as image classification and recognition, setting new benchmarks for efficiency in DL architectures. However, the impact of XCEPTION extends far beyond its prowess in traditional CV tasks. Its versatility has led to widespread adoption across diverse domains, including object detection, image segmentation, and image captioning. The flexibility and efficiency of XCEPTION empower researchers and practitioners to tackle a wide range of challenges with ease, driving innovation and unlocking new possibilities in AI. As we embarked on our experimentation journey, we recognized the importance of optimizing the preprocessing phase to maximize the effectiveness of DL models. Augmentation emerged as a pivotal technique in our arsenal, offering a powerful means to enhance the model's generalization capabilities by introducing diverse transformations to the original data. In our efforts to prepare images for the COVID-19 Radiography database, we approached augmentation with meticulous care. We employed a variety of techniques, including rotation, scaling, flipping, and translation, to augment the dataset and enrich its diversity. Additionally, we leveraged techniques such as Gaussian noise injection and brightness adjustments to simulate real-world variations and improve the model's robustness to noise and lighting conditions. Through careful experimentation and refinement, we optimized our augmentation pipeline to enhance the balance between diversity, ensuring that the augmented data accurately reflected the variability present in real-world scenarios. This meticulous approach not only enhanced the performance of our DL models but also underscored the importance of thoughtful preprocessing in achieving optimal results. XCEPTION represents a groundbreaking advancement in DL architecture, offering a compelling blend of efficiency and performance. Its adoption across diverse domains underscores its versatility and impact, while techniques such as augmentation play a crucial role in maximizing the effectiveness of DL models. As we continue to push the boundaries of AI, innovations like XCEPTION and thoughtful preprocessing techniques will undoubtedly shape the future of the field, driving progress and unlocking new opportunities for exploration and discovery.

We embarked on our experimentation journey by delving into the realm of preprocessing activities, a crucial phase in the optimization of DL models. Among the arsenal of techniques, augmentation stands tall as a formidable approach, enriching the model's performance by fostering enhanced generalization capabilities through the application of diverse transformations on the original data. In our quest to prepare images for the COVID-19 database, we meticulously undertook the following steps:

- Augmentation techniques: Leveraging the potential of augmentation, we employed a spectrum of transformations on the images. This encompassed rotations within a range of $\pm 10\%$, scaling variations spanning $\pm 10\%$, and translations in both horizontal and vertical planes by $\pm 10\%$. Furthermore, to enrich the dataset, we introduced a zoom effect, fluctuating by $\pm 15\%$ along both axes. These techniques not only diversify the dataset but also enhance its robustness, enabling our model to generalize better across various scenarios and improve its performance in real-world applications.
- Data transformation: We meticulously convert raw images into pixel arrays, a foundational step in our computational journey. Essential to this process is normalization, a pivotal procedure where we meticulously adjust the pixel values to gracefully reside within the confined range of

[0, 1]. This meticulous scaling ensures uniformity and consistency, laying the groundwork for subsequent analyses and modeling endeavors. By embracing this critical step, we not only streamline our data for optimal computational efficiency but also enhance the interpretability and robustness of our analytical outcomes.

- Enhancing image quality: Employing the adaptive histogram equalization technique was pivotal in our efforts to enhance image quality. This method, a sophisticated form of histogram equalization, effectively addresses issues like distortion and uneven brightness levels. By analyzing the histogram of pixel intensities and redistributing them to achieve a more balanced distribution, it optimizes images for further processing stages. This process not only improves visual clarity but also aids in feature extraction and pattern recognition tasks. As a result, our approach not only enhances the esthetic appeal of images but also significantly boosts the efficacy of subsequent analytical processes.
- Standardization: Standardization played a pivotal role in optimizing the image preprocessing of the proposed dataset. Understanding the significance of uniformity, we meticulously resized the normalized images to regulate dimension of 224 × 224 pixels. This dimension aligns seamlessly with the layer input requirements of each pretrained CNN model integrated into our pipeline. By adhering to this standardized dimension, we ensured compatibility across various models, facilitating smoother data processing and enhancing the efficiency of our image analysis tasks. This meticulous approach underscores our commitment to maximizing the potential of our database through streamlined and optimized processes.

For the subsequent training and validation phases, we partitioned the dataset, allocating 80% for training and reserving the remaining 20% for validation purposes. During the training phase, we opted for the stochastic gradient descent (SGD) optimizer, supplemented with momentum set at 0.9 and employing a gradient threshold method based on the L2 norm. Our training regimen encompassed a minimum batch size of 32 and a maximum epoch count capped at 50. The learning rate remained fixed at 0.0003 throughout the training process. Furthermore, to curtail overfitting, we introduced a factor for L2 regularization (weight decay) set at 0.0001, ensuring the robustness and generalization prowess of our trained models. Fig. 5.7 illustrates SIIM-FISABIO-RSNA COVID-19 dataset.

The experimentation phase took place on Kaggle, utilizing the high computing capabilities of the NVIDIA Tesla P100 GPU for training and verifying the suggested architectures, along with their necessary components and software libraries. In this section, we explore the results achieved in localizing anomalies and carrying out multiclassification assignments on the images. Furthermore, a thorough examination of the experimental results from these assignments is presented, illuminating the progress made in crafting accurate and reliable object detection architecture for identifying abnormalities in the proposed images.

To evaluate the efficacy of the proposed pretrained models, we employed various metrics including confusion matrix criteria and receiver-operating characteristic (ROC) curves. These metrics encompass crucial measurements such as Accuracy (ACC), Precision (P), Recall (R), and F1-score (F1), as outlined in Eqs. (5.1–5.4).

$$\mathrm{ACC} = \frac{\mathrm{TP} + \mathrm{TN}}{\mathrm{TP} + \mathrm{TN} + \mathrm{FP} + \mathrm{FN}} \tag{5.1}$$

$$P = \frac{\mathrm{TP}}{\mathrm{TP} + \mathrm{FP}} \tag{5.2}$$

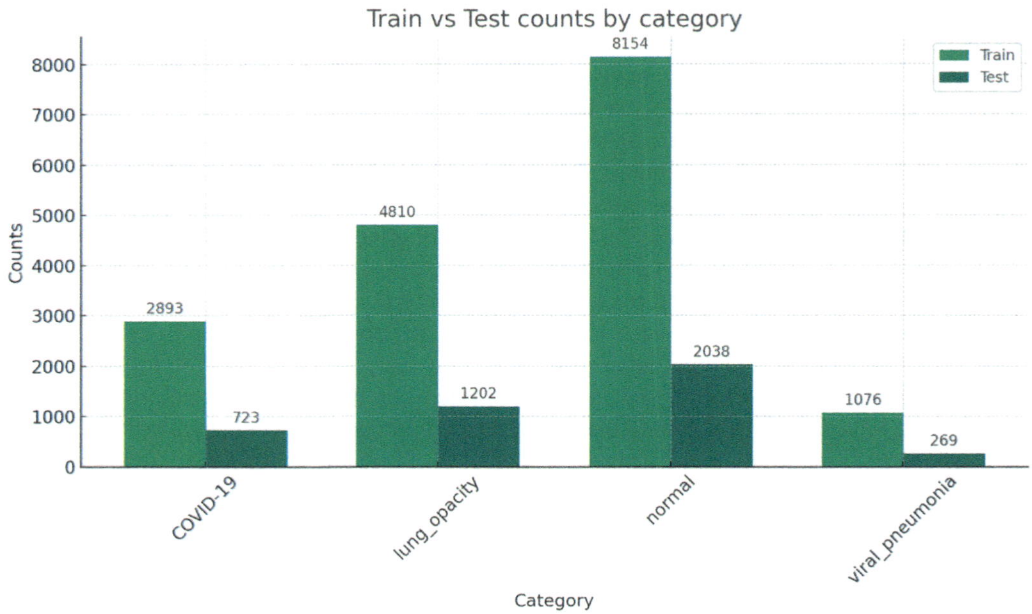

FIGURE 5.7

This bar graph illustrates the distribution of training and testing data across four categories: COVID-19, lung opacity, normal, and viral pneumonia. It highlights the total counts for each category, demonstrating the dataset's composition used in medical imaging studies.

$$R = \frac{\mathrm{TP}}{\mathrm{TP} + \mathrm{FN}} \tag{5.3}$$

$$\mathrm{F1} = 2 \times \frac{(P \times R)}{(P + R)} \tag{5.4}$$

Fig. 5.8 provides a thorough summary of the outcomes derived from analyzing abnormalities in CXR images using multiclassification methods. The assessment entails comparing different models based on various confusion metrics. The results emphasize the effectiveness of the proposed models in accurately classifying four distinct patient conditions: normal, lung opacity, viral pneumonia, and COVID-19. Notably, the models show a capability in prioritizing normal images, followed by lung opacity, COVID-19, and viral pneumonia images. Among these models, ResNet50 emerges as a strong performer, with F1 scores ranging from 0.80 to 0.91 across all categories. Particularly impressive is its ability to identify COVID-19 cases, with the highest F1-score of 0.91, indicating superior classification in this class. Furthermore, ResNet50 demonstrates commendable precision and recall values across all categories, suggesting its capacity to accurately identify positive cases while minimizing false positives. Similarly, VGG19 shows respectable performance, with F1 scores ranging from 0.85 to 0.91 across the four classes. Like ResNet50, VGG19 excels in identifying COVID-19 cases, displaying the highest F1-score within this class. Precision and recall values for COVID-19 and viral pneumonia classes are notably high, affirming the model's accuracy in

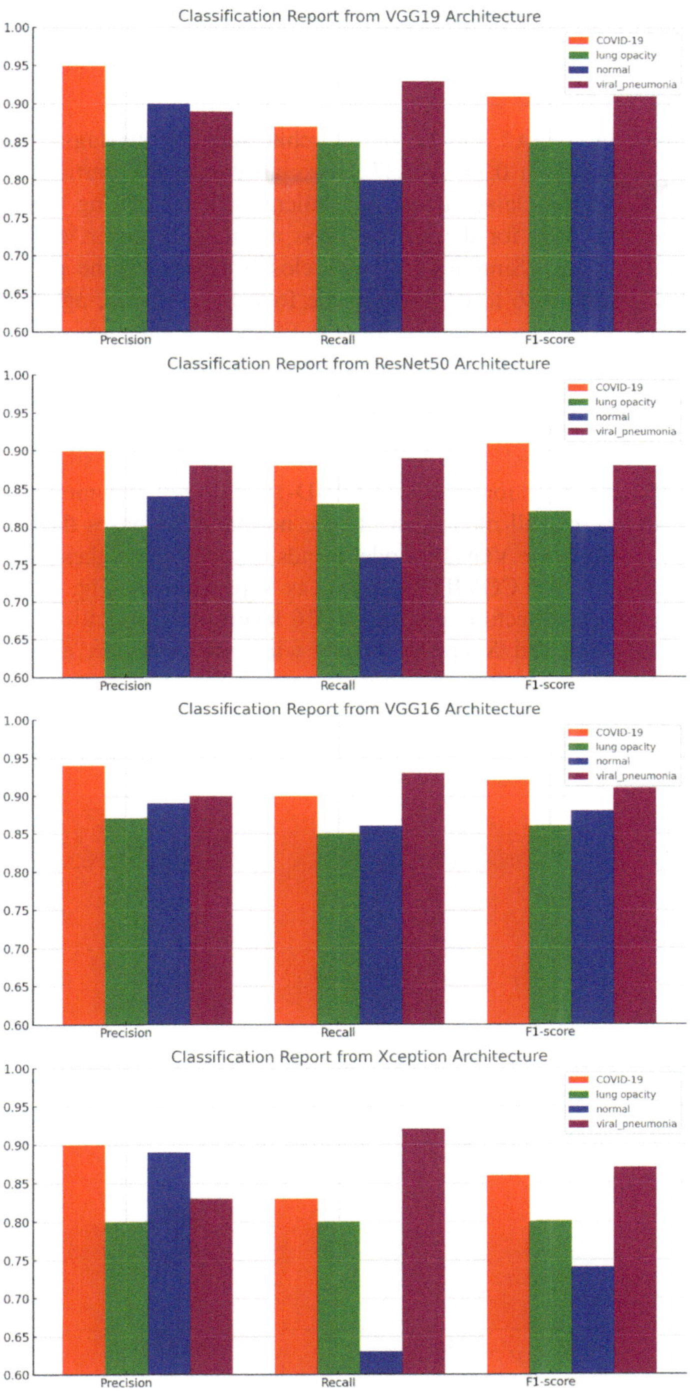

FIGURE 5.8

This graph displays the classification performance metrics—Precision, Recall, and F1-score—for four different classes (COVID-19, lung opacity, normal, and viral pneumonia) using four different deep learning architectures: VGG19, ResNet50, VGG16, and Xception. Each bar represents a metric for a specific class, illustrating how each model varies in identifying these conditions, allowing for a direct comparison of their effectiveness across various classes and metrics.

identifying these cases. In contrast, the Xception architecture slightly lags behind its counterparts, yielding F1 scores ranging from 0.74 to 0.87 across all categories. Particularly concerning is its lower F1-score for the normal class, indicating challenges in identifying this category accurately. The precision and recall values for the normal class are notably lower, suggesting limitations in identifying true negative cases. Similarly, VGG16 closely resembles the performance of VGG19, with F1 scores ranging from 0.86 to 0.92 across the four classes. Once again, the model excels in identifying COVID-19 cases, achieving the highest F1-score within this class. The precision and recall values for COVID-19 and viral pneumonia classes remain high, further confirming the model's accuracy in identifying positive cases. Overall, all four models demonstrate commendable performance, with F1 scores ranging from 0.74 to 0.92 across all categories. However, subtle performance differences are noted, with VGG19 and VGG16 showing slightly better performance compared to ResNet50 and Xception models. COVID-19 and viral pneumonia classes are comparatively easier to identify across all models, while the normal class poses the greatest challenge for the Xception model. Notably, the VGG16 model stands out with the highest accuracy of 92.1% and excels in multiclassification of COVID-19 cases, as supported by Fig. 5.8. The superiority of VGG16 lies in its simpler architecture, comprising 16 layers, which facilitates easier training compared to VGG19, ResNet50, and Xception models with more complex architectures. The use of smaller 3×3 filters in VGG16 enables learning of more detailed features, crucial for effective analysis of CXR images. Additionally, the incorporation of max pooling after every two convolution layers in VGG16 helps in reducing the spatial dimensionality of feature maps. Fig. 5.9 illustrates the accuracy for the four pretrained models.

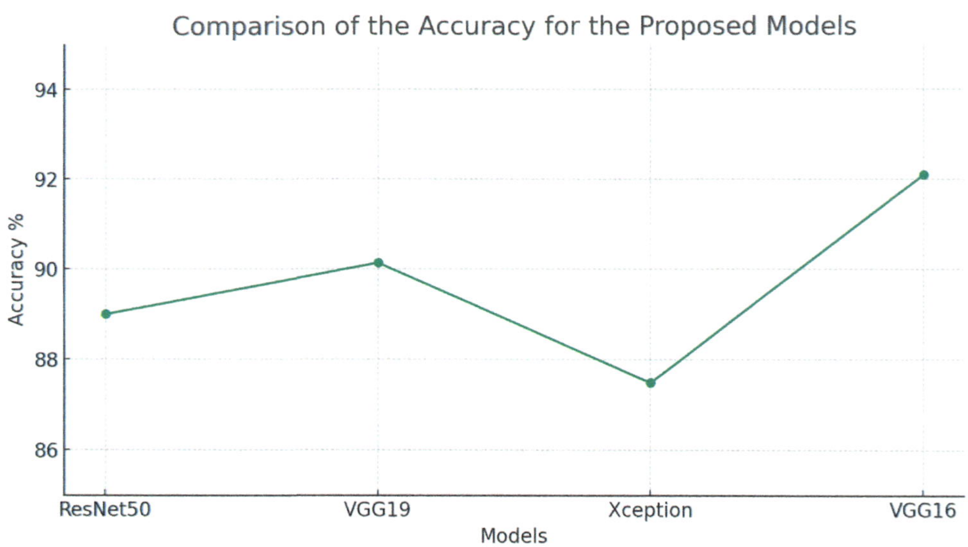

FIGURE 5.9

This graph representing the comparison of accuracy for the proposed models: ResNet50, VGG19, Xception, and VGG16. The graph uses markers to denote the accuracy percentage for each model, providing a clear visualization of the performance trend across the models.

5.5.2 Localization of abnormalities on chest X-ray images

Various trials were carried out on each model utilizing a proposed preprocessing method involving image cropping and rotation. This preprocessing aimed to improve the models' performance by exposing them to images in various orientations and sizes, mimicking real-world scenarios where medical images may differ in rotation and cropping. The outcomes of these trials shed light on the performance of three notable object detection models: Faster R-CNN, YOLOv7, and YOLOv8x. The results reveal that the mean average precision (mAP) attained by each model is capped at 0.49 for Faster R-CNN, 0.47 for YOLOv7, and 0.46 for the YOLOv8x model. These figures offer insights into the effectiveness of each model in accurately identifying abnormalities in CXR images. However, it is crucial to delve deeper into the implications of these results and grasp the challenges encountered by object detection models when applied to medical imaging, particularly CXRs. CXRs pose a unique set of challenges for CV models due to their intricate nature. Unlike natural images, which usually depict distinct objects against a relatively uniform background, CXRs often display overlapping organs, structures, and subtle disease manifestations. This complexity stems from the intricacies of human anatomy and the interactions of X-rays with various tissues and organs. One of the main hurdles faced by object detection models when analyzing CXRs is the presence of overlapping anatomical structures. Organs such as the heart, lungs, ribs, and blood vessels can overlap in X-ray images, making it difficult for models to accurately delineate boundaries and identify individual abnormalities. Additionally, the subtle variations in grayscale intensity and texture further complicate the task of distinguishing between normal and abnormal regions. Moreover, the manifestation of diseases in CXRs can vary significantly from patient to patient. While some abnormalities may exhibit characteristic patterns or shapes, others may present as subtle deviations from normal anatomy. This variability necessitates robust feature extraction and classification mechanisms capable of capturing both common abnormalities and rare, atypical manifestations. Furthermore, the inherent noise and artifacts present in X-ray images pose additional challenges for object detection models. Artifacts such as motion blur, scatter radiation, and hardware imperfections can obscure important anatomical details and mimic pathological findings, leading to false positives or false negatives in the detection process. In light of these challenges, the modest mAP scores obtained by the object detection models underscore the need for further research and refinement in medical imaging applications. While the tested models demonstrate promising capabilities, there is still room for improvement, particularly in addressing the complexities specific to CXR analysis. Future work may involve exploring advanced feature extraction techniques, incorporating domain-specific knowledge into model architectures, and leveraging larger, more diverse datasets to enhance model generalization and robustness. The experiments conducted on Faster R-CNN, YOLOv7, and YOLOv8x models highlight both the potential and limitations of object detection in CXR analysis. While the models demonstrate reasonable performance, the challenges posed by the intricate nature of CXRs necessitate continued research and innovation to realize their full potential in clinical practice.

5.5.3 Ensembled models for enhancing localization of abnormalities

The SIIM-FISABIO-RSNA COVID-19 dataset shows an imbalance in class distribution, where the number of annotations differs across various classes. This discrepancy can negatively impact the performance in underrepresented classes, leading to decreased mean average precision. To address this issue and improve overall performance, we utilize the weighted box fusion (WBF) technique. This method employs ensemble strategies by combining predicted confidence scores and bounding boxes from multiple object detection models. The WBF technique utilizes confidence scores from all proposed bounding boxes to create average boxes. Initially, it computes the Intersection over Union (IoU) between pairs of bounding boxes to measure their overlap, as defined in Eq. (5.5). Then, weights are assigned to each bounding box based on its confidence score and IoU with other boxes. Finally, a weighted average of the bounding boxes is computed to obtain the final prediction, as depicted in Fig. 5.10.

$$\mathrm{IoU}(b_1, b_2) = \frac{\mathrm{area}(b_1 \cap b_2)}{\mathrm{area}(b_1 \cup b_2)} \tag{5.5}$$

Assuming you have N object detectors in your ensemble, and each detector produces a set of bounding boxes with their corresponding confidence scores, the WBF (Eq. 5.6) is:

$$B^* = \sum_{i=1}^{N} w_i B_i \tag{5.6}$$

In the context of object detection, the fused set of bounding boxes B_i is derived from the individual sets of bounding boxes produced by each detector i, where w_i represents the weight assigned to each detector based on its performance and reliability. The determination of these weights can be approached through various methods, such as assessing precision and recall on a validation set or utilizing mAP scores derived from a test set. It is crucial to normalize these weights so that their collective sum equals 1. Following weight computation, the final set of bounding boxes B^* is obtained by aggregating the bounding boxes from each detector in a linear manner, where each contribution is scaled by its respective weight.

The mean average precision was employed to evaluate the performance of object detection, particularly focusing on CXR images. mAP accounts for the influence of different confidence thresholds on detection accuracy. Confidence scores are assigned by object detectors to each identified

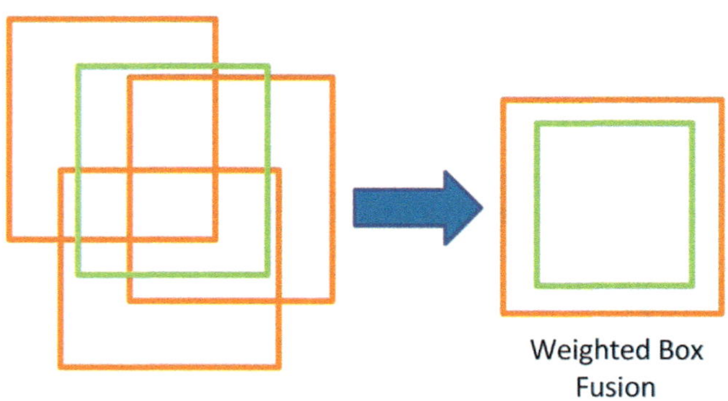

FIGURE 5.10

Diagram illustrating the weighted box fusion (WBF) technique for combining multiple bounding boxes within an ensemble.

object, indicating the algorithm's confidence in its correctness. By adjusting the threshold for considering an object as detected, mAP captures the intricate balance between precision and recall, providing valuable insights into the algorithm's efficacy across various operational points, as illustrated in Eqs. (5.7) and (5.8) where k stands for the number of queries, and AP_i denotes the average precision (AP) for a specific query (i).

$$\text{Average Precision (AP)} = \int_{r=0}^{1} p(r)dr \tag{5.7}$$

$$\text{mAP} = \frac{1}{k}\sum_{i}^{k} \text{AP}_i \tag{5.8}$$

In this study, an ensemble approach was employed to enhance COVID-19 detection, integrating multiple object detectors and evaluating them using the SIIM-FISABIO-RSNA COVID-19 dataset. Initially, the combination of YOLOv7 and EfficientNet was examined, resulting in an improvement of the mean average precision to 0.58 mAP@0.5. Subsequently, a more comprehensive system was devised by introducing Faster R-CNN to augment the ensemble, resulting in the amalgamation of EfficientNet, YOLOv7, and Faster R-CNN. This integration led to a further enhancement in mAP, reaching 0.612 mAP@0.5, as depicted in Fig. 5.11. Ensemble models, by nature, amalgamate the strengths of multiple individual models to mitigate their respective weaknesses, thereby enhancing

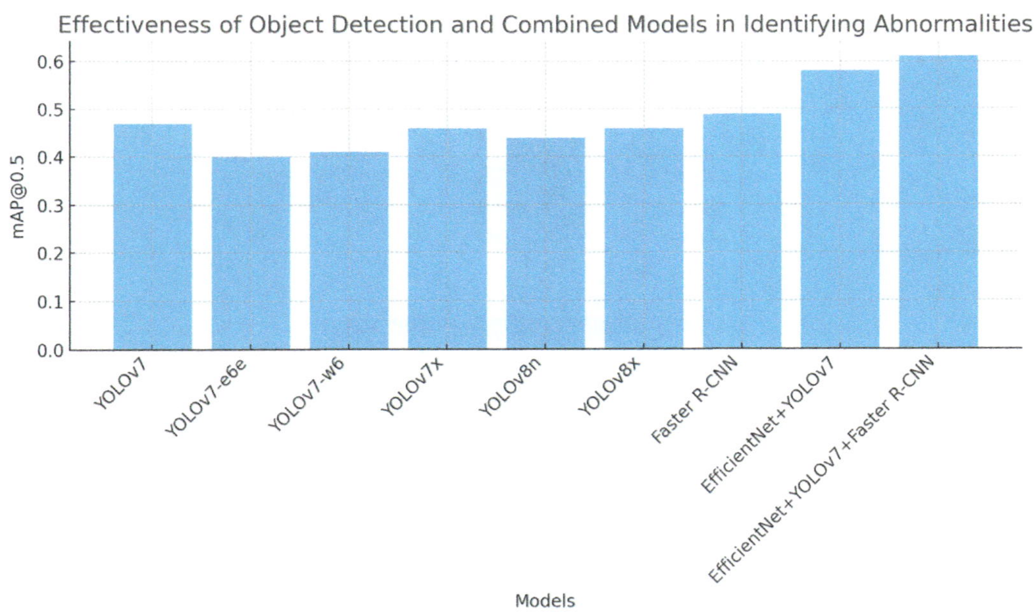

FIGURE 5.11

This figure represents the effectiveness of various object detection models in identifying abnormalities, measured by the metric mAP@0.5. The graph compares traditional models like YOLO and Faster R-CNN with combined models such as EfficientNet + YOLOv7, highlighting the superior performance of the latter in this task.

overall performance. In this specific scenario, the EfficientNet model, renowned for its efficacy in image classification, was fused with YOLOv7 and Faster R-CNN, both prominent object detection models with distinctive attributes. YOLOv7 excels in real-time processing and speed, whereas Faster R-CNN boasts higher accuracy albeit at a slower pace. Through this amalgamation, the ensemble models leverage the swiftness of YOLOv7 and the precision of Faster R-CNN, while capitalizing on EfficientNet's classification capabilities. The evaluation metric of mAP gauges the precision of a model across various levels of recall, providing insight into its ability to accurately identify objects of interest. As evidenced, the ensemble model EfficientNet + YOLOv7 achieves a mAP of 0.58, surpassing the performance of any individual object detection model. Furthermore, the inclusion of Faster R-CNN in the ensemble, resulting in EfficientNet + YOLOv7 + Faster

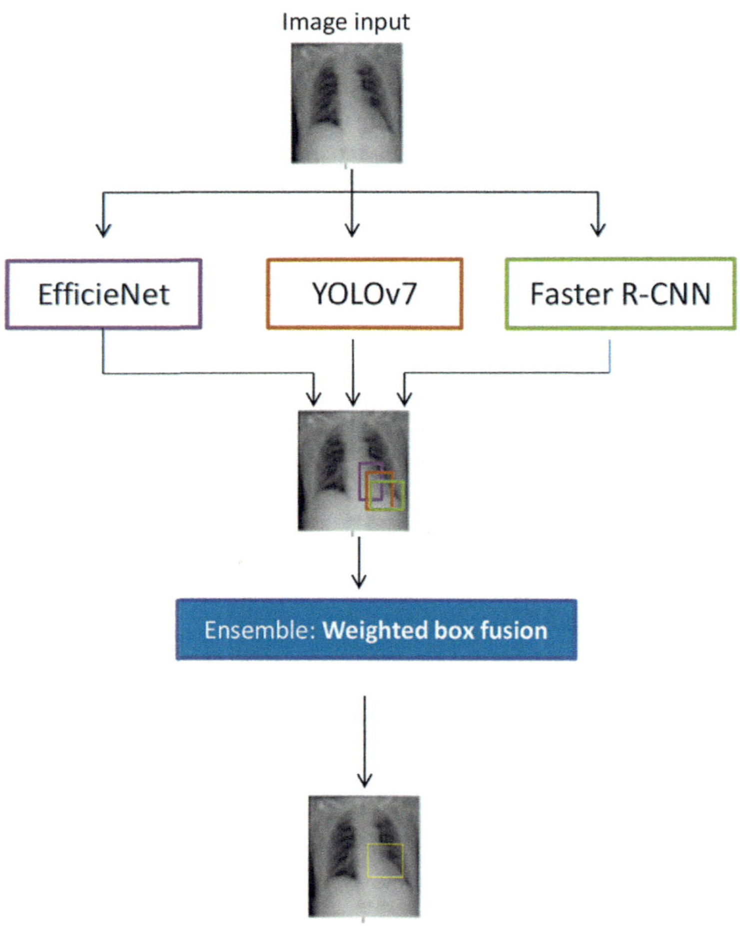

FIGURE 5.12

The ultimate ensemble models incorporate EfficientNet, YOLOv7, and Faster R-CNN to pinpoint and identify objects in chest X-ray images.

R-CNN, yields a higher mAP of 0.612, indicative of superior performance. The rationale behind the efficacy of ensemble models lies in their ability to exploit the strengths of diverse models, ultimately leading to more accurate and efficient detection of abnormalities. Fig. 5.12 shows the ultimate ensemble models incorporate EfficientNet, YOLOv7, and Faster R-CNN to pinpoint and identify objects in CXR images.

References

Aslan, M. F., Sabanci, K., Durdu, A., & Unlersen, M. F. (2022). COVID-19 diagnosis using state-of-the-art CNN architecture features and Bayesian optimization. *Computers in Biology and Medicine*, *142*. Available from http://www.elsevier.com/locate/compbiomed, https://doi.org/10.1016/j.compbiomed.2022.105244.

Attallah, O. (2022). ECG-BiCoNet: An ECG-based pipeline for COVID-19 diagnosis using bi-layers of deep features integration. *Computers in Biology and Medicine*, *142*, 105210. Available from https://doi.org/10.1016/j.compbiomed.2022.105210.

Basu, S., Mitra, S., & Saha, N. (2020). Deep learning for screening COVID-19 using chest X-ray images. *IEEE symposium series on computational intelligence*, SSCI, Institute of Electrical and Electronics Engineers Inc. India. http://ieeexplore.ieee.org/xpl/mostRecentIssue.jsp?punumber = 9308061.

Bhowal, P., Sen, S., Yoon, J. H., Geem, Z. W., & Sarkar, R. (2021). Choquet integral and coalition game-based ensemble of deep learning models for COVID-19 screening from chest X-ray images. *IEEE Journal of Biomedical and Health Informatics*, *25*(12), 4328–4339. Available from https://doi.org/10.1109/JBHI.2021.3111415, http://ieeexplore.ieee.org/xpl/RecentIssue.jsp?punumber = 6221020.

Cao, G. Song, W., & Zhao, Z. (2019) Gastric cancer diagnosis with mask R-CNN. *Proceedings - 2019 11th international conference on intelligent human-machine systems and cybernetics, IHMSC*. Institute of Electrical and Electronics Engineers Inc. China. http://ieeexplore.ieee.org/xpl/mostRecentIssue.jsp?punumber = 8936461.

Chen, H., Jiang, Y., Loew, M., & Ko, H. (2022). Unsupervised domain adaptation based COVID-19 CT infection segmentation network. *Applied Intelligence*, *52*(6), 6340–6353. Available from https://doi.org/10.1007/s10489-021-02691-x, http://www.springer.com/journal/10489.

Chiao, J.-Y., Chen, K.-Y., Liao, K. Y.-K., Hsieh, P.-H., Zhang, G., & Huang, T.-C. (2019). Detection and classification the breast tumors using mask R-CNN on sonograms. *Medicine*, *98*(19), e15200. Available from https://doi.org/10.1097/md.0000000000015200.

Chowdhury, M. E. H., Rahman, T., Khandakar, A., Mazhar, R., Kadir, M. A., Mahbub, Z. B., Islam, K. R., Khan, M. S., Iqbal, A., Emadi, N. A., Reaz, M. B. I., & Islam, M. T. (2020). Can AI help in screening viral and COVID-19 pneumonia? *IEEE Access*, *8*, 132665–132676. Available from http://ieeexplore.ieee.org/xpl/RecentIssue.jsp?punumber = 6287639, https://doi.org/10.1109/ACCESS.2020.3010287.

Dong, D., Tang, Z., Wang, S., Hui, H., Gong, L., Lu, Y., Xue, Z., Liao, H., Chen, F., Yang, F., Jin, R., Wang, K., Liu, Z., Wei, J., Mu, W., Zhang, H., Jiang, J., Tian, J., & Li, H. (2021). *The role of imaging in the detection and management of COVID-19: A review. IEEE Reviews in Biomedical Engineering* (14, pp. 16–29). Available from http://ieeexplore.ieee.org/xpl/RecentIssue.jsp?punumber = 4664312, https://doi.org/10.1109/RBME.2020.2990959.

Elhanashi, A., Lowe, D., Saponara, S., & Moshfeghi, Y. (2022). Deep learning techniques to identify and classify COVID-19 abnormalities on chest X-ray images. *Proceedings of SPIE - the international society for optical engineering*. SPIE, Italy. http://spie.org/x1848.xml.

Geetha, R., Balasubramanian, M., & Devi, K. R. (2022). COVIDetection: Deep convolutional neural networks-based automatic detection of COVID-19 with chest x-ray images. *Research on Biomedical Engineering*, *38*(3), 955–964. Available from https://doi.org/10.1007/s42600-022-00230-2, https://link.springer.com/journal/42600.

Hou, J., & Gao, T. (2021). Explainable DCNN based chest X-ray image analysis and classification for COVID-19 pneumonia detection. *Scientific Reports*, *11*(1). Available from https://doi.org/10.1038/s41598-021-95680-6, http://www.nature.com/srep/index.html.

Jaiswal, A., Gianchandani, N., Singh, D., Kumar, V., & Kaur, M. (2021). Classification of the COVID-19 infected patients using DenseNet201 based deep transfer learning. *Journal of Biomolecular Structure and Dynamics*, *39*(15), 5682–5689. Available from https://doi.org/10.1080/07391102.2020.1788642, http://www.tandfonline.com/loi/tbsd20.

Jiang, H., Tang, S., Liu, W., & Zhang, Y. (2021). Deep learning for COVID-19 chest CT (computed tomography) image analysis: A lesson from lung cancer. *Computational and Structural Biotechnology Journal*, *19*, 1391–1399. Available from http://www.csbj.org, https://doi.org/10.1016/j.csbj.2021.02.016.

Karim, M. R., Dohmen, T., Cochez, M., Beyan, O., Rebholz-Schuhmann, D., & Decker, S. (2020). DeepCOVIDExplainer: Explainable COVID-19 diagnosis from chest X-ray images. *Proceedings - 2020 IEEE international conference on bioinformatics and biomedicine, BIBM*. Institute of Electrical and Electronics Engineers Inc. Germany. http://ieeexplore.ieee.org/xpl/mostRecentIssue.jsp?punumber = 9312958.

Li, X., Tan, W., Liu, P., Zhou, Q., Yang, J., & Pavone, L. (2021). Classification of COVID-19 chest CT images based on ensemble deep learning. *Journal of Healthcare Engineering*, *2021*, 1–7. Available from https://doi.org/10.1155/2021/5528441.

Lin, K., Zhao, H., Lv, J., Li, C., Liu, X., Chen, R., & Zhao, R. (2020). Discrete dynamics in nature and society, face detection and\nsegmentation based on improved mask R-CNN. *Discrete Dynamics in Nature and Society*.

Liu, M., Dong, J., Dong, X., Yu, H., & Qi, L. (2018). Segmentation of lung nodule in CT images based on mask R-CNN. *9th International conference on awareness science and technology, iCAST*. Institute of Electrical and Electronics Engineers Inc. China. http://ieeexplore.ieee.org/xpl/mostRecentIssue.jsp?punumber = 8501354.

Minaee, S., Kafieh, R., Sonka, M., Yazdani, S., & Jamalipour Soufi, G. (2020). Deep-COVID: Predicting COVID-19 from chest X-ray images using deep transfer learning. *Medical Image Analysis*, *65*, 101794. Available from https://doi.org/10.1016/j.media.2020.101794.

Mulay, S., Deepika, G., Jeevakala, S., Ram, K., & Sivaprakasam, M. (2019). *Liver segmentation from multi-modal images using HED-mask R-CNN* (pp. 68–75). Springer Science and Business Media LLC. Available from https://doi.org/10.1007/978-3-030-37969-8_9.

Narin, A., Kaya, C., & Pamuk, Z. (n.d.). Automatic detection of coronavirus disease (Covid-19) using X-ray images and deep convolutional neural networks, 2020 arXiv preprint.

Nguyen, D. H., Le, T. H., Tran, T. H., Vu, H., Le, T. L., & Doan, H. G. (2018). Hand segmentation under different viewpoints by combination of mask r-cnn with tracking. *Proceedings of the 5th Asian conference on defence technology, ACDT*. Institute of Electrical and Electronics Engineers Inc. Vietnam. http://ieeexplore.ieee.org/xpl/mostRecentIssue.jsp?punumber = 8580229.

Rahman, T., Khandakar, A., Qiblawey, Y., Tahir, A., Kiranyaz, S., Kashem, S. B. A., Islam, M. T., Maadeed, S. A., Zughaier, S. M., Khan, M. S., & Chowdhury, M. E. H. (2020). Exploring the effect of image enhancement techniques on COVID-19 detection using chest X-rays images. *arXiv*. Available from https://doi.org/10.48550/arxiv.2012.02238, https://arxiv.org.

Reis, K. W., & Oliveira-Esquerre, K. P. Diagnosis of patients with blood cell count for COVID-19: an explainable artificial intelligence approach. *Journal of Health Informatics*. 13 (n.d.).

Sethi, R., Mehrotra, M., Sethi, D. (2020). Deep learning based diagnosis recommendation for COVID-19 using chest X-Rays images. *Proceedings of the 2nd international conference on inventive research in computing applications, ICIRCA*. Institute of Electrical and Electronics Engineers Inc. India. http://ieeexplore.ieee.org/xpl/mostRecentIssue.jsp?punumber = 9169741.

Sethy, P. K., Behera, S. K., Ratha, P. K., & Biswas, P. (2020). Detection of coronavirus disease (COVID-19) based on deep features and support vector machine. *International Journal of Mathematical, Engineering and Management Sciences*, *5*(4), 643–651. Available from https://doi.org/10.33889/IJMEMS.2020.5.4.052, http://www.ijmems.in/volumes/volume5/number4/52-IJMEMS-20-46-54-643-651-2020.pdf.

Shi, F., Wang, J., Shi, J., Wu, Z., Wang, Q., Tang, Z., He, K., Shi, Y., & Shen, D. (2021). Review of artificial intelligence techniques in imaging data acquisition, segmentation, and diagnosis for COVID-19. *IEEE Reviews in Biomedical Engineering*, *14*, 4–15. Available from https://doi.org/10.1109/rbme.2020.2987975.

Shibata, T., Teramoto, A., Yamada, H., Ohmiya, N., Saito, K., & Fujita, H. (2020). Automated detection and segmentation of early gastric cancer from endoscopic images using mask R-CNN. *Applied Sciences*, *10* (11), 3842. Available from https://doi.org/10.3390/app10113842.

Shu, J. H., Nian, F. D., Yu, M. H., & Li, X. (2020). An improved mask R-CNN model for multiorgan segmentation. *Mathematical Problems in Engineering*, *2020*. Available from http://www.hindawi.com/journals/mpe/contents.html, https://doi.org/10.1155/2020/8351725.

Tang, S., Wang, C., Nie, J., Kumar, N., Zhang, Y., Xiong, Z., & Barnawi, A. (2021). EDL-COVID: Ensemble deep learning for COVID-19 case detection from chest X-ray images. *IEEE Transactions on Industrial Informatics*, *17*(9), 6539–6549. Available from https://doi.org/10.1109/TII.2021.3057683, http://ieeexplore.ieee.org/xpl/RecentIssue.jsp?punumber = 9424.

Wang, S., Kang, B., Ma, J., Zeng, X., Xiao, M., Guo, J., Cai, M., Yang, J., Li, Y., Meng, X., & Xu, B. (2020). A deep learning algorithm using CT images to screen for corona virus disease (COVID-19). *medRxiv*. Available from https://www.medrxiv.org/, https://doi.org/10.1101/2020.02.14.20023028.

Ying, S., Zheng, S., Li, L., Zhang, X., Zhang, X., Huang, Z., Chen, J., Zhao, H., Wang, R., Chong, Y., Shen, J., Zha, Y., & Yang, Y. (2020). Deep learning enables accurate diagnosis of novel coronavirus (COVID-19) with CT images. *medRxiv*. Available from https://www.medrxiv.org/, https://doi.org/10.1101/2020.02.23.20026930.

Zhang, K., Liu, X., Shen, J., Li, Z., Sang, Y., Wu, X., Zha, Y., Liang, W., Wang, C., Wang, K., Ye, L., Gao, M., Zhou, Z., Li, L., Wang, J., Yang, Z., Cai, H., Xu, J., Yang, L., … Wang. (2020). Clinically applicable AI system for accurate diagnosis, quantitative measurements, and prognosis of COVID-19 pneumonia using computed tomography. *Cell*, *181*(6), 1423. Available from https://doi.org/10.1016/j.cell.2020.04.045.

CHAPTER

Real-time stroke detection based on deep learning and federated learning 6

6.1 Background

Stroke is a major global health concern, being a primary cause of death and disability. The early recognition and accurate diagnosis of stroke symptoms are vital to enhancing patient outcomes. This introductory segment will discuss the identification and diagnostic procedures for stroke, underscoring the significance of quick intervention (Basu, 2014; Díez-Tejedor & Fuentes, 2003; Hayes & Carroll, 1986; Powers et al., 2019). A stroke, or cerebrovascular accident, happens when the brain's blood supply is disrupted, causing brain cell damage or death. There are primarily two types of strokes: ischemic, resulting from an obstruction in a brain-supplying blood vessel, and hemorrhagic, caused by bleeding within the brain. The signs and symptoms of a stroke can be recalled with the acronym FAST: face drooping, arm weakness, speech difficulty, time to call emergency services. Additional symptoms include sudden numbness or weakness on one side of the body, confusion, difficulties with speech or understanding, problems with vision, dizziness, loss of balance or coordination, and an unexplained severe headache (Jauch et al., 2013). When symptoms suggest a stroke, it is crucial for healthcare providers to quickly confirm the diagnosis and identify the stroke type to begin the appropriate treatment. Diagnostic tools and methods include imaging techniques, such as computed tomography (CT) scans, magnetic resonance imaging (MRI), and angiography, which are utilized to visualize the brain and assess its electrical activity, along with blood tests to check for underlying causes like high cholesterol or clotting disorders (Merino & Warach, 2010). Immediate action is crucial in stroke management to limit brain damage and enhance outcomes. The "time is brain" philosophy highlights the need for swift evaluation and treatment to maintain brain function. For ischemic strokes, prompt delivery of thrombolytic therapy (like tissue plasminogen activator) or mechanical thrombectomy may be necessary to reopen the blocked artery. In hemorrhagic stroke cases, urgent neurosurgical procedures are required to manage bleeding and alleviate brain pressure. Early intervention is vital in stroke management, as it helps limit brain damage and enhances recovery prospects. The principle of "time is brain" underscores the urgency of quick assessment and treatment to preserve brain functionality. For ischemic strokes, timely treatment might involve thrombolytic therapy (such as tissue plasminogen activator) or mechanical clot removal to restore blood flow. In hemorrhagic strokes, early neurosurgical intervention may be required to stop the bleeding and alleviate brain pressure.

Imaging techniques like CT and MRI are crucial in diagnosing stroke. CT scans are primarily used to exclude hemorrhagic stroke, whereas MRIs are particularly effective in identifying ischemic strokes and distinguishing them from other nonstroke conditions. The application of DL in image and video recognition has brought transformative changes to how computers analyze visual information (Elhanashi et al., 2022; Elhanashi, Saponara, Dini, et al., 2023; Saponara et al., 2021). Moreover, DL has drastically improved classification and modulation processes, significantly

Deep Learning in Action: Image and Video Processing for Practical Use. DOI: https://doi.org/10.1016/B978-0-443-30078-3.00006-8

outperforming traditional techniques (Zheng et al., 2022). Techniques, such as perfusion imaging and diffusion-weighted imaging are increasingly recognized for their potential to improve the precision of stroke diagnoses (Campbell et al., 2019). DL, especially through the use of convolutional neural networks (CNNs), has markedly enhanced diagnostic accuracy and patient management across various medical imaging fields, including ophthalmology, respiratory imaging, and breast health. It has enabled effective diagnosis of conditions like diabetic retinopathy, lung nodules, and breast cancer using medical imaging technologies, such as retinal fundus photography, CT scans, and mammograms. However, despite these advancements, challenges remain, including the development of reliable quantitative imaging biomarkers, concerns about data quality and bias, and the opaque nature of DL algorithms. Initiatives to tackle these issues and boost the clinical value of DL in medical imaging are in progress (Aggarwal et al., 2021; Elhanashi, Saponara, Zheng, et al., 2023; Varoquaux & Cheplygina, 2022).

6.1.1 Stroke as a critical health issue

Stroke is a critical health issue with significant global impact, posing substantial challenges to healthcare systems, economies, and patients' quality of life. It is the second leading cause of death worldwide and a major cause of long-term disability (The top 10 causes of death, 2018). Strokes occur when the blood supply to part of the brain is interrupted or reduced, preventing brain tissue from getting oxygen and nutrients, and leading to the death of brain cells within minutes. There are two main types of strokes: ischemic stroke, caused by a blockage in an artery, and hemorrhagic stroke, caused by a rupture of a blood vessel (American Stroke Association Types of Stroke, 2021) Ischemic strokes are the most common, accounting for about 87% of all strokes (Benjamin et al., 2019). Risk factors for stroke include high blood pressure, diabetes, high cholesterol, smoking, and atrial fibrillation. Lifestyle factors, such as physical inactivity, poor diet, and excessive alcohol consumption also contribute to stroke risk (Mozaffarian et al., 2015). Additionally, genetic factors and age play significant roles, with the risk increasing substantially in people over 65 years old (Feigin et al., 2014). The burden of stroke is not evenly distributed; low- and middle-income countries bear a disproportionately high share of stroke morbidity and mortality, largely due to less access to healthcare, lower awareness, and fewer preventive measures. The consequences of stroke extend beyond the immediate health effects. Survivors often face significant challenges, including physical disability, cognitive impairment, and emotional difficulties. Rehabilitation can be a long and arduous process, requiring multidisciplinary care from physiotherapists, occupational therapists, speech therapists, and psychologists (Langhorne et al., 2011). Despite advances in acute stroke management, such as thrombolysis and thrombectomy for ischemic stroke, many patients do not receive these treatments due to late arrival at the hospital or lack of specialized stroke centers (Powers et al., 2018). Prevention is crucial in reducing the burden of stroke. Primary prevention focuses on managing risk factors, such as hypertension, diabetes, and hyperlipidemia through lifestyle changes and medication (Campbell et al., 2019). Public health campaigns aimed at smoking cessation, promoting physical activity, and healthy eating are essential in reducing the incidence of stroke. Secondary prevention involves preventing recurrent strokes in patients who have already experienced one. This includes the use of antiplatelet or anticoagulant therapy, controlling blood pressure, and lifestyle modifications (Hankey, 2014). The economic impact of stroke is substantial, involving direct medical costs, long-term rehabilitation expenses, and indirect costs, such as loss of productivity and informal care provided by family members (Kaur et al., 2014). In the United States alone, the estimated annual cost of stroke is around $46 billion, including healthcare services, medications, and missed days of work. The personal impact on patients and their families is equally profound, often leading to a reduced quality of life and increased caregiver burden. Effective stroke management requires a comprehensive approach, integrating prevention, acute care, and rehabilitation. Acute stroke care involves rapid diagnosis using imaging techniques, such as CT and MRI scans, and immediate treatment to restore blood flow in ischemic strokes or control bleeding in hemorrhagic strokes. The implementation of stroke units, specialized hospital wards dedicated to the care of stroke patients, has been shown to improve outcomes significantly. These units provide coordinated care by a team of healthcare professionals specializing in stroke management. Rehabilitation is an integral part of stroke recovery, aiming to help patients regain independence and improve their quality of life. Rehabilitation strategies are tailored to individual needs and may include exercises to improve motor skills, training in daily living activities, and cognitive therapy to address memory, attention, and problem-solving deficits (Cramer et al., 2011). Innovations in stroke rehabilitation, such as the use of virtual reality, robotics, and brain–computer interfaces, hold promise for enhancing recovery. Support for stroke survivors and their families is also crucial. This includes providing information about stroke and recovery, connecting them with support groups, and offering psychological support to cope with the emotional aftermath of a stroke. Public awareness campaigns are vital for improving the recognition of stroke symptoms and the importance of seeking immediate medical help. The acronym FAST is widely used to educate the public on the signs of stroke and the need for urgent intervention. Despite progress, many challenges remain in the fight against stroke. Disparities in stroke care and outcomes persist across different socioeconomic and racial groups (Howard et al., 2011). Research into new treatments, including neuroprotective agents and regenerative therapies, is ongoing, aiming to improve outcomes for stroke patients (Zhang et al., 2013). Policy initiatives to improve stroke care infrastructure, increase funding for stroke research, and enhance public health strategies are essential in addressing this critical health issue. In conclusion, stroke represents a major global health challenge with profound medical, economic, and social implications. Comprehensive strategies encompassing prevention, acute care, rehabilitation, and support for survivors are essential to reduce the burden of stroke. Continued efforts in research, public health policy, and healthcare delivery are needed to improve stroke outcomes and quality of life for stroke patients and their families.

6.1.2 Current challenges in stroke detection

Stroke detection faces several challenges today, with significant implications for patient outcomes and healthcare systems globally. One of the primary challenges is the timely and accurate identification of stroke symptoms. Early detection is crucial for effective treatment, particularly in administering thrombolytic therapy within a narrow therapeutic window. However, symptoms of stroke can be varied and nonspecific, often leading to delays in diagnosis. Common symptoms like sudden numbness, confusion, trouble speaking, and severe headaches are sometimes mistaken for other medical conditions (Johnston, 2007). This diagnostic challenge is compounded in rural and underserved areas where access to advanced medical imaging technology is limited. Imaging technologies like CT and MRI are essential for confirming a stroke diagnosis, determining its type (ischemic or hemorrhagic), and guiding treatment. Yet, these resources are not universally available, and there can be significant delays in obtaining the necessary scans. In urban areas with better access to these technologies, the challenge often lies in the availability of radiologists who can promptly interpret the images, particularly during off-hours or in high-volume settings. Another critical challenge in stroke detection is the differentiation between stroke types. Ischemic strokes, caused by a blockage in a blood vessel (Wardlaw et al., 2014), require different management compared to hemorrhagic strokes, which are caused by bleeding in the brain (Donnan et al., 2008). Misclassification can lead to inappropriate treatment and potentially worsen patient outcomes. Advanced imaging techniques, such as perfusion imaging and diffusion-weighted imaging, have improved the accuracy of stroke type identification, but their use is still limited by availability and the need for specialized training Additionally, the implementation of telestroke services, which use telemedicine to provide remote diagnosis and consultation, has shown promise in addressing some of these challenges, particularly in remote and underserved regions. However, the adoption of telestroke is uneven, often hindered by logistical, financial, and regulatory barriers (Demaerschalk et al., 2009). Another significant hurdle in stroke detection is public awareness and education. Many individuals are not familiar with the signs of stroke, or the urgency required in seeking medical attention. Public health campaigns aimed at increasing awareness of stroke symptoms and the importance of rapid response, such as the FAST campaign, have been somewhat effective, but gaps in knowledge persist, particularly among high-risk populations. Furthermore, disparities in stroke detection and treatment are evident across different demographic groups. Studies have shown that minorities and individuals from lower socioeconomic backgrounds often experience delays in stroke recognition and treatment (Tong et al., 2002). These disparities are attributed to a combination of factors, including lower health literacy, limited access to healthcare, and potential biases within the healthcare system. Addressing these disparities requires targeted interventions that consider cultural, economic, and systemic factors. In addition to these challenges, the evolving landscape of stroke care presents new obstacles. Advances in neuroimaging and biomarkers hold promise for more precise and rapid stroke detection, but integrating these technologies into routine clinical practice is complex and costly. Moreover, the development of artificial intelligence (AI) and machine learning algorithms for stroke detection is a burgeoning field, offering the potential to enhance diagnostic accuracy and efficiency (Davenport & Kalakota, 2019). However, the implementation of AI in clinical settings raises issues related to data privacy, algorithmic bias, and the need for extensive validation and training of healthcare professionals. The regulatory framework for the approval and oversight of AI tools in medicine is still evolving, adding another layer of complexity to their adoption (Topol, 2019). Finally, the COVID-19 pandemic has posed additional challenges for stroke detection and management. During the pandemic, many individuals have delayed seeking medical care due to fear of exposure to the virus, leading to an increase in the number of patients presenting with advanced stroke symptoms (Hess et al., 2020). The pandemic has also strained healthcare resources, impacting the timely diagnosis and treatment of stroke patients. Telemedicine has played a crucial role during this period, but the rapid shift to virtual care has highlighted the need for robust infrastructure and training to support its effective use. In conclusion, while there have been significant advancements in stroke detection technologies and strategies, numerous challenges remain. Timely and accurate diagnosis is hindered by varied symptoms, limited access to advanced imaging, and disparities in healthcare delivery. Public awareness campaigns and the adoption of telemedicine offer potential solutions but require broader implementation and support. Additionally, emerging technologies such as AI promise to revolutionize stroke detection but bring their own set of challenges. Addressing these issues requires a multifaceted approach, encompassing technological innovation, healthcare policy reform, and targeted public health interventions to ensure equitable and effective stroke care for all.

6.1.3 The need for real-time detection

In today's fast-paced, interconnected world, the ability to detect and respond to events in real time has become increasingly crucial across various domains, from cybersecurity and fraud prevention to traffic management and emergency response systems. As technology continues to advance and the volume of data generated grows exponentially, the need for real-time detection has become more pressing than ever before. Real-time detection systems enable organizations and individuals to identify and address issues as they occur, minimizing the potential for harm, loss, or disruption. In the realm of cybersecurity, for example, real-time detection is essential for identifying and mitigating cyber threats before they can cause significant damage to networks, systems, and sensitive data. Similarly, in the financial sector, real-time fraud detection systems are crucial for identifying and preventing fraudulent transactions as they happen, protecting both businesses and consumers from financial losses. In the healthcare industry, real-time monitoring and detection systems can help healthcare providers identify and respond to patient emergencies more quickly, potentially saving lives. In the transportation sector, real-time traffic monitoring and detection systems can help optimize traffic flow, reduce congestion, and improve overall efficiency. As the world becomes increasingly interconnected and data-driven, the need for real-time detection will only continue to grow, driving innovation and advancements in various fields. However, the implementation of real-time detection systems is not without its challenges. One of the primary challenges is the sheer volume of data that must be processed and analyzed in real time. With the proliferation of connected devices and the increasing amount of data generated by various sources, real-time detection systems must be able to handle and process vast amounts of data quickly and efficiently. This requires advanced algorithms, powerful computing resources, and efficient data storage and retrieval methods. Another challenge is the need for accurate and reliable data. Real-time detection systems rely on the accuracy of the data they receive, and any inaccuracies or inconsistencies in the data can lead to false positives or false negatives, which can have serious consequences. To address this challenge, organizations must invest in data quality assurance measures, such as data validation, cleansing, and normalization, to ensure that the data used by real-time detection systems is accurate and reliable. Privacy and security concerns are also a significant challenge when it comes to real-time detection systems. As these systems collect and process large amounts of data, there is a risk of data breaches, unauthorized access, and misuse of sensitive information. To mitigate these risks, organizations must implement robust security measures, such as encryption, access controls, and data governance policies, to protect the data used by real-time detection systems. Despite these challenges, the benefits of real-time detection systems are clear and compelling. By enabling organizations and individuals to identify and respond to events as they occur, real-time detection systems can help reduce the impact of negative events, improve decision-making, and enhance overall efficiency and effectiveness. As the demand for real-time detection continues to grow, we can expect to see ongoing advancements in the field, with new technologies and approaches emerging to address the challenges and capitalize on the opportunities presented by real-time detection. From the development of more powerful and efficient algorithms to the integration of AI and machine learning, the future of real-time detection looks bright, with the potential to transform the way we live, work, and interact with the world around us. Real-time stroke detection is a critical aspect of modern healthcare systems, where timely intervention can significantly impact patient outcomes. The need for real-time stroke detection stems from the time-sensitive nature of strokes, where every minute counts in preserving brain function and preventing long-term disabilities. By utilizing advanced technologies, such as AI, machine learning algorithms, and wearable devices, healthcare providers can now monitor patients continuously and detect early signs of stroke onset. These real-time detection systems enable rapid assessment and intervention, leading to improved patient care and better prognosis. Additionally, real-time stroke detection allows for immediate communication between healthcare professionals, facilitating quick decision-making and coordination of treatment plans. Furthermore, these systems can provide valuable data for research purposes, helping to enhance our understanding of stroke mechanisms and improve future diagnostic and therapeutic strategies. In essence, the need for real-time stroke detection underscores the importance of leveraging technology to enhance healthcare delivery, optimize patient outcomes, and advance medical knowledge in the field of stroke management.

6.2 Federated learning for healthcare

Federated learning (FL) represents a paradigm shift in how machine learning models are trained and deployed, particularly within the healthcare sector where data privacy and security are of paramount importance. Traditional machine learning approaches require centralized data storage, which poses significant risks to patient confidentiality and data security. FL, on the other hand, enables collaborative model training across multiple decentralized data sources without necessitating the transfer of raw data, thus maintaining data locality and privacy (Yang et al., 2019). This decentralized approach aligns well with the stringent regulatory requirements in healthcare, such as the Health Insurance Portability and Accountability Act in the United States and the General Data Protection Regulation (GDPR) in Europe, which impose strict guidelines on data sharing and privacy (Li et al., 2020). By leveraging FL, healthcare organizations can collaboratively build robust machine learning models while ensuring that sensitive patient data remains on-premise. This is particularly beneficial for training predictive models for rare diseases, where data is inherently sparse and distributed across various institutions. The aggregation of these diverse datasets through FL can significantly enhance the predictive accuracy and generalizability of the models, as demonstrated in studies where FL was used to improve diagnostic algorithms for conditions such as diabetic retinopathy and brain tumors. Furthermore, FL addresses the issue of data heterogeneity, which is prevalent in healthcare due to differences in data collection methods, patient demographics, and clinical practices. Advanced FL techniques, such as federated averaging (FedAvg) and differential privacy, help mitigate these discrepancies by enabling the integration of heterogeneous data sources while preserving individual data characteristics. Despite its advantages, implementing FL in healthcare is not without challenges. One significant hurdle is the computational and communication overhead associated with FL, as it requires frequent communication between local nodes and the central server to update the global model. This can be particularly taxing for healthcare institutions with limited computational resources. Moreover, ensuring the security of the FL framework itself is critical, as adversarial attacks can target the model parameters during transmission, potentially compromising the integrity of the entire system. To counteract these threats, robust encryption techniques and secure multiparty computation are employed to safeguard the model updates and ensure that no individual participant can reverse-engineer the original data (Bonawitz et al., 2017). Another challenge is the potential bias in federated models, which can arise from unbalanced or nonrepresentative data contributions from participating institutions. This can lead to models that perform well on data from certain institutions but poorly on others, thereby undermining the overall effectiveness of the FL approach. To address this, advanced strategies, such as federated transfer learning and personalized FL have been developed, allowing for the adaptation of the global model to local data distributions and ensuring more equitable model performance across diverse healthcare settings (Chen et al., 2020). Additionally, the integration of FL with electronic health records and other clinical data systems necessitates sophisticated data harmonization and preprocessing pipelines to ensure compatibility and interoperability across different healthcare information technology (IT) infrastructures. The collaborative nature of FL also requires a high level of trust and cooperation among participating entities, which can be facilitated through clear data governance frameworks and legal agreements. Furthermore, the application of FL extends beyond predictive analytics to other areas of healthcare, such as genomics and personalized medicine. For instance, FL has been used to develop predictive models for genetic predispositions to certain diseases, enabling the pooling of genomic data from multiple research centers without exposing individual genetic information. This collaborative approach accelerates the discovery of genetic markers and the development of targeted therapies. In personalized medicine, FL can help in creating personalized treatment plans by leveraging diverse patient data from various sources, thereby improving the accuracy and effectiveness of treatment recommendations. The adoption of FL in healthcare is also being propelled by advancements in edge computing and the Internet of Things, which facilitate the seamless integration of FL with real-time patient monitoring systems and wearable devices. This enables continuous model updates and real-time predictive analytics, enhancing patient care and management. Despite the promising potential of FL in healthcare, its implementation requires careful consideration of ethical, legal, and social implications, including the management of patient consent, data ownership, and the equitable distribution of benefits derived from federated models. In conclusion, FL represents a transformative approach to machine learning in healthcare, offering a solution to the perennial challenges of data privacy and security. By enabling collaborative model training across decentralized data sources, FL enhances predictive model accuracy and generalizability while maintaining data locality. The successful implementation of FL in healthcare hinges on addressing challenges related to computational overhead, security, data bias, and interoperability. As advancements in FL techniques and supporting technologies continue to evolve, the integration of FL into healthcare systems holds the promise of revolutionizing patient care through more accurate, secure, and collaborative data analytics.

6.2.1 Understanding federated learning

FL is a novel approach to machine learning that seeks to address the privacy and security concerns inherent in traditional centralized data processing methods by enabling the training of models across multiple decentralized devices or servers without the need to transfer raw data to a central location. Fig. 6.1 shows the illustration of FL. This paradigm shift aims to keep data localized on

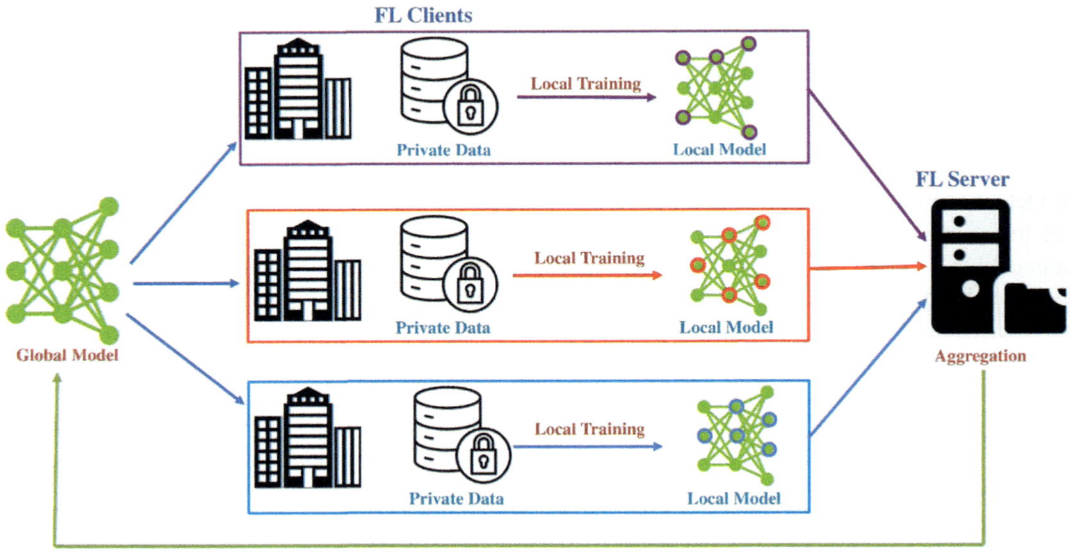

FIGURE 6.1

An illustration of federated learning.

individual devices, such as smartphones or edge servers, while still benefiting from collaborative learning. In traditional machine learning, data from various sources is aggregated into a central server where the training of models takes place. However, this centralized approach presents significant privacy risks, as the transmission and storage of large volumes of sensitive data can lead to potential breaches and misuse. FL mitigates these risks by allowing devices to train a shared global model using their local data, only sharing the model updates, such as gradients, with the central server, which then aggregates these updates to improve the global model. This decentralized approach not only enhances privacy by keeping data on the devices where it is generated but also reduces the bandwidth and storage requirements associated with transferring large datasets. Furthermore, FL supports a more inclusive model training process by leveraging the computational resources of multiple devices, which can be particularly beneficial in scenarios where data is sparse or distributed across numerous sources. The process of FL typically involves multiple rounds of communication between the central server and the participating devices. Each round begins with the central server sending the current global model to the devices. The devices then perform training on their local data and compute model updates, which are sent back to the central server. The server aggregates these updates to refine the global model, and the process repeats. This iterative cycle continues until the model reaches a satisfactory level of performance. One of the key challenges in FL is ensuring that the aggregated model updates are effective and robust. This requires sophisticated algorithms to handle the heterogeneity of data and computing power across devices. For instance, different devices may have varying amounts of data, computational capabilities, and network conditions, which can affect the consistency and efficiency of model updates. To address these challenges, FL employs techniques, such as FedAvg, which combines model updates from multiple devices by averaging them, and differential privacy, which adds noise to the updates to protect individual data points from being inferred. Another critical aspect of FL is its application across various domains. In healthcare, for example, FL can enable collaborative research and model training across different institutions without compromising patient privacy. Hospitals can train predictive models on patient data locally and share only the model parameters, thus complying with data protection regulations while benefiting from collective learning. Similarly, in finance, FL allows institutions to improve fraud detection models by training on distributed datasets across banks without exposing sensitive customer information. Additionally, FL can enhance personalized services on mobile devices. For instance, personalized language models on smartphones can be trained using the user's data without it leaving the device, thus providing improved user experiences while maintaining data privacy. The success of FL also hinges on its ability to operate efficiently in real-world environments, which involves dealing with issues, such as intermittent connectivity, asynchronous updates, and the need for scalable and secure communication protocols. As research and development in FL progress, innovations continue to emerge, focusing on improving the efficiency, scalability, and security of the learning process. Advanced techniques like federated metalearning, which aims to create models that can quickly adapt to new tasks, and federated reinforcement learning, which extends FL to reinforcement learning scenarios, are being explored. These advancements have the potential to further expand the applicability and effectiveness of FL. Moreover, FL aligns with the growing emphasis on data sovereignty and regulatory compliance. With regulations such as the GDPR in Europe and the California Consumer Privacy Act in the United States, organizations are increasingly required to manage and process data in a way that protects individual privacy rights. FL provides a framework that inherently supports these regulatory requirements by minimizing the need for data centralization. Despite its promising advantages, FL is not without its limitations and challenges. The complexity of managing decentralized training processes, ensuring the security of model updates, and achieving consensus among heterogeneous devices are significant hurdles that researchers and practitioners must overcome. Additionally, the potential for bias in FL models, due to the nonuniform distribution of data across devices, is an area of ongoing investigation. Addressing these challenges requires a multidisciplinary effort, combining insights from machine learning, distributed systems, cryptography, and data privacy. In conclusion, FL represents a transformative approach to machine learning, offering a viable solution to the privacy and security concerns associated with traditional centralized data processing. By enabling the collaborative training of models across decentralized devices while keeping data localized, FL has the potential to revolutionize various sectors, from healthcare and finance to personalized services on mobile devices. As research and innovation in this field continue to advance, FL is poised to play a pivotal role in the future of secure and privacy-preserving machine learning.

6.2.2 Privacy and security concerns in federated learning

Privacy and security concerns in FL are multifaceted and demand a comprehensive understanding to mitigate potential risks effectively. FL, a decentralized approach to machine learning, enables multiple parties to collaboratively train a model without sharing their raw data. This method enhances privacy by keeping data local; however, it also introduces unique challenges. One of the primary privacy concerns is the risk of inference attacks. Even though data is not directly shared, gradients or model updates transmitted during training can leak sensitive information. Adversaries can exploit these updates to reconstruct individual data points or infer specific attributes about the data. Various techniques, such as differential privacy and secure multiparty computation, have been proposed to address these issues, but they often come with trade-offs in terms of model accuracy and computational overhead. Another significant privacy concern is the potential for membership inference attacks, where an attacker aims to determine whether a particular data point was part of the training set. This can be particularly problematic in scenarios involving sensitive information, such as medical records or financial data. Ensuring that FL systems are robust against such attacks requires careful consideration of the model's structure and the incorporation of privacy-preserving mechanisms. Security concerns in FL are equally critical and include the threat of model poisoning attacks. In such attacks, a malicious participant can inject poisoned data or model updates into the training process, leading to biased or incorrect models. This can have severe implications, especially in applications where model predictions directly impact decision-making, such as in autonomous driving or healthcare diagnostics. Detecting and mitigating model poisoning requires sophisticated anomaly detection techniques and robust aggregation methods that can identify and exclude malicious contributions. Another security issue is the susceptibility to adversarial attacks, where an attacker crafts specific inputs to deceive the model into making incorrect predictions. This type of attack can be particularly dangerous in FL settings, where the diversity of data sources and lack of centralized control make it harder to detect and defend against such inputs. FL also faces challenges related to the integrity and authenticity of the data. Ensuring that data used in training is legitimate and has not been tampered with is crucial for maintaining the trustworthiness of the resulting model. This necessitates robust authentication and verification mechanisms to validate the sources of data and their contributions. Additionally, the decentralized nature of FL complicates the enforcement of data governance policies. Organizations need to ensure that all participants adhere to regulatory requirements and organizational policies regarding data usage and sharing. This can be particularly challenging in cross-border collaborations where legal and regulatory frameworks differ. Effective governance in FL requires transparent policies, clear guidelines, and mechanisms for compliance monitoring. The communication infrastructure used in FL also poses security challenges. Data and model updates are transmitted over potentially insecure networks, making them vulnerable to interception and tampering. Implementing secure communication protocols, such as end-to-end encryption, is essential to protect data in transit and prevent unauthorized access. However, encryption alone is not sufficient; there must also be mechanisms to ensure the integrity and authenticity of the transmitted updates. FL systems must be designed with resilience in mind to withstand various types of attacks and failures. This includes incorporating redundancy, fault-tolerance, and continuous monitoring to detect and respond to anomalies promptly. The complexity of FL environments necessitates a multidisciplinary approach to security and privacy, involving expertise from fields, such as cryptography, data science, and network security. Moreover, the ethical implications of FL cannot be overlooked. The potential for bias and discrimination in federated models is a significant concern, as biased data from individual participants can lead to biased model outcomes. Ensuring fairness and equity in FL requires deliberate efforts to include diverse data sources and to apply techniques that mitigate bias. Transparency and accountability are also crucial in fostering trust among participants. Clear documentation of the FL process, including data sources, model updates, and decision-making criteria, can help build confidence in the system. Participants need assurance that their data is being used responsibly and that they have recourse in case of misuse. Finally, the dynamic nature of FL environments means that privacy and security measures must be continuously updated and adapted to evolving threats. This requires ongoing research, development, and collaboration among stakeholders to stay ahead of potential vulnerabilities. In conclusion, while FL offers significant advantages in terms of privacy and efficiency, it also presents unique privacy and security challenges that must be carefully managed. Addressing these concerns requires a holistic approach that balances the need for privacy, security, and model performance. By implementing robust privacy-preserving techniques, secure communication protocols, and rigorous governance frameworks, FL can be leveraged effectively while minimizing risks. Continuous vigilance, research, and innovation are essential to ensure that FL systems remain secure and trustworthy in an ever-changing threat landscape.

6.2.3 Benefits and challenges

FL approach has garnered significant interest due to its unique advantages and inherent challenges. One of the primary benefits of FL is enhanced privacy and security. Since data never leaves the local devices, the risk of data breaches and unauthorized access is significantly reduced. This makes FL particularly appealing in sensitive domains, such as healthcare, finance, and personal data applications. Moreover, FL allows for the utilization of diverse and distributed data sources, leading to models that are more generalized and robust. This diversity helps in capturing various patterns and anomalies that might be missed if the data were centralized. Another advantage is reduced latency in model training and inference. As data processing is done locally, the need to transfer large datasets to a central server is eliminated, which can lead to faster decision-making processes. FL also facilitates cost savings associated with data storage and transmission. By processing data locally, the bandwidth and storage requirements on central servers are minimized, potentially reducing operational costs. Additionally, FL supports continuous learning and model updates without significant downtime, as updates are done incrementally on local devices. Despite these advantages, FL comes with a set of challenges. One of the foremost challenges is communication overhead. Coordinating updates from numerous devices and aggregating them into a global model requires substantial communication bandwidth, which can be particularly taxing in environments with limited connectivity. Another challenge is the heterogeneity of data and devices. Variations in data distribution across devices, as well as differences in computational power and storage, can lead to inconsistencies in model performance and training efficiency. Ensuring that all devices contribute effectively to the global model without overwhelming less capable devices is a complex task. Moreover, FL faces difficulties in maintaining model accuracy and fairness. The nonindependent and identically distributed nature of local datasets can cause biased model updates, potentially leading to a global model that does not perform well across all data distributions. Another significant challenge is the need for robust and efficient algorithms for model aggregation and update. The aggregation process must account for the varying quality and reliability of updates from different devices. Additionally, ensuring the security and integrity of model updates is crucial, as malicious actors could potentially manipulate local updates to degrade the global model's performance. This necessitates the development of sophisticated techniques for anomaly detection and robust aggregation. FL also poses challenges in terms of scalability. As the number of participating devices increases, the complexity of coordination and model management escalates. Efficiently handling a large number of devices while maintaining the quality and efficiency of the global model is a significant challenge. Furthermore, FL requires mechanisms for efficient handling of stragglers, devices that are slower in computing and communicating updates. These stragglers can delay the overall training process, and strategies to mitigate their impact are essential for timely model convergence. The implementation of FL also demands a robust infrastructure that supports secure communication, effective data management, and seamless integration of model updates. This infrastructure must be resilient to network failures and capable of handling the dynamic nature of device participation. Another consideration is the energy consumption associated with local training. FL can be resource-intensive, particularly on battery-powered devices, necessitating optimizations to reduce energy usage and ensure sustainable operations. In summary, while FL offers numerous benefits, such as enhanced privacy, reduced latency, cost savings, and the ability to leverage diverse data sources, it also presents substantial challenges including communication overhead, data and device heterogeneity, maintaining model accuracy and fairness, ensuring robust aggregation, scalability issues, handling stragglers, and infrastructure requirements. Addressing these challenges requires ongoing research and innovation in algorithms, infrastructure, and practical deployment strategies. Despite these hurdles, the potential of FL to revolutionize how we train and deploy machine learning models makes it a promising area of exploration in the quest for more secure, efficient, and equitable AI solutions.

Benefits of FL:

1. Enhanced privacy and security.
2. Utilization of diverse and distributed data sources.
3. Reduced latency in model training and inference.
4. Cost savings associated with data storage and transmission.
5. Continuous learning and model updates without significant downtime.

Challenges of FL:

1. Communication overhead.
2. Heterogeneity of data and devices.
3. Maintaining model accuracy and fairness.
4. Need for robust and efficient algorithms for model aggregation and update.
5. Scalability issues.
6. Handling stragglers.
7. Infrastructure requirements.
8. Energy consumption associated with local training.

6.3 Real-time stroke detection system

In the experimental setup for real-time stroke detection, a sophisticated integration of advanced DL technologies is employed to enhance accuracy while preserving privacy. This research involves the examination of various architectures of you look only once (YOLO)v8 models, a state-of-the-art neural network architecture designed for real-time object detection. These proposed models are specifically utilized to detect strokes by identifying facial paralysis and distinguishing nonstroke conditions from the faces of individuals in the images. A key aspect of this research is the use of FL, a decentralized training methodology that allows collaborative model training across multiple clients

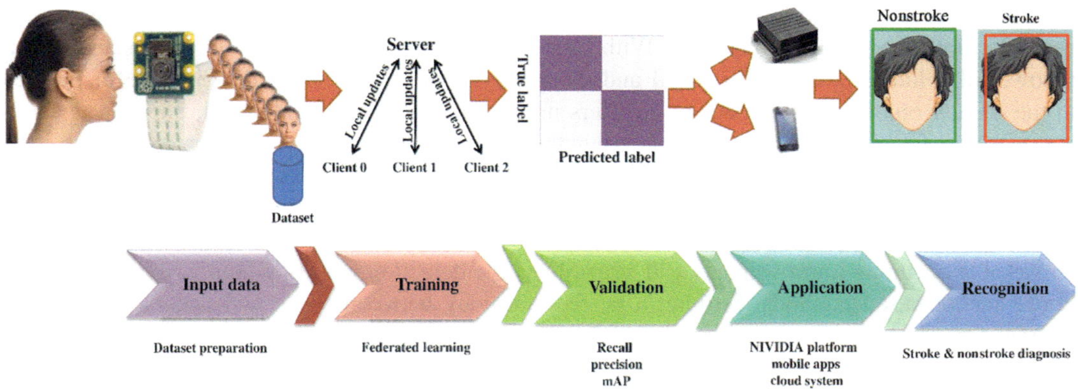

FIGURE 6.2

The proposed system for utilizing real-time deep learning model and federated learning for stroke and nonstroke detection.

without compromising the confidentiality of sensitive data. The experimental setup features a central server that oversees the training process and coordinates interactions with three distinct clients, each contributing valuable data to improve the model's performance. To further optimize the system's capabilities, NVIDIA platforms are utilized to evaluate the inference of the deployed models. This setup facilitates the rapid assessment of the proposed models, thereby enabling real-time stroke detection and diagnosis. The system is designed to efficiently process the recognition of individuals' faces, promptly identifying stroke signs, and ensuring timely medical intervention. This approach not only enhances the accuracy of stroke detection but also maintains the privacy of the data used in the training process. As depicted in Fig. 6.2, the proposed framework illustrates the utilization of real-time DL models for both stroke and nonstroke detection, demonstrating the effectiveness of combining cutting-edge neural network architectures with FL to achieve a robust and efficient real-time stroke detection system. The overarching goal of this research is to develop a reliable and privacy-preserving method for early stroke detection, which is crucial for timely medical response and improved patient outcomes. By leveraging the advanced capabilities of YOLOv8 and FL, the study presents a comprehensive solution that addresses the challenges of real-time medical diagnosis, ensuring that individuals exhibiting signs of stroke are quickly identified and provided with necessary medical attention. This innovative approach not only advances the field of medical diagnostics but also highlights the potential of DL technologies in transforming healthcare delivery, particularly in critical and time-sensitive scenarios, such as stroke detection.

6.3.1 Design and architecture

The YOLOv8 architectures mark the forefront of the YOLO series, specializing in the real-time detection of individual faces. This model excels in real-time object detection due to its faster speed, increased accuracy, and anchor-free design. Leveraging computer vision, neural networks, DL, and image processing techniques, YOLOv8 delivers outstanding object recognition capabilities. Its multiscale prediction and enhanced backbone network further boost its performance, making it a versatile tool for various applications. With faster and more precise results, YOLOv8 stands out as a powerful solution in the fields of AI and computer vision, representing the pinnacle of progress in the YOLO object detector lineage. It offers unparalleled precision and speed, building upon the legacy of its forerunners by integrating groundbreaking features and enhancements, making it the go-to choose for a broad spectrum of object detection challenges across different settings. The advanced backbone and neck architectures significantly improve feature extraction, thus boosting overall efficiency. With the introduction of an anchor-free split Ultralytics head, YOLOv8 achieves remarkable accuracy improvements and streamlines the detection workflow, outperforming conventional anchor-based methods. Striking a perfect harmony between speed and accuracy, it is ideal for real-time detection needs in various application areas. The model provides a wide range of pretrained options, facilitating the selection of the most suitable one for specific requirements. As the most compact variant in the YOLOv8 series, it is engineered for a wide array of detection tasks, from simple object identification to more complex challenges, such as instance segmentation, detection of key points, orientation of objects, and categorization. The architecture is a refined version of the CSPDarknet53, incorporating 53 convolutional layers and cross-stage partial connections to bolster the flow of information between layers. The YOLOv8 head consists of several convolutional layers leading to fully connected layers, tasked with predicting bounding boxes, objectness scores, and class probabilities for identified objects. A distinct feature of YOLOv8 is its self-attention mechanism within the head, enabling the model to focus on specific parts of an image and adjust feature significance according to the relevance of the task. Remarkably adept at detecting objects across multiple scales, it uses a feature pyramid network to identify objects of diverse sizes and scales within an image effectively. This multilayered pyramid facilitates the detection of both large and small objects, underscoring YOLOv8 adaptability and thoroughness in object detection. The architecture and capabilities of YOLOv8 are visually depicted in Fig. 6.3. This comprehensive and highly efficient model stands out in its ability to handle diverse datasets and ease of training, making it a preferred choice for various applications. The YOLOv8 architecture excels in scenarios requiring real-time processing and high accuracy, from autonomous driving and surveillance to healthcare and retail. Its robust performance and ease of integration into existing systems underscore its significance as a transformative tool in object detection. The combination of speed, accuracy, and versatility in the YOLOv8 models makes them indispensable in modern computer vision tasks. With its refined architecture and advanced features, YOLOv8 not only continues the legacy of the YOLO series but also sets a new standard in object detection technology. The integration of innovative components, such as the anchor-free Ultralytics head and self-attention mechanisms demonstrates a significant leap in the field, ensuring that YOLOv8 remains at the cutting edge of technological advancements. This model's design philosophy emphasizes both performance and usability, catering to a wide range of users from researchers to industry professionals. The modularity of YOLOv8 allows for easy customization and optimization, enabling users to tailor the model to their specific needs and applications. Whether for academic research or commercial deployment, YOLOv8 offers a robust framework that can be adapted to meet the demands of various object detection tasks. Its efficiency in processing and high accuracy rates make it an invaluable asset in developing intelligent systems that require real-time decision-making capabilities. The continual evolution of the YOLO series, culminating in the YOLOv8 architecture, reflects the ongoing advancements in AI and machine learning, driving forward the capabilities of computer vision

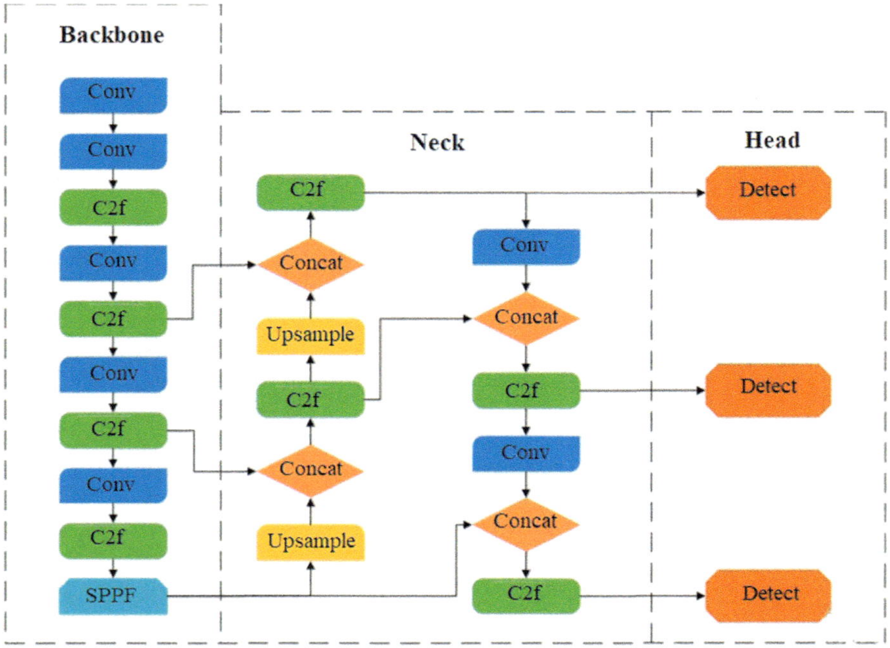

FIGURE 6.3

The YOLOv8 architecture incorporates a modified CSPDarknet53 as its core framework. It introduces the C2f module as a replacement for the CSPLayer found in YOLOv5, enhancing its structure. To speed up the computation process, it employs a spatial pyramid pooling fast (SPPF) layer, which consolidates features into a uniform-size map (The top 10 causes of death, 2018). A diagram of a software flowchart.

systems. As a testament to its innovation and effectiveness, YOLOv8 has garnered widespread adoption and acclaim in the tech community, solidifying its position as a leader in object detection technology.

In the architecture's initial setup, a significant modification is introduced by replacing the 6×6 convolution in the stem with a more conventional 3×3 convolution, thereby altering the primary building block. Additionally, the C2f module is substituted for the C3 module, as depicted in Fig. 6.4. The accompanying image provides a comprehensive summary of this module, highlighting key parameters: "f" denotes the feature count, "e" signifies the expansion rate, and CBS represents a combination of Convolution, Batch Normalization, and a Sigmoid Linear Unit (SiLU) operation. In the C2f configuration, the outputs from all Bottleneck stages are integrated. Each Bottleneck stage comprises two 3×3 convolutions linked by residual connections, forming a more complex and robust structure. Unlike C2f, the C3 module uses only the output from the final Bottleneck stage, thus simplifying the architecture. The Bottleneck component in question is similar to the one found in YOLOv5, with a notable exception: the initial convolution's kernel size is increased from 1×1 to 3×3. This adjustment underscores a gradual shift in YOLOv8 towards reintegrating the ResNet block, which is known for its efficacy in DL architectures due to its ability to mitigate the

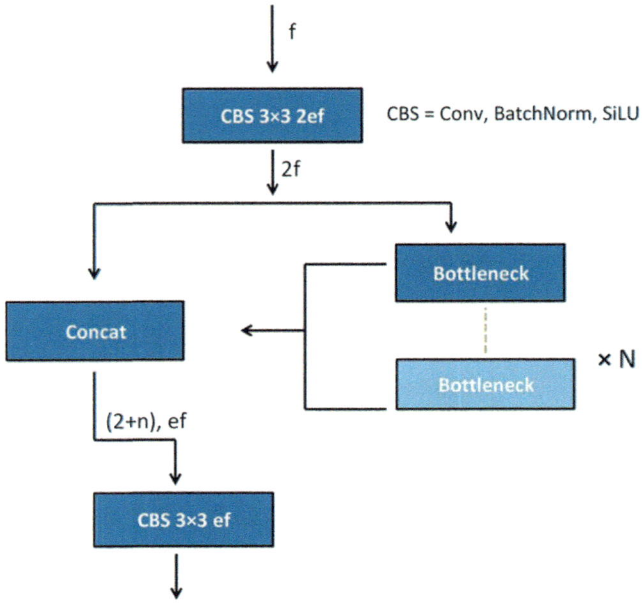

FIGURE 6.4

The c2f layer for YOLOv8 architecture.

vanishing gradient problem through residual connections. This transition back to the ResNet block implies a strategic move to harness its advantages, including improved gradient flow and better feature reuse. The design choices reflect a deliberate effort to enhance the model's performance by leveraging the strengths of well-established components like the ResNet block while introducing nuanced improvements. This combination of retaining proven techniques and incorporating new optimizations aims to achieve a more efficient and effective architecture. The replacement of the 6×6 convolution with a 3×3 convolution in the stem not only simplifies the model but also aligns it with contemporary CNN design practices, which favor smaller, more frequent convolutions to capture finer details. Furthermore, the transition from C3 to C2f indicates a shift toward more comprehensive feature integration. By merging outputs from all Bottleneck stages, the C2f configuration can potentially capture a wider range of features, enhancing the model's ability to generalize from diverse data patterns. The expanded use of the 3×3 convolution, particularly in the initial stages of the architecture, may also contribute to improved computational efficiency and reduced complexity, making the model more accessible for deployment in various applications. The integration of Batch Normalization and SiLU within the CBS structure further underscores the model's emphasis on maintaining normalized activations and leveraging advanced activation functions to enhance learning dynamics. The SiLU function, in particular, combines the properties of Rectified linear unit (ReLU) and Sigmoid activations, offering benefits in terms of smooth gradients and preventing dead neurons. These architectural refinements collectively aim to optimize the performance and adaptability of the model, reflecting a thoughtful balance between innovation and established best practices in DL. By incrementally integrating these changes, the architecture seeks to build on the strengths of previous models like YOLOv5 while addressing specific limitations and enhancing overall capability. The strategic use of the ResNet block highlights an awareness of its proven benefits in deep networks, ensuring robust performance through effective gradient propagation and feature reuse. This architectural evolution signifies a progressive step toward creating a more versatile and powerful model, capable of handling a broad spectrum of tasks with greater precision and efficiency. In summary, the architectural adjustments, from the replacement of the 6×6 convolution with a 3×3 convolution to the substitution of C2f for C3, alongside the integration of the ResNet block and advanced activation functions, collectively enhance the model's robustness, efficiency, and adaptability, paving the way for improved performance across various applications.

In the network's neck section, feature concatenation is executed directly without necessitating uniform channel dimensions, an approach that effectively reduces both the parameter count and overall tensor sizes, thereby streamlining the network's complexity. This design philosophy underscores the optimization of neural network structures by minimizing redundant computations and resource consumption. Table 6.1 elucidates a comparative analysis of various YOLOv8 versions: YOLOv8x, YOLOv8l, YOLOv8m, YOLOv8s, and YOLOv8n, each distinguished by their complexity and performance metrics. These versions, despite their differences, uniformly process images with an input size of 640 pixels, ensuring consistency in image resolution across all models. The number of parameters, expressed in millions (M), serves as an indicator of each model's capacity to learn from data, while the computational workload during inference is quantified by floating-point operations per second (FLOPs), measured in billions (B). YOLOv8x, the most sophisticated model, is equipped with 68.2 million parameters and necessitates 257.8 billion FLOPs, showcasing its high learning capacity and significant computational complexity. On the opposite end of the spectrum, YOLOv8n is the simplest model, containing a mere 3.2 million parameters and requiring 8.7 billion FLOPs, reflecting its minimal complexity and lower computational demands. This spectrum of complexity and performance from YOLOv8n to YOLOv8x allows for a diverse range of applications, catering to both lightweight deployments with limited computational resources and high-accuracy scenarios necessitating substantial computational power. By providing these varying levels of complexity and performance, the YOLOv8 series accommodates a broad array of deployment environments, from edge devices with stringent resource constraints to powerful cloud-based systems demanding top-tier accuracy. The thoughtful engineering behind these models ensures that each version is tailored to specific operational needs, optimizing performance without compromising on the quality of results. This modularity in design not only facilitates adaptability but also enhances the efficiency of deployment, making the YOLOv8 series a versatile tool in the field of

Table 6.1 Comparison of various YOLOv8 models, categorized by their model size, the number of parameters (in millions M), and floating-point operations per second (FLOPs) in billions B.

Model	Size (pixels)	Params (M)	FLOPs (B)
YOLOv8x	640	68.2	257.8
YOLOv8l	640	43.7	165.2
YOLOv8m	640	25.9	78.9
YOLOv8s	640	11.2	28.6
YOLOv8n	640	3.2	8.7

computer vision. The direct feature concatenation in the neck section exemplifies a strategic choice to enhance network efficiency, further reinforced by the careful balancing of parameters and computational load across different YOLOv8 versions. This balance is crucial for achieving optimal performance in real-world applications, where computational resources and accuracy requirements vary significantly. The approach adopted by YOLOv8 models underscores a commitment to delivering high-performance neural networks that are both resource-efficient and scalable, ensuring their applicability across a wide spectrum of use cases. From autonomous vehicles requiring rapid, accurate object detection to mobile applications necessitating minimal latency and resource usage, the YOLOv8 series stands out as a robust solution. The architecture's adaptability, combined with the strategic use of feature concatenation, positions YOLOv8 as a leading choice in scenarios where both performance and efficiency are paramount. In summary, the design and engineering of the YOLOv8 series, highlighted by direct feature concatenation and a carefully balanced parameter and FLOPs distribution, embody an advanced understanding of neural network optimization. This results in models that not only perform exceptionally well across various tasks but also adapt seamlessly to the specific demands of different deployment environments, making them an invaluable asset in the toolkit of computer vision practitioners.

6.3.2 Data preprocessing and augmentation

The dataset utilized in this chapter is composed of two distinct categories of images. One category encompasses individuals diagnosed with acute stroke, while the other comprises individuals who do not have such a diagnosis. In total, the dataset includes 3745 images, offering a substantial resource for analysis. Table 6.1 provides the primary description for the proposed dataset of stroke and nonstroke images. To enhance the efficacy of the model, various data augmentation methods were implemented. These techniques aim to expand the dataset by creating modified versions of the existing images. Specifically, augmentation involved operations, such as flipping, rotating, and scaling the images. By applying these transformations, the dataset becomes more diverse and resilient, better reflecting a wider range of real-world scenarios. By augmenting the dataset in this manner, the model's accuracy is expected to improve. The diverse representations provided by augmented data can help the model generalize better to unseen instances, thereby enhancing its performance when classifying images of individuals with or without acute stroke. In essence, data augmentation enriches the dataset, allowing the model to learn from a wider spectrum of image variations and complexities. Fig. 6.2 illustrates the distribution of the two classes within the proposed dataset. These visual aids are invaluable for evaluating model performance, detecting class imbalances or dependencies, and guiding decisions related to model refinement and data handling strategies. Class frequency refers to the distribution of data points among different categories or classes within a dataset. When considering normalized height and width space for stroke and nonstroke datasets, it indicates the number of data points falling within specific height and width ranges. Typically, labels denote the assigned categories or classes for each data point, distinguishing between stroke and nonstroke instances in relevant datasets. A height–width graph typically illustrates data point distributions based on their height and width values, often presented as a scatter plot with height on the x-axis and width on the y-axis. Alternatively, an x–y graph can visualize the data, particularly if additional features beyond height and width are involved, with each data point representing a point in a multidimensional space where each axis corresponds to a different feature. These visual representations aid in understanding the distribution and relationship of data points, facilitating better model training and evaluation. The data used in this research encompasses two primary categories: images of individuals diagnosed with acute stroke and images of those without such a diagnosis. This dataset, consisting of 3745 images, provides a substantial base for thorough analysis. Table 6.1 offers a detailed description of the proposed dataset, categorizing it into stroke and nonstroke images.

To optimize the model's effectiveness, several data augmentation techniques were employed. These methods serve to broaden the dataset by generating altered versions of the current images, including operations like flipping, rotating, and scaling. These transformations enhance the dataset's diversity and robustness, better representing a variety of real-world situations. This augmentation process is crucial for improving the model's accuracy, as it allows the model to generalize more effectively to new, unseen instances. In other words, by enriching the dataset with a wider array of image variations and complexities, data augmentation helps the model learn more comprehensively. Fig. 6.5 showcases the distribution of the two classes within the proposed dataset. These visual aids are critical for assessing model performance, identifying class imbalances or dependencies, and guiding decisions on model refinement and data management strategies.

Class frequency concerns the distribution of data points across different categories or classes within a dataset. When analyzing normalized height and width spaces for stroke and nonstroke datasets, it represents the number of data points within particular height and width ranges. Labels typically designate the categories or classes assigned to each data point, differentiating between stroke and nonstroke cases in relevant datasets. A height–width graph usually depicts data point distributions based on their height and width values, often using a scatter plot with height on the x-axis and width on the y-axis. Alternatively, an x–y graph can be utilized to visualize the data, especially if additional features beyond height and width are considered, with each data point representing a position in a multidimensional space where each axis corresponds to a different feature. These visual tools are essential for comprehending data point distributions and relationships, thereby enhancing model training and evaluation processes.

The dataset employed in this research includes images from two key categories: those of individuals diagnosed with acute stroke and those of individuals without such a diagnosis. In total, the dataset comprises 3745 images, providing a significant resource for analysis. Table 6.2 delivers a comprehensive description of the proposed dataset, distinguishing between stroke and nonstroke images.

To improve the model's performance, various data augmentation methods were used. These techniques aim to expand the dataset by producing modified versions of the existing images. Specifically, augmentation involved operations like flipping, rotating, and scaling the images. These transformations increase the dataset's diversity and resilience, mirroring a broader range of real-world scenarios. By augmenting the dataset in this way, the model's accuracy is expected to improve. The diverse representations from augmented data can help the model generalize better to new instances, enhancing its performance when classifying images of individuals with or without acute stroke. Essentially, data augmentation enriches the dataset, allowing the model to learn from a wider range of image variations and complexities. Fig. 6.2 demonstrates the distribution of the two classes within the proposed dataset. These visual aids are invaluable for evaluating model performance, detecting class imbalances or dependencies, and guiding decisions related to model refinement and data handling strategies.

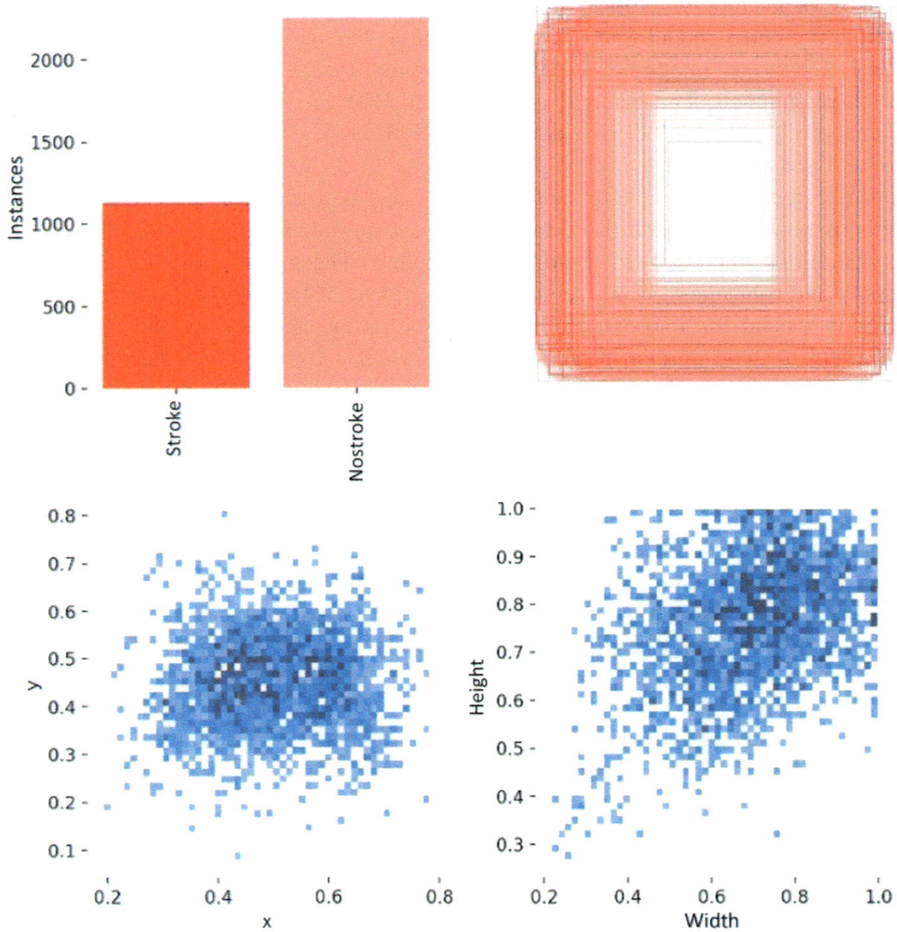

FIGURE 6.5

Visualization of class distribution in the proposed dataset, with the upper bar graph showing a higher number of instances for "nostroke" than "stroke."

Table 6.2 The main description and parameters for stroke and nonstroke dataset.

Parameters	Specifications
Image type	JPG
Images with stroke	1245
Images with nonstroke	2500
Total images	3745

Class frequency pertains to the distribution of data points among different categories or classes within a dataset. When considering normalized height and width space for stroke and nonstroke datasets, it indicates the number of data points falling within specific height and width ranges. Typically, labels denote the assigned categories or classes for each data point, distinguishing between stroke and nonstroke instances in relevant datasets. A height–width graph usually illustrates data point distributions based on their height and width values, often presented as a scatter plot with height on the x-axis and width on the y-axis. Alternatively, an $x-y$ graph can visualize the data, especially if additional features beyond height and width are involved, with each data point representing a point in a multidimensional space where each axis corresponds to a different feature. These visual representations aid in understanding the distribution and relationship of data points, facilitating better model training and evaluation.

The dataset utilized in this research comprises images from two primary categories: individuals diagnosed with acute stroke and those without such a diagnosis. This dataset, which includes 3745 images, offers a substantial foundation for detailed analysis. Table 6.1 provides a thorough description of the proposed dataset, categorizing it into stroke and nonstroke images. To enhance the model's efficacy, various data augmentation techniques were employed. These methods aim to expand the dataset by generating modified versions of the existing images, such as flipping, rotating, and scaling. By applying these transformations, the dataset becomes more diverse and resilient, better reflecting a wide range of real-world scenarios. This augmentation process is critical for improving the model's accuracy, as it helps the model generalize more effectively to new, unseen instances. Data augmentation enriches the dataset with a broader spectrum of image variations and complexities, enabling the model to learn more comprehensively. Fig. 6.4 illustrates the distribution of the two classes within the proposed dataset. These visual aids are essential for assessing model performance, identifying class imbalances or dependencies, and guiding decisions related to model refinement and data handling strategies. Class frequency refers to the distribution of data points across different categories or classes within a dataset. When analyzing normalized height and width spaces for stroke and nonstroke datasets, it represents the number of data points within specific height and width ranges. Labels typically designate the categories or classes assigned to each data point, differentiating between stroke and nonstroke cases in relevant datasets. A height–width graph usually depicts data point distributions based on their height and width values, often using a scatter plot with height on the x-axis and width on the y-axis. Alternatively, an $x-y$ graph can be utilized to visualize the data, especially if additional features beyond height and width are considered, with each data point representing a position in a multidimensional space where each axis corresponds to a different feature. These visual tools are crucial for understanding data point distributions and relationships, thereby enhancing model training and evaluation processes.

6.3.3 Distributed model and federated learning

In this research, we employed FL to train our proposed model, taking advantage of its decentralized nature. FL allows multiple clients to collaboratively train a model without sharing their raw data, thus preserving data privacy. Our objective was to simulate an FL environment with three clients operating on a single machine, where both the server and all three clients share central processing unit (CPU), graphics processing unit (GPU), and memory resources. In this setup, each client runs an instance of FlowerClient, leading to a total of three instances in memory. Running this configuration on a single machine can strain memory resources, even if only a subset of clients participates in each FL round.

We leveraged the FLOWER platform, which facilitates efficient communication between clients and the server by transmitting only model updates instead of raw data. This significantly reduces communication overhead, making FLOWER suitable for environments with limited bandwidth or high-latency connections. Additionally, FLOWER ensures that raw data remains on local devices, sharing only model updates in the form of weight differentials with the central server. This approach safeguards sensitive information against data breaches and unauthorized access. Our proposed method implements an FL system for object detection using the YOLOv8n model, involving three clients and a server. Each client is responsible for training a YOLOv8n model on its local data using the Ultralytics library. The (DetectionTrainer) class handles the specifics of the training process. Each client's dataset is stored in the "data/clients/{idx}" directory, and the clients periodically train their local models, calculating metrics, such as mean Average Precision (mAP), recall, precision, and loss. During the FL process, each client sends its model parameters to the server.

The server orchestrates the FL process within the FLOWER framework, aggregating model updates from the three clients using the FedAvg strategy provided by the flwr library. The FL process iterates over a specified number of epochs, with the server engaging in communication with the clients. After each round, the server aggregates the model updates, evaluates the federated model, and logs the results in the "results" directory. The server's primary role is to oversee and coordinate the training process, ensuring the participation of the clients.

The clients, while structurally similar, differ mainly in the data they hold. Each client has data pertaining to distinct classes of stroke and nonstroke cases. The distributed DL workflow in our system can be outlined in four phases:

1. **Receive updated model:** clients establish a secure connection with the server to ensure data integrity and privacy. The server then transmits the latest version of the global machine learning model using efficient communication protocols to minimize latency.
2. **Local model training**: clients preprocess their local datasets, addressing outliers, handling missing values, and performing feature scaling as needed to enhance data quality. They then utilize their computational resources to train the model locally, applying techniques, such as mini-batch gradient descent or FL to effectively manage the datasets.
3. **Model evaluation:** following the training phase, clients conduct thorough evaluations of the trained model using various metrics like accuracy, precision, recall, and F1 score, tailored to their specific application requirements. They meticulously analyze the model's predictions on their local datasets, performing detailed error analyses to identify instances of incorrect predictions. This iterative process helps refine the model's predictive capabilities and overall performance.
4. **Send updated weights:** after completing local model training and evaluation, clients securely transmit the updated model weights back to the server for aggregation, ensuring data confidentiality. The server aggregates the received updates from multiple clients using techniques such as FedAvg to synthesize a new global model. The server then performs additional validation checks on the aggregated model to verify its integrity and stability before deploying it for further inference or subsequent training rounds.

This FL setup ensures a robust and efficient training process, maintaining data privacy while leveraging distributed computational resources. The integration of the YOLOv8n model for object detection demonstrates the system's capability to handle complex tasks, making it suitable for various applications requiring secure and efficient model training across multiple data sources.

Moreover, by keeping data localized and only sharing model updates, our approach mitigates the risk of data breaches and unauthorized access, which is crucial in sensitive domains, such as healthcare. This FL framework not only enhances the model's performance through collaborative training but also ensures that data privacy and security are upheld throughout the process. Our results indicate that this method effectively balances the trade-offs between data privacy, communication efficiency, and model performance, making it a promising solution for distributed machine learning tasks.

6.3.4 Training setup and optimization

Training YOLOv8 models for effective object detection involves a meticulous optimization process of various hyperparameters. These hyperparameters are critical in determining the performance and efficiency of the model. In this extended discussion, we will delve into the specifics of these hyperparameters and their roles, the training environment, and the overall impact on the YOLOv8 model's object detection capabilities. The image size, set to 640 pixels, is a fundamental hyperparameter that influences the dimensions of input images as shown in Table 6.3. This parameter is crucial for feature extraction and localization. A larger image size can potentially capture more detail, improving the model's ability to detect smaller objects. However, this comes at the cost of increased computational requirements. Conversely, a smaller image size reduces the computational load but may miss finer details.

The batch size, specified as 32, determines the number of samples processed before the model's parameters are updated. This hyperparameter significantly affects computational efficiency and convergence stability. A larger batch size can lead to more stable gradient updates and efficient use of hardware, but it also demands more memory. Smaller batch sizes can reduce memory usage but may lead to noisier gradient estimates and longer training times. The training duration is divided into 30 epochs, where an epoch represents a complete iteration over the entire dataset. This iterative process is essential for refining the model's performance. More epochs generally allow the model

Table 6.3 Hyperparameters for tuning YOLOv8 models.

Hyperparameter	Value
Image size	640
Batch size	32
Number of epochs	30
Mosaic	0.8
Mixup	0.2
Learning rate	10–5
Optimizer	AdamW
Cache	False

to learn more thoroughly from the data, but excessive epochs can lead to overfitting, where the model performs well on training data but poorly on unseen data. The mosaic parameter, set at 0.8, introduces a data augmentation technique that blends multiple images. This technique enhances generalization and robustness by presenting the model with varied contexts and object configurations within a single training image. Mosaic augmentation helps the model to learn more robust features that can generalize better to new, unseen images. Mixup, assigned a value of 0.2, is another data augmentation technique that linearly interpolates between pairs of images and their labels. This technique diversifies the training dataset, making the model more resilient to variations in the data. Mixup can be particularly effective in reducing overfitting and improving the model's ability to generalize from limited training data. The learning rate, set at 10^{-5}, is a critical hyperparameter that controls the step size in updating model parameters during training. A well-chosen learning rate ensures that the model converges efficiently to a minimum of the loss function. Too high a learning rate can cause the model to converge too quickly to a suboptimal solution, while too low a learning rate can make the training process excessively slow. The AdamW optimizer is employed to adjust the model weights, effectively minimizing the defined loss function. AdamW combines the benefits of both adaptive learning rate methods and weight decay regularization, leading to more robust and efficient training. The choice of optimizer plays a significant role in achieving faster convergence and better overall model performance. The cache parameter, set to False, controls whether datasets are cached in memory. Caching can significantly speed up the training process by reducing data loading times. However, it also increases memory consumption. For large datasets or limited memory environments, it might be beneficial to disable caching to avoid memory issues. All experiments were conducted using AWS EC2 G4 instances equipped with 8 NVIDIA T4 GPUs, featuring 96 CPUs and a network bandwidth of 100 Gbps. This high-performance computing environment is essential for handling the computational demands of training YOLOv8 models. The use of multiple GPUs allows for parallel processing, significantly reducing training times and enabling the handling of larger datasets. Fine-tuning these hyperparameters is pivotal for orchestrating the training process to yield a YOLOv8 model optimized for object detection tasks. The interplay between different hyperparameters must be carefully balanced to ensure optimal performance. For instance, adjusting the learning rate in conjunction with the batch size can lead to more stable and efficient training. Similarly, the choice of data augmentation techniques like mosaic and mixup can enhance the model's ability to generalize, thereby improving its performance on real-world object detection tasks. By systematically optimizing these hyperparameters, the YOLOv8 model can achieve a high level of accuracy and efficiency in object detection. The training procedure, supported by powerful computing resources, ensures that the model can handle complex and large-scale datasets, making it suitable for a wide range of applications in various industries.

6.3.5 Experiment results and discussion

Figs. 6.6 and 6.7 illustrate the performance of the five YOLOv8 models across four key metrics: precision, recall, F1 score, and mAP. All models exhibit rapid improvement during the initial epochs, indicating swift learning in the early stages. For YOLOv8l and YOLOv8m, precision, recall, and F1 scores plateau near the maximum value of 1.0, highlighting their accuracy and strong balance between precision and recall. Their mAP also stabilizes at a high level, suggesting consistent reliability across various classes. YOLOv8n shows a more pronounced learning curve with substantial metric

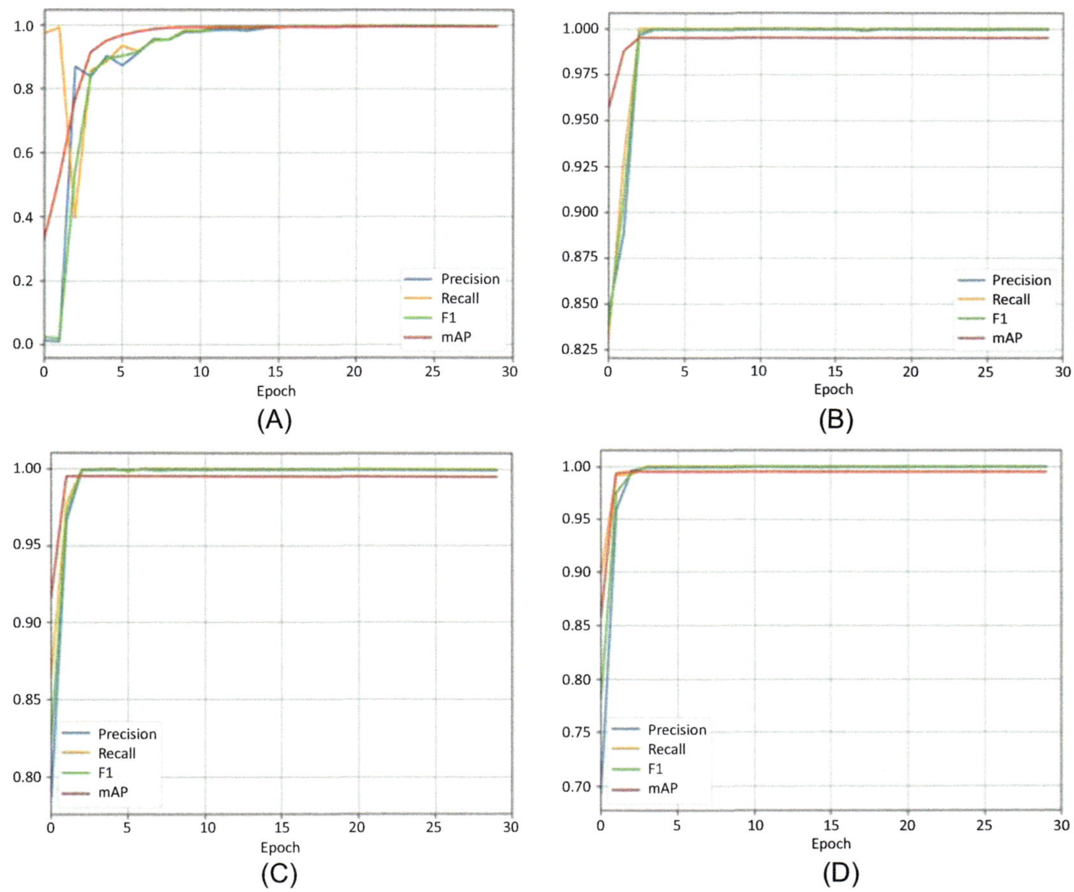

FIGURE 6.6

The performance of YOLOv8 models verses other YOLO architectures, which illustrates recall, precision, mAP, and F1: (A) YOLOv8n, (B) YOLOv8l, (C) YOLOv8m, (D) YOLOv8s.

improvements before stabilization, though its overall metric values, especially mAP, are lower than the other models, indicating reduced object detection performance. YOLOv8s mirrors the trends of YOLOv8l and YOLOv8m, achieving and maintaining high metric values, suggesting effectiveness and stability. Similarly, YOLOv8x demonstrates high performance across all metrics, akin to YOLOv8l and YOLOv8m, signifying robustness with high precision and recall. Overall, except for the slightly less effective YOLOv8n, the models quickly achieve and maintain high precision, recall, and F1 scores, with mAP also indicating strong predictive power across different thresholds. YOLOv8n, being a simplified model prioritizing speed and efficiency with fewer parameters, offers lower accuracy compared to the more complex YOLOv8x, YOLOv8l, YOLOv8m, and YOLOv8s, which, with more parameters and computational power, excel in complex pattern recognition and key metrics. YOLOv8n is beneficial for fast processing in resource-constrained environments, whereas

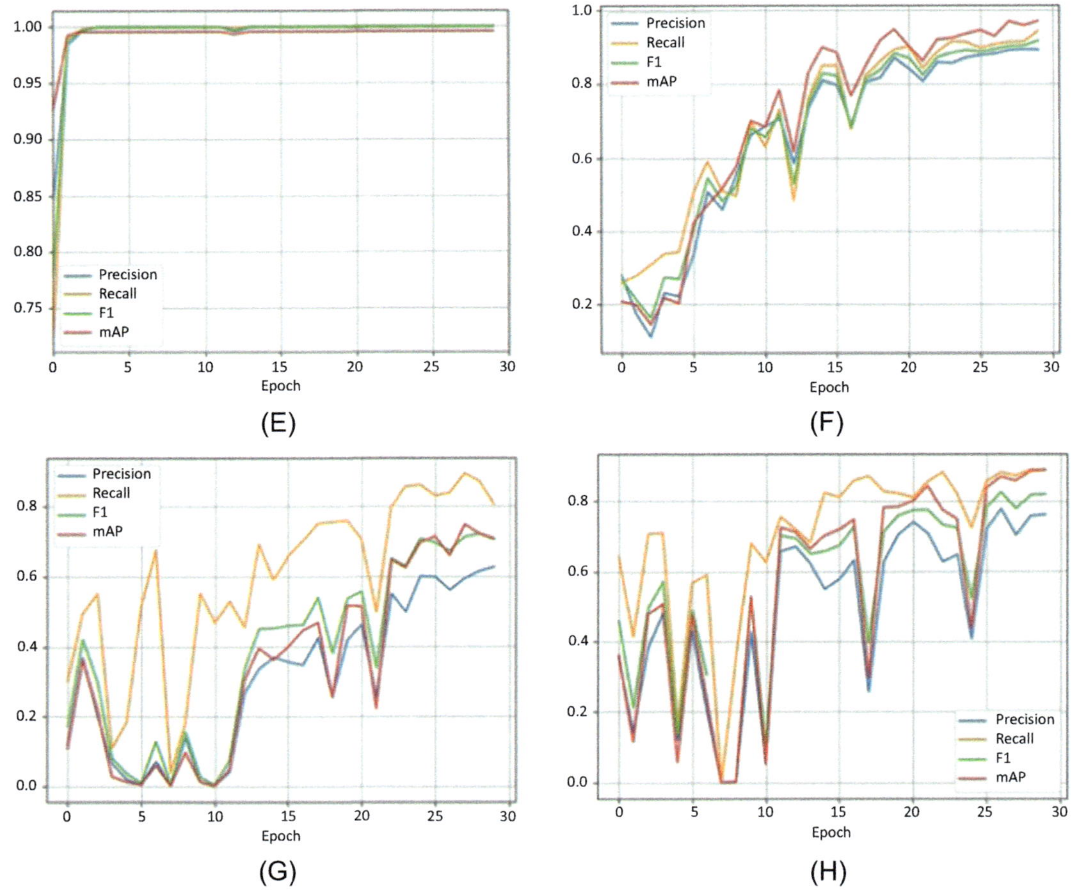

FIGURE 6.7

The performance of YOLOv8 models verses other YOLO architectures, which illustrates recall, precision, mAP, and F1: (E) YOLOv8x, (F) YOLOv5n, (G) YOLOv7, (H) YOLOv7x.

the larger models are preferable for high-accuracy tasks where resources are sufficient. In this research, we compared the proposed YOLOv8 models with YOLOv5n, YOLOv7, and YOLOv7x, all trained for the same number of epochs (Donnan et al., 2008) to ensure a fair comparison. The experimental results showed that YOLOv5n outperformed both YOLOv7 and YOLOv7x. However, the YOLOv8 models demonstrated superior performance over these architectures, excelling in multiple key metrics, including mAP, recall, precision, and F1 score, as depicted in Fig. 6.5. This enhanced performance underscores the advancements in the YOLOv8 models, making them a suitable choice for stroke and nonstroke applications.

FL is a machine learning approach where a model is trained across multiple decentralized edge devices (clients) without sharing data, thereby enhancing privacy, and reducing data centralization. The server coordinates the process by aggregating the client models to form a global model. In this

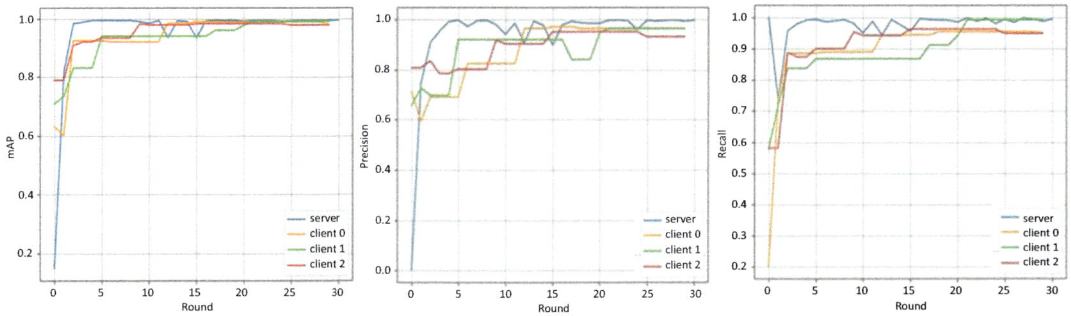

(A) (B) (C)

FIGURE 6.8

The performance evolution which include (A) mean Average Precision (mAP), (B) precision, and (C) recall scores across multiple rounds of training for three clients and server in a federated learning system.

context, mAP, precision, and recall are key performance metrics. The mAP metric, used in ranking tasks, object detection, and information retrieval, shows that the server and all clients improve rapidly within the first five rounds of training, with the server and client 0 achieving stable performance while clients 1 and 2 show some variability, likely due to more complex and variable data. Precision, defined as the ratio of true positive predictions to total positive predictions, climbs sharply initially and then plateaus, indicating a stable number of false positives. The server maintains the highest precision, reflecting the accuracy of the aggregated model. Recall, the ratio of true positive predictions to actual positives, also increases rapidly at the beginning, with the server exhibiting the highest recall, demonstrating its superior ability to detect true positives. Overall, the server consistently outperforms the clients across all metrics, which is expected in FL as the server model benefits from aggregated updates from all clients. Key observations include rapid learning in initial rounds, stabilization of metrics with the server showing the least variance, variability in client performance due to local data differences, and convergence of client performance toward the server's over time. Fig. 6.8 illustrates the performance, including mAP, precision, and recall scores, across multiple training rounds for three clients and the server in an FL system.

6.4 Implementation on NVIDA platforms

NVIDIA's Jetson platform offers a range of powerful and efficient AI computing devices designed to bring DL to the edge. These devices cater to various performance needs and power constraints, making AI accessible across a wide array of applications, from robotics to embedded systems. At the entry level, the Jetson Nano is a compact yet capable device, providing a cost-effective solution for AI projects limited by power and space. For more demanding tasks, the Jetson Xavier AGX offers a significant performance boost with its advanced GPU architecture and AI accelerators, ideal for tasks requiring higher computational throughput. At the top of the line is the Jetson Orin, the latest addition that represents the cutting edge in edge AI performance, delivering breakthrough

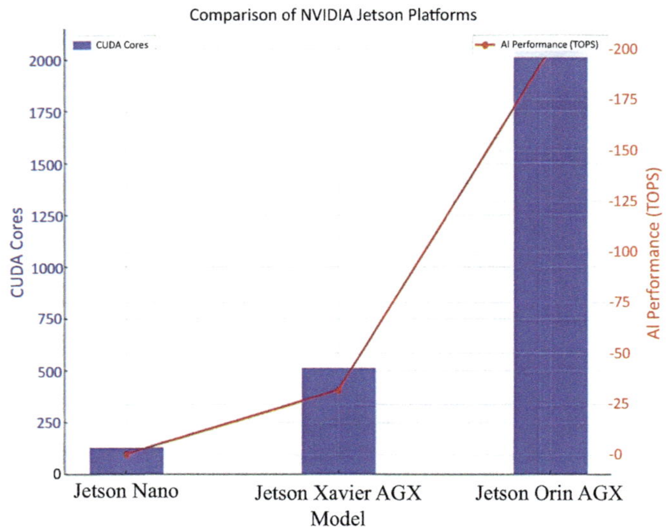

FIGURE 6.9

A comparative analysis of NVIDIA Jetson platforms, which illustrates number of CUDA cores and artificial intelligence performance (measured in TOPS, Tera Operations Per Second) across three models: Jetson Nano, Jetson Xavier AGX, and Jetson Orin AGX.

capabilities for autonomous machines with the highest performance and energy efficiency for AI, robotics, and other compute-intensive tasks.

Each platform in the series is engineered for flexibility, scalability, and ease of integration, essential for innovators developing the next generation of intelligent machines. A comparative analysis of the NVIDIA Jetson Nano, Jetson AGX Xavier, and Jetson Orin platforms highlights their CUDA cores and AI performance (TOPS, Tera Operations Per Second). The bar plot indicates a significant increase in CUDA cores across the models, enhancing parallel computing capabilities. The line plot shows AI performance, with Jetson Orin demonstrating a substantial leap, reaching up to 200 TOPS, compared to Jetson Nano's 0.5 TOPS and Jetson AGX Xavier's 32 TOPS. This progression underscores the evolution in processing power and AI capabilities, with Jetson Orin offering vastly superior performance for demanding AI applications and computational tasks. Fig. 6.9 presents a comparative analysis of the NVIDIA Jetson platforms, showing the number of CUDA cores and AI performance capacity (quantified in TOPS) among the three variants: Jetson Nano, Jetson Xavier AGX, and Jetson Orin AGX.

6.4.1 The importance of NVIDIA GPUs for real-time inference

Fig. 6.10 presents a comparison of real-time detection frames per second (FPS) among various YOLOv8 models running on three NVIDIA Jetson platforms: Nano, Xavier AGX, and Orin. The data clearly shows that the Jetson Xavier AGX and Jetson Orin significantly outperform the Jetson Nano in terms of FPS. This highlights their superior processing power and efficiency in handling

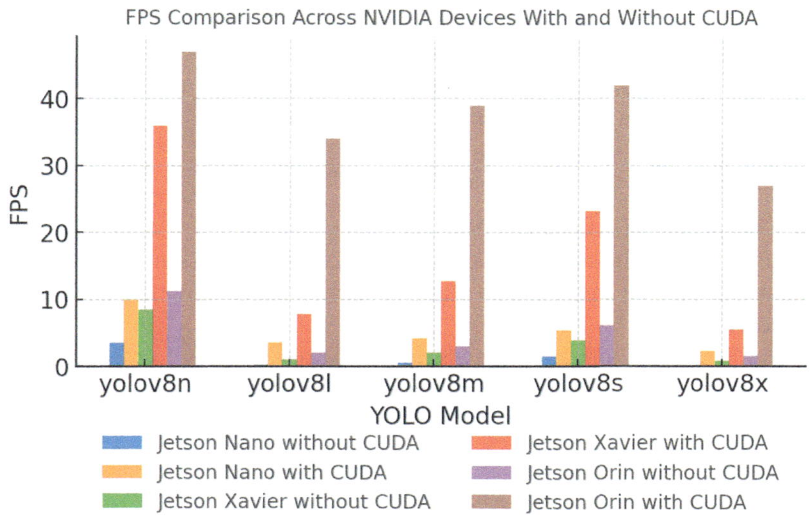

FIGURE 6.10

This figure illustrates the frames per second (FPS) performance for different YOLO models (yolov8n, yolov8l, yolov8m, yolov8s, and yolov8x) across three NVIDIA Jetson devices (Nano, Xavier, and Orin) with and without CUDA acceleration. Output image.

these tasks. The study compared the performance of the proposed approach on NVIDIA devices with and without CUDA utilization. The findings emphasize the crucial role of CUDA and GPU acceleration in executing YOLOv8 models to meet real-time requirements. CUDA markedly enhances the speed, allowing YOLOv8 models to process data at a much faster rate. By leveraging the parallel processing power of GPUs, CUDA reduces execution time, enabling real-time object detection and analysis. It is evident that the YOLOv8n model achieves the highest FPS on all three platforms, indicating its status as the fastest model for real-time detection. This is consistent with its streamlined design, which prioritizes speed and efficiency. Consequently, despite its lower accuracy metrics, YOLOv8n is highly suitable for applications where real-time processing is critical. In contrast, the YOLOv8x model, which is the most computationally intensive, exhibits the lowest FPS across all platforms. This demonstrates that while YOLOv8x offers the best accuracy metrics, its complexity makes it less appropriate for scenarios requiring high-speed object detection. The other models, YOLOv8l, YOLOv8m, and YOLOv8s, display a gradation in FPS performance, with more complex models (e.g., YOLOv8l) being slower than simpler ones (e.g., YOLOv8s). Performance on the Jetson Xavier AGX and Jetson Orin is significantly better than on the Jetson Nano, the least powerful of the three hardware platforms.

The graph illustrates the trade-off between accuracy and speed among the YOLOv8 models and underscores the importance of selecting the appropriate model and hardware platform based on specific application requirements. Real-time detection of strokes using the proposed DL object detection models is crucial for timely medical intervention and improved patient outcomes. The proposed models, especially the YOLOv8n architecture, are designed to quickly and accurately identify stroke indicators from facial features. By processing data in real-time, these models can provide immediate feedback to healthcare professionals, enabling rapid decision-making. This rapid analysis is essential in emergency situations where every second counts. The ability to differentiate between stroke and nonstroke cases on the spot helps prioritize treatment, reduce the risk of long-term damage, and potentially save lives.

Analysis of the importance of GPU on NVIDIA platforms

1. Performance boost with GPU and CUDA:
   a. The NVIDIA Jetson platforms, particularly Xavier AGX and Orin, demonstrate superior FPS performance compared to the Jetson Nano, underscoring the benefits of enhanced processing power and efficiency.
   b. CUDA's utilization significantly speeds up the execution of YOLOv8 models by leveraging GPU parallel processing capabilities, reducing the time required for real-time object detection.
2. Model-specific performance:
   a. YOLOv8n stands out as the fastest model, making it ideal for applications requiring rapid processing despite its lower accuracy.
   b. YOLOv8x, though the most accurate, is the slowest, highlighting the trade-off between accuracy and speed. This makes it less suitable for real-time applications.
3. Platform capabilities:
   a. The Jetson Xavier AGX and Orin platforms provide much better performance than the Jetson Nano, making them preferable for high-speed processing tasks.
   b. The choice of hardware platform should align with the application's specific needs, balancing speed, and computational power.
4. Critical application in healthcare:
   a. In medical applications, such as stroke detection, the ability to process data in real-time is vital for timely intervention.
   b. The YOLOv8n model's ability to quickly identify stroke indicators can significantly enhance patient outcomes by enabling swift and accurate decision-making in emergency situations.

The comparison of YOLOv8 models on different NVIDIA Jetson platforms highlights the importance of GPU acceleration and CUDA in achieving real-time performance. Selecting the appropriate model and hardware platform is crucial, especially in critical applications like healthcare, where rapid and accurate detection can save lives. The study underscores the need for balancing accuracy and speed to meet the specific demands of various real-time applications.

6.4.2 NVIDIA computation cost analysis

Power consumption measurement has been carried across three NVIDIA platforms: Jetson Nano, Jetson Xavier AGX, and Jetson Orin. The Jetson Nano demonstrates remarkable energy efficiency, consistently showing low power usage across all YOLO models. This characteristic makes it an ideal candidate for power-sensitive applications. On the other hand, the Jetson Orin, although being the most power-hungry, presumably offers superior computational performance. This trade-off might be justified for demanding tasks where processing speed is crucial. The Jetson Xavier AGX stands in between, offering a moderate balance between power consumption and performance.

6.4.2.1 Power consumption trends

The progression from YOLOv8l to YOLOv8m and further models shows a trend of increasing power requirements. This trend suggests that these models are more computationally intensive and exploit the hardware's capabilities to a greater extent. This increasing trend is most pronounced with the Jetson Orin, which shows a substantial leap in power consumption for the latest models. This indicates its capability to unleash the full potential of advanced YOLO models, albeit at a greater energy cost.

This data is vital for selecting the appropriate hardware for proposed models where both the performance and the power budget need to be optimized. Fig. 6.11 illustrates the power consumption across various YOLO models when deployed on NVIDIA's Jetson hardware platforms: Nano, Xavier AGX, and Orin.

6.4.2.2 Temperature analysis across platforms

The temperature data provided for different YOLOv8 models across NVIDIA Jetson platforms (Nano, Xavier AGX, and Orin) show some interesting trends as illustrated in Tables 6.4–6.6.

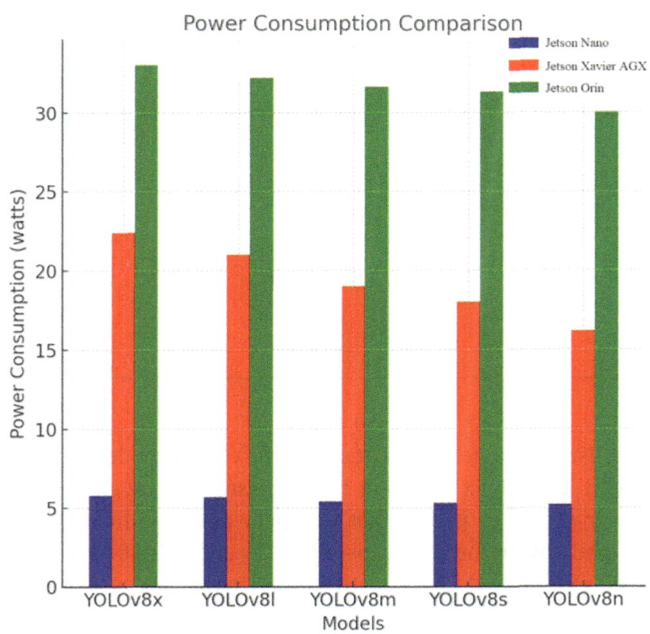

FIGURE 6.11

Comparison of power consumption across NVIDIA Jetson platforms (Nano, Xavier AGX, and Orin) running different YOLOv8 models, demonstrating the varying energy requirements of each model on the respective hardware.

Table 6.4 Operational temperatures of YOLOv8 models on the NVIDIA Jetson Nano platform.

Jetson Nano	Temperature (°C)
YOLOv8x	54
YOLOv8l	45
YOLOv8m	43.5
YOLOv8s	42.7
YOLOv8n	40

Table 6.5 Operational temperatures of YOLOv8 models on the NVIDIA Jetson Xavier AGX platform.

Jetson Xavier AGX	Temperature (°C)
YOLOv8x	43
YOLOv8l	41
YOLOv8m	40
YOLOv8s	39
YOLOv8n	37

Table 6.6 Operational temperatures of YOLOv8 models on the NVIDIA Jetson Xavier Orin platform.

Jetson Orin	Temperature (°C)
YOLOv8x	42
YOLOv8l	40
YOLOv8m	39
YOLOv8s	39
YOLOv8n	36

Starting with the Jetson Nano, the temperatures for the YOLO models are higher compared to the other two platforms, with YOLOv8x reaching the highest temperature at 54°C. This indicates that while the Nano is power-efficient, it does not dissipate heat as effectively. This is due to a less robust cooling system and lower thermal capacity. However, there is a clear downward trend in temperature from YOLOv8x to YOLOv8n, with the latter running at a cooler 40°C. This indicates that the newer models are more efficient in terms of heat generation and dissipation. The Jetson Xavier AGX shows a consistently cooler operational temperature across all YOLO models when compared to the Jetson Nano, indicating better thermal management. The temperatures range from 43°C for YOLOv8x to 37°C for YOLOv8n. The lower temperatures suggest that the Xavier AGX is more capable of handling the computational demands of the YOLO models efficiently, thereby generating less heat. The Jetson Orin records temperatures similar to the Xavier AGX but is marginally cooler across all models except for YOLOv8s, where it equals the AGX at 39°C. This could be due to efficient power usage that translates into less heat output. YOLOv8n runs coolest on the Orin at 36°C.

Below are detailed tables of the operational temperatures for the YOLOv8 models on each NVIDIA Jetson platform:

6.4.2.3 Analysis of computation cost

6.4.2.3.1 Jetson Nano

- Power consumption: the Jetson Nano's low power usage across all YOLO models makes it highly energy-efficient. This platform is particularly suitable for applications where power consumption is a critical concern, such as in battery-powered devices or edge computing scenarios.
- Temperature: despite its efficiency, the Nano's higher operational temperatures indicate a less effective heat dissipation mechanism. This suggests that while it conserves power, it might require additional cooling solutions for prolonged high-performance tasks.

6.4.2.3.2 Jetson Xavier AGX

- Power consumption: the Xavier AGX balances power consumption and performance. It provides a moderate power usage profile, making it a versatile option for various applications that need a compromise between efficiency and performance.
- Temperature: with better thermal management than the Nano, the Xavier AGX runs cooler, indicating its ability to handle intensive computations more effectively without generating excessive heat. This makes it a reliable choice for applications that demand sustained high performance without overheating risks.

6.4.2.3.3 Jetson Orin

- Power consumption: the Orin's significant power consumption, especially with advanced YOLO models, highlights its high computational capabilities. This platform is ideal for tasks requiring maximum processing power and speed, albeit with a higher energy cost.
- Temperature: despite its high power usage, the Orin manages to maintain relatively low temperatures, similar to or even cooler than the Xavier AGX. This efficient heat management implies that the Orin can sustain high-performance operations without compromising on thermal efficiency.

The choice of NVIDIA Jetson platform for running YOLO models depends on the specific requirements of the application in terms of power consumption, computational performance, and thermal management. The Jetson Nano is best suited for power-sensitive applications with limited computational demands. The Jetson Xavier AGX offers a balanced solution for moderate power and performance needs. The Jetson Orin, with its superior computational power and efficient thermal management, is ideal for high-performance tasks where energy consumption is less of a concern.

References

Aggarwal, R., Sounderajah, V., Martin, G., Ting, D. S. W., Karthikesalingam, A., King, D., Ashrafian, H., & Darzi, A. (2021). Diagnostic accuracy of deep learning in medical imaging: A systematic review and meta-analysis. *NPJ Digital Medicine*, *4*(1). Available from https://doi.org/10.1038/s41746-021-00438-z.

American Stroke Association Types of Stroke (2021). https://www.stroke.org/en/about-stroke/types-of-stroke.

Basu, A. P. (2014). Early intervention after perinatal stroke: Opportunities and challenges. *Developmental Medicine & Child Neurology*, *56*(6), 516–521. Available from https://doi.org/10.1111/dmcn.12407.

Benjamin, E. J., Muntner, P., Alonso, A., Bittencourt, M. S., Callaway, C. W., Carson, A. P., Chamberlain, A. M., Chang, A. R., Cheng, S., Das, S. R., Delling, F. N., Djousse, L., Elkind, M. S. V., Ferguson, J. F., Fornage, M., Jordan, L. C., Khan, S. S., Kissela, B. M., Knutson, K. L., ... Virani, S. S. (2019). Heart disease and stroke statistics-2019 update: A report from the American Heart Association. *Circulation*, *139* (10), e56. Available from https://doi.org/10.1161/CIR.0000000000000659.

Bonawitz, K., Ivanov, V., Kreuter, B., Marcedone, A., McMahan, H. B., Patel, S., Ramage, D., Segal, A., & Seth K. (2017) Practical secure aggregation for privacy-preserving machine learning. *Proceedings of the ACM conference on computer and communications security*, 1175–1191. Available from https://doi.org/10.1145/3133956.3133982.

Campbell, B. C. V., De Silva, D. A., Macleod, M. R., Coutts, S. B., Schwamm, L. H., Davis, S. M., & Donnan, G. A. (2019). Ischaemic stroke. *Nature Reviews Disease Primers*, *5*(1). Available from https://doi.org/10.1038/s41572-019-0118-8, http://www.nature.com/nrdp/.

Chen, Y., Xue, M., & Shi, W. (2020). Personalized federated learning for intelligent IoT applications: A cloud-edge based framework. *IEEE Open Journal of the Computer Society*, *1*, 55–67.

Cramer, S. C., Sur, M., Dobkin, B. H., O'Brien, C., Sanger, T. D., Trojanowski, J. Q., Rumsey, J. M., Hicks, R., Cameron, J., Chen, D., Chen, W. G., Cohen, L. G., deCharms, C., Duffy, C. J., Eden, G. F., Fetz, E. E., Filart, R., Freund, M., Grant, S. J., ... Vinogradov, S. (2011). Harnessing neuroplasticity for clinical applications. *Brain*, *134*(6), 1591–1609. Available from https://doi.org/10.1093/brain/awr039.

Davenport, T., & Kalakota, R. (2019). The potential for artificial intelligence in healthcare. *Future Healthcare Journal*, *6*(2), 94–98. Available from https://doi.org/10.7861/futurehosp.6-2-94.

Demaerschalk, B. M., Miley, M. L., Kiernan, T. E. J., Bobrow, B. J., Corday, D. A., Wellik, K. E., Aguilar, M. I., Ingall, T. J., Dodick, D. W., Brazdys, K., Koch, T. C., Ward, M. P., & Richemont, P. C. (2009). Stroke telemedicine. *Mayo Clinic Proceedings*, *84*(1), 53–64. Available from https://doi.org/10.4065/84.1.53, http://www.mayoclinicproceedings.com/content/84/1/53.full.pdf + html.

Donnan, G. A., Fisher, M., Macleod, M., & Davis, S. M. (2008). Stroke. *The Lancet*, *371*(9624), 1612–1623. Available from https://doi.org/10.1016/S0140-6736(08)60694-7, http://www.journals.elsevier.com/the-lancet/.

Díez-Tejedor, E., & Fuentes, B. (2003). Acute care in stroke: The importance of early intervention to achieve better brain protection. *Cerebrovascular Diseases*, *17*(Suppl. 1), 130–137. Available from https://doi.org/10.1159/000074805.

Elhanashi, A., Saponara, S., & Zheng, Q. (2023). Classification and localization of multi-type abnormalities on chest X-rays images. *IEEE Access*, *11*, 83264–83277. Available from https://doi.org/10.1109/ACCESS.2023.3302180, http://ieeexplore.ieee.org/xpl/RecentIssue.jsp?punumber = 6287639.

Elhanashi, A., Lowe, D., Saponara, S., & Moshfeghi, Y. (2022). Deep learning techniques to identify and classify COVID-19 abnormalities on chest x-ray images. Proceedings of SPIE 12102, real-time image processing and deep learning 2022.

Elhanashi, A., Saponara, S., Dini, P., Zheng, Q., Morita, D., & Raytchev, B. (2023). An integrated and real-time social distancing, mask detection, and facial temperature video measurement system for pandemic monitoring. *Journal of Real-Time Image Processing*, *20*(5). Available from https://doi.org/10.1007/s11554-023-01353-0.

Feigin, V. L., Forouzanfar, M. H., Krishnamurthi, R., Mensah, G. A., Connor, M., Bennett, D. A., Moran, A. E., Sacco, R. L., Anderson, L., Truelsen, T., O'Donnell, M., Venketasubramanian, N., Barker-Collo, S., Lawes, C. M. M., Wang, W., Shinohara, Y., Witt, E., Ezzati, M., & Naghavi, M. (2014). Global and regional burden of stroke during 1990–2010: Findings from the global burden of disease study 2010. *The Lancet*, *383*(9913), 245–255. Available from https://doi.org/10.1016/S0140-6736(13)61953-4, http://www.journals.elsevier.com/the-lancet/.

Hankey, G. J. (2014). Secondary stroke prevention. *The Lancet Neurology*, *13*(2), 178–194. Available from https://doi.org/10.1016/S1474-4422(13)70255-2.

Hayes, S. H., & Carroll, S. R. (1986). Early intervention care in the acute stroke patient. *Archives of Physical Medicine and Rehabilitation*, *67*(5), 319–321.

Hess, D. C., Eldahshan, W., & Rutkowski, E. (2020). COVID-19-Related Stroke. *Translational Stroke Research*, *11*(3), 322–325. Available from https://doi.org/10.1007/s12975-020-00818-9, http://www.springer.com/biomed/neuroscience/journal/12975.

Howard, V. J., Kleindorfer, D. O., Judd, S. E., McClure, L. A., Safford, M. M., Rhodes, J. D., Cushman, M., Moy, C. S., Soliman, E. Z., Kissela, B. M., & Howard, G. (2011). Disparities in stroke incidence contributing to disparities in stroke mortality. *Annals of Neurology*, *69*(4), 619–627. Available from https://doi.org/10.1002/ana.22385.

Jauch, E. C., Saver, J. L., Adams, H. P., Bruno, A., Connors, J. J. B., Demaerschalk, B. M., Khatri, P., McMullan, P. W., Qureshi, A. I., Rosenfield, K., Scott, P. A., Summers, D. R., Wang, D. Z., Wintermark, M., & Yonas, H. (2013). Guidelines for the early management of patients with acute ischemic stroke: A guideline for healthcare professionals from the American Heart Association/American Stroke Association. *Stroke*, *44*(3), 870–947. Available from https://doi.org/10.1161/STR.0b013e318284056a, https://www.ahajournals.org/journal/str.

Johnston, S. C. (2007). Clinical practice. Transient ischemic attack. *New England Journal of Medicine*, *347*(21), 1687–1692.

Kaur, G., Prinja, S., Lakshmi, P. V. M., & Kumar, R. (2014). The societal and family burden of stroke in India. *WHO South-East Asia Journal of Public Health*, *3*(3–4), 81–88.

Langhorne, P., Bernhardt, J., & Kwakkel, G. (2011). Stroke rehabilitation. *The Lancet*, *377*(9778), 1693–1702. Available from https://doi.org/10.1016/s0140-6736(11)60325-5.

Li, T., Sahu, A. K., Talwalkar, A., & Smith, V. (2020). Federated learning: Challenges, methods, and future directions. *IEEE Signal Processing Magazine*, *37*(3), 50–60. Available from https://doi.org/10.1109/MSP.2020.2975749, http://ieeexplore.ieee.org/xpl/RecentIssue.jsp?punumber = 79&year = 2008.

Merino, J. G., & Warach, S. (2010). Imaging of acute stroke. *Nature Reviews Neurology*, *6*(10), 560–571. Available from https://doi.org/10.1038/nrneurol.2010.129.

Mozaffarian, D., Benjamin, E. J., Go, A. S., Arnett, D. K., Blaha, M. J., Cushman, M., De Ferranti, S., Després, J. P., Fullerton, H. J., Howard, V. J., Huffman, M. D., Judd, S. E., Kissela, B. M., Lackland, D. T., Lichtman, J. H., Lisabeth, L. D., Liu, S., Mackey, R. H., Matchar, D. B., … Turner, M. B. (2015). Heart disease and stroke statistics-2015 update: A report from the American Heart Association. *Circulation*, *131*(4), e29. Available from https://doi.org/10.1161/CIR.0000000000000152, http://circ.ahajournals.org.

Powers, W. J., Rabinstein, A. A., Ackerson, T., Adeoye, O. M., Bambakidis, N. C., Becker, K., Biller, J., Brown, M., Demaerschalk, B. M., Hoh, B., Jauch, E. C., Kidwell, C. S., Leslie-Mazwi, T. M., Ovbiagele, B., Scott, P. A., Sheth, K. N., Southerland, A. M., Summers, D. V., & Tirschwell, D. L. (2019). Guidelines for the early management of patients with acute ischemic stroke: 2019 update to the 2018 guidelines for the early management of acute ischemic stroke a guideline for healthcare professionals from the American Heart Association/American Stroke Association. *Stroke*, *50*(12), E344. Available from https://doi.org/10.1161/STR.0000000000000211, http://stroke.ahajournals.org/.

Powers, W. J., Rabinstein, A. A., Ackerson, T., Adeoye, O. M., Bambakidis, N. C., Becker, K., Biller, J., Brown, M., Demaerschalk, B. M., Hoh, B., Jauch, E. C., Kidwell, C. S., Leslie-Mazwi, T. M., Ovbiagele, B., Scott, P. A., Sheth, K. N., Southerland, A. M., Summers, D. V., & Tirschwell, D. L. (2018). 2018 Guidelines for the early management of patients with acute ischemic stroke: A guideline for healthcare professionals from the American Heart Association/American Stroke Association. *Stroke*, *49*(3), e46. Available from https://doi.org/10.1161/STR.0000000000000158.

Saponara S. Elhanashi A. & Gagliardi, A. (2021). Reconstruct fingerprint images using deep learning and sparse autoencoder algorithms. Proceedings of SPIE 11736 – the international society for optical engineering http://spie.org/x1848.xml, https://doi.org/10.1117/12.2585707.

The top 10 causes of death. (2018). https://www.who.int/news-room/fact-sheets/detail/the-top-10-causes-of-death.

Tong, D., Reeves, M. J., Hernandez, A. F., Zhao, X., Olson, D. M., Fonarow, G. C., & Schwamm, L. H. (2002). Times from symptom onset to hospital arrival in the get with the guidelines–stroke program. *Circulation: Cardiovascular Quality and Outcomes*, *5*(2), 207–213.

Topol, E. J. (2019). High-performance medicine: The convergence of human and artificial intelligence. *Nature Medicine*, *25*(1), 44–56. Available from https://doi.org/10.1038/s41591-018-0300-7, http://www.nature.com/nm/index.html.

Varoquaux, G., & Cheplygina, V. (2022). Machine learning for medical imaging: Methodological failures and recommendations for the future. *NPJ Digital Medicine*, *5*(1). Available from https://doi.org/10.1038/s41746-022-00592-y.

Wardlaw, J. M., Murray, V., Berge, E., & del Zoppo, G. J. (2014). Thrombolysis for acute ischaemic stroke. *Cochrane Database of Systematic Reviews*, *2014*(7). Available from https://doi.org/10.1002/14651858.CD000213.pub3, http://as.wiley.com/WileyCDA/Brand/id-6.html.

Yang, Q., Liu, Y., Chen, T., & Tong, Y. (2019). Federated machine learning: Concept and applications. *ACM Transactions on Intelligent Systems and Technology*, *10*(2). Available from https://doi.org/10.1145/3298981, http://dl.acm.org/citation.cfm?id = J1318.

Zhang, R. L., Zhang, Z. G., & Chopp, M. (2013). Ischemic stroke and neurogenesis in the subventricular zone. *Neuropharmacology*, *55*(4), 569–575.

Zheng, Q., Zhao, P., Wang, H., Elhanashi, A., & Saponara, S. (2022). Fine-grained modulation classification using multi-scale radio transformer with dual-channel representation. *IEEE Communications Letters*, *26*(6), 1298–1302. Available from https://doi.org/10.1109/LCOMM.2022.3145647, https://ieeexplore.ieee.org/servlet/opac?punumber = 4234.

CHAPTER

Efficient identification of bag-breakup in continuous airflow via video analysis

7

7.1 Overview of bag break detection

In recent years, the pressing issues of global warming and air pollution have transcended national borders, evolving into complex international dilemmas (Alessio et al., 2021; Xiao & Gao, 2021). A significant contributor to air pollution stems from automobile emissions, which not only release greenhouse gases such as CO_2 but also emit a mix of hazardous substances including NO_x (nitrogen oxides), hydrocarbons, carbon monoxide, particulate matter, and other pollutants, thereby severely contaminating the air we breathe. Consequently, there has been a steady escalation in the stringency of regulations governing automobile emissions year by year. To mitigate the emission of hazardous substances, it is imperative to achieve a precise air–fuel ratio of 14.7:1 during combustion, a ratio that optimally balances air and fuel to ensure efficient burning without excess or deficiency. This theoretical air–fuel ratio is pivotal in curbing the release of harmful pollutants into the atmosphere. To attain this precise ratio, O_2 sensors are strategically installed in the exhaust pipes of automobiles. These sensors function by monitoring the oxygen concentration in the exhaust gas, facilitating real-time adjustments to the air–fuel mixture to maintain it close to the ideal ratio. However, environmental conditions, particularly during winter, pose unique challenges to this delicate balance. The lower ambient air temperature in winter correlates with a decrease in the temperature of the exhaust pipe wall. When hot exhaust gas, laden with water vapor, traverses the exhaust pipe, the water vapor cools and condenses on the inner walls of the pipe. Over time, this condensate accumulates, leading to the formation of water pools inside the pipe. As the exhaust gas disperses the accumulated condensate, it is released into the atmosphere. Regrettably, this process is not without consequences. The condensate, when in contact with the O_2 sensor, can compromise its performance, diminishing its ability to accurately regulate the air–fuel ratio. In severe cases, this may even result in damage to the sensor, further exacerbating the emission control challenges. Moreover, the accumulation of condensate within the exhaust pipe presents additional hazards. Under subzero conditions, the condensate may freeze, obstructing the proper flow of exhaust gases. This impediment not only compromises the vehicle's performance but also poses a potential safety hazard on the road. Understanding the mechanisms governing the dispersion of condensate is paramount in addressing these issues. By elucidating the factors influencing condensate dispersion, researchers and policymakers can develop targeted strategies to mitigate its adverse effects on emission control systems. While advancements in emission control technology have significantly reduced the environmental impact of automobiles, challenges persist, particularly in adverse weather conditions. Addressing these challenges demands a multifaceted approach that encompasses technological innovation, regulatory measures, and ongoing research into understanding the

Deep Learning in Action: Image and Video Processing for Practical Use. DOI: https://doi.org/10.1016/B978-0-443-30078-3.00007-X

complexities of emission control systems. Only through concerted efforts can we hope to mitigate the detrimental effects of automobile emissions on our environment and public health. The breakup process is segmented into three phases as depicted in Fig. 7.1A deformation and bag growth phase, where the droplet changes from its original spherical form into a liquid disk, developing a progressively thickening bag-like membrane; (B) bag rupture phase, in which the bag splits, forming a liquid torus ring along with numerous micro-sized droplets; and (C) torus breakup phase, during which the torus ring disintegrates into several smaller droplets.

Object detection stands as a cornerstone task within the realm of computer vision. In recent years, the field has witnessed significant strides, particularly with the advent of deep learning-based models, promising heightened accuracy and expedited detection speeds. A multitude of such models has been proposed, highlighting advancements in the domain. (For a comprehensive survey of recent developments, refer to (Cherapanamjeri & Rao, 2022; Jiao et al., 2019; Kaur & Singh, 2023; Liu et al., 2020)). However, the practical application of deep learning-based object detection models poses myriad challenges, especially in specialized domains where images encapsulate distinct scientific phenomena or originate from industrial contexts. Securing an extensive corpus of annotated data for such applications proves arduous. Unlike natural scene images, which may lend themselves to crowdsourced annotations, specialized domains often necessitate expert annotation, rendering the process both laborious and costly. Consequently, amassing sizable, annotated datasets for training data-hungry deep-learning models becomes either infeasible or impractical. Moreover, the presence of rare object classes or phenomena exacerbates the class imbalance predicament, impeding the learning process and jeopardizing its reliability.

Object detection models have emerged as pivotal tools in computer vision, employed widely in various everyday and specialized tasks. These models are designed to identify and locate objects within images, a capability that has found applications ranging from autonomous driving to content moderation. However, despite their widespread adoption and utility, there are significant challenges associated with their development and evaluation that need to be thoroughly addressed to enhance their effectiveness and adaptability. One of the primary challenges in the development and evaluation of object detection models is the nature of the datasets commonly used for their testing and validation. The assessment of these models occurs within the confines of datasets comprised of natural images, such as

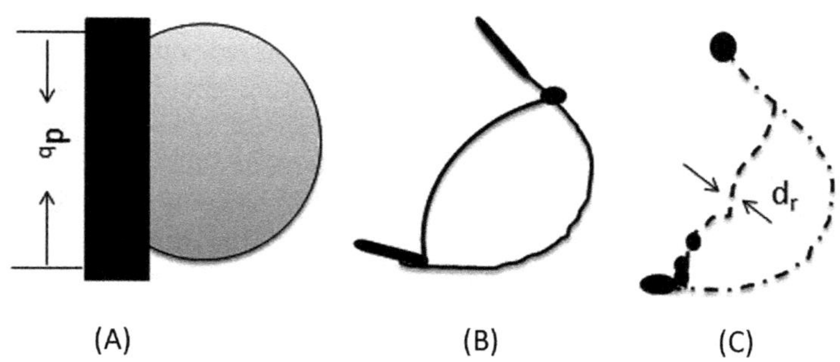

FIGURE 7.1

Workflow of bag-breakup process: (A) deformation and bag growth phase, (B) bag rupture phase, and (C) torus breakup phase.

the PASCAL visual object classes (VOC) and the common objects in context (COCO). These datasets are immensely valuable for foundational research and have played a critical role in advancing the field of object detection. They provide a diverse array of images featuring everyday objects in natural settings, which are essential for training models to recognize and interact with objects that most humans encounter regularly. However, the features encapsulated by such datasets diverge from the contexts and requirements of more specialized applications in scientific or industrial domains. For example, in a manufacturing setting, object detection models might be required to recognize and differentiate between highly similar machine parts, a task for which the generalist datasets such as PASCAL VOC and COCO may not provide sufficient training data. Similarly, in scientific research, models might need to detect and analyze objects under microscopes or in aerial images, scenarios that are underrepresented in conventional object detection datasets. This divergence raises significant concerns about the efficacy of object detection methods when applied outside the standard benchmark datasets. The criticality of certain model components and features such as the type of convolutional layers used, the architecture of the model, or the training algorithm may not translate effectively to specialized applications. For instance, a feature that significantly improves detection accuracy in natural images may have little to no impact on the detection of industrial components or scientific specimens.

To address these gaps and shed light on the performance of object detection models in nonstandard contexts, our study focuses on evaluating two representative object detection models using a dataset that is distinct from those comprised of natural images. This approach allows us to directly assess how well these models perform when they are applied to a domain that is not typically represented in mainstream object detection studies.

Our methodology involves a detailed analysis of two well-regarded models in the field of object detection. The first model is known for its efficiency and speed, making it suitable for applications where real-time processing is crucial, such as video surveillance or autonomous vehicle navigation. The second model is recognized for its high accuracy and robustness, characteristics that are vital for applications demanding high precision, such as defect detection in manufacturing or disease identification in medical imaging.

For the study, we use a modest-sized dataset sourced from a specific domain that diverges from natural images. This dataset has been curated to reflect the unique challenges and characteristics of the target application, including the types of objects present and the typical imaging conditions. By using such a dataset, we can more accurately gauge the models' detection capabilities and their practical utility in specialized settings.

Our analysis consists of several key components:

1. **Detection accuracy:** We evaluate how accurately each model identifies and locates objects within the dataset. This includes assessing the models' sensitivity (true positive rate) and specificity (true negative rate), as well as their overall accuracy in terms of correctly identified objects versus total objects present.
2. **Component impact analysis**: We dissect the impact of various components of the object detection models on their detection accuracy. This involves manipulating specific elements of the models such as adjusting layer configurations, altering training procedures, or modifying feature extractors and observing the resultant changes in performance. This analysis helps identify which components are crucial for maintaining high performance in nonstandard imaging conditions and which might be less relevant.

3. **Comparative analysis**: By comparing the performance of the two models, we aim to draw conclusions about their relative strengths and weaknesses in handling domain-specific challenges. This comparison will also provide insights into whether certain model architectures or configurations are more adaptable to specialized applications than others.

The results of this study are expected to contribute valuable insights into the applicability and optimization of object detection models in fields where traditional datasets are not representative of the actual application context. By understanding the limitations and potential of these models in specialized domains, researchers and practitioners can better tailor object detection systems to meet specific needs, leading to more robust and effective solutions across a wider range of applications. This research not only advances our knowledge in the field of object detection but also bridges the gap between generic object recognition tasks and specialized, high-stakes applications where precision and reliability are paramount.

The dataset employed in this study comprises fundamental experimental images depicting droplet dispersion phenomena within an automobile exhaust pipe. Termed as "bag-breakup," the target of detection constitutes a form of droplet dispersal. In contrast to natural scene images wherein multiple detection targets may inhabit a single frame or obtaining a plethora of target-laden images proves facile, our dataset diverges. Each image typically hosts one, at most two, detection targets, amidst a collection of thousands of images devoid of any discernible targets. Moreover, the visual similarity between the detection targets (bag-breakups) and the background poses a formidable challenge, unlike the relative ease of discerning objects from their surroundings in natural scene images. Of paramount importance is the real-time processing capability requisite for handling the copious experimental data generated daily, input as a continuous video stream into the system. To address these multifaceted challenges and offer pragmatic guidance to practitioners grappling with analogous hurdles, we proffer a repertoire of solutions and architectural choices tailored to such contexts.

The main contribution of this research is as the followings:

1. This chapter delves into the intricate difficulties that arise while implementing deep learning-based object detection strategies within niche areas such as scientific or industrial environments. It emphasizes the application of these advanced computational techniques to a particularly challenging subject within fluid dynamics the phenomenon of bag-breakup observed in droplet dispersion. This phenomenon is critical to understand because it has significant implications for various scientific and industrial processes, including inkjet printing, pesticide spraying, and fuel injection systems. In scientific and industrial settings, the characteristics and demands of the imagery are fundamentally different from those found in more commonly studied natural scenes. Images from these specialized domains typically feature complex backgrounds, variable lighting conditions, and dynamic changes, which are not usually present in standard datasets used for training deep-learning models. Furthermore, the objects of interest, such as droplets undergoing bag-breakup, are often smaller, faster moving, and have less defined shapes compared to objects in natural scenes, adding another layer of complexity to their detection. The research presented in this chapter aims to bridge the gap between the typical performance of object detection models trained on general datasets and their effectiveness in specialized contexts. It explores various approaches to enhance the accuracy and reliability of detecting the bag-breakup phenomenon in droplet dispersion images. This

includes adjusting existing deep-learning architectures to better accommodate the unique aspects of the imagery found in these domains, such as developing custom layers or loss functions that can focus more precisely on the small, fast-changing features typical of fluid phenomena. To address these challenges, the chapter reviews a series of experiments that systematically tweak different parameters and configurations within a deep-learning framework. These experiments are designed to ascertain which modifications yield the most significant improvements in performance when applied to the specialized task of detecting bag-breakup. For instance, it discusses the impact of using high-speed cameras to capture clearer images of the fast-moving droplets and the potential benefits of employing image preprocessing techniques to reduce background noise and enhance the visibility of the breakup events. Additionally, the research evaluates different training strategies, such as supervised, semisupervised, and unsupervised learning, to determine which is most effective in this context. It considers the use of synthetic data to augment the limited amount of real-world data typically available in specialized domains. This synthetic data is generated through simulations that closely mimic the fluid dynamics observed in bag-breakup, providing a richer dataset for training deep-learning models. The findings underscore the necessity of domain-specific adaptations in both the data handling and algorithmic aspects of deep-learning applications. By customizing the training process and the model architecture to better reflect the unique properties of the target phenomenon and the imaging conditions, the researchers demonstrate that it is possible to significantly improve object detection performance in specialized domains.

2. In this chapter, we explore the effectiveness of two advanced object detection techniques, RetinaNet and You Only Look Once version 7 (YOLOv7), within specialized domain applications. Object detection, a critical component in various technological sectors, involves identifying and locating objects within digital images. Specialized domains refer to specific areas where standard object detection models may struggle due to unique challenges such as varying lighting conditions, unusual object shapes, or cluttered backgrounds. The study begins by selecting RetinaNet and YOLOv7 due to their state-of-the-art performance in general object detection tasks. RetinaNet is renowned for its focal loss function, which effectively addresses class imbalance by focusing more on hard-to-classify objects. On the other hand, YOLOv7, an iteration of the YOLO series, is celebrated for its speed and accuracy, making it a suitable candidate for real-time detection tasks. The evaluation process in the study is twofold: quantitative and qualitative analysis. Quantitative analysis involves measuring the precision, recall, and overall accuracy of the models across various datasets curated from the specialized domains. These metrics provide a numerical basis for comparing the performance of the two models. Qualitative analysis, meanwhile, examines how well the models perform under the operational conditions specific to the specialized domains, such as detecting objects in low light or capturing details in high-motion scenarios. One of the pivotal aspects of this research is identifying and implementing strategies to overcome the challenges inherent in specialized domain imagery. These challenges often stem from the unique characteristics of the images, such as atypical object presentations or complex environmental factors. For example, in medical imaging, objects of interest, such as tumors, might appear significantly different based on the imaging technique used, such as MRI or CT scans. Similarly, in aerial surveillance, factors such as altitude and weather can severely impact the visibility and appearance of objects. The research delineates specific adjustments and enhancements needed for RetinaNet and YOLOv7

to function optimally within these challenging environments. Adjustments may include tuning the models to focus on smaller or partially visible objects and enhancing their ability to distinguish objects from noisy backgrounds. Furthermore, the study explores the integration of domain-specific knowledge into the training process, such as using annotated datasets that are representative of the real-world conditions of each domain. Through the comprehensive evaluation, the study provides valuable insights into the suitability of RetinaNet and YOLOv7 for specialized domain applications. The findings highlight which model performs better under specific conditions and what modifications are necessary to maximize their effectiveness. This kind of insight is crucial for practitioners and researchers who are looking to deploy object detection technologies in specialized fields, ensuring that they choose the most appropriate model and adapt it effectively to meet their specific needs.

3. This chapter provides a detailed examination of how two advanced object detection models, RetinaNet and YOLOv7, are applied to the complex task of recognizing and classifying the bag-breakup phenomenon in fluid dynamics. The exploration of these models in such a specialized context sheds light on the essential techniques required for precise object detection within niche areas of research and application. The bag-breakup phenomenon is a specific fluid dynamic event where a fluid-filled bag disintegrates under certain conditions, such as changes in pressure or velocity. This process is significant in various scientific and industrial applications, where understanding and controlling such events can lead to better product designs or improved processes. Capturing this phenomenon through visual detection systems poses a unique challenge due to the dynamic and transient nature of fluids, making standard object detection models less effective without significant adaptation. In tackling this challenge, the chapter initially outlines the operational principles of RetinaNet and YOLOv7, focusing on their algorithmic structures and how they can be adapted to better suit the detection of fluid dynamics phenomena. Although the intrinsic details of these models are complex, their effectiveness in standard object detection tasks has been well documented, making them promising candidates for this specialized application. The analysis begins with a series of experiments designed to assess the adaptability and accuracy of each model in detecting bag-breakup. Various scenarios are constructed to simulate the conditions under which bag-breakup occurs, and the models are tasked with identifying and classifying these events from video footage. The performance metrics used in these as key indicators of model efficacy in correctly identifying and categorizing objects within images. One of the critical aspects discussed is the customization of the models to enhance their sensitivity to the fluid's dynamic properties. This involves tweaking the models' hyperparameters, enhancing their convolutional neural networks (CNNs) to better capture the fluid's motion, and training them on a dataset specifically curated to include various stages and types of bag-breakup. The training process also emphasizes the importance of high-quality, annotated data in teaching the models to recognize such a complex and variable phenomenon accurately. Following the experimentation phase, the chapter delves into the comparative analysis of RetinaNet and YOLOv7. This includes a discussion on the strengths and weaknesses of each model in this application, such as RetinaNet's higher precision at the cost of speed versus YOLOv7's faster processing times with slightly reduced accuracy. Such insights are crucial for researchers and practitioners when choosing the right model for their specific needs.

7.1.1 Bag-breakup in continuous airflow

Bag-breakup in continuous airflow stands as a pivotal phenomenon within the domain of fluid dynamics, holding profound implications across various industrial and scientific realms. This intricate process occurs within the context of complex systems such as automotive exhausts, industrial chimneys, and environmental ventilation mechanisms, where the interplay between fluid dynamics and material properties gives rise to distinctive visual patterns. At its core, bag-breakup entails the disintegration of liquid masses, typically droplets or aerosols, suspended within a continuous airflow. The dynamics governing this phenomenon encompass a rich tapestry of fluid mechanics principles, encompassing factors such as inertial forces, surface tension, viscosity, and turbulence. Understanding and accurately characterizing bag-breakup phenomena are of paramount importance across diverse fields, including automotive engineering, environmental science, aerosol research, and industrial process optimization. In the automotive sector, for instance, the efficient combustion of fuel relies heavily on the effective dispersion of fuel droplets within the exhaust stream, necessitating a nuanced comprehension of bag-breakup dynamics to enhance engine performance and minimize emissions. Similarly, in environmental engineering, the dispersal of pollutants and particulate matter hinges on the intricacies of bag-breakup phenomena within atmospheric airflow patterns, thereby influencing air quality assessments and regulatory frameworks. Moreover, in industrial processes involving spray drying, coating, or atomization, precise control over droplet size distribution, achieved through an understanding of bag-breakup mechanisms, underpins product quality and process efficiency. Despite its significance, the study of bag-breakup in continuous airflow presents formidable challenges owing to the complex interplay of factors governing fluid behavior and the transient nature of the phenomenon. Traditional experimental techniques often fall short in capturing the intricacies of bag-breakup dynamics in real-time and under varying operating conditions, necessitating the development of advanced computational models and high-resolution imaging techniques to unravel its complexities. Furthermore, the inherent variability and nonlinear nature of bag-breakup phenomena demand a multidisciplinary approach that integrates insights from fluid dynamics, materials science, computational modeling, and experimental characterization. Overcoming these challenges requires concerted efforts from researchers and engineers across disparate disciplines, coupled with advancements in computational resources, experimental methodologies, and collaborative research frameworks. By elucidating the fundamental principles underpinning bag-breakup in continuous airflow and developing predictive models capable of simulating its behavior across diverse settings (Morita et al., 2023), researchers can unlock new avenues for innovation in fields ranging from energy and transportation to environmental sustainability and healthcare. Thus the study of bag-breakup phenomena not only enriches our understanding of fundamental fluid dynamics principles but also holds immense potential for addressing pressing societal challenges and driving technological advancements in the years to come (Zhao et al., 2019). Fig. 7.2 illustrates the apparatus employed to capture images during the droplet dispersal experiments.

7.1.2 Factors affecting bag-breakup

Droplet dispersion, particularly within the context of automotive exhaust systems, presents a fascinating yet intricate phenomenon. Central to this process is "bag-breakup," a crucial event wherein droplets disintegrate, impacting emissions and environmental considerations. Understanding the

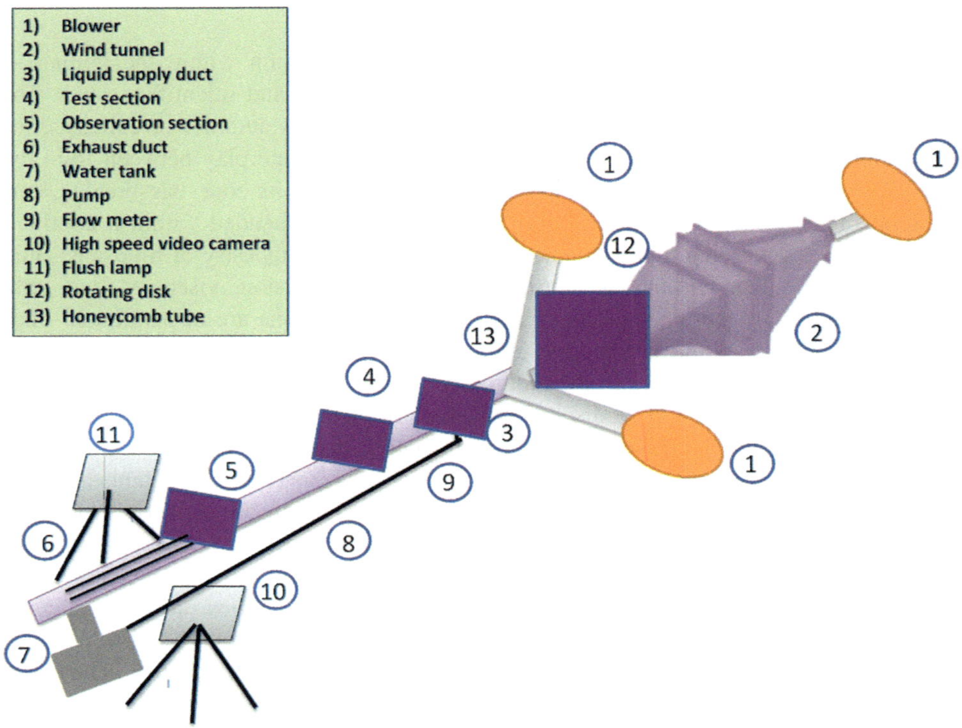

FIGURE 7.2

The apparatus employed to capture images during the droplet dispersal experiments.

factors influencing bag-breakup is paramount for optimizing combustion efficiency, reducing pollutant emissions, and advancing automotive engineering. In this article, we delve into the multifaceted dynamics governing bag-breakup, exploring the interplay of various factors shaping this phenomenon.

7.1.2.1 Fluid dynamics and flow characteristics

Fluid dynamics and flow characteristics form the foundation of droplet dispersion, emphasizing the complex interplay of forces that govern droplet behavior. The flow characteristics within an exhaust system, such as turbulence levels, velocity profiles, and pressure differentials, are crucial determinants of how droplets behave and interact. High turbulence within the system can lead to increased droplet breakup, as the shear forces exerted during turbulent flows tend to cause droplets to fragment into smaller sizes. This process is critical in many industrial and natural processes where the size and distribution of droplets can impact system efficiency and environmental interactions. On the other hand, laminar flow regimes, characterized by smoother and more streamlined flow, tend to support droplet coalescence, where droplets merge to form larger ones, thus delaying breakup events. The presence of laminar flow can be beneficial or detrimental, depending on the desired outcome in a specific application, such as in painting or in the delivery of aerosol medications, where larger droplets might be necessary for effective performance. Understanding these nuances of fluid flow within systems like exhausts is pivotal not only for engineering applications but also for environmental sciences, where droplet dynamics can influence pollutant dispersion and rainfall patterns. The behavior of droplets under different flow conditions also has significant implications for the design of equipment such as sprayers and nozzles, which rely on precise droplet sizes and dispersion patterns to achieve optimal functionality. Moreover, the study of fluid dynamics and droplet behavior extends into fields such as meteorology and respiratory medicine, where the understanding of droplet interaction with air currents can aid in predicting weather patterns and in designing better protective measures against airborne diseases. This interdisciplinarity of fluid dynamics demonstrates its universal applicability and critical role in advancing technology and environmental stewardship. As such, a thorough grasp of the flow characteristics within an exhaust system or any similar fluid dynamic environment is essential for scientists and engineers as they innovate and troubleshoot in their respective fields, aiming to optimize performance and mitigate negative impacts on health and the environment (Moraveji & Toghraie, 2017).

7.1.2.2 Droplet properties

The physical and chemical properties of droplets wield considerable influence over the bag-breakup process, a phenomenon critical in various industrial and natural environments where the integrity and distribution of droplets impact processes such as spray cooling, pesticide application, and rain formation. Droplet size, composition, surface tension, and viscosity are key parameters that dictate their susceptibility to breakup under varying conditions. Smaller droplets are particularly noteworthy, characterized by their higher surface area-to-volume ratios, which make them more prone to breakup due to increased surface forces that act more significantly relative to their volume compared to larger droplets. This susceptibility is crucial in environments where droplets interact dynamically with their surroundings, such as in atmospheric clouds where small droplets can easily split and merge, affecting weather patterns and cloud dynamics. The composition of droplets also plays a pivotal role, in influencing their physical behavior and chemical reactivity. Droplets consisting of different chemical substances may exhibit varied responses to environmental stresses; for instance, oil-based droplets might behave differently from water-based ones due to differences in chemical properties and interactions with ambient elements. Moreover, the surface tension of droplet a measure of the cohesive force at the surface that holds a droplet together significantly affects their stability. Lower surface tension reduces the energy required to deform a droplet, thereby enhancing its tendency to breakup under mechanical or thermal stresses. Viscosity, another crucial property, dictates the internal resistance to flow within the droplet; lower viscosity implies that the droplet material is less resistant to deformation, further facilitating breakup. Additionally, the presence of surfactants or contaminants can radically alter the intrinsic properties of droplets. Surfactants reduce the surface tension, potentially leading to more significant deformation and subsequent breakup under less forceful conditions. Contaminants, depending on their nature, might alter the viscosity or add to the complexity of the chemical makeup of the droplets, thereby influencing the breakup process in unpredictable ways. These elements combined depict a complex interplay of physical and chemical factors that determine the behavior of droplets in a myriad of conditions, highlighting the importance of understanding these properties in predicting and controlling the outcomes of processes involving liquid dispersal. Thus in practical applications, manipulating these droplet properties can optimize processes such as fuel injection in engines, where fine control over droplet breakup can lead to more efficient fuel combustion and reduced emissions. In ecological systems, such knowledge assists in better-predicting precipitation patterns and enhancing cloud seeding efforts, crucial for managing water resources and understanding climate dynamics. Overall, the study of droplet properties not only provides insights into their fundamental physics but also serves as a cornerstone in improving various technological and environmental applications where control over liquid fragmentation is paramount (Buranasuksombat et al., 2011; Hubbard et al., 1975; Yan et al., 2019).

7.1.2.3 Environmental conditions

Environmental conditions, including temperature, humidity, and atmospheric pressure, significantly influence droplet behavior and, consequently, the process of bag-breakup. In environments where temperatures are elevated, particularly within exhaust systems, there is an increased tendency for droplet evaporation, which results in a reduction in droplet size and promotes the likelihood of breakup. This is because higher temperatures provide the energy needed to overcome the cohesive forces holding the droplet together, thereby facilitating its disintegration into smaller droplets. In contrast, higher levels of humidity can counteract the effects of temperature by impeding evaporation. The presence of more water vapor in the air reduces the evaporative drive as the air is already saturated or near saturated with moisture, leading to less energy available for evaporation. This results in larger droplets that are more prone to coalesce with other droplets rather than breaking up, thus delaying the breakup process. Moreover, variations in atmospheric pressure also play a crucial role in the dynamics of droplet behavior. Lower atmospheric pressure, which often corresponds to higher altitudes or specific meteorological conditions, can decrease the air density, and thus reduce the resistance against droplet movement, facilitating faster breakup. Conversely, higher pressure increases the density of the air, enhancing the aerodynamic forces acting on the droplet and delaying its breakup. Understanding how these environmental factors interact is essential for a comprehensive grasp of bag-breakup phenomena, as these conditions collectively determine the stability and disintegration patterns of droplets in real-world settings. This knowledge is vital for industries and applications where precise control of droplet dispersion and size is critical, such as in spray drying processes, pesticide application in agriculture, or fuel injection systems in automotive engines.

7.1.2.4 Combustion characteristics

The combustion characteristics within an engine cylinder play a crucial role in influencing the formation and behavior of droplets before they enter the exhaust system, with factors such as fuel composition, injection timing, and combustion efficiency having a significant impact on the droplet size distribution and concentration. When combustion is incomplete or when fuel–air mixing is suboptimal, there tends to be a formation of larger droplets, which are more likely to undergo breakup. On the other hand, when the combustion process is efficient, it leads to the formation of smaller, more uniform droplets that are less prone to breakup. Understanding the complex interplay between combustion dynamics and droplet formation is essential for elucidating the mechanisms behind bag-breakup, as it helps in identifying the specific conditions under which droplets behave in certain ways. This knowledge is critical for optimizing engine performance and reducing emissions, as well as for improving the design and functionality of exhaust systems. By analyzing how numerous factors affect droplet behavior, researchers and engineers can develop strategies to control and manipulate these factors to achieve desired outcomes, such as minimizing pollutant emissions or enhancing fuel efficiency. Additionally, insights gained from studying combustion characteristics and their impact on droplet dynamics can also contribute to advancements in other areas, such as the development of new fuels and combustion technologies, leading to more environmentally friendly and sustainable combustion systems.

7.1.2.5 Impact of engine design and operating conditions

The design and operating parameters of the engine play a pivotal role in shaping droplet dispersion and subsequent bag-breakup phenomena. Engine geometry, fuel injection systems, and operating temperatures profoundly influence droplet trajectories and residence times within the combustion chamber. Variations in engine load, speed, and operating conditions can alter droplet size distribution and concentration, modulating breakup kinetics. Furthermore, exhaust gas recirculation systems and aftertreatment devices can affect droplet properties and behavior, influencing breakup dynamics downstream. Understanding the holistic influence of engine design and operating conditions is indispensable for optimizing bag-breakup processes.

The complexities surrounding bag-breakup in droplet dispersion, it becomes evident that a myriad of factors converge to shape this phenomenon. From fluid dynamics and droplet properties to environmental conditions and combustion characteristics, each element intricately influences breakup dynamics. By comprehensively understanding these factors and their interplay, researchers and engineers can devise strategies to optimize combustion efficiency, mitigate pollutant emissions, and propel advancements in automotive technology. As we delve deeper into this intricate realm, unlocking the mysteries of bag-breakup holds promise for a greener, more sustainable future (Cheng, 2000; Gonca & Dobrucali, 2016).

7.1.3 Importance of bag-breakup detection in automotive safety

In the realm of automotive safety, advancements in technology have continuously reshaped and redefined the landscape. Among the myriad of safety features and systems integrated into modern vehicles, the detection of phenomena such as bag-breakup holds particular significance. Bag-breakup, a crucial aspect of droplet dispersion within automobile exhaust systems, plays a pivotal role in ensuring both environmental sustainability and the safety of motorists and pedestrians alike.

Droplet dispersion, a phenomenon intricately linked with engine performance and emissions control, occurs within the confines of an automobile's exhaust system. As combustion takes place within the engine, various byproducts are produced, including water vapor. Within the exhaust system, water vapor condenses into droplets, forming liquid pools commonly referred to as "bags". The breakup of these bags is a critical juncture in the emission process, influencing pollutant dispersion and, the environmental impact of the vehicle.

From a safety standpoint, the detection and monitoring of bag-breakups assume paramount importance. Detecting the onset of bag-breakup enables initiative-taking measures to be taken to mitigate potential hazards. The dispersion of droplets, particularly in the vicinity of the exhaust system, can pose a risk of contamination to surrounding components and surfaces. Moreover, in extreme cases, the failure to detect and address bag-breakup can lead to hazardous emissions being released into the environment, compromising air quality and public health.

In the context of vehicle emissions control, effective bag-breakup detection facilitates adherence to stringent regulatory standards governing pollutant emissions. Regulatory bodies worldwide impose stringent limits on the emissions of pollutants such as particulate matter and NO_x. Failure to comply with these regulations not only exposes manufacturers to legal ramifications but also contributes to environmental degradation and public health concerns. By ensuring the timely detection and mitigation of bag-breakups, automotive manufacturers can uphold their commitment to environmental stewardship and regulatory compliance.

Furthermore, the integration of bag-breakup detection systems aligns with the broader trend toward vehicle automation and intelligent transportation systems. In an era characterized by the proliferation of autonomous driving technologies, the ability of vehicles to self-monitor and respond to environmental cues assumes unprecedented importance. Bag-breakup detection systems, when integrated with onboard sensors and control mechanisms, empower vehicles to autonomously regulate their emissions, optimizing performance while minimizing environmental impact. Beyond its implications for vehicle emissions control and environmental sustainability, bag-breakup detection holds intrinsic value in enhancing overall vehicle safety. The automotive exhaust system encompasses a myriad of components and subsystems, each playing a crucial role in the vehicle's operation. Detecting anomalies such as bag-breakup provides valuable insights into the health and integrity of the exhaust system, enabling preemptive maintenance and repairs to prevent catastrophic failures. Moreover, the integration of bag-breakup detection systems dovetails with broader initiatives aimed at enhancing road safety and reducing accidents. By equipping vehicles with advanced sensing and detection capabilities, manufacturers can augment existing safety systems, such as collision avoidance and lane departure warning systems. The ability to detect and respond to potential hazards in real-time enhances the overall safety and reliability of vehicles, thereby reducing the incidence of accidents and mitigating their consequences. The detection of bag-breakup within automotive exhaust systems epitomizes the intersection of environmental sustainability, regulatory compliance, and vehicle safety. By leveraging advanced sensing technologies and intelligent algorithms, automotive manufacturers can proactively monitor and mitigate the risks associated with bag-breakups, thereby enhancing both the environmental performance and safety of their vehicles. As we continue to navigate towar a future characterized by autonomous mobility and sustainable transportation, the importance of bag-breakup detection in automotive safety cannot be overstated (Cadwallader & Herring, 1999).

7.1.4 Challenges in identifying bag-breakup

Identifying and accurately detecting phenomena such as bag-breakup poses significant challenges in various scientific and industrial applications. Bag-breakup, a form of droplet dispersion occurring within automobile exhaust pipes, presents a particularly intricate puzzle for researchers and practitioners alike. At the heart of this challenge lies the inherent complexity of the visual patterns associated with bag-breakup, which often closely resemble the background against which they occur. Unlike the straightforward discrimination between objects and their surroundings in natural scene images, distinguishing bag-breakup instances amidst visually similar backgrounds demands a nuanced approach. Compounding this issue is the scarcity of annotated data tailored to such specialized domains. Unlike crowd-sourced annotations feasible for natural scene images, annotating images depicting bag-breakup typically necessitates expert intervention, rendering the process laborious and resource-intensive. Consequently, the acquisition of large-scale annotated datasets requisite for training deep-learning models becomes a formidable task. Moreover, the presence of rare classes of objects or phenomena further exacerbates the challenge, giving rise to class imbalance issues that impede the learning process and compromise detection accuracy. Evaluating the efficacy of object detection models poses a challenge. Existing evaluation frameworks rely on datasets comprising natural scene images, such as PASCAL VOC and COCO, whose features diverge significantly from those encountered in scientific or industrial contexts. Thus the suitability of state-of-the-art object detection methods for specialized applications remains ambiguous, necessitating rigorous scrutiny and adaptation. Real-time processing capabilities emerge as another pivotal consideration in the identification of bag-breakup. Managing the sheer volume of experimental data generated daily, often in the form of continuous video streams, demands robust and efficient processing mechanisms. In response to these multifaceted challenges, researchers and practitioners are compelled to explore innovative solutions and architectural choices tailored to the idiosyncrasies of specialized domains. These may encompass novel algorithmic approaches, leveraging contextual information across sequential frames to enhance detection accuracy, or the development of domain-specific datasets and evaluation frameworks to benchmark model performance accurately. By navigating these challenges adeptly, researchers and practitioners can pave the way for more reliable and effective identification of bag-breakup phenomena, facilitating advancements in diverse scientific and industrial domains.

7.2 Methodology

In this study, we delve into the nuances and challenges of applying deep learning-based object detection methods to special domain applications, such as scientific and industrial images, which significantly differ from natural scene images commonly used for evaluation. We focus on the detection of a specific fluid phenomenon, bag-breakup, in images of droplet scatter in a scenario that presents distinct characteristics compared to natural images. To address this, we employ two advanced and well-established object detection techniques, namely, RetinaNet and YOLOv7. Our methodology involves a comprehensive analysis where we evaluate the strategies needed to adapt these methods effectively to the unique properties of the target images. Both quantitative and qualitative evaluations are conducted to assess the performance and efficacy of these methods in the specialized domain. Furthermore, we introduce a novel approach aimed at enhancing detection accuracy by leveraging information from multiple consecutive frames. This new method seeks to capitalize on temporal dependencies within the image sequences, potentially capturing dynamic aspects of the fluid phenomenon more effectively. By doing so, we aim to offer a more robust and accurate detection mechanism tailored to the specific challenges posed by nonnatural images. Through our meticulous exploration and experimentation, we shed light on the intricacies involved in adapting object detection techniques to diverse image domains. The insights derived from this study are intended to be invaluable for researchers and practitioners venturing into applications where images exhibit significant deviations from natural scenes. We believe that our findings not only contribute to the advancement of object detection methodologies but also provide practical guidance for addressing the complexities associated with specialized image datasets.

7.2.1 Dataset collection and description

In this research endeavor, we embarked on the collection and analysis of a comprehensive dataset consisting of experimental images captured under diverse conditions. These conditions encompassed varying wind speeds, pipe geometries, and other parameters to capture the full spectrum of droplet dispersal phenomena. The primary objective was to visually ascertain the frequency of droplet scattering in the captured images. It is noteworthy that the occurrence of droplet scattering was observed in a mere 1/1000 to 1/10,000 of the total experimental images. A total of 808 images have been utilized in this research. This low incidence rate necessitated the meticulous visual inspection of an extensive number of images, rendering the process exceedingly time-intensive and arduous for researchers. Recognizing the challenges inherent in manual image inspection, our study pivoted toward the development and deployment of an automated system capable of detecting droplet scattering. To achieve this, we employed an advanced object detection methodology rooted in deep-learning techniques. Our investigation delineated four distinct types of scattering phenomena: ligament, bag-breakup, multimode, and impact. Among these, our focus was primarily directed toward the detection of bag-breakup events due to their significance and prevalence in the observed experimental data.

A bag-breakup event occurs when the liquid film experiences inertial forces exerted by the surrounding gas phase. This phenomenon results in the droplet expanding akin to a balloon, culminating in its fragmentation. The term "bag-breakup" is derived from the visual resemblance of the ruptured droplet to a deflated bag now of fragmentation. An illustrative example of a bag-breakup event is depicted in Fig. 7.3, providing a tangible representation of this specific scattering phenomenon. By concentrating our efforts on bag-breakup detection, we aimed to contribute a focused and in-depth analysis to the broader understanding of droplet scattering mechanisms. The utilization of

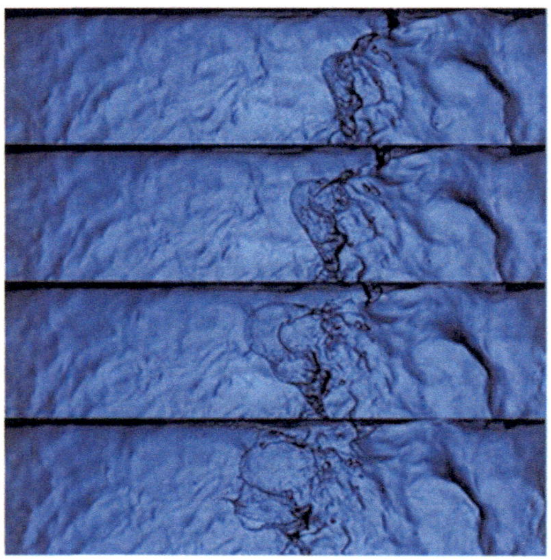

FIGURE 7.3

Example of a bag-breakup: the bag is visible moving from right to left.

deep learning-based object detection methods facilitated the accurate identification and classification of bag-breakup events within the collected dataset. This approach not only expedited the analysis process but also enhanced the reliability and consistency of the detection results. Our study underscores the pivotal role of automated systems in expediting the detection and analysis of rare scattering phenomena in experimental datasets. Through the meticulous collection and examination of images captured under varied conditions, coupled with the deployment of innovative deep-learning techniques, we endeavored to elucidate the intricacies of bag-breakup events and their implications in droplet dispersal mechanisms. This research serves as a steppingstone toward the development of robust tools and methodologies for advancing the field of droplet scattering analysis, paving the way for future innovations and discoveries in this domain.

7.2.2 Data preprocessing

In the context of the problem addressed in this paper, as well as in similar industrial and scientific applications, we encounter a unique challenge. The object of interest that requires detection belongs to a rare class or phenomenon, observable in only a minuscule subset of all images. Most of these images predominantly feature the background class, devoid of any target, while those showcasing the target usually exhibit only a singular instance of the object. This stands in stark contrast to conventional scenarios where target objects, such as cars or faces, are abundant in natural scenes, with multiple objects often present in a single image, facilitating easier acquisition and labeling of training data. The predominant representation of the background class in our images results in a significant class imbalance, posing challenges that can impede the learning process, rendering it unreliable. While two-stage detectors mitigate this issue by eliminating most background regions during the region proposal stage, one-stage detectors necessitate addressing this imbalance directly. One effective solution to this problem is the focal loss, as proposed by Lin et al. Focal Loss modifies the traditional cross−entropy loss by introducing a term (1 - pt), reducing the loss for samples with high confidence, corresponding to the predominant background class. This adjustment emphasizes the training of challenging samples belonging to the target class, which inherently has fewer training samples available. Consequently, RetinaNet, despite being a one-stage detector, achieves accuracy comparable to two-stage detectors while maintaining the advantage of computational efficiency. Another obstacle in training deep learning-based object detection methods is the substantial data requirement. Unlike general cases utilizing natural scene images, securing large, annotated datasets for our specific task is challenging and costly, as annotations are often provided solely by experts. This limitation makes extensive data collection impractical. To address this, fine-tuning strategies are employed, utilizing pretrained weights from large datasets as initial values for the target dataset. This approach enables achieving high detection accuracy even when training with limited data.

Furthermore, data augmentation proves invaluable in enhancing model robustness when training with restricted datasets. Beyond conventional augmentation techniques such as image rotation and flipping, innovative methods such as mosaic augmentation have emerged, allowing the amalgamation of multiple training images. These augmentation strategies not only amplify the dataset but also diversify the training samples, enriching the model's understanding and improving its generalization capabilities. Thus a combination of specialized loss functions, fine-tuning, and advanced data augmentation techniques forms a holistic approach to address the challenges inherent in detecting rare classes in object detection tasks.

7.2.3 The proposed deep-learning models

The proposed deep-learning models discussed in this research focus on enhancing detection speed, a critical requirement in many industrial and scientific applications where vast amounts of data need to be processed within tight time constraints. Object detection methods can broadly be categorized into two types: (1) two-stage object detection models, exemplified by faster-Region-based Convolutional Neural Networks (RCNN), which involves a separate region proposal stage followed by classification and regression tasks to determine the object's class and bounding box; and (2) one-stage object detection models such as Single Shot Detector (SSD), YOLO, EfficientDet, and recent transformer-based methods, which predict object classes and bounding boxes directly from input images without the need for a preliminary region proposal stage. Due to the additional time needed for region proposal computation in two-stage models, one-stage models offer much faster detection speeds, making them a preferable choice for applications prioritizing speed. In recent years, module-level reparameterization has emerged as a significant area of research, focusing on substituting the multibranch structures used during training with simpler modules during inference. This substitution reduces memory access costs and accelerates the inference process. The state-of-the-art YOLOv7 model employs this approach, which we will compare in this study with the widely used RetinaNet model, serving as our baseline. RetinaNet is a straightforward yet conceptually sound one-stage model that comprises a backbone feature pyramid network (FPN) and subnetworks for object classification and box regression. On the other hand, YOLOv7 is a one-stage model incorporating various recent architectural designs and learning techniques, utilizing Efficient Layer Aggregation Network (ELAN) as its backbone, and has demonstrated superior performance compared to previous object detection models in terms of both detection speed and accuracy.

7.2.4 Training and validation

In the pursuit of enhancing object detection capabilities, we embarked on the training and validation of two distinct one-stage object detection models: the advanced YOLOv7 and the established RetinaNet, which serves as a comparative baseline. YOLOv7, representing the innovative advancements in object detection, was pitted against the more traditional yet reliable RetinaNet. Our dataset, sourced from various videos, was meticulously partitioned into training, validation, and test subsets to facilitate a comprehensive evaluation of model performance. Specifically, the training set comprised 597 images, the validation set had 65 images, and the test set encompassed 146 images. To maintain uniformity and consistency during the training and validation processes, all images were standardized to a resolution of 800×800 pixels. In the RetinaNet model, we employed the Adam optimization algorithm for the model training process. The learning rate was meticulously set at 1×10^{-5}, aiming to strike a balance between rapid convergence and stability. The hyperparameters, denoted as $\Theta 1$ and $\Theta 2$, were established as $\Theta 1 = 0.9$ and $\Theta 2 = 0.999$, respectively. Furthermore, to streamline the training process and enhance model robustness, a batch size of 8 was chosen. To augment the dataset and introduce variability into the training samples, two augmentation techniques were incorporated: vertical flipping and color jittering. Conversely, in the

YOLOv7 model, the data augmentation strategy was slightly modified. Specifically, the default horizontal flipping was substituted with vertical flipping, while all other parameters and settings remained unaltered. This adjustment was made to diversify the training data and potentially improve the model's ability to generalize across different scenarios. Both models underwent an intensive training regimen spanning 100 epochs, ensuring that they were exposed to a diverse range of training samples to optimize their detection capabilities. Through this rigorous training and validation process, we aimed to assess and compare the performance of YOLOv7 and RetinaNet in object detection tasks, shedding light on their respective strengths and limitations in handling complex visual data. To initiate the training process, all input images were resized to the uniform resolution of 800 $\times$ 800 pixels. This resolution was chosen based on preliminary experiments that suggested an optimal balance between processing speed and image detail sufficiency for object detection accuracy. Standardizing image size is crucial as it ensures that all features within the images maintain consistent proportions and are similarly processed by the CNNs during feature extraction. The choice of Adam optimizer was influenced by its efficiency in handling sparse gradients and its adaptive learning rate capabilities, which make it well-suited for deep-learning tasks involving large datasets with complex image data. Setting the learning rate to a low value of 1×10^{-5} was a strategic decision aimed at minimizing the risk of overshooting minimal loss during training, thereby stabilizing the training trajectory. The use of specific hyperparameters, $\Theta 1 = 0.9$ and $\Theta 2 = 0.999$, helped in controlling the exponential decay rates of moving averages, which is a critical factor in the momentum component of Adam.

Choosing a batch size of 8 was a compromise between computational demand and the need for sufficient gradient approximation per update. Smaller batch sizes can lead to more noise in the gradient estimates, which, while sometimes beneficial for escaping local minima, can also cause instability in the training process. Data augmentation, involving vertical flipping and color jittering, was introduced to artificially expand the diversity of the dataset. These techniques simulate different lighting conditions and orientations that the model might encounter in real-world scenarios, thereby enhancing its generalizability and robustness. The adjustment to include vertical flipping instead of the standard horizontal flipping in YOLOv7 was intended to evaluate the hypothesis that different augmentation strategies could yield improvements in model generalization. This change was particularly geared toward exploring whether such modifications could enhance the model's performance in detecting objects in uncommon orientations, an aspect critical for practical applications where objects may not always be ideally positioned. The training regimen of 100 epochs was established to provide many opportunities for the models to converge toward optimal performance. An epoch in machine learning is a complete pass through the entire training dataset, and extending this to a substantial number of cycles ensures that the models sufficiently learn and adapt to the nuances of the data. This extended training period is crucial for deep-learning models such as YOLOv7 and RetinaNet, which rely heavily on feature learning capabilities to detect and classify objects within images accurately. The assessment of model performance posttraining involved evaluating the precision, recall, and mean average precision (mAP) across various intersection over union (IoU) thresholds. These metrics provide a comprehensive insight into how well the models perform in terms of not only detecting the objects but also how accurately they are able to localize them within the images. Precision measures the accuracy of the predictions (i.e., the proportion of positive identifications that were correct), while recall assesses the model's ability to find all relevant cases (i.e., the proportion of actual positives that were correctly identified). The mAP provides an average over multiple thresholds, giving a single performance score that reflects detection accuracy at various levels of IoU. The comparative analysis between YOLOv7 and RetinaNet aims to highlight the relative strengths and weaknesses of each model in various operational scenarios. For instance, RetinaNet might excel in scenarios with high background noise and complex object textures, whereas YOLOv7 might perform better in environments with dynamic object movements and varying scales. This understanding aids in selecting the appropriate model depending on specific use-case requirements, such as surveillance, autonomous driving, or medical imaging.

7.3 Experimental results

In the experimental study, we focused on the rapid detection of bag-breakups in both pulsating and steady airflow conditions using video analysis paired with deep-learning techniques. The outcomes of this research were notably promising, highlighting the application's accuracy and efficiency in identifying bag-breakups from the captured video footage. This highlights the significant potential of this innovative approach in real-time monitoring and control systems across various industrial domains. The deep-learning algorithms employed in the study demonstrated remarkable accuracy. These algorithms were adept at recognizing the specific incidents of bag-breakups within the video footage, a task that typically requires high precision to avoid false alarms and missed detections. The efficiency of these algorithms was also highlighted, as they processed video data rapidly, allowing for real-time analysis which is a critical requirement in many industrial applications. The performance of the deep-learning model was rigorously evaluated under a range of airflow conditions, which included both pulsating and steady states. This was essential to assess the model's robustness and adaptability across different operational scenarios that might be encountered in real-world settings. Notably, the model exhibited high sensitivity and specificity in its operational capability. It effectively distinguished between intact bags and those undergoing breakups, even amidst the complex dynamics of changing airflow. This precision is crucial for timely interventions in processes where the integrity of bags is directly tied to operational efficiency and safety. In many industrial processes, the integrity of bags is paramount. A failure in a bag can lead to significant operational disruptions or pose safety risks. Therefore the ability of the model to accurately detect breakups as they occur and do so in real-time is highly valuable. It allows for immediate corrective actions to be taken before there are serious consequences, maintaining continuous operation and minimizing potential downtime. Another significant aspect of the study was the computational efficiency of the proposed method. The ability to analyze video data quickly and make decisions in real-time is crucial for industries where delays can lead to increased operational costs or safety hazards. The model's rapid processing capabilities ensure that the flow of operations is maintained, and system downtimes are significantly reduced. The integration of video analysis with deep-learning techniques formed a synergistic approach that leveraged the strengths of both technologies. Video analysis provided a rich data source that included temporal and spatial details of the bags under various conditions, while deep learning offered the tools to interpret this data effectively and learn from it to make accurate predictions and detections. The combination of these technologies allowed the model to perform exceptionally well under diverse airflow conditions. This adaptability is especially important in industrial settings where environmental factors and operational conditions can vary widely and unpredictably. The ability to maintain high performance across such a range of conditions underscores the robustness of the solution. The experimental results validate the viability and effectiveness of the developed methodology. They pave the way for the broader implementation of such systems in industrial settings, particularly in roles that require constant monitoring of equipment and materials, such as in the filtration and packaging industries. These sectors stand to benefit immensely from the enhanced monitoring capabilities and improved operational integrity that the system offers.

7.3.1 Evaluation metrices

The average precision (AP) stands as a pivotal yardstick for evaluating the outcomes of experiments, particularly in the realm of object detection. This metric derives from the precision–recall (PR) curve, a graphical representation of the relationship between precision and recall, fundamental in assessing the efficacy of detection results. At its core, AP quantifies the area beneath this curve, offering a succinct measure of model performance. The journey to compute AP begins with the identification of object areas that exhibit a noteworthy IoU score compared to a predetermined threshold. These areas are then matched with their corresponding ground truth bounding boxes, laying the groundwork for subsequent evaluation. Following this, each detected region, distinguished by its confidence level, undergoes scrutiny. The region boasting the highest confidence among all associated with a specific ground truth bounding box earns the coveted title of true positive (TP), provided its confidence surpasses a set threshold denoted as β. Conversely, any other detected regions are deemed false positives (FP). This meticulous classification sets the stage for the PR curve's construction. By systematically varying the confidence threshold β and tallying the counts of TP and FP detections, a PR curve is meticulously crafted. This curve offers a nuanced perspective on the model's performance, illustrating the trade-offs between precision and recall across different confidence thresholds. The AP, then, emerges as the integral of this curve, encapsulating the model's overall efficacy in object detection. This methodological approach furnishes a robust framework for scrutinizing the performance of object detection models. By delineating the precision and recall rates across varying confidence thresholds, it empowers practitioners with granular insights essential for informed decision-making. Whether optimizing models or validating their effectiveness, AP serves as a beacon, guiding the trajectory of refinement and enhancement. The computation of AP transcends mere numerical calculation; it symbolizes a comprehensive evaluation paradigm. It signifies the culmination of meticulous analysis, reflective of the model's ability to discern objects amidst the visual cacophony. As such, AP stands not merely as a metric but as a testament to the rigor and precision underlying the pursuit of excellence in object detection.

7.3.2 Comparative analysis

We conducted a comparative analysis of object detection models, emphasizing the importance of meticulous precision in determining the exact location of objects using bounding box coordinates on images. However, when dealing with complex shapes, such as bag-breakups, characterized by intricate texture patterns and visual appearances, the exact bounding box becomes challenging to define. This complexity leads to considerable variations in annotations among different annotators. In contrast, natural scene images present more uniform object boundaries, with annotators agreeing on the correct boundaries for objects such as cars. An illustrative example is presented in Fig. 7.4, where the model's prediction is commendable; nevertheless, the IoU score a metric measuring the overlap ratio between predicted and ground truth bounding boxes is low. This discrepancy highlights the difficulty in precisely defining the boundaries of bag-breakup objects, resulting in inconsistencies among annotations. Consequently, unlike the standard IoU threshold of 0.5 commonly used for natural scene images, a lower threshold of 0.2 is also considered suitable for this specific task. The rationale behind this adjustment stems from the substantial variations in annotations among individual annotators, making it unreasonable to expect a high overlap between detection and ground truth. Evaluative results, as depicted in Fig. 7.5, reveal the AP metrics for different models employed in the experiment. The RetinaNet model utilizes ResNet-34-FPN as its backbone, while the YOLOv7 model adheres to its conventional implementation. Notably, altering the IoU threshold during evaluation yielded a 10.1% improvement in AP for RetinaNet and a 4.9% enhancement for YOLOv7. Furthermore, the state-of-the-art YOLOv7 model demonstrated superior performance, outpacing RetinaNet by 8.9% when using an IoU threshold of 0.5. This performance gap was mitigated to 3.7% when utilizing the reduced IoU threshold of 0.2, underscoring the importance of adapting the IoU threshold to the nature of the data. The challenges posed by the complex shapes of bag-breakup objects and the variations in annotations necessitate careful consideration of the IoU threshold during model evaluation. Tailoring the threshold to better suit the intricacies of the data can significantly impact the performance metrics, as evidenced by the notable improvements observed in the evaluation of the RetinaNet and YOLOv7 models. Thus adapting evaluation criteria to account for the specificities of the data under study is crucial for achieving accurate and reliable object detection results.

In the comprehensive assessment of model performance various evaluation metrics such as precision, recall, and the F1 score, which encapsulates both precision and recall, are presented. These

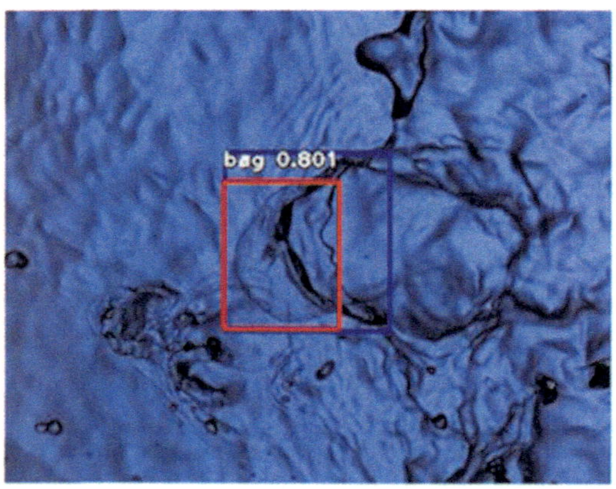

FIGURE 7.4

Detection of bag-breakup in an image, illustrating an instance where despite excellent detection accuracy, the intersection over union (IoU) remains low. The predicted area by the model is marked in red, while the actual annotation appears in blue. The number displayed above the predicted bounding box indicates the model's confidence level.

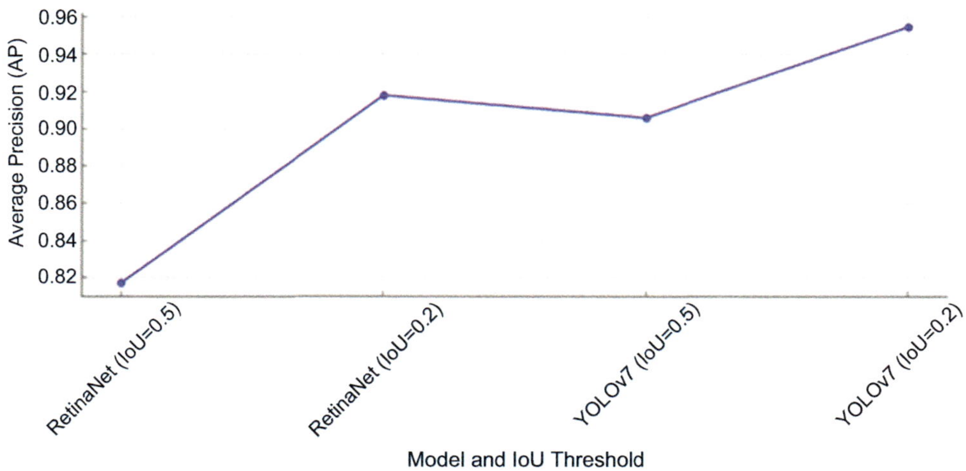

FIGURE 7.5

Line graph depicting the average precision (AP) of RetinaNet and YOLOv7 models at different intersection over union (IoU) thresholds of 0.5 and 0.2. The graph illustrates the variations in AP with changes in IoU, highlighting the superior performance at lower IoU thresholds for both models.

metrics are plotted against the model's confidence level. YOLOv7 demonstrates superior accuracy in terms of both precision and recall compared to RetinaNet. Furthermore, YOLOv7 exhibits less variability in accuracy when the IoU threshold is adjusted. This consistent performance could be attributed to YOLOv7 incorporation of the IoU-related loss in its bounding box regression loss function, whereas RetinaNet employs only the smooth L1 Loss. This analysis underscores the significance of considering these evaluation metrics and threshold adjustments for optimal model performance in object detection tasks. As we delve into the intricacies of model evaluation, precision, recall, and the F1 score emerge as vital indicators of a model's effectiveness in correctly identifying objects within an image. Precision measures the accuracy of positive predictions made by the model, indicating the proportion of TPs among all positive predictions. Recall, on the other hand, assesses the model's ability to capture all relevant instances, representing the proportion of TPs that were correctly identified. The F1 score, a harmonic means of precision and recall, provides a balanced assessment of a model's performance, particularly useful when dealing with imbalanced datasets. YOLOv7 shines, showcasing superior precision and recall compared to its counterpart, RetinaNet. This superiority becomes even more pronounced as the IoU threshold is adjusted. The IoU threshold plays a crucial role in determining whether a detected bounding box accurately captures an object. By integrating IoU-related loss into its regression function, YOLOv7 demonstrates robustness against variations in this threshold, resulting in more consistent performance across different scenarios. This nuanced understanding underscores the importance of fine-tuning these thresholds to strike a balance between detection accuracy and computational efficiency. During this study, we utilized a relatively modest dataset comprising approximately 800 images. However, through the process of fine-tuning the pretrained versions of YOLOv7 and RetinaNet on our dataset, we managed to attain an impressive AP exceeding 0.9 on the test data. This achievement prompted us to delve deeper into the efficacy of various training strategies and model components specifically tailored for small-scale datasets, such as the one employed in our study. To this end, we conducted further experiments by training both models from scratch under diverse conditions, subsequently evaluating the resultant changes in accuracy. Our findings from training YOLOv7 from scratch are presented in Fig. 7.6. The training regimen spanned 3000 epochs, with convergence observed between 1000 and 2000 epochs. Notably, YOLOv7 exhibited a remarkable AP exceeding 0.9 even without the benefit of pretraining on a larger dataset. However, the exclusion of mosaic augmentation led to a decline in AP by approximately 0.2 points. This underscores the pivotal role of mosaic augmentation in bolstering the efficacy of training on diminutive datasets within this domain.

Fig. 7.7 outlines the results of our experimental endeavors, where we embarked on training the RetinaNet model from the ground up. This endeavor involved harnessing two distinct backbones ResNet-18-FPN and ResNet-34-FPN. Departing from the conventional fine-tuning strategy, we opted for a more aggressive approach by increasing the learning rate tenfold, setting it at 1×10^{-4}, and subjecting the model to an extended training regime spanning 100 epochs. Remarkably, convergence was attained in approximately 50 epochs for both ResNet-18-FPN and ResNet-34-FPN, indicating the efficacy of the training protocol in reaching a stable state. However, despite these concerted efforts, the AP scores obtained remained subdued. For ResNet-18-FPN and ResNet-34-FPN, the APs stood at 0.621 and 0.654, respectively. Comparatively, these figures trailed behind the levels of accuracy achieved through the fine-tuning of pretrained models by more than 0.2 points. This stark disparity accentuates the indispensability of the fine-tuning process and reinforces the notion that pretrained weights provide robust initializations for the model.

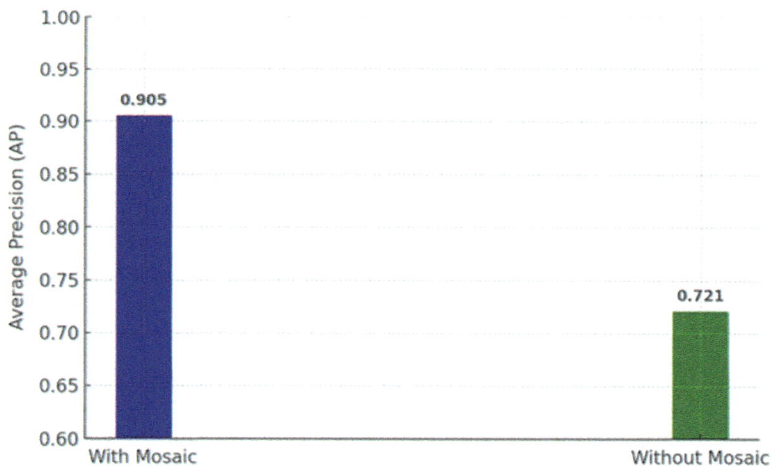

FIGURE 7.6

Comparison of YOLOv7 performance with and without mosaic augmentation. This graph illustrates the average precision (AP) scores for the YOLOv7 model trained with mosaic augmentation (AP = 0.905) and without mosaic augmentation (AP = 0.721). The model demonstrates significantly better performance when mosaic augmentation is applied, emphasizing its effectiveness in enhancing model accuracy.

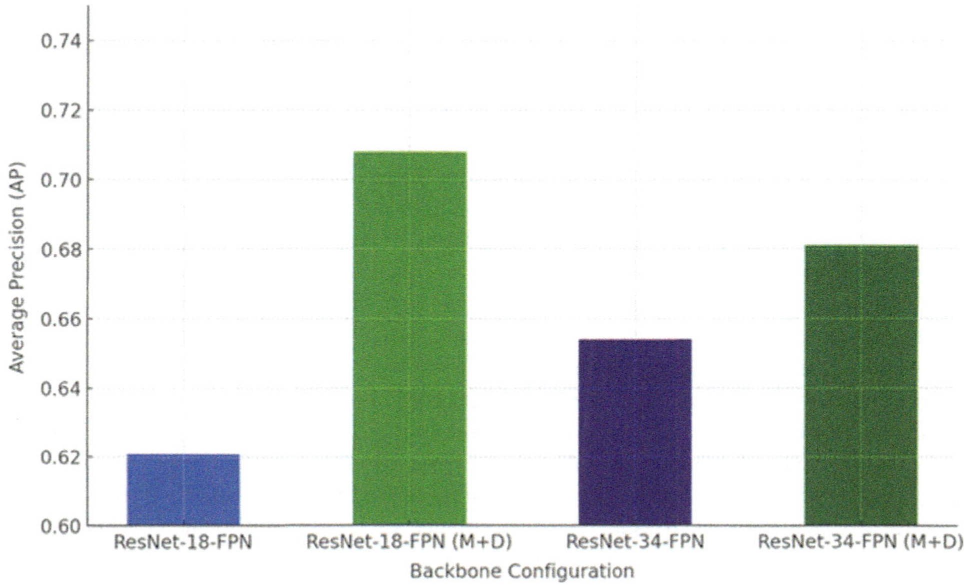

FIGURE 7.7

Average precision (AP) scores for RetinaNet with different backbone configurations. This bar graph illustrates the AP scores for RetinaNet using ResNet-18-FPN and ResNet-34-FPN backbones. The configurations include training from scratch without any augmentations (royal blue and dark blue), and with both mosaic augmentation and DIoU loss (forest green and dark green). The enhancements yield higher AP scores, demonstrating the effectiveness of these methods in improving model performance.

Such robustness persists even when confronted with datasets originating from domains significantly different from the natural scene images used for pretraining. Our study underscores the critical importance of employing meticulous model training and validation techniques, especially when dealing with limited datasets. Such practices are essential for optimizing performance and promoting generalizability across diverse domains. By adhering to rigorous methodologies, we can mitigate the risk of overfitting and ensure that our models exhibit robust performance across a spectrum of real-world scenarios. Furthermore, our findings highlight the need for a nuanced understanding of the interplay between model architecture, training strategies, and dataset characteristics. This holistic approach is pivotal for unlocking the full potential of deep-learning models and harnessing their capabilities to address real-world challenges effectively. While training models from scratch offer flexibility and control over the learning process, it necessitates careful consideration of numerous factors to achieve optimal results. By leveraging insights gleaned from both successes and setbacks, we can refine our methodologies and pave the way for advancements in the field of computer vision and beyond.

Examining the results in Fig. 7.8, it's apparent that RetinaNet achieves its highest AP value of 0.97 when configured with N set to 5 and i set to 4. This configuration represents the optimal balance between frame stacking and interval settings, resulting in superior detection performance. The significant improvement over YOLOv7 underscores the effectiveness of our proposed method in enhancing detection accuracy. Conversely, Fig. 7.9 illustrates the AP values obtained by YOLOv7 across varying N and i settings. While YOLOv7 demonstrates the potential to improve its detection accuracy by adopting our proposed method, the magnitude of enhancement is comparatively modest. The best AP value for YOLOv7 is 0.961, achieved with N set to 5 and i to 3, indicating a 0.6% enhancement over its conventional usage. While this improvement is noteworthy, it falls short of the performance achieved by RetinaNet under similar configurations. Further insights into the detection outcomes are demonstrated where bag-breakup detection scenarios from RetinaNet are observed. A comparison between RetinaNet's conventional usage and its implementation with our proposed method highlights the efficacy of our approach. In the visual representation, detections are delineated within red boxes, while ground truths are encased in blue. The numerical values above the boxes represent the model's confidence level, with only detections surpassing a 0.4 confidence threshold being displayed. This visual depiction reinforces the superior detection capabilities of RetinaNet when leveraging our proposed methodology. The experimental results underscore the efficacy of our proposed method in enhancing object detection performance, particularly when applied to RetinaNet. By optimizing the configuration parameters N and i, significant improvements in AP are achieved, surpassing the performance of the conventional YOLOv7 framework. This not only highlights the importance of advanced techniques in object detection but also underscores the potential for further advancements in the field.

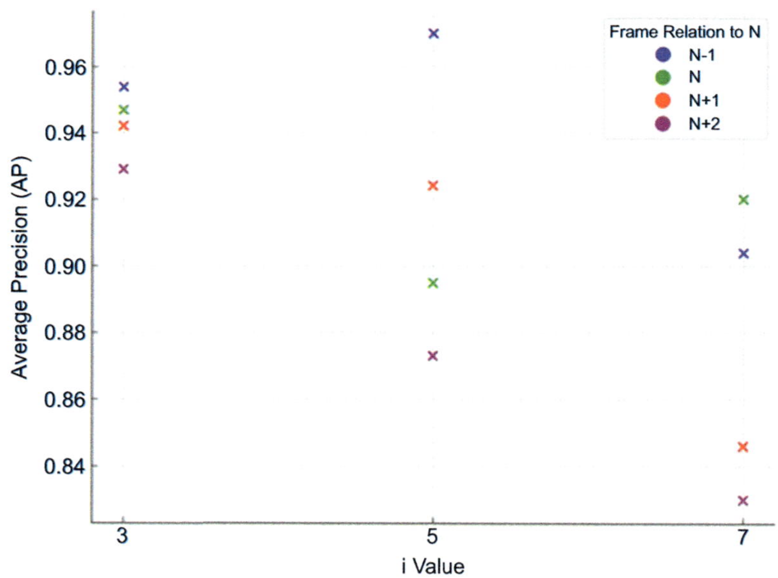

FIGURE 7.8

This graph displays the average precision (AP) obtained by RetinaNet for different values of NN and i. Each color represents a different frame relative to NN (e.g., $N-1$ N − 1, NN, $N+1$ N + 1, $N+2$ N + 2). The scatter plot shows how AP varies with the inclusion of information from neighboring frames. As you can see, there are variations in AP depending on both the parameter i and the frame position relative to NN.

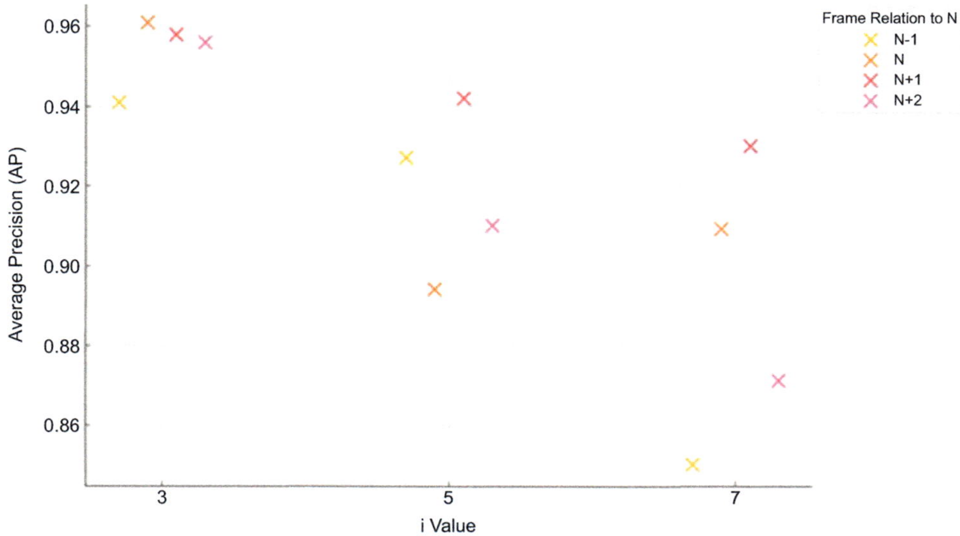

FIGURE 7.9

This graph illustrates the impact of utilizing neighboring frame information on the average precision (AP) performance of YOLOv7 for object detection. The AP values are plotted for different frame configurations (N − 1, N, N + 1, N + 2) across various values of (*i*). Each set of data points represents how the inclusion of additional contextual frames influences detection accuracy, demonstrating the potential benefits and limitations of frame integration at various levels.

Fig. 7.8 presents a detailed analysis of the AP results achieved by RetinaNet across different configurations of N and i, representing the number of frames stacked together and the interval length before and after the detection frame T. The comparison with the conventional YOLOv7 framework reveals promising advancements in detection accuracy. Notably, RetinaNet outperforms YOLOv7 by 1.5%, highlighting its efficacy in object detection tasks.

The absence of such ambiguous regions is conspicuous. In these images, both RetinaNet and YOLOv7, two robust object detection algorithms, perform admirably well without falling prey to false positive detections. This comparison highlights the efficacy of the proposed method in enhancing detection precision, particularly in environments where conventional methods might falter due to image intricacies. Going deeper into the implications of these findings, it becomes apparent that the effectiveness of object detection algorithms is contingent not only on their inherent capabilities but also on the complexities of the visual data they encounter. Images that present clear and unambiguous depictions of objects pose minimal challenges to algorithms, allowing them to perform with confidence. However, in real-world scenarios, ambiguity often prevails, manifesting in images where object boundaries blur, and contextual cues are sparse. In such scenarios, the proposed method emerges as a promising solution, offering a pathway to navigate through the uncertainty. By leveraging temporal information across consecutive frames, the method transcends the limitations of single-frame analysis, unraveling subtle patterns and contextual cues that elude conventional approaches. This temporal coherence proves instrumental in distinguishing genuine object instances from spurious identifications, thereby bolstering the overall robustness and reliability of the detection system. Moreover, the findings underscore the symbiotic relationship between algorithmic sophistication and contextual awareness. While state-of-the-art algorithms demonstrate impressive performance metrics under ideal conditions, their true efficacy is evaluated in real-world scenarios, where ambiguity and uncertainty abound. The ability to glean insights from temporal dynamics proves indispensable, enabling algorithms to discern meaningful patterns amidst the noise of uncertainty. Looking ahead, the insights garnered from this analysis pave the way for future advancements in object detection research. By embracing a comprehensive approach that integrates temporal dynamics with spatial context, researchers can unlock new frontiers in detection precision and robustness. Furthermore, the findings emphasize the importance of dataset diversity, highlighting the necessity for training data that captures the rich diversity of real-world scenarios, replete with all its intricacies and ambiguities. Through a meticulous examination of image data and algorithmic performance, the study elucidates the pivotal role of temporal coherence in mitigating FP and enhancing detection precision. Armed with these insights, researchers can chart a course toward more resilient and dependable object detection systems, capable of navigating the complexities of the real world with confidence.

7.3.3 Error analysis and misdetection cases

In the field of image analysis, particularly in computer vision tasks, the imbalance between the classes of foreground and background within datasets poses a significant challenge. This imbalance refers to the uneven distribution of samples between these classes, which can skew the learning process of machine learning models. Typically, natural scene images exhibit a more balanced distribution of foreground and background elements. However, in our study, we encountered a pronounced class imbalance within the dataset utilized for our analysis, deviating markedly from this norm. To quantify the impact of this class imbalance on the accuracy of our model, we devised a series of experiments. These experiments aimed to compare the performance of our model when trained with and without the integration of focal loss, a widely recognized technique employed to mitigate the adverse effects of class imbalance. Focal loss functions by downweighting the loss assigned to well-classified examples, thereby emphasizing the importance of hard-to-classify examples, such as those belonging to the minority class. Our experimental setup involved training the model using both conventional loss functions and focal loss, and subsequently evaluating their respective performances using metrics such as AP. The rationale behind AP lies in its ability to measure the PR trade-off, making it a suitable metric for assessing the efficacy of our model in capturing both foreground and background instances accurately. The results of our experiments, as illustrated in Fig. 7.10, revealed a compelling trend. When focal loss was integrated into the training process, we observed a noteworthy improvement in the AP metric, with an increase of 4.5% compared to the model trained without focal loss. This enhancement underscores the effectiveness of focal loss in ameliorating the challenges posed by class imbalance, particularly within the context of our specific dataset. Delving deeper into the implications of these findings, it becomes apparent that focal loss serves as a valuable tool in bolstering the performance of machine learning models when confronted with imbalanced datasets. By dynamically adjusting the contribution of individual training samples to the overall loss function, focal loss enables the model to prioritize learning from difficult-to-classify instances, thus fostering a more robust and discriminative

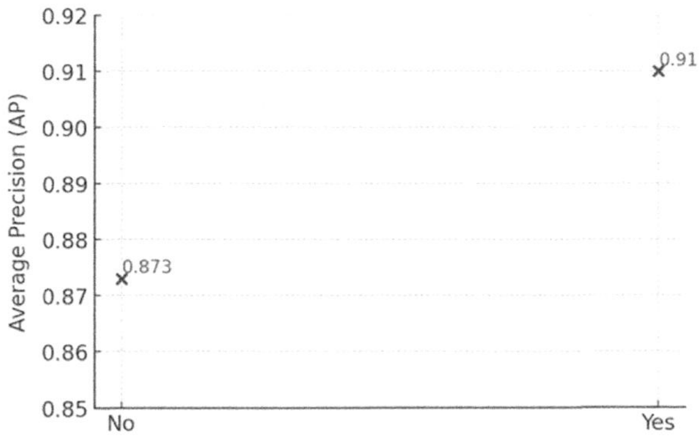

FIGURE 7.10

This figure illustrates the influence of focal loss on the average precision (AP) for mitigating class imbalance. The dots represent the AP values with and without the application of focal loss. As you can see, the AP is higher when focal loss is applied.

representation of both foreground and background elements. Furthermore, the observed improvement in AP signifies a more nuanced understanding of the intricacies within the dataset. In essence, the integration of focal loss empowers the model to allocate greater attention to the minority class, thereby mitigating the biases inherent in imbalanced datasets and facilitating more equitable learning outcomes across all classes. Beyond its immediate implications for our specific study, these findings hold broader significance within the realm of machine learning research and application. As the proliferation of large-scale datasets continues to fuel advancements in artificial intelligence, the prevalence of class imbalance remains a pervasive challenge that must be addressed to ensure the reliability and generalizability of machine learning models. This study sheds light on the critical role of focal loss in mitigating the adverse effects of class imbalance within datasets, particularly in the context of image analysis tasks. Through rigorous experimentation and empirical validation, we have demonstrated its efficacy in enhancing model performance, as evidenced by the notable improvement in AP. Moving forward, the integration of focal loss stands poised to catalyze further advancements in the field of machine learning, enabling more robust and equitable solutions across a diverse array of applications.

To assess the impact of reparameterization in YOLOv7, we examined the inference speed both with and without reparameterization. We conducted our tests using an Intel Xeon W-2223 CPU and an NVIDIA GeForce RTX 3090 GPU. The tests were conducted on images sized 800 × 800 pixels. According to the data presented in Fig. 7.11, YOLOv7 can perform extremely fast inference without reparameterization. However, when reparameterization is applied, the inference speed increases by 1.1 times, enabling real-time processing when using a GPU.

Additionally, for a comprehensive evaluation of the YOLOv7 model's efficacy in detecting instances of bag-breakup, we present several visual representations in Fig. 7.12. These depictions serve to elucidate the model's performance, with predicted instances highlighted by red bounding boxes and ground truth annotations delineated by blue boxes. The upper segment of Fig. 7.12 showcases successful detections of bag-breakup occurrences, while the lower portion accentuates instances of FP areas erroneously identified as bag-breakups despite lacking genuine representation.

FIGURE 7.11

This graph represents the influence of reparameterization on inference speed. The dots represent the inference speeds with and without reparameterization. As indicated, the speed improves when reparameterization is applied.

Upon closer examination, it becomes apparent that the prevalent FP manifest predominantly in two distinct categories. The first category, as exemplified by case (C), pertains to the erroneous detection of minute areas situated at the periphery of the image. This phenomenon is inherently linked to the utilization of mosaic augmentation techniques during the model's training phase. Mosaic augmentation, by design, combines multiple images to create a single training sample, resulting in instances where portions of the bounding box extend beyond the boundaries of the original image. Consequently, the residual portions of these bounding boxes inadvertently serve as signals, potentially leading to the occurrence of FP along the edges of the image. To address this inherent limitation, it is imperative to incorporate a postprocessing step aimed at discerning and excluding diminutive bounding boxes situated in proximity to the image periphery. By implementing such a postprocessing mechanism, the model can effectively distinguish genuine instances of bag-breakup from spurious detections resulting from the aforementioned artifact of mosaic augmentation. This strategic intervention not only enhances the model's precision but also fosters greater robustness in its ability to accurately discern instances of bag-breakup across diverse environmental conditions and image compositions. Moreover, it is essential to underscore the significance of continuous refinement and optimization efforts aimed at bolstering the YOLOv7 model's performance in real-world applications. As technological advancements and novel methodologies continue to emerge within the realm of computer vision and deep learning, ongoing research endeavors hold the promise of further enhancing the model's efficacy and applicability across a myriad of domains and use cases. The illustrative examples presented in Fig. 7.12 offer valuable insights into the performance of the YOLOv7 model in the context of bag-breakup detection. Through meticulous analysis and strategic interventions, such as the implementation of postprocessing mechanisms to mitigate the effects of mosaic augmentation artifacts, the model's accuracy and reliability can be significantly augmented. By embracing a proactive approach toward refinement and optimization, researchers and practitioners can propel the evolution of deep-learning methodologies, thereby unlocking new frontiers in the realm of computer vision and pattern recognition. The identification and mitigation of FP in image analysis, particularly in scenarios involving complex phenomena such as bag-breakup events, presents a formidable challenge. In this section, we

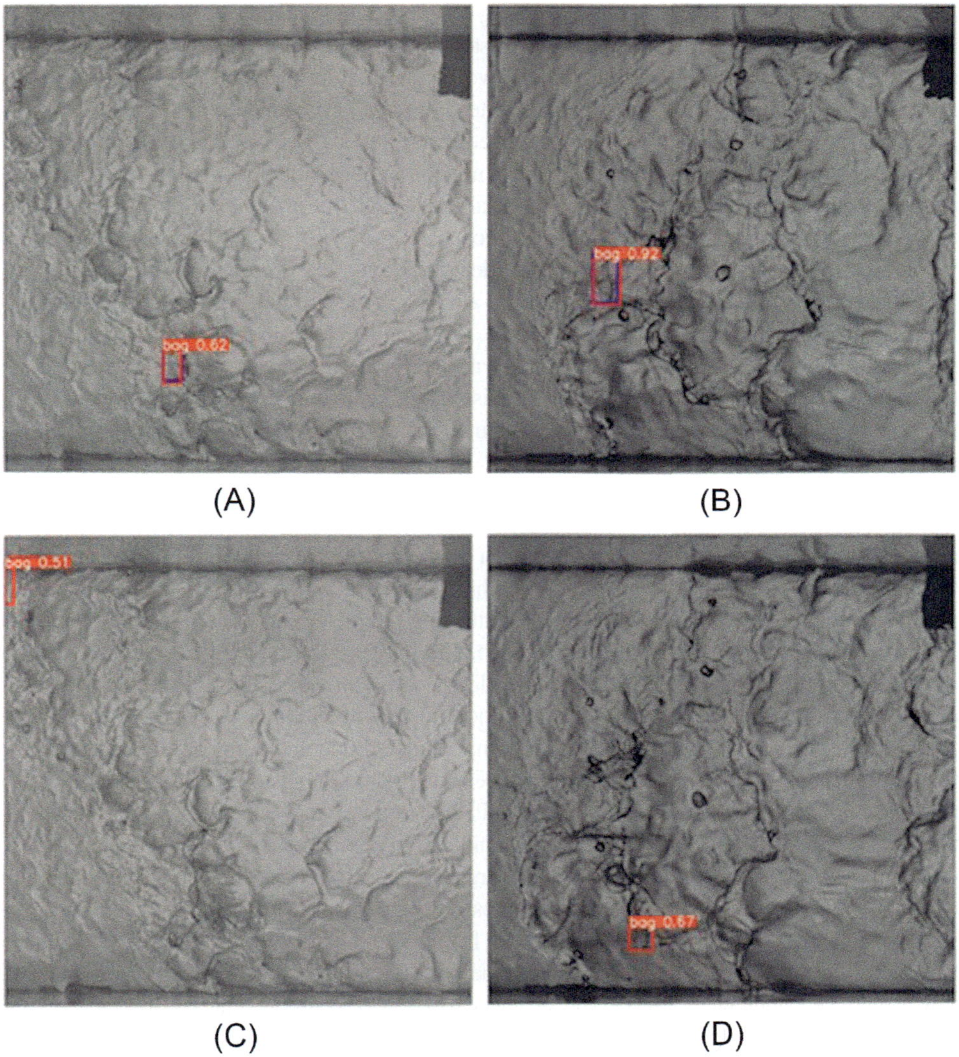

FIGURE 7.12

Example of YOLOv7 detection: Predictions are displayed in red boxes, and accurate labels are in blue boxes. (A) and (B) successful detections; (C) a case of false positives near the image's edge; (D) a false detection in an area with a similar texture that is not an actual bag-breakup.

delve deeper into the second category of FP, as depicted in Fig. 7.5D, where the similarity between the image texture of FP and genuine bag-breakup instances complicates accurate identification, even for domain experts. To effectively address such intricate cases, a more sophisticated approach is required, one that goes beyond simple image analysis techniques. This necessitates the integration of information from adjacent image frames, enabling a holistic understanding of the sequential progression of a bag-breakup event from initiation to cessation. By leveraging the temporal evolution of bag-breakup events captured across multiple frames, we gain valuable insights that can aid in distinguishing genuine instances from FP. This temporal context provides crucial clues about the dynamic nature of bag-breakup events, including the trajectory, speed, and pattern of debris dispersion, which are often indicative of a genuine event. We introduced a novel methodology inspired by these observations, which offers a promising strategy to effectively address such intricate false positive scenarios. This methodology capitalizes on the temporal coherence of bag-breakup events, exploiting the sequential nature of image data to enhance the accuracy of detection and classification. At its core, the proposed methodology employs advanced machine learning algorithms, specifically designed to analyze sequential data and extract meaningful temporal features. By training these algorithms on annotated datasets containing both genuine bag-breakup events and various types of FP, the model learns to discern subtle differences in temporal patterns that distinguish genuine events from artifacts. Furthermore, the methodology incorporates techniques from computer vision and signal processing to preprocess the image data, enhancing its suitability for temporal analysis. This may involve techniques such as motion estimation, optical flow analysis, and frame interpolation, which help to mitigate noise and artifacts while preserving important temporal information. Once preprocessed, the sequential image data is fed into the machine learning model, which processes it in a sequential manner, analyzing each frame in the context of its temporal neighbors. This sequential analysis enables the model to capture the temporal dynamics of bag-breakup events, identifying characteristic patterns that differentiate them from FP. In addition to temporal analysis, the methodology also leverages contextual information from adjacent image frames to further refine the classification process. By considering the spatial relationships between neighboring frames and incorporating contextual cues such as object trajectories and spatial coherence, the model gains a more comprehensive understanding of the scene dynamics.

This contextual information serves to corroborate the temporal analysis, providing additional evidence to support the classification decision. For example, if the temporal analysis indicates a rapid and coherent dispersion of debris particles consistent with a genuine bag-breakup event, the model may further verify this by examining the spatial consistency of debris trajectories across adjacent frames. By integrating temporal and contextual cues in this manner, the proposed methodology offers a robust solution to the challenge of distinguishing genuine bag-breakup events from FP. Its ability to capture the dynamic evolution of events over time, combined with a contextual understanding of scene dynamics, enables it to effectively discriminate between genuine instances and artifacts with high accuracy. The second category of FP in bag-breakup event detection presents a complex challenge that requires a nuanced approach incorporating temporal and contextual analysis. The methodology introduced a promising solution to this challenge, leveraging advanced machine learning techniques to analyze sequential image data and extract meaningful temporal and spatial features. By exploiting the temporal coherence of bag-breakup events and incorporating contextual cues from adjacent frames, the methodology enables accurate identification and classification of genuine events while minimizing FP.

References

Alessio, H. M., Bassett, D. R., Bopp, M. J., Parr, B. B., Patch, G. S., Rankin, J. W., Rojas-Rueda, D., Roti, M. W., & Wojcik, J. R. (2021). Climate change, air pollution, and physical inactivity: Is active transportation part of the solution? *Medicine & Science in Sports & Exercise*, *53*(6), 1170–1178. Available from https://doi.org/10.1249/mss.0000000000002569.

Buranasuksombat, U., Kwon, Y. J., Turner, M., & Bhandari, B. (2011). Influence of emulsion droplet size on antimicrobial properties. *Food Science and Biotechnology*, *20*(3), 793–800. Available from https://doi.org/10.1007/s10068-011-0110-x.

Cadwallader, L. C., & Herring, J. S. (1999). Safety issues with hydrogen as a vehicle fuel. *INEEL/EXT-99-00522*. Idaho National Lab (INL).

Cheng, S. W. S. (2000). The impacts of engine operating conditions and fuel compositions on the formation of combustion chamber deposits. *SAE Technical Papers*. SAE International. Available from http://papers.sae.org/ https://doi.org/10.4271/2000-01-2025.

Cherapanamjeri, J., & Rao, B. N. K. (2022). Neural networks based object detection techniques in computer vision. In *4th International Conference on Inventive Research in Computing Applications, ICIRCA 2022—Proceedings* (pp. 1092–99). Institute of Electrical and Electronics Engineers Inc. Available from http://ieeexplore.ieee.org/xpl/mostRecentIssue.jsp?punumber = 9985450, https://doi.org/10.1109/ICIRCA54612.2022.9985581.

Gonca, G., & Dobrucali, E. (2016). The effects of engine design and operating parameters on the performance of a diesel engine fueled with diesel-biodiesel blends. *Journal of Renewable and Sustainable Energy*, *8*(2). Available from https://doi.org/10.1063/1.4944457.

Hubbard, G. L., Denny, V. E., & Mills, A. F. (1975). Droplet evaporation: Effects of transients and variable properties. *International Journal of Heat and Mass Transfer*, *18*(9), 1003–1008. Available from https://doi.org/10.1016/0017-9310(75)90217-3.

Jiao, L., Zhang, F., Liu, F., Yang, S., Li, L., Feng, Z., & Qu, R. (2019). A survey of deep learning-based object detection. *IEEE Access*, *7*, 128837–128868. Available from https://doi.org/10.1109/access.2019.2939201.

Kaur, R., & Singh, S. (2023). A comprehensive review of object detection with deep learning. *Digital Signal Processing*, *132*, 103812. Available from https://doi.org/10.1016/j.dsp.2022.103812.

Liu, L., Ouyang, W., Wang, X., Fieguth, P., Chen, J., Liu, X., & Pietikäinen, M. (2020). Deep learning for generic object detection: A survey. *International Journal of Computer Vision*, *128*(2), 261–318. Available from https://doi.org/10.1007/s11263-019-01247-4.

Moraveji, A., & Toghraie, D. (2017). Computational fluid dynamics simulation of heat transfer and fluid flow characteristics in a vortex tube by considering the various parameters. *International Journal of Heat and Mass Transfer*, *113*, 432–443. Available from https://doi.org/10.1016/j.ijheatmasstransfer.2017.05.095.

Morita, D., Raytchev, B., Elhanashi, A., Kawaguchi, M., Ogata, Y., Higaki, T., Kaneda, K., Nakashima, A., & Saponara, S. (2023). Fast detection of bag-breakups in pulsating and steady airflow using video analysis and deep learning. *Journal of Real-Time Image Processing*, *20*(6). Available from https://doi.org/10.1007/s11554-023-01363-y. Available from, https://www.springer.com/journal/11554.

Xiao, X., & Gao, M. (2021). *Overview of climate change, air pollution, and human health. Air Pollution, Climate, and Health: An Integrated Perspective on Their Interactions* (pp. 3–12). Elsevier. Available from https://www.sciencedirect.com/book/9780128201237, https://doi.org/10.1016/B978-0-12-820123-7.00003-6.

Yan, X., Zhang, L., Sett, S., Feng, L., Zhao, C., Huang, Z., Vahabi, H., Kota, A. K., Chen, F., & Miljkovic, N. (2019). Droplet jumping: Effects of droplet size, surface structure, pinning, and liquid properties. *ACS Nano*, *13*(2), 1309–1323. Available from https://doi.org/10.1021/acsnano.8b06677, http://pubs.acs.org/journal/ancac3.

Zhao, H., Wu, Z. W., Li, W. F., Xu, J. L., & HaiFeng, L. (2019). Interaction of two drops in the bag breakup regime by a continuous air jet. *Fuel*, *236*, 843–850. Available from https://doi.org/10.1016/j.fuel.2018.09.067.

CHAPTER

Conclusions and recommendations 8

In this book, the synthesis of advanced neural network architectures and their transformative applications in image and video processing is thoroughly explored, underscoring the profound impact these technologies have on diverse sectors. As we conclude this comprehensive examination, it is evident that DL has revolutionized the way images and videos are processed, analyzed, and interpreted, driving significant advancements across various practical domains. The overarching conclusion drawn from the discussions and analyses presented is that DL methodologies, particularly convolutional neural networks (CNNs) and their variants, have demonstrated unparalleled capabilities in handling the complexities and nuances of visual data. These advancements are not merely theoretical but have translated into tangible improvements in fields such as healthcare, where DL algorithms are used for early and accurate diagnosis of diseases through medical imaging where real-time video processing is crucial for navigation and safety; and entertainment, where enhanced image and video quality enrich user experiences. One of the pivotal insights gleaned from this exploration is the importance of large, annotated datasets in training robust and accurate DL models. The success of DL in image and video processing heavily relies on the availability of extensive datasets that capture the diversity and intricacies of real-world scenarios. This necessitates concerted efforts in data collection, annotation, and preprocessing, highlighting the need for collaboration across industries and research institutions to create and share high-quality datasets. Moreover, the book underscores the critical role of object detection and data augmentation techniques in addressing the challenges posed by limited data, enabling models to generalize better and perform effectively even in data-scarce environments. The practical implications of these technological advancements are vast and multifaceted. In healthcare, DL models have shown remarkable success in automating and enhancing diagnostic processes, leading to more accurate and timely detection of conditions such as COVID-19, retinal diseases, and neurological disorders. The integration of DL into medical imaging workflows not only improves diagnostic accuracy but also alleviates the workload of medical professionals, allowing them to focus on more complex cases. In the field of surveillance application, DL enables real-time analysis of video feeds from vehicle-mounted cameras, facilitating critical functions such as object detection of fire and smoke on real-time basis. The reliability and efficiency of these systems are paramount for the safety and viability of surveillance applications, underscoring the essential role of DL in the future of transportation. The entertainment industry has also been significantly impacted by DL, with applications ranging from video content recommendation to high-definition video streaming and immersive virtual reality experiences. DL algorithms enhance the quality and personalization of content delivery, creating more engaging and tailored experiences for users. Furthermore, the ability to automatically generate and enhance visual content opens up new creative possibilities, allowing artists and content creators to push the boundaries of their craft. Despite these remarkable advancements, the book also highlights several challenges and areas for future research. One of the primary concerns is the interpretability

Deep Learning in Action: Image and Video Processing for Practical Use. DOI: https://doi.org/10.1016/B978-0-443-30078-3.00008-1

and transparency of DL models. The "black box" nature of these models poses significant challenges in understanding their decision-making processes, which is crucial for critical applications such as healthcare and autonomous driving. There is an ongoing need for developing methods to elucidate the inner workings of DL models, making their predictions more interpretable and trustworthy. Additionally, the ethical implications of DL in image and video processing cannot be overlooked. Issues related to privacy, data security, and algorithmic bias need to be addressed to ensure that the deployment of these technologies is fair, responsible, and aligned with societal values.

Chapter 1 presented a comprehensive exploration of the multifaceted domain of artificial intelligence (AI), delving into its definition, evolution, and various subfields, particularly focusing on machine learning (ML) and DL. This conclusion synthesizes the key points discussed across the different sections, underscoring the transformative potential of AI technologies in addressing real-world challenges and driving innovation across industries. The chapter began by providing an overview of AI, emphasizing its growing importance in today's technological landscape. AI, defined as the capability of machines to mimic human intelligence, has undergone significant evolution from its early theoretical foundations to its current state, characterized by sophisticated algorithms and applications. The progression from rule-based systems to learning algorithms marks the pivotal shift in AI's development trajectory. AI's evolution has been marked by several milestones, starting from symbolic AI, which involved explicit programming of rules, to the advent of ML, where systems learn from data. This section highlighted key historical developments, such as the Dartmouth conference, which coined the term AI, and the subsequent AI winters and springs, reflecting periods of both stagnation and rapid advancement. The resurgence of AI in recent years can be attributed to breakthroughs in computational power, data availability, and algorithmic innovations. ML Fundamentals were introduced as a subset of AI focused on the development of algorithms that enable computers to learn from and make predictions based on data. This section elucidated the core concepts of ML, including supervised learning, unsupervised learning, and reinforcement learning, each playing a crucial role in different types of AI applications. Supervised learning involves training a model on labeled data, unsupervised learning on unlabeled data to discover hidden patterns, and reinforcement learning on interactions with an environment to maximize cumulative reward. Expanding on the fundamentals, the discussion on ML types provided insights into the various approaches within ML, such as, classification, object detection, and dimensionality reduction. Each type serves distinct purposes; for instance, regression predicts continuous outcomes, while classification deals with discrete categories. Clustering groups similar data points, and dimensionality reduction simplifies data without losing essential information, enhancing the efficiency of subsequent processing steps. We discussed DL, a subset of ML that has revolutionized AI through its ability to model complex patterns in data using multilayered neural networks. The fundamentals of DL were explored, highlighting the architecture of deep neural networks composed of multiple layers that automatically learn representations from data. The discussion underscored the importance of activation functions, backpropagation, and optimization techniques in training deep networks effectively. An overview of object detection, classification, and segmentation elucidated how these techniques apply DL models to identify, categorize, and delineate objects within images. Object detection locates objects within an image, classification assigns labels to entire images, and segmentation partitions images into meaningful regions, enabling detailed analysis and interpretation. The section on computer vision applications demonstrated how DL has empowered advancements in fields like medical imaging, and facial recognition. These applications leverage the robust pattern recognition capabilities of DL models to interpret and analyze visual data with unprecedented accuracy and speed. An overview highlighted how image and video data are integral to diverse applications, from security surveillance to entertainment, enabling machines to perceive and interpret the visual world similarly to humans. The evolution of visual processing was traced, showing the transition from simple image processing techniques to advanced DL methods that offer superior performance in tasks like object recognition, motion tracking, and scene understanding. The discussion on differentiating between image and video data explained the distinct characteristics and processing requirements of static images versus dynamic video sequences, each presenting unique challenges and opportunities for AI models. An exploration of common image formats and their properties provided insights into various file types, such as JPEG, and PNG, detailing their use cases and implications for storage, compression, and quality. The importance of bridging the gap between theory and practice was emphasized, highlighting how academic research in AI is translated into real-world solutions that address practical problems, driving societal progress. The role of AI in solving real-world challenges was discussed, showcasing applications in healthcare, surveillance applications, Image restoration, and more, where AI systems enhance efficiency, accuracy, and decision-making.

Chapter 2 proposed a video-based fire and smoke detection technique to be implemented as a fire safety monitoring system in a low-cost and low-power single-board computer. The aim was to develop an efficient and effective fire and smoke detection system that could be deployed on embedded platforms like the Raspberry Pi and NVIDIA Jetson Nano, which are known for their affordability and low power consumption. The study involved examining two different DL object detection algorithms: the regional convolutional neural network (R-CNN) and you only look once version II (YOLOv2). These algorithms were chosen for their distinct approaches to object detection, which could potentially offer insights into the most suitable method for fire and smoke detection in a real-time surveillance context. We created lightweight DL architectures specifically tailored for these embedded systems. The primary goal was to reduce the total weight of the final deep architecture while maintaining high accuracy in detection and ensuring fast processing times. This was crucial because embedded systems like the Raspberry Pi and Jetson Nano have limited computational resources and memory. By optimizing the DL models, we aimed to achieve a balance between performance and resource utilization. In our experiments, we observed that YOLOv2 outperformed the R-CNN model in terms of both accuracy and real-time detection capabilities. This is a significant finding because it highlights the effectiveness of YOLOv2 approach, which involves processing the entire image at once rather than focusing on generated region proposals, as in the R-CNN method. This holistic view of the image allows YOLOv2 to leverage contextual information, thereby reducing the occurrence of false positives in fire and smoke detection. False positives are a common challenge in fire detection systems, and reducing them is critical for the reliability of such systems in real-world applications. The proposed approach also demonstrated an improvement in handling videos with no fire or smoke objects, further validating the effectiveness of YOLOv2. This improvement can be attributed to the algorithm's ability to use contextual clues from the entire image, which helps in accurately distinguishing between actual fire and smoke and other similar-looking objects or phenomena. This capability is particularly important in environments where various factors, such as lighting conditions and background clutter, can complicate the detection process. We compared YOLOv2 with a state-of-the-art real-time object detection system that can classify and locate multiple objects in a single camera image. Our custom YOLOv2 network was trained using existing datasets from the literature and tested against both classical and DL algorithms. The results were impressive, with YOLOv2 achieving the best performance in terms of accuracy, F1 score, recall, and precision. These metrics are essential for evaluating the effectiveness of a detection system, as they provide a comprehensive view of its ability to correctly identify and locate objects of interest. One challenge with the proposed models is that YOLOv2 does not focus on small objects, creating a spatial constraint that limits the number of predictions per grid cell. This limitation is inherent to the design of YOLOv2, which uses a fixed grid to divide the image and predict bounding boxes. As a result, small objects that occupy less space within a grid cell may not be detected accurately. Despite this limitation, YOLOv2 overall performance remains superior due to its speed and accuracy in detecting larger objects. During our experiments, we encountered limitations in executing the R-CNN model on the Raspberry Pi and Jetson platforms as standalone applications. This was primarily due to the lack of support for code generation for the R-CNN model on these embedded systems. The R-CNN model requires significant computational power and memory, which are beyond the capabilities of low-cost embedded platforms. In contrast, YOLOv2 was successfully implemented on the NVIDIA Jetson Nano, and we compared its frames-per-second real-time detection performance with other methodologies. The results of our experiments validated the effectiveness of the YOLOv2 model, confirming that the proposed implementation is viable in a real Internet of Things (IoT) environment. This is a significant finding because it demonstrates the feasibility of deploying advanced DL models for fire and smoke detection on affordable and low-power embedded platforms. Such implementations are crucial for extending fire safety monitoring to a wide range of applications, including residential, commercial, and industrial settings. This chapter shows that a video-based fire and smoke detection system using YOLOv2 is highly effective for deployment on low-cost and low-power embedded systems. The key advantages of this approach include:

1. **High accuracy and speed:** YOLOv2 ability to process the entire image at once and leverage contextual information results in high accuracy and fast detection speeds, making it suitable for real-time applications.
2. **Low resource consumption:** By optimizing the DL architecture, we ensured that the system could run efficiently on embedded platforms with limited computational resources and memory.
3. **Reduced false positives:** YOLOv2 holistic view of the image helps reduce false positives, enhancing the reliability of the fire and smoke detection system.
4. **Feasibility for IoT environments:** The successful implementation of YOLOv2 on the NVIDIA Jetson Nano demonstrates the feasibility of deploying advanced DL models in IoT environments, expanding the potential applications of such systems.

However, it is important to note the limitation of YOLOv2 in detecting small objects, which could be a consideration in certain scenarios. Future work could focus on addressing this limitation by exploring hybrid models or enhancing YOLOv2 architecture to improve its performance with small objects. Additionally, further research could investigate the integration of other sensors and data sources to complement video-based detection and enhance overall system robustness. Overall, our proposed video-based fire and smoke detection technique represents a significant advancement in fire safety monitoring systems, providing a practical, efficient, and reliable solution for real-time detection on low-cost embedded platforms.

Chapter 3 discussed a real-time AI platform for people detection and social distancing classification of individuals based on thermal imaging cameras. This platform aims to minimize the spread of COVID-19 by eliminating physical contact among individuals. You Only Look Once version IV (YOLOv4)-tiny and YOLOv2 DL models were proposed for object recognition in this chapter. YOLOv4-tiny is a simple neural network architecture, making it suitable for low-cost embedded devices. The YOLOv4-tiny algorithm has also been implemented to monitor social distancing from a bird's-eye view, eliminating the issue of perspective view from the video camera. The proposed approach is applied to video captured by thermal imaging cameras to detect people, classify social distancing, and simultaneously measure people's skin temperature. We defined the safe condition with green color for the bounding boxes, while the unsafe condition has been determined with two different levels of violation: Alert and Risk, which have been marked with yellow and red colors respectively.

The final prototype algorithms were used in low-cost NVIDIA Jetson devices (Xavier and Jetson Nano) as end-edge devices. YOLOv4-tiny showed promising results for real-time detection, making it suitable for human recognition systems. We integrated the social distancing approach with a mask detection algorithm, executed on a single NVIDIA board, to assess the robustness of low-cost embedded systems in running multiple DL models in parallel, simultaneously. The main contributions of the proposed work are that it efficiently ensures safe social distancing between individuals. The developed DL models were validated through multiple experiments and achieved reasonable accuracy and user acceptance. Jetsons have low power consumption relative to their computing power, but they can be set to different power modes. For social distancing activities, we performed different experiments on Jetson Nano and Jetson Xavier AGX with different power modes. The highest real-time performance was obtained on Jetson Xavier AGX when the power mode was set to the maximum value (30 watts). This chapter noted that claims of improved real-time performance lead to increased power demands. For instance, although graphics processing unit (GPU) architectures in Jetson Xavier AGX provide better real-time measurement, continued performance increases can negate gains in efficiency, and the graphics processing units (GPUs) continue to consume large amounts of power. Therefore this is a limitation of this chapter: to accelerate a complex algorithm for social distancing applications (DL object detection and distance measurement), the many-core GPU has been utilized in Jetson platforms. However, low-cost embedded systems require more energy to process the deployed approaches. The integration of thermal imaging with AI-based models for detecting and managing social distancing offers a significant advancement in public health monitoring, especially during pandemics. Thermal imaging provides the dual benefits of noncontact temperature measurement and the ability to detect individuals in various lighting conditions. This characteristic is particularly advantageous in scenarios like airports, hospitals, and public transportation hubs where continuous monitoring is essential. By employing YOLOv4-tiny and YOLOv2, the system can perform robustly even on hardware with limited processing power, ensuring wider accessibility and implementation feasibility. In our experiments, the use of thermal cameras proved to be a game-changer. These cameras can detect heat signatures, making it possible to identify individuals and assess their body temperatures simultaneously. This dual functionality is crucial for monitoring both the presence of individuals and potential fever, a common symptom of COVID-19. The color-coded system—green for safe, yellow for alert, and red for risk—provides an intuitive and immediate visual cue to operators, enhancing the system's usability which include:-

1. **Real-Time Detection and Social Distancing Classification:** The research developed a real-time AI platform utilizing thermal imaging cameras and DL models (YOLOv4-tiny and YOLOv2) to detect people and classify social distancing. This approach minimizes COVID-19 spread by reducing physical contact and provides an effective, noncontact method for monitoring public health.

2. **Integration of Thermal Imaging and AI:** The system combines thermal imaging with AI-based models, enabling dual functionality of detecting individuals and measuring their skin temperature. This feature is crucial for identifying potential feverish individuals, enhancing the system's application in high-traffic public areas like airports and hospitals.
3. **Efficient Performance on Low-Cost Embedded Devices:** The YOLOv4-tiny model demonstrated efficient real-time performance on low-cost NVIDIA Jetson devices (Nano and Xavier AGX). Despite their low power consumption, these devices effectively handled multiple DL tasks, proving their viability for widespread implementation in monitoring systems.
4. **Enhanced Safety Measures with Mask Detection:** The research integrated a mask detection algorithm with the social distancing approach, running simultaneously on a single NVIDIA board. This integration ensures that individuals not only maintain safe distances but also wear masks, addressing multiple transmission vectors of COVID-19 and significantly enhancing the overall effectiveness of the platform.

Moreover, the YOLOv4-tiny model's performance on NVIDIA Jetson devices showcases the balance between computational efficiency and accuracy. The Jetson Nano and Xavier AGX, despite their low power consumption, were able to handle real-time data processing effectively. This capability is vital for applications requiring immediate response and decision-making, such as crowd management in public spaces. The mask detection feature integrated with the social distancing algorithm adds another layer of safety. By ensuring individuals not only maintain appropriate distances but also wear masks, the system addresses multiple vectors of virus transmission. This holistic approach increases the overall effectiveness of the measures put in place to mitigate the spread of COVID-19. While the research demonstrated promising results, it also highlighted some limitations. The increased power demands associated with achieving higher real-time performance on the Jetson Xavier AGX indicate a trade-off between efficiency and processing power. Although GPUs offer substantial computational benefits, their high energy consumption can be a drawback, particularly for prolonged usage in large-scale deployments. This limitation suggests that future research should focus on optimizing algorithms to balance performance and energy efficiency better. Another critical aspect of this chapter is the potential for scalability and adaptability. The modular nature of the developed system allows for easy updates and integration of additional features, such as advanced behavioral analysis and integration with broader smart city infrastructure. This adaptability ensures the system can evolve with changing public health requirements and technological advancements. The real-time AI platform for people detection and social distancing classification using thermal imaging cameras represents a significant step forward in public health technology. By leveraging DL models like YOLOv4-tiny and YOLOv2, the system provides an effective, efficient, and scalable solution for monitoring and managing social distancing. The integration of mask detection further enhances its utility in preventing COVID-19 spread. Despite the challenges related to power consumption, the research demonstrated the feasibility and effectiveness of using low-cost embedded systems for complex DL tasks. Future work should focus on optimizing these systems for better energy efficiency and exploring additional functionalities to enhance their application in diverse real-world scenarios. The platform not only addresses immediate public health needs but also lays the groundwork for more advanced, AI-driven health monitoring solutions in the future.

Chapter 4 highlighted a novel approach to fingerprint image reconstruction based on DL architectures. In this study, we proposed two autoencoders incorporating sparse and CNN algorithms by modeling the fingerprint image recovery challenge by extracting the features of the input image and replicating well-designed details in the output image. CNN performance is strongly influenced by the quality of a fingerprint image and its local and global structures. The accuracy of the proposed CNN model depends on the amount and quality of the training images. In addition, CNN architectures have some disadvantages, such as poor generalization ability, a requirement for a huge training dataset. The proposed algorithm uses poor-quality original raw fingerprint images. The CNN autoencoder performed very effectively in replicating fingerprint features from the images, overcoming the sparse autoencoder and other state-of-the-art methods in calculating the cumulative match features between the estimated and original features.

We tested the proposed algorithm on four different fingerprint databases (Dataset I, Dataset II, Dataset III, and Dataset IV) and achieved a recognition rate of 98.1%, 97%, 95.9%, and 95.02%, respectively. In fact, analyzing the experimental results obtained, the Convolutional Autoencoder is the most suitable technique for recovering complex contextual fingerprint features, since it improved and sharpened the fingerprint features on real fingerprint images such as FVC2004 and SOCOFing databases. The measured memory size of the proposed CNN autoencoder is much smaller than the state-of-the-art AI methods, and this makes it suitable for driving low-cost embedded devices. Therefore the CNN autoencoder is a viable option for biometric authentication and identification applications. We see two different directions that can further improve the performance of this model, one of which is the integration of the proposed approach with fingerprint scanners such as Lumidigm and Secugem sensors, which will provide the final result on how the model performs when reconstructing the images. In addition, it could consider other data augmentation techniques using histogram-based operations and other geometric transformations to improve the mean squared error value for the proposed approach. The DL revolution has opened new vistas in many fields, and fingerprint image reconstruction is no exception. The implementation of a novel approach using DL architectures in Chapter 4 highlights significant advancements. In our study, we proposed two autoencoders that incorporate sparse and CNN algorithms, addressing the fingerprint image recovery challenge by extracting and replicating the features of the input image with exceptional detail in the output image. This method capitalizes on the strength of CNNs, although their performance is heavily influenced by the quality of the fingerprint image and its structural intricacies. The precision of the proposed CNN model is contingent upon the volume and quality of the training images. Despite some inherent drawbacks of CNN architectures, such as limited generalization ability and the necessity for extensive training datasets, our proposed algorithm demonstrates resilience by using low-quality original raw fingerprint images.

The effectiveness of the CNN autoencoder is notable in its ability to replicate fingerprint features from images, outperforming the sparse autoencoder and other leading methods in matching estimated features with original ones. Testing across four distinct fingerprint databases yielded impressive recognition rates of 98.1%, 97%, 95.9%, and 95.02%, respectively. Such high recognition rates indicate the robustness of the Convolutional Autoencoder, making it the most appropriate technique for recovering complex fingerprint features. This is particularly evident in its application to real fingerprint images from databases like FVC2004 and SOCOFing, where it significantly enhances and sharpens fingerprint features.

1. **Innovative deep learning approach:** The chapter introduces a novel approach to fingerprint image reconstruction using DL architectures, specifically two autoencoders incorporating sparse and CNN algorithms. This method effectively extracts and replicates fingerprint features, even from poor-quality images.

2. **High recognition rates across databases:** The proposed CNN autoencoder model demonstrated impressive recognition rates of 98.1%, 97%, 95.9%, and 95.02% across four different fingerprint databases (Dataset I, Dataset II, Dataset III, and Dataset IV), highlighting its robustness and effectiveness.
3. **Superior to traditional methods:** The CNN autoencoder outperformed sparse autoencoders and other state-of-the-art methods in matching estimated features with original fingerprint features, making it a highly suitable technique for recovering complex contextual fingerprint details.
4. **Efficiency and practical application:** The model's memory efficiency is superior to current AI methods, making it suitable for low-cost embedded devices. This efficiency opens up potential applications in biometric authentication and identification systems.
5. **Future enhancements:** The chapter suggests two main directions for further improvement: integrating the model with advanced fingerprint scanners like Lumidigm and Secugem sensors to assess real-world performance, and employing various data augmentation techniques to refine the model's accuracy and robustness.

Furthermore, the proposed CNN autoencoder's memory efficiency surpasses that of current AI methods, suggesting its suitability for deployment in low-cost embedded devices. This efficiency opens up vast potential for practical applications in biometric authentication and identification systems. Future improvements to this model could come from two main directions. Firstly, integrating the proposed approach with advanced fingerprint scanners such as Lumidigm and Secugem sensors would offer critical insights into its performance in real-world scenarios. Secondly, exploring various data augmentation techniques, including histogram-based operations and geometric transformations, could further refine the model's accuracy by improving the mean squared error values. This chapter explored a sophisticated approach to fingerprint image reconstruction using DL, specifically focusing on the strengths of CNN architectures. Despite some inherent challenges associated with CNNs, such as the need for extensive training data and their generalization limitations, our proposed CNN autoencoder model proved to be highly effective. It demonstrated superior performance in replicating and enhancing fingerprint features from poor-quality images, outperforming traditional sparse autoencoders and other state-of-the-art methods. The model's success across multiple fingerprint databases, with high recognition rates, underscores its robustness and suitability for real-world applications. Furthermore, the efficiency in memory usage makes it an attractive option for implementation in low-cost embedded devices, which is crucial for the widespread adoption of biometric authentication systems. To further enhance the performance of the proposed model, integrating it with advanced fingerprint scanners could provide valuable insights into its practical effectiveness. Additionally, employing diverse data augmentation techniques could improve the model's accuracy and robustness, making it even more reliable for biometric identification.

The advancements presented in this study mark a significant step forward in fingerprint image reconstruction using DL. The proposed CNN autoencoder offers a promising solution for accurate and efficient fingerprint recovery, paving the way for improved biometric authentication and identification systems. With further refinements and real-world integrations, this approach has the potential to revolutionize the field and set new standards for fingerprint recognition technology.

Chapter 5 presented a comprehensive study on leveraging DL techniques to enhance the detection and localization of abnormalities in chest X-ray images, specifically targeting conditions such as bronchopneumonia and COVID-19. The critical importance of accurately interpreting these images cannot be overstated, given that misinterpretations can lead to false negatives or positives, adversely affecting patient care. The chapter proposed two primary DL approaches: multiclassification and object detection models, aimed at classifying and localizing different abnormalities in chest X-ray images. These models were rigorously trained on extensive datasets and validated on independent test sets to ensure their robustness and reliability.

The first key contribution of this chapter is the development and application of two distinct DL techniques: multiclassification and object detection, utilizing CNNs. These techniques allow for the automatic learning and extraction of relevant features from chest X-ray images, facilitating accurate classification and localization of abnormalities. By employing CNNs, the models can discern complex patterns within the images, enhancing their diagnostic accuracy. The multiclassification approach developed in this study categorizes chest X-ray images into four distinct classes: COVID-19, normal, lung opacity, and viral pneumonia. This categorization is crucial for clinicians as it enables them to differentiate between various respiratory diseases and healthy lungs, thereby aiding in the precise diagnosis and appropriate treatment of patients. The classification model demonstrated high accuracy, reflecting its potential as a reliable tool in medical diagnostics. A novel ensemble model approach was also introduced, which combines the results of three object detection model EfficientNet, you only look once version VII (YOLOv7), and Faster R-CN using weighted box fusion techniques. This ensemble method significantly improved the mean average precision (mAP) and reduced the risk of overfitting. By leveraging the strengths of multiple models, the ensemble approach provided more robust and accurate detection of multiple abnormalities in chest X-ray images. Advanced image preprocessing techniques were employed to enhance the quality and consistency of the chest X-ray images. These techniques included augmentation, cropping, rotation, and normalization, all of which contributed to the improved performance of the proposed models. Preprocessing minimized the search space, reduced artifacts, and eliminated irrelevant details, such as patient information and recording procedure data, that could potentially confuse the models. The motivation behind this research is to enhance medical diagnosis and patient care by developing accurate algorithms capable of efficiently classifying and localizing various abnormalities in chest X-rays. Early and precise diagnosis is critical for timely treatment, better patient outcomes, and reduced healthcare costs. By leveraging DL approaches, this chapter aims to significantly improve the efficiency and accuracy of diagnosing chest-related medical conditions.

Despite the promising results, the research encountered several challenges, primarily related to the datasets. Medical imaging datasets often suffer from class imbalance, where one class is significantly underrepresented. This imbalance can lead to biased predictions and reduced performance of DL models. Additionally, acquiring medical imaging datasets is costly and involves ethical considerations, limiting the size of the datasets available for training and validation. Another significant finding is that while ensemble models outperform single-object models in detecting multiple abnormalities, they also come with certain drawbacks. Ensemble models are computationally expensive and time-consuming due to the need to train and store multiple models and combine their outputs. This complexity results in increased memory requirements and system demands. Moving forward, there is a concerted effort to enhance the accuracy of the proposed models by refining preprocessing techniques, balancing the number of classes in the datasets, and exploring other DL architectures for both multiclassification and object detection. This ongoing work aims to further improve the diagnostic capabilities of these models, making them even more effective tools in clinical settings. In conclusion, this chapter presented a thorough exploration of DL techniques for classifying and localizing abnormalities in chest X-ray images. The multiclassification and object detection models proposed in this research demonstrated significant potential in improving the accuracy and efficiency of medical diagnoses. By addressing the challenges related to dataset imbalances and the computational complexity of ensemble models, future research can build on these findings to develop even more robust diagnostic tools. The ultimate goal is to assist radiologists in providing accurate and timely diagnoses, thereby enhancing patient outcomes and reducing the burden on healthcare systems.

This chapter presented an in-depth analysis of the methodologies, findings, and implications of using DL for chest X-ray image analysis. Key points include:

1. **Implementation of deep learning techniques:** The research successfully implemented CNN-based models for multiclassification and object detection, demonstrating their capability to learn and extract relevant features for accurate diagnosis.
2. **Multiclassification model:** The classification model differentiated between COVID-19, normal lungs, lung opacity, and viral pneumonia, providing a valuable tool for clinicians to diagnose multiple respiratory conditions.
3. **Ensemble model approach:** Combining EfficientNet, YOLOv7, and Faster R-CNN models through weighted box fusion techniques led to improved detection accuracy and reduced overfitting, showcasing the advantages of ensemble methods.
4. **Advanced preprocessing techniques:** The use of augmentation, cropping, rotation, and normalization improved the quality and consistency of the chest X-ray images, contributing to the enhanced performance of the models.
5. **Challenges and limitations:** The research highlighted the issues of class imbalance and the computational demands of ensemble models, suggesting areas for future improvement.
6. **Future directions:** Efforts to refine preprocessing techniques, balance dataset classes, and explore new DL architectures are ongoing, with the aim of further improving diagnostic accuracy and efficiency.

Chapter 6 presented an innovative, real-time stroke detection system utilizing DL and federated learning (FL) to address the critical need for timely and accurate stroke diagnosis. Strokes, being life-threatening medical emergencies, demand immediate intervention to reduce mortality and long-term disabilities. Traditional stroke detection methods rely heavily on the manual interpretation of medical images, which is both time-consuming and prone to human error. To overcome these limitations, our research introduces a novel approach that leverages the power of DL and the privacy-preserving benefits of FL. The primary objective of this chapter is to develop an efficient and accurate model capable of discerning between stroke and nonstroke cases in real-time, thus facilitating healthcare professionals in making well-informed decisions. By focusing on facial paralysis observed in images, our methodology utilizes you only look once version VIII (YOLOv8) models to identify intricate patterns and features associated with strokes. These models are trained on comprehensive datasets that include both stroke and nonstroke cases, enhancing their ability to detect strokes accurately and quickly.

One of the significant advancements in our research is the adoption of FL. This decentralized training approach allows the model to learn from data distributed across various clients without compromising patient privacy. By decentralizing the training process, sensitive patient information remains localized, addressing privacy concerns while maintaining the model's performance. This approach is particularly important in the healthcare sector, where data privacy is paramount.

Our proposed methodology has been implemented on NVIDIA platforms, utilizing their advanced GPU capabilities to enable real-time processing and analysis. This implementation showcases the practical feasibility of real-time stroke detection, demonstrating remarkable speed and accuracy. The combination of DL and FL in our system not only improves the timeliness of stroke detection but also ensures that patient data is kept secure.

The main key-points of this chapter are as follows

1. **Novel real-time stroke detection system:** We introduce a real-time stroke detection system based on facial paralysis images. By automating the stroke detection process, the system has the potential to significantly reduce the time required for diagnosis and treatment initiation, which is crucial for improving patient outcomes.
2. **Comprehensive datasets and YOLOv8 models:** The study emphasizes the importance of using comprehensive datasets that include both stroke and nonstroke faces for effective model training. By leveraging the advanced architectural improvements of YOLOv8 models, the system can enhance real-time processing capabilities. Extensive training on diverse datasets enables the model to discern intricate patterns and features associated with strokes, improving its accuracy and responsiveness.
3. **Federated learning for privacy preservation:** By adopting a FL technique, the model can learn from data distributed across various clients without compromising patient privacy. This decentralized approach ensures that sensitive patient information remains localized while maintaining model performance.
4. **Implementation on NVIDIA platforms:** The practical feasibility of the proposed methodology is demonstrated through its implementation on NVIDIA platforms. By harnessing advanced GPU capabilities, the system achieves remarkable speed and accuracy, revolutionizing stroke diagnosis and treatment with efficient analysis.

In addition to these contributions, our research highlights the potential for further optimization and improvements. YOLOv8 models have shown promising results in terms of mAP, recall, and precision. However, the YOLOv8n model, designed to prioritize speed and efficiency, achieves slightly lower accuracy compared to other models due to its simplified architecture with fewer parameters and reduced computational requirements. This trade-off between computational efficiency and accuracy is a significant challenge that needs to be addressed for broader applications.

To further optimize our approach, we plan to convert the proposed model to TensorFlow Lite. This conversion will enhance real-time detection capabilities and reduce power consumption, making the system more viable for deployment on low-cost embedded devices. Additionally, we will continue our research and experimentation with the latest object detection models, such as you only look once version IX (YOLOv9), which has recently been released. The implications of this chapter are profound, offering a pathway to enhancing patient outcomes by enabling healthcare professionals to make quicker, more informed decisions. The integration of DL and FL in stroke detection presents a significant advancement in medical diagnostics, promising to save lives and elevate the quality of healthcare services in the neurology field. By addressing the limitations of traditional stroke detection methods and leveraging cutting-edge technologies, our research contributes to the ongoing efforts to improve stroke diagnosis and treatment. This chapter has presented an innovative approach to real-time stroke detection, combining the strengths of DL and FL. The proposed system offers a solution that is both efficient and privacy-conscious, addressing the critical need for timely and accurate stroke diagnosis. By utilizing YOLOv8 models trained on comprehensive datasets and implementing the system on NVIDIA platforms, we have demonstrated the practical feasibility of our approach. The adoption of FL ensures that patient data remains secure, addressing privacy concerns while maintaining model performance. The advancements in DL and FL presented in this research have the potential to revolutionize stroke diagnosis and patient care. By automating the detection process and enabling real-time analysis, our system can significantly reduce the time required for diagnosis and treatment initiation, ultimately improving patient outcomes. The ongoing optimization efforts, including the conversion to TensorFlow Lite and exploration of the latest object detection models, will further enhance the system's performance and broaden its applicability.

This chapter not only contributes to the field of stroke diagnosis but also underscores the importance of interdisciplinary collaboration in addressing complex medical challenges. By integrating advanced computational techniques with clinical expertise, we can develop innovative solutions that improve patient care and save lives. The proposed real-time stroke detection system represents a significant step forward in the application of AI in healthcare, demonstrating the transformative potential of technology in the fight against life-threatening conditions like stroke.

Chapter 7 presented an in-depth exploration of object detection methods, specifically focusing on their application in detecting bag-breakup phenomena in images of droplet scattering. Object detection methods based on DL have made significant progress in recent years and have been employed successfully in numerous applications. However, their efficacy and accuracy in specialized domains remain unclear due to their predominant evaluation on datasets comprising natural images. This study aims to bridge this gap by evaluating the performance of object detection techniques in a specialized domain, where image characteristics differ substantially from those of natural scenes.

Our investigation centered around the bag-breakup phenomenon, a fluid dynamics event where droplets scatter and form bag-like structures before breaking up. Detecting this phenomenon in images presents unique challenges due to the distinct visual properties of the images compared to natural scenes. For this purpose, we employed two state-of-the-art object detection methods, RetinaNet and YOLOv7, and explored strategies to optimize their performance in this specialized context. We conducted both quantitative and qualitative evaluations to assess the effectiveness of these methods and proposed a new approach to enhance detection accuracy by leveraging information from multiple consecutive frames.

The significance of this chapter extends beyond the immediate application of bag-breakup detection. Global environmental concerns, such as global warming and air pollution, have become critical issues. Automobile emissions contribute significantly to these problems, releasing not only greenhouse gases like CO_2 but also harmful substances like NOx, HC, CO, and particulate matter. Stringent regulations on automobile emissions necessitate precise control of the air-fuel ratio in engines, typically achieved through the use of O_2 sensors in exhaust systems. These sensors monitor oxygen concentration to maintain the optimal air-fuel ratio, which is crucial for minimizing harmful emissions.

However, in colder climates, the exhaust pipe temperature decreases, leading to condensation of water vapor in the exhaust gases. This condensate can adhere to O_2 sensors, impairing their performance or even causing damage. Additionally, if the condensate freezes, it can obstruct the exhaust flow, further exacerbating emission control issues. Understanding the dispersion mechanism of condensate in exhaust systems is thus vital for improving emission controls. Returning to the specific focus of our study, the detection of bag-breakup in droplet scattering images exemplifies the broader challenges faced in specialized domains. These images differ significantly from natural scenes in texture, structure, and visual properties, posing a unique set of challenges for object detection methods. Despite these challenges, our findings demonstrate that with appropriate strategies, state-of-the-art object detection methods can achieve high accuracy and real-time performance even with limited training data. Our quantitative and qualitative evaluations of RetinaNet and YOLOv7 revealed several key insights. Both methods showed strong performance in detecting bag-breakup phenomena, but each had its strengths and weaknesses. RetinaNet, with its focus on accuracy, performed well in identifying the intricate structures of bag-breakup events. YOLOv7, designed for real-time applications, excelled in speed without significantly compromising accuracy. These findings suggest that the choice of detection method should consider the specific requirements of the application, balancing accuracy and real-time performance. To address the challenge of false positives, we proposed a novel method that utilizes information from several consecutive frames. This approach helps to distinguish between actual bag-breakup events and regions with similar visual structures, which are difficult to discriminate in single-frame analysis. By integrating temporal information, this method enhances detection accuracy, reducing false positives and improving overall reliability. Our study provides practical insights for researchers and practitioners in specialized domains. The strategies and methods discussed here can be applied to other applications where image characteristics differ from those of natural scenes. For instance, in industrial inspection, medical imaging, or scientific research, where image textures and structures may vary widely, adopting a multiframe approach and carefully selecting detection methods can significantly enhance performance. The task of automatic detection of bag-breakup in images of droplet scattering can be accomplished with high accuracy and in real-time using state-of-the-art object detection methods. Despite the challenges posed by the unique characteristics of these images, the strategies discussed in this study, including the use of consecutive frames for enhanced accuracy, provide a robust framework for tackling similar problems in other specialized domains. This chapter underscores the importance of adapting object detection methods to the specific requirements of the application domain, offering valuable guidance for future efforts in diverse fields. To further build on this work, future research could explore the integration of additional contextual information, such as environmental conditions or fluid properties, to improve detection accuracy. Moreover, extending the evaluation to other specialized domains could validate the generalizability of the proposed strategies. As DL continues to evolve, incorporating advances such as attention mechanisms or more sophisticated temporal models could further enhance the performance of object detection methods in specialized applications. Ultimately, the insights gained from this study highlight the potential of DL-based object detection methods to address complex problems in specialized domains. By tailoring these methods to the unique characteristics of the images and leveraging additional information, researchers and practitioners can achieve significant improvements in accuracy and reliability, paving the way for new applications and advancements in various fields.

"Deep Learning in Action: Image and Video Processing for Practical Use" equips readers with a comprehensive understanding of both fundamental and advanced DL concepts tailored specifically to image and video processing. The book provides practical applications that translate theoretical knowledge into real-world tasks such as object detection, image and video classification. Readers gain hands-on experience through detailed examples and projects using popular frameworks like Mathlab and PyTorch. It covered essential techniques and algorithms, including convolutional neural networks (CNNs), and autoencoders, while emphasizing the importance of data preparation and augmentation. The book delves into model training, hyperparameter tuning, and optimization strategies to enhance model performance. Additionally, it guides readers on evaluating models using various metrics, ensuring robust and reliable outcomes. Practical insights into deploying models in production environments highlight considerations for scalability and efficiency. Case studies and industry applications offer real-world context and inspiration, while discussions on future trends and research directions keep readers abreast of the latest advancements in DL for image and video processing. The Book covered:-

1. **Comprehensive understanding of deep learning:** Gain a thorough understanding of the fundamentals and advanced concepts of DL, particularly in the context of image and video processing. This includes learning about neural network architectures, such as CNNs, and their specific applications to visual data. Understand how DL models can be trained and optimized for various tasks, and explore the latest research developments and their practical implications in real-world scenarios.
2. **Practical applications:** Learn how to apply DL techniques to real-world image and video processing tasks, such as object detection, image classification, and video segmentation. Explore practical applications including people detection in crowded spaces, fire and smoke classification for early hazard detection, medical applications like COVID-19 detection in radiology images, and image restoration for enhancing complex fingerprint images. These examples demonstrate the transformative potential of DL in various industries and scenarios.
3. **Hands-on experience:** Acquire hands-on experience through practical examples and projects that demonstrate the implementation of DL models using popular frameworks like Mathlab and PyTorch. These projects reinforce theoretical concepts and cultivate skills in data preprocessing, model architecture design, and fine-tuning for specific tasks such as image recognition or video analysis. This practical approach fosters a deeper understanding of how to apply DL techniques effectively in diverse real-world scenarios, preparing practitioners for complex challenges in the field.
4. **Techniques and algorithms:** Understand the various algorithms and techniques used in DL for image and video analysis, including CNNs, which excel in spatial hierarchies; pretrained models, offering efficient learning capabilities; you only look once (YOLO) detectors, known for their real-time object detection speed; and the R-CNN architecture, combining region proposal methods with CNNs for accurate object localization. These methods empower practitioners with versatile tools for addressing complex visual recognition tasks across different scales and domains.
5. **Data preparation and augmentation:** Learn about data preparation techniques, including data augmentation, preprocessing, and the importance of having a well-curated dataset for training DL models. Data augmentation involves techniques like image rotation, flipping, and color manipulation to increase dataset diversity and improve model generalization. Preprocessing steps such as normalization and resizing ensure data consistency and compatibility with model requirements. A well-curated dataset, free of biases and noise, lays a solid foundation for training robust DL models capable of handling real-world complexities effectively.
6. **Model training and optimization:** Gain insights into model training processes, hyperparameter tuning, and optimization strategies to enhance the performance and accuracy of DL models.

Understand the nuances of fine-tuning neural network architectures for specific tasks, optimizing learning rates, and implementing regularization techniques to prevent overfitting. Explore advanced optimization algorithms like Adam and SDG to expedite training and improve generalization. Mastering these techniques ensures models are robust and efficient in real-world applications.

7. **Evaluation and metrics:** Understand how to evaluate the performance of DL models using various metrics and validation techniques such as confusion matrix, recall, mAP, precision, and receiver operating characteristic (ROC) curve analysis. These metrics provide quantitative insights into different aspects of model performance. The confusion matrix, for instance, breaks down the model's predictions versus actual labels, enabling assessment of true positives, true negatives, false positives, and false negatives. Recall measures the model's ability to correctly identify all relevant instances, while precision indicates the proportion of correctly identified instances among all predicted instances. mAP considers precision across multiple thresholds and is crucial for tasks like object detection. ROC analysis plots the trade-off between true positive rate and false positive rate, providing a comprehensive view of classification performance. These evaluation tools collectively ensure the reliability and robustness of DL models, guiding adjustments and optimizations to achieve desired outcomes effectively.
8. **Deployment strategies:** Learn about the deployment of DL models in production environments, including considerations for scalability, efficiency, and real-time processing, and assessing them on different types of embedded devices such as NVIDIA GPUs and Raspberry Pi. Understanding how to optimize models for deployment on these devices involves balancing computational requirements with hardware limitations, ensuring efficient inference while maintaining accuracy. This section explores techniques for model optimization, leveraging hardware-specific optimizations like CUDA cores on NVIDIA GPUs or optimizing inference pipelines for the ARM architecture used in Raspberry Pi, thus enabling practical deployment across diverse embedded platforms.

Glossary

Artificial Intelligence (AI) A field of computer science aiming to create intelligent systems capable of simulating human cognitive functions such as learning, problem-solving, perception, and language understanding.

Deep Learning A subset of machine learning that utilizes artificial neural networks with multiple layers to learn and extract intricate patterns from large datasets automatically.

Machine Learning (ML) An approach to data analysis that automates the building of analytical models by using algorithms that iteratively learn from data to find patterns and make decisions.

Supervised Learning A type of machine learning where models are trained on labeled data to learn the relationship between input data and the corresponding output, such as classification and regression tasks.

Unsupervised Learning Machine learning technique where models are trained on unlabeled data to discover patterns or structures within the data, including clustering and dimensionality reduction.

Semi-supervised Learning A learning approach that uses a combination of labeled and unlabeled data to improve model accuracy, particularly useful when labeled data is scarce or expensive to obtain.

Reinforcement Learning (RL) Machine learning paradigm where agents learn to make decisions by interacting with an environment, receiving rewards or penalties based on their actions, aimed at maximizing cumulative reward over time.

Convolutional Neural Network (CNN) A type of deep neural network particularly suited for processing and analyzing visual data such as images by automatically learning spatial hierarchies of features.

Crowded Environments Areas with high concentrations of people, requiring precise monitoring to ensure public safety.

Social Distancing Compliance Adherence to prescribed physical distancing measures to mitigate the spread of diseases like COVID-19.

Surveillance Systems Integrated systems for monitoring and maintaining security and safety in public spaces.

Cutting-edge Technology Advanced technological innovations that enhance accuracy and efficiency.

Public Safety Measures and protocols aimed at safeguarding the well-being of individuals within public spaces.

Euclidean Distance A mathematical formula used for precise measurement of spatial distances.

Thermal Cameras Devices capable of detecting heat signatures to monitor temperatures and detect individuals.

Bounding Boxes Rectangular frames used to encapsulate and identify objects within images.

Confusion Matrix Tabular representation of model predictions against actual outcomes, used for performance evaluation.

Autoencoder A type of neural network designed to learn efficient representations of data by compressing input into a lower-dimensional code and then reconstructing it.

Feature Extraction The process of automatically identifying and selecting relevant characteristics from raw data, such as images, to facilitate learning and decision-making in machine learning models.

Sparse Autoencoder An autoencoder variant that enforces sparsity in its hidden layer activations, encouraging the model to identify and utilize the most significant features of the data.

Fingerprint Recognition The process of identifying individuals based on unique patterns present in their fingerprints, crucial for security and biometric authentication systems.

Mean Squared Error (MSE) A measure used to assess the average squared difference between the estimated values and the actual values.

Multi-classification A method of categorizing data into more than two classes or categories, used here for distinguishing between different types of abnormalities in chest X-rays.

Object Detection The process of identifying and locating specific objects within images, crucial for pinpointing abnormalities like tumors or cysts in chest X-rays.

Pulmonary Abnormalities Irregularities or diseases affecting the lungs, such as pneumonia, tuberculosis, or lung cancer.

Fine-tuning A technique in machine learning where a pretrained model is adjusted or trained further for a specific task or dataset.

Diagnostic Accuracy The degree to which diagnostic tests are able to correctly identify presence or absence of a condition.

Efficiency How effectively a method or system performs its intended tasks, often considering speed and resource usage.

Ensemble Model A model that integrates predictions from multiple individual models to improve overall performance.

Weighted Box Fusion A technique in object detection where bounding boxes from different models are combined based on their respective confidence scores.

Mean Average Precision (mAP) A metric used to evaluate the accuracy of object detection algorithms.

Overfitting A modeling error where a machine learning model performs well on training data but poorly on new, unseen data.

Image Augmentation Techniques used to artificially increase the diversity of data available for training models, without collecting additional data.

Federated Learning A decentralized approach to machine learning where multiple parties collaboratively train a model without sharing raw data.

Inference Attacks Attempts to infer sensitive information from model outputs or updates in federated learning.

Normalization Adjusting images to a standard format or intensity range, ensuring consistency and facilitating comparison across different images.

Pre-processing Techniques applied to raw data or images to prepare them for analysis, enhancing quality and usability.

Automation The use of technology to perform tasks with minimal human intervention, crucial in medical image analysis for consistency and efficiency.

Patient Outcomes The results and effects of medical treatment or intervention on a patient's health condition.

Healthcare Resources Assets and facilities allocated for providing medical care and treatment.

Early Diagnosis Detecting health conditions in their initial stages, often leading to more effective treatments and improved outcomes.

Prompt Intervention Timely medical action taken upon detection of a health issue, aimed at preventing further complications.

Data Augmentation Techniques such as flipping, rotating, and scaling images to diversify the dataset.

Class Frequency Distribution of data points among different categories within a dataset.

Class Imbalances Unequal distribution of data points across different categories in a dataset.

Flower (FL framework) Platform facilitating efficient communication between clients and servers in federated learning.

FlowerClient Client instance in federated learning using the Flower framework.

Federated Averaging (FedAvg) Strategy to aggregate model updates in federated learning.

Bag Breakup A fluid dynamics phenomenon where a fluid-filled bag disintegrates due to external conditions like pressure or velocity changes.

Quantitative Analysis Analysis based on numerical data to measure precision, recall, and accuracy of models.

Qualitative Analysis Assessment of model performance based on nonnumerical factors, such as visual quality and robustness in challenging conditions.

Hyperparameters Parameters of a model that are set before the learning process begins, influencing the model's performance and learning dynamics.

Video Footage Analysis Examination and processing of video data to extract meaningful information, often used in surveillance and scientific research.

Real-time Detection Immediate analysis and identification of objects or events as they occur, crucial for applications requiring instant feedback or response.

Index

Note: Page numbers followed by "*f*" and "*t*" refer to figures and tables, respectively.

D

E

9780443300783